D. H. Lawrence

The Complete Poems of
D. H. Lawrence

with an Introduction and Notes by
DAVID ELLIS

Wordsworth Poetry Library

In loving memory of
MICHAEL TRAYLER
the founder of Wordsworth Editions

3

Readers who are interested in other titles from
Wordsworth Editions are invited to visit our website at
www.wordsworth-editions.com

For our latest list and a full mail-order service, contact
Bibliophile Books, 5 Thomas Road, London E14 7BN
Tel: +44 (0)20 7515 9222 Fax: +44 (0)20 7538 4115
E-mail: orders@bibliophilebooks.com

ISBN 978-1-85326-417-7

First published 1994 by Wordsworth Editions Limited
8B East Street, Ware, Hertfordshire SG12 9HJ

Typeset in Great Britain by Antony Gray
Printed and bound by Clays Ltd, St Ives plc

INTRODUCTION

When Lawrence was about to publish his *Collected Poems* in 1928 he was worried that their often highly personal nature would disconcert anyone unfamiliar with the details of his life and times. 'Even the best poetry,' he wrote, 'when it is at all personal, needs the penumbra of its own time and place and circumstance to make it full and whole.' And he went on: 'If we knew a little more of Shakespeare's self and circumstance how much more complete the Sonnets would be to us, how their strange, torn edges would be softened and merged into the whole body.'[1]

As this volume shows, Lawrence's *Collected Poems* are never as enigmatic and self-consciously ambivalent as Shakespeare's *Sonnets* and the alert reader can deduce from them a good deal about the circumstances of his life. In the early section, for example, there are a number of dialect poems, among them 'Whether or not' and 'Violets'. Reviewing the collection in which these two poems originally appeared, Ezra Pound wrote in his usual forthright manner that when Lawrence ceased to discuss 'his own disagreeable sensations', and concentrated instead on 'low-life narrative', there was no English poet under forty who could then 'get within a shot of him'.[2] Lawrence's ability to write so convincingly in dialect was of course a consequence of what, up until his time, was an exceedingly rare characteristic of great English writers, a working-class background (it was no wonder that he was such an admirer of Robert Burns). Had he been born any earlier than 1885 it is hard to see how a miner's son, from a small mining village near Nottingham called Eastwood, could have overcome the cultural and financial disadvantages of his childhood. But a flurry of new educational measures in the late nineteenth and early twentieth centuries meant that Lawrence was able to win a scholarship to Nottingham Grammar School in 1898 and some time later he became a pupil teacher in an Eastwood elementary school. He then won a place on a one-year teacher training course at Nottingham University and in October 1908

---

1 See the Appendix to this volume for this quotation (p. 620) and others from Lawrence's various introductions and prefaces to collections of his poetry.
2 *Literary Essays of Ezra Pound*, London 1954, p. 387

joined the staff of an elementary school in Croydon, not far from the old Crystal Palace ('the great blue palace at Sydenham' as he calls it in the first part of 'Dreams Old and Nascent'). While the dialect poems in the early part of this volume are a sign of Lawrence's social origins, those which deal with his life as a schoolteacher testify to social advancement and the triumph of his mother's determination that he should not, like so many of his contemporaries, follow his father down the pit.

The contents of Collected Poems do then give a rough indication of Lawrence's outward, material progress, but in his Introductory Note to them he was more concerned with the kind of information a reader might need in order to appreciate that they also made up 'a biography of an emotional and inner life'. That he was unusually attached to his mother, and that her death had a devastating effect on him, will be clear enough from several poems in what follows; but his relations with other women can seem confusing and, for obvious reasons of propriety, Lawrence is not very helpful in the first of his Introductions when he refers without elaboration to 'the poems to Miriam . . . to Helen, and to the other woman, the woman of "Kisses in the Train" and "Hands of the Betrothed" '. As most readers of Sons and Lovers will be aware, Miriam was Jessie Chambers, an Eastwood girl whom he had known from his early teens and with whom he had a long and, in its latter stages, anguished relationship. Helen was Helen Corke, who also taught in a London elementary school and whose written account of her affair with a married man, which had ended with his suicide, provided the basis for Lawrence's second novel, The Trespasser. The woman of 'Kisses in the Train' (and 'Hands of the Betrothed') was Louie Burrows, whom he had first met when he was a pupil teacher and to whom he became engaged during the dark days in December 1910 when his mother lay dying. The story of Lawrence's relationships with these women is complicated – for quite long periods he was simultaneously involved with all three – and they preoccupied him sufficiently to prompt the thought that the early Lawrence is above all a love poet, even if the 'love' concerned is as much if not more a matter of pain, sorrow and guilt as of happiness and joy. One topic related to love on which Lawrence is eloquent is sexual frustration (although he eventually persuaded Jessie Chambers into a sexual relationship which proved unsatisfactory to them both, it is doubtful whether Helen Corke ever slept with him and Louie Burrows certainly didn't). A poem like 'The Hands of the Betrothed', for example, seems to throb with repressed sexual feeling and may well have the kind of quality Pound meant when he referred to 'disagreeable sensations'; but then, by the time he wrote that phrase, Pound was a member of a free-living London set whereas Lawrence (despite his period in Croydon) was a dyed-in-the-wool provincial who brought to his writing all the strengths and drawbacks of an English nonconformist background.

Lawrence's willingness to talk about his sexual frustration, if only in a highly allusive, roundabout way, is characteristic of a certain rawness of feeling in many of the early poems which helped to create the sense that he was avant-garde. At the start of his career as a poet he was very loosely associated with a number of young men who, following the accession of George V in 1910, were known as the 'Georgians'. A new reign, the implication was, would also mean a new era in poetry. It is one of the cruel ironies of literary history that a word which was meant to indicate all that was fresh, innovative and exciting in the poetry of the time should have later come to signal what is now recognisable as the fag-end of Romanticism, its 'last oozings' to invoke an appropriate phrase from Keats's 'Ode to Autumn'. Lawrence may often distinguish himself from the other Georgians by the nature of his subject-matter but the manner he adopts in his early poetry is like theirs in being uncomfortably literary, fully of poeticisms, archaic diction, stale metaphors. If there were a prize for the worse poem ever written by a great writer there are several pieces in the early part of this volume – 'Letter from Town; On a Grey Morning in March', for instance – which would be strong contenders. When he came to collect his poems in 1928, Lawrence altered the earlier ones considerably (the appearance of the word 'cunt' on p. 50 would have been unthinkable to his pre-war self, even in a dialect poem). One or two of them, such as 'Virgin Youth', he rewrote completely, and he clarified and generally improved many others. But he could not, and probably did not want to hide the conflict in his early work between his urgent preoccupations as a young man and a poetic style which had become outdated, an unsuitable medium for 'modern' concerns.

In Lawrence's move to a more direct, colloquial and powerful poetic idiom there are three major and very different influences at work, one of which is the First World War. Because of his poor health he never experienced life in the trenches, being finally graded 'C' in September 1918 (fit only for sedentary, non-combat duties) after a series of increasingly humiliating medical examinations. But he declared his opposition to the war early, followed public affairs

intensely, and suffered a certain degree of persecution because of the
'unpatriotic' nature of his behaviour and views. After the banning of
his fourth novel, *The Rainbow*, in 1915 he found it more and more
difficult to make a living in an England whose social and therefore
cultural life was so completely distorted by the war effort. Increasingly
isolated, desperately poor and often ill, he was left when hostilities
finally ceased in November 1918 a quite different man from the
successful and optimistic young writer of four years before. Like
many of his contemporaries who *had* seen action, he felt bitter and
alienated and recognised that, as a writer, it was no longer possible
to express oneself like a latter-day Shelley or Keats in a world so
many of whose previous values, securities and complacencies had
been destroyed.

But new poetic styles, appropriate to the urgent needs of the most
gifted and sensitive young minds of a particular period, cannot be
plucked out of thin air. As Lawrence makes abundantly clear in his
Preface to the 1920 American edition of his *New Poems*, the writer
who most helped him to see his way forward was Walt Whitman. It
was Whitman above all who made him feel that poetry did not have
to rhyme or be written in regular metre, who introduced him to the
advantages of free verse. He felt that just as Whitman had 'pruned
away his clichés' he himself could 'get rid of the stereotyped
movements and the old hackneyed associations of sound or sense . . .
break down those artificial conduits and canals through which we do
so love to force our utterance'.[3] The first collection in which
Lawrence makes extensive use of free verse is called *Look! We Have
Come Through!* (1917), but that title is a reminder of the third major
factor in the development in his new poetic manner since it refers
principally to his relationship with Frieda von Richthofen.

At the end of 1911 Lawrence became so ill that he was obliged to
give up his schoolteaching. During his convalescence he decided on
a change of life: that he would break off his engagement with Louie
Burrows, earn what he could as a writer and, more immediately, see
if he could find a job abroad as a language assistant. In March 1912
he went for help and advice to a man who had taught him languages
at the university, Professor Ernest Weekley, and proceeded to fall in
love with his wife. Strikingly good looking, interested in ideas,
sexually uninhibited and, for someone brought up as Lawrence had
been, distinctly exotic, Frieda Weekley was the daughter of a minor

3 See the Appendix, p. 617.

German aristocrat (while she was living with Lawrence in England during the war it hardly helped their cause that one of her distant von Richthofen cousins was the legendary German fighter pilot known as 'the Red Baron'). Frieda introduced Lawrence to new feelings and experiences, not merely because the two of them lived mostly abroad before the war broke out; and for the next few years he devoted himself to working out a satisfactory relationship with her. As many of the poems in *Look! We Have Come Through!* suggest, this was not an easy matter. Frieda von Richthofen, Weekley or Lawrence (as she became in July 1914) was an emancipated, fiercely independent woman with a shrewd understanding of her partner's psychological weaknesses and peculiarities. A characteristic of Lawrence from the beginning of his writing career was a willingness to acknowledge in himself feelings that most other people would choose to ignore, but in confronting Frieda he was forced to investigate his own nature even more deeply, strip away ornamentation and abandon all forms of posturing. It is this effort which makes itself felt linguistically in *Look! We Have Come Through!*, a collection full of poems which, if they are not always pleasing, at least suggest a writer who is not striking appropriately poetic poses but being as honest and sincere as he can possibly be.

The circumstances of the war forced on Lawrence a new directness and urgency, the example of Whitman encouraged him to be less conventional, and his life with Frieda obliged him to uncover and develop what he increasingly felt was his real nature. If the advantages of his new manner are not felt by every reader of *Look! We Have Come Through!*, it may be because some of the poems in which it is most evident are almost too intimate, uncomfortably private. ('I don't mind his having come through,' Bertrand Russell is reported to have said of its title, 'but why should I look?')[4] Yet in Lawrence's next collection, *Birds, Beasts and Flowers*, which contains many of his most successful and best known poems, the difference from his early work is unmistakable. Lawrence is often a love poet in his early poems but he is perhaps even more predominantly a poet of Nature. The trouble is that in the early phase of his writing career, Nature seems all too often a mere adjunct of himself, that he is guilty to an excessive extent of what Ruskin called 'the pathetic fallacy': the attribution of human characteristics and feelings to natural phenomena. Typical is a poem like 'Weeknight Service', in which the

4 See *Ottoline at Garsington*, edited by Gathorne Hardy, p. 94.

'silver moon' is described as being 'up there in the sky / Serenely smiling at naught', 'patient Night / Sits indifferent, hugged in her rags', and 'the wise old trees / Drop their leaves with a faint, sharp hiss of contempt'. The general effect is of a man purporting to describe the outside world but in fact always talking about himself. In the new mood of rigorous self-investigation prompted by the war and life with Frieda, Lawrence diagnosed this solipsism as a dangerous weakness in himself. 'I was so weary of the world,' he wrote in 'New Heaven and Earth', 'I was so sick of it, / everything was tainted with myself, / skies, trees, flowers, birds, water'. . . , and he went on to describe how touching his wife in bed allowed him to escape from self-enclosure into a 'new world', a 'new earth' of difference where he could properly recognise the otherness of his environment. It is this otherness he celebrates in *Birds, Beasts and Flowers*, most memorably in poems such as 'Bare Almond Trees', 'Humming Bird' or 'Snake', but perhaps most obviously and clearly in a poem like 'Fish', where he has to admit that this 'grey, monotonous soul in the water', with which he shares the world, is a being he does not know as he once confidently thought he did: 'I didn't know his God'.

The natural world of *Birds, Beasts and Flowers* is a 'new earth' for Lawrence because he more clearly recognises the differences and, in some cases, the unbridgeable gap between himself and its other inhabitants whether they be animal, vegetable or mineral. Yet language is a distinctively human attribute so that any writing or talking about Nature will inevitably impose on the non-human environment some degree of human concern. This is evident enough in one of the major triumphs of the collection, the six tortoise poems. The acuteness of observation in these poems is remarkable – in the first of them a baby tortoise has never been so vividly evoked.

> You draw your head forward, slowly, from your little wimple
> And set forward, slow-dragging, on your four-pinned toes,
> Rowing slowly forward.
> Whither away, small bird?
> Rather like a baby working its limbs,
> Except that you make slow, ageless progress
> And a baby makes none.
>
> The touch of the sun excites you,
> And the long ages, and the lingering chill
> Make you pause to yawn,
> Opening your impervious mouth,

> Suddenly beak-shaped, and very wide, like some suddenly
>   gaping pincers;
> Soft red tongue, and hard thin gums,
> Then close the wedge of your little mountain front,
> Your face, baby tortoise.

The tortoise poems illustrate as well as any others the skill with which Lawrence is able to manipulate his free-verse form, shortening and lengthening lines to control a poem's pace, constructing a sequence of rhythmic units without falling into regular stanzaic form, and skilfully mingling formal diction with the vernacular. Variation in tone is very important to them, with humour or wit – not the most notable features of his early poetry – playing a major role. Staggered by the lack of family feeling between the female tortoise and her offspring, or pretending to be staggered, the narrator exclaims, 'It is no use my saying to him in an emotional voice: / "This is your Mother, she laid you when you were an egg," ' adding slyly at the beginning of the next movement, 'He does not even trouble to answer: "Woman, what have I to do with thee?" ' As this example illustrates, the poems benefit also from Lawrence's dramatic sense. As well as being a novelist and short-story writer he was of course a dramatist (one or two of his plays are still performed today), and many of the poems in *Birds, Beasts and Flowers* – 'Peach', for example, or 'Mosquito' and 'Man and Bat' – are structured around an implied dramatic situation. In the tortoise sequence there is an implied drama taking place between the narrator/poet and the female companion in whose company he is observing the tortoises, and an overt drama among the tortoises themselves.

It is as Lawrence describes or rather creates the drama of the tortoises that the tendency of language to make us all inescapably anthropomorphic becomes especially evident. What he admires is the way in which, as soon as the baby tortoise is born – deposited on the ground 'as if he were no more than droppings' – he is independent, a courageous explorer of his environment, untrammelled by family obligations and feelings. Yet inscribed on his shell is the cross he has to bear, the urge to procreate. As a young man Lawrence had read and been very impressed by a translation of Schopenhauer's *Metaphysics of Love*, in which sexual feeling figures as an overpowering instinct to which human beings are blindly and unknowingly subjugated. For him, the tortoise is similarly a victim of sex desire, driven on by grim necessity and exposing himself in the process to humiliation and the loss of his independence. From being the 'lonely rambler, the stoic, dignified stalker through the chaos' of the world, he becomes a sad creature ridiculously clinging on to the 'scaly ankle' of the much larger female. 'Alas,' Lawrence comments, 'the spear is through the side of his isolation. / His adolescence saw him crucified into sex.' The word 'adolescence' suggests how far at this point in the sequence the tortoises have been incorporated into the human world despite the brilliance at its beginning of a descriptive notation which can often strike us as 'objective'. Of an incorporating tendency also of course is the way in which they are here associated with Western culture's founding narrative, as they are in the use of 'Woman what have I to do with thee?' (Christ's words to his mother at the marriage in Cana). Tortoises do not experience 'adolescence' and religion can mean nothing to them. Lawrence has projected on to these creatures his own concerns but, as any detailed comparison would show, in a manner much more controlled and self-aware than the projections in his early verse. The tortoises are certainly allegorised but they none the less stick in the mind as very much themselves. The poems which describe them are required reading for anyone who can only think of Lawrence in terms of Lady Chatterley's Lover, but they also illustrate, as well as any others could, the ability his mature poetic manner gave him to move with ease through a variety of different poetic registers. If readers of this volume read nothing else, they should read these.

The place names at the bottom of many of the poems in Birds, Beasts and Flowers give some indication of the Lawrences' movements once the war was over and they were finally able to leave England in 1919. Some of the poems were written in Fiesole near Florence but many more in Taormina, Sicily, where they had rented a villa. In February 1922 they set off for America, the long way round. One episode during their six weeks' stay in what is now Sri Lanka is recorded in 'Elephant' (while they were living in Kandy the Prince of Wales paid an official visit there), and it was a trip to the Sidney Zoo which later gave rise to 'Kangaroo'. The place names 'Taos' and 'Lobo' indicate that it was to New Mexico the Lawrences quickly moved once they had reached the United States, yet many of the discussions which took place before the publication of Birds, Beasts and Flowers in 1923 had to be carried on by letter when they were on the first of two visits to Mexico in the spring and summer of 1922. Once this volume had appeared Lawrence wrote very little poetry until he and

Frieda were back in Europe and his publisher's invitation to collect together all his previous work helped revive his interest.

The poems Lawrence began to write after *Collected Poems* had appeared were different from those he had written before. He called them 'pansies' because, as Ophelia says in *Hamlet,* 'pansies, that's for thoughts' (the English word does in fact derive from the French 'pensées'), but also because he *wanted* them to be regarded as ephemeral — 'A flower passes, and that perhaps is the best of it.'[5] A typical pansy or thought poem would be 'Self-Pity': 'I never saw a wild thing / Sorry for itself. / A small bird will drop frozen dead from a bough / without ever having felt sorry for itself'; or 'Forget': 'To be able to forget is to be able to yield / to God who dwells in deep oblivion. / Only in sheer oblivion are we with God. / For when we know in full, we have left off knowing'; but the form itself is highly malleable and allows for the expression of all kinds of thought or feeling. It can be used by Lawrence for lyrical *aperçus* of great beauty, for the expression of a moving private despair, but also for social and political commentary. Never very long, if not often as short as 'Self-Pity' or 'Forget', *Pansies* allowed Lawrence to rail against the evils of modern industrial society, our obsession with money, the curse of the English class system or the cerebral nature of our lives; but they also provided him with the occasion for sad, elegiac reflections on the after-life of love or the failure of desire. Although they tend to form themselves into small groups, dominated by a particular subject or theme, they are constantly variable, with an exquisitely worded observation at one extreme balanced by cheerful doggerel at the other. It takes all sorts. One useful function the pansy performed for Lawrence was that of a safety valve, allowing him the opportunity for short, sharp bursts of indignation, many of which were directed at the British system of censorship. He had often had difficulties with the censor, particularly during the war when *The Rainbow* was suppressed; but these increased enormously after the appearance of *Lady Chatterley's Lover* in 1928. He had published this novel privately in Florence but ran into difficulties as he began to send it by post to customers in England. In a demonstration of their concern, the authorities not only confiscated various copies of *Lady Chatterly* but also illegally seized a typescript of *Pansies* which Lawrence had sent to his agent. Later, in the summer of 1929, they were to close down an exhibition of his

5 See the Appendix, p. 628.

paintings, which was being held in London, chiefly because he had refused to follow convention and deprive his nude figures of pubic hair. By that time, his *Pansies* were about to appear, in an official edition, from which a number of poems such as 'The Noble Englishman' or 'Don't Look at Me' had been omitted, and also, a little later, in a privately printed, unexpurgated one. But Lawrence was continuing to write in the same vein except that those poems which expressed his indignation at English society (his final visit to England in the summer of 1926 had coincided with the General Strike), and what was implied about it by the censorship system, he referred to as 'nettles'. A slim volume of his *Nettles* appeared on 13 March 1930 just eleven days after his death.

This volume of Lawrence's complete poems reprints *Collected Poems*, the unexpurgated *Pansies*, and *Nettles*, all those collections (that is) which he himself prepared for the press; but it also includes the two notebooks in which he was working when he died. These were edited by Richard Aldington and Pino Orioli and published under the title *Last Poems* in October 1932, the name Aldington had given to one of the notebooks while he called the other 'More Pansies'. This distinction is not entirely accurate but it works well enough. In the 'More Pansies' notebook Lawrence does seem to be continuing what had become a kind of diary of his thoughts and feelings in verse, whereas, in the other, there is much more emphasis on death, religion, the last things. The preoccupation with illness and death indicates a reason why he chose the 'pansy' form which is additional to any he himself gives. With his health failing, short poems were an appropriate medium of self-expression for someone who was obliged to spend long stretches of the day in bed. He had rarely been free of illness for long. The doctor who examined him when he was forced to give up teaching thought that he would be threatened with consumption if he ever went back to a school. Thereafter he was often ill with respiratory and chest problems but it was not until he was in Mexico City, in the early months of 1925, that he was officially diagnosed as tubercular. Although he refused to accept this diagnosis, always referring when he was ill to the flu or trouble with his bronchials (rather than his lungs), the evidence for pulmonary tuberculosis grew increasingly strong. He found sustained physical effort more and more difficult, coughed persistently and grew ever more thin. Enfeebled as he was, the amount of writing he did was remarkable, but there is no doubt that for a man so creative, and with such a constant need to articulate his thoughts and feelings on a wide variety of subjects, the short poem was an ideal medium.

Dr Johnson recounts, surely with some irony, that when Addison knew he had only a short time to live he sent for a young friend of 'very irregular life' in order that he might see 'how a Christian can die'.[6] Lawrence's last poems show us how someone of a naturally religious temperament, who could no longer accept the dogmas of Christianity, faced up to the prospect of death. Several different religious scenarios are invoked, in addition to the Christian one: the Greek or Roman descent into the underworld in 'Bavarian Gentians', for example, or the Etruscan ship of death in the poem of that title; and Lawrence often relies also on the idea of death as part of a natural and cyclical process of renewal, the winter before the inevitable return of spring. At no point does he commit himself fully to belief in an after-life but he plays with the notion as part of an intensely imaginative struggle to come to terms with his imminent dissolution. Several of the last poems are rightly famous and they are no doubt made more effective by a general knowledge of the time and circumstance, if not the place (Bandol and then Vence in the South of France), of their composition. But time and circumstance are not everything. The *Oxford Book of English Verse* used to include a poem by Chidiock Tichbourne with an epigraph which ran, 'Written with his own hand in the Tower before his execution'. Tichbourne was executed in 1586 and it is the circumstances in which his poem was composed which add lustre to an otherwise unexceptional piece. Lawrence's 'Shadows', on the other hand, would remain a great poem even if we were to learn that it dated from a time when he was in rude health, or if we knew nothing about its author. Biographical information does often increase our appreciation of literature but, if the literature is good enough, we can usually do without it.

Lawrence is now known principally as the author of *Lady Chatterley's Lover* yet he wrote many other novels (several of which are much better than this, his last one), a large number of excellent short stories and some of the best novellas or tales in the language. In addition to his plays, he was also responsible for a volume of literary criticism, a host of philosophical essays and three travel books. It is perhaps no wonder therefore that his poetry is somewhat neglected.

6 Samuel Johnson, *Lives of the English Poets*, Everyman edition, London 1925, Vol. I. p. 346

A few famous poems are regularly anthologised but there are many more which deserve to be and anyone who happened to be led by 'Snake' into exploring the rest of *Birds, Beasts and Flowers* would be in for a pleasant surprise.

Yet Lawrence's achievement in other literary forms is not the only reason for the uncertainty of his reputation as a poet. Another is that, in breaking away from the Georgians and their ilk, he did not take the route indicated by Pound and Eliot. He never, that is, became a modernist, even though several of his poems appeared in Imagist anthologies during the war; and it was modernism which was to dominate poetry for many decades after the war was over – as far at least as literary critics were concerned. It is possible to isolate two principal ways in which Lawrence's revolutionary poetic practice differed from that of the modernists. In the first place, he had little sympathy with their emphasis on craftsmanship, that insistence on the necessary hard grind of writing poetry which is especially associated with Pound although it was Eliot who famously said, 'No verse is free for a man who wants to do a good job.'[7] In the second, he was dismissive of Eliot's doctrine of impersonality, the attempt to bring a certain classical austerity and restraint back to poetry and avoid post-Romantic displays of personal feeling. For Eliot and Pound direct autobiographical expression was so closely associated with lax, post-Romantic gush that they would have no truck with it.

Both these modernist positions were impossible for Lawrence in that, as the Preface to the American edition of *New Poems* clearly shows, the chief feature of the aesthetic he developed under the influence of Whitman was spontaneity. Like Wordsworth, he always writes about poetry as if, once the poet was possessed of the right feelings, the appropriate words would naturally come. Honing this or that phrase, debating with oneself over this or that word, or endlessly checking the rhythms, were in any case activities inevitably destructive of spontaneous expression. With these beliefs, the impulse Lawrence felt when preparing his *Collected Poems* to revise and even rewrite some of them became a problem. He solved it by suggesting that in his early days his creative demon was sometimes stifled by the commonplace youth which he had in part then been: 'A young man is afraid of his demon and puts his hand over the demon's mouth sometimes and speaks for him.' This meant that in altering

7 T. S. Eliot, *On Poetry and Poets*, London 1957, p. 37

his early poems he felt that he was merely giving them the form they should really have always had, and removing from them the effects of youthful inhibition. As he puts it: 'It is not for technique these poems are altered: it is to say the real say.'[8]

The commitment to spontaneity not only meant that Lawrence could not sympathise with Pound's emphasis on artistry but also that he had no time at all for his and Eliot's celebration of impersonality. He rightly identified Flaubert as the modern originator of the impersonality doctrine but felt no admiration for the success with which this writer was supposed to have removed all traces of his own voice from *Madame Bovary*. Self-effacement or self-disguise he tended to regard as a subtle form of conceit and the classical precedents which were sometimes invoked in defence of impersonality he regarded as 'bunkum, but still more *cowardice*'.[9] These at least are the terms he used when his friend John Middleton Murry was attacked for his 'Romanticism' in Eliot's journal *The Criterion*, and they would certainly have seemed to him appropriate for the manipulation of pronouns which, in Eliot's fine poem 'Portrait of a Lady' (for example), prevents the reader from identifying the precise nature of the autobiographical impulse. In contrast to Eliot, Lawrence felt that, since all literature was in its essence self-expression, the more openly and frankly confessional a poet was the better. Exposing to the reader what you really felt and thought was to him more important than 'art'.

The consequences of these beliefs are that, on some occasions, the subject matter of a poem is more interesting to Lawrence than it could ever be to the reader while, on others, felicity of expression is sacrificed to the urge to communicate. Thus, although there is plenty of ore in this volume it does not come without a good deal of dross. Lawrence had remarkable gifts for lyrical as well as dramatic expression but so keen is he to communicate that sometimes his poems are only distinguished as such by a striking phrase ('the upholstered dead that sit in deep armchairs'), or might just as well have been written out in prose. In his later work especially, what defines a poem is less its form than the occasion which gave rise to it: one, that is, which seemed to him to require brief rather than extended comment. But just as his technical deficiencies can sometimes disappoint so too can

8 See the Appendix, p. 622.
9 *The Letters of D. H. Lawrence*, Vol. IV, edited by Warren Roberts, James T. Boulton and Elizabeth Mansfield, p. 500

the nature of these brief comments – or rather they can often irritate, particularly those which relate to social or political matters. Lawrence could have said with Lord Byron, 'I have simplified my politics into an utter detestation of all existing government,'[10] but his spleen can occasionally make him appear foolish, he has thoughts on leadership which can now sound slightly sinister, and the alternatives he offers to what was and still is the general state of things can seem self-indulgently utopian. Neither politically correct nor 'reasonable', Lawrence usually hits the nail on the head but he can also give the impression of a man swinging his hammer wildly in all directions, merely to express his pent-up rage.

The undoubted unevenness of Lawrence's work is a strong argument in favour of selections of his poetry, yet it is important that once in a while he should also be seen as he is, warts an' all. Although their social backgrounds were antithetical, it is not only on political matters that Lawrence shares many characteristics with his fellow Midlander Lord Byron (the Byrons' country seat was not far from Eastwood); and in Matthew Arnold's attempt to sum up Byron there are, therefore, many phrases which might be applied to Lawrence also. Arnold notes, for example, how difficult it is to separate Byron's work from his personality, he complains of the 'slovenliness and tunelessness' of some of his verse, yet he also stresses how important Byron was and still can be as the old social order breaks up. As this inevitable process continues, he says,

> . . . we shall turn our eyes again, and to more purpose, upon this passionate and dauntless soldier of the forlorn hope, who . . . waged against the conservation of the old impossible world so fiery [a] battle; waged it till he fell, – waged it with such splendid and imperishable excellence of sincerity and strength.[11]

The idiom is old-fashioned but it conveys well the intensity of Lawrence, his courage, and above all the searching honesty with which he scrutinised both the outside world and himself.

DAVID ELLIS
University of Kent at Canterbury

---

10 quoted by Matthew Arnold in his essay on Byron, in *Essays in Criticism: Second Series*, London 1888, p. 195
11 ibid., p. 202

SUGGESTIONS FOR FURTHER READING

Two early books entirely devoted to Lawrence's poetry are Tom Marshall, *The Psychic Mariner* (London 1970), and Sandra Gilbert, *Acts of Attention* (Cornell University Press, 1972). A decade later came Gail Porter Mandell, *The Phoenix Paradox: A Study of Renewal Through Change in the 'Collected Poems' and 'Last Poems' of D. H. Lawrence* (Southern Illinois University Press, 1984). There is a selection of articles on the poetry in Volume 4 of *D. H. Lawrence: Critical Assessments*, ed. David Ellis and Ornella De Zordo (Robertsbridge: Helm Information, 1992), and more recent pieces can be found in *Approaches to Teaching the Works of D. H. Lawrence*, ed. Elizabeth M. Sargent and Garry Watson (Modern Languages Association of America, 2001). Mara Kalnins has written an excellent introduction to a selection of Lawrence's poetry in the Everyman series (1992) and Keith Sagar has done the same for the selection published in the Penguin Poetry Library (1986). The numerous articles Sagar has published on the poetry all have interest and value, as does anything by Christopher Pollnitz, the editor of the coming Cambridge edition of the Complete Poems. There is an essay on the poetry by Helen Sword in *The Cambridge Companion to D. H. Lawrence*, ed. Ann Fernihough (Cambridge University Press, 2001), pp. 119–35, and two other essays which the reader might find useful are R. P. Draper, 'The Poetry of D. H. Lawrence', in *D. H. Lawrence: New Studies*, ed. Christopher Heywood (New York 1987), and Holly Laird, 'Excavating the Early Poetry of D. H. Lawrence', in the *D. H. Lawrence Review*, Vol. 23 (Summer/Fall, 1991), pp. 111–28. Anyone who wants to follow up various suggestions made in my Introduction should consult 'Verse or Worse: The Place of Pansies in Lawrence's Poetry', in David Ellis and Howard Mills, *D. H. Lawrence's Non-Fiction: Art, Thought and Genre* (Cambridge University Press, 1988), pp. 146–70, and my essay on *Birds, Beasts and Flowers*, in *A Companion to Twentieth-Century Poetry*, ed. Neil Roberts (Blackwell, Oxford 2001), pp. 392–402. The lecture which James Fenton gave on Lawrence when he was professor of poetry at Oxford – 'Men, Women and Beasts' – is interesting and has been published in Fenton's *The Strength of Poetry* (Oxford University Press, 2001), pp. 165–86.

CONTENTS

UNRHYMING POEMS

ANIMALS

GHOSTS

PANSIES

The Complete Poems of D. H. Lawrence

RHYMING POEMS

The Wild Common

The quick sparks on the gorse-bushes are leaping
Little jets of sunlight texture imitating flame;
Above them, exultant, the peewits are sweeping:
They have triumphed again o'er the ages, their screamings proclaim.

Rabbits, handfuls of brown earth, lie
Low-rounded on the mournful turf they have bitten down to the quick.
Are they asleep? – Are they living? – Now see, when I
Lift my arms, the hill bursts and heaves under their spurting kick!

The common flaunts bravely; but below, from the rushes
Crowds of glittering king-cups surge to challenge the blossoming
    bushes;
There the lazy streamlet pushes
His bent course mildly; here wakes again, leaps, laughs, and gushes

Into a deep pond, an old sheep dip,
Dark, overgrown with willows, cool, with the brook ebbing through so
    slow;
Naked on the steep, soft lip
Of the turf I stand watching my own white shadow quivering to and fro.

What if the gorse-flowers shrivelled, and I were gone?
What if the waters ceased, where were the marigolds then, and the
    gudgeon?
What is this thing that I look down upon?
White on the water wimples my shadow, strains like a dog on a string,
    to run on.

How it looks back, like a white dog to its master!
I on the bank all substance, my shadow all shadow looking up to me,
    looking back!
And the water runs, and runs faster, runs faster,
And the white dog dances and quivers, I am holding his cord quite
    slack.

But how splendid it is to be substance, here!
My shadow is neither here nor there; but I, I am royally here!
I am here! I am here! screams the peewit; the may-blobs burst out in a
    laugh as they hear!
Here! flick the rabbits. Here! pants the gorse. Here! say the insects far
    and near.

Over my skin in the sunshine, the warm, clinging air
Flushed with the songs of seven larks singing at once, goes kissing me
    glad.
You are here! You are here! We have found you! Everywhere
We sought you substantial, you touchstone of caresses, you naked lad!

Oh but the water loves me and folds me,
Plays with me, sways me, lifts me and sinks me, murmurs:
    Oh marvellous stuff!
No longer shadow! – And it holds me
Close, and it rolls me, enfolds me, touches me, as if never it could
    touch me enough.

Sun, but in substance, yellow water-blobs!
Wings and feathers on the crying, mysterious ages, peewits wheeling!
All that is right, all that is good, all that is God takes substance! a
    rabbit lobs
In confirmation, I hear sevenfold lark-songs pealing.

Dog-Tired

If she would come to me here
        Now the sunken swaths
        Are glittering paths
To the sun, and the swallows cut clear
Into the setting sun! if she came to me here!

If she would come to me now,
Before the last-mown harebells are dead;
While that vetch-clump still burns red!
Before all the bats have dropped from the bough
To cool in the night; if she came to me now!

The horses are untackled, the chattering machine
Is still at last. If she would come
We could gather up the dry hay from
The hill-brow, and lie quite still, till the green
Sky ceased to quiver, and lost its active sheen.

I should like to drop
On the hay, with my head on her knee,
And lie dead still, while she
Breathed quiet above me; and the crop
Of stars grew silently.

I should like to lie still
As if I was dead; but feeling
Her hand go stealing
Over my face and my head, until
This ache was shed.

From a College Window

The glimmer of the limes, sun-heavy, sleeping,
    Goes trembling past me up the College wall.
Below, the lawn, in soft blue shade is keeping
    The daisy-froth quiescent, softly in thrall.

Beyond the leaves that overhang the street,
    Along the flagged, clean pavement summer-white,
Passes the world with shadows at their feet
    Going left and right.

Remote, although I hear the beggar's cough,
    See the woman's twinkling fingers tend him a coin,
I sit absolved, assured I am better off
    Beyond a world I never want to join.

Discord in Childhood

Outside the house an ash tree hung its terrible whips,
And at night when the wind rose, the lash of the tree
Shrieked and slashed the wind, as a ship's
Weird rigging in a storm shrieks hideously.

Within the house two voices arose, a slender lash
Whistling she-delirious rage, and the dreadful sound
Of a male thong booming and bruising, until it had drowned
The other voice in a silence of blood, 'neath the noise of the ash.

Cherry Robbers

Under the long dark boughs, like jewels red
  In the hair of an Eastern girl
Hang strings of crimson cherries, as if had bled
  Blood-drops beneath each curl.

Under the glistening cherries, with folded wings
  Three dead birds lie:
Pale-breasted throstles and a blackbird, robberlings
  Stained with red dye.

Against the haystack a girl stands laughing at me,
  Cherries hung round her ears.
Offers me her scarlet fruit: I will see
  If she has any tears.

Dream-Confused

  Is that the moon
At the window so big and red?
No-one in the room?
No-one near the bed?

  Listen, her shoon
Palpitating down the stair!
– Or a beat of wings at the window there?

A moment ago
She kissed me warm on the mouth;
The very moon in the south
Is warm with a ruddy glow;
The moon, from far abysses
Signalling those two kisses.

And now the moon
Goes clouded, having misunderstood.
And slowly back in my blood
My kisses are sinking, soon
To be under the flood.

We misunderstood!

Renascence

We have bit no forbidden apple,
    Eve and I,
Yet the splashes of day and night
Falling round us, no longer dapple
The same valley with purple and white.

This is our own still valley,
    Our Eden, our home;
But day shows it vivid with feeling,
And the pallor of night does not tally
With dark sleep that once covered the ceiling.

The little red heifer: to-night I looked in her eyes;
    She will calve to-morrow.
Last night, when I went with the lantern, the sow was grabbing her
    litter
With snarling red jaws; and I heard the cries
Of the new-born, and then, the old owl, then the bats that flitter.

And I woke to the sound of the wood-pigeon, and lay and listened
    Till I could borrow
A few quick beats from a wood-pigeon's heart; and when I did rise
Saw where morning sun on the shaken iris glistened.
And I knew that home, this valley, was wider than Paradise.

I learned it all from my Eve,
     The warm, dumb wisdom;
She's a quicker instructress than years;
She has quickened my pulse to receive
Strange throbs, beyond laughter and tears.

So now I know the valley
     Fleshed all like me
With feelings that change and quiver
And clash, and yet seem to tally,
Like all the clash of a river
     Moves on to the sea.

Virgin Youth

Now and again
The life that looks through my eyes
And quivers in words through my mouth,
And behaves like the rest of men,
Slips away, so I gasp in surprise.

And then
My unknown breasts begin
To wake, and down the thin
Ripples below the breast an urgent
Rhythm starts, and my silent and slumberous belly
In one moment rouses insurgent.

My soft, slumbering belly,
Quivering awake with one impulse and one will,
Then willy nilly
A lower me gets up and greets me;
Homunculus stirs from his roots, and strives until,
Risen up, he beats me.

He stands, and I tremble before him.
– Who then art thou? –
He is wordless, but sultry and vast,
And I can't deplore him.
– Who art thou? What hast
Thou to do with me, thou lustrous one, iconoclast? –

How beautiful he is! without sound,
Without eyes, without hands;
Yet, flame of the living ground
He stands, the column of fire by night.
And he knows from the depths; he quite
Alone understands.

Quite alone, he alone
Understands and knows.
Lustrously sure, unknown
Out of nowhere he rose.

I tremble in his shadow, as he burns
For the dark goal.
He stands like a lighthouse, night churns
Round his base, his dark light rolls
Into darkness, and darkly returns.

Is he calling, the lone one? Is his deep
Silence full of summons?
Is he moving invisibly? Does his steep
Curve sweep towards a woman's?

Traveller, column of fire,
It is vain.
The glow of thy full desire
Becomes pain.

Dark, ruddy pillar, forgive me! I
Am helplessly bound
To the rock of virginity. Thy
Strange voice has no sound.

We cry in the wilderness. Forgive me, I
Would so gladly lie
In the womanly valley, and ply
Thy twofold dance.

Thou dark one, thou proud, curved beauty! I
Would worship thee, letting my buttocks prance.
But the hosts of men with one voice deny
Me the chance.

They have taken the gates from the hinges
And built up the way. I salute thee
But to deflower thee. Thy tower impinges
On nothingness. Pardon me!

Study

Somewhere the long mellow note of the blackbird
Quickens the unclasping hands of hazel.
Somewhere the wind-flowers fling their heads back
Stirred by an impetuous wind. Some ways'll
All be sweet with white and blue violet –
     (*Hush now, hush! Where am I? – Biuret*[1] *–*)

On the green wood's edge a shy girl hovers
From out of the hazel-screen on to the grass,
Where wheeling and screaming the petulant plovers
Wave frighted. – Who comes? – A labourer, alas!
     (*Work, work, you fool –*)

Somewhere the lamp hanging low from the ceiling
Lights the soft hair of a girl as she reads,
And the red firelight steadily reeling
Puts the hard hands of my friend to sleep.
And the white dog snuffs the warmth, appealing
For the man to heed lest the girl shall weep.

    Tears and dreams for them; for me
    Bitter science – the exams are near.
    I wish I did it more willingly!
    I wish you did not wait, my dear,
    For me to come; since work I must.
    Though it's all the same when we are dead –
        I wish I was only a bust,
            All head – !

Twilight

Darkness comes out of the earth
    And swallows dip into the pallor of the west;
From the hay comes the clamour of children's mirth;
    Wanes the old palimpsest.

The night-stock oozes scent,
    And a moon-blue moth goes flittering by:
All that the worldly day has meant
    Wastes like a lie.

The children have forsaken their play;
    A single star in a veil of light
Glimmers: litter of day
    Is gone from sight.

Love on the Farm

What large, dark hands are those at the window
Grasping in the golden light
Which weaves its way through the evening wind
    At my heart's delight?

Ah, only the leaves! But in the west
I see a redness suddenly come
Into the evening's anxious breast –
    'Tis the wound of love goes home!

The woodbine creeps abroad
Calling low to her lover:
    The sun-lit flirt who all the day
    Has poised above her lips in play
    And stolen kisses, shallow and gay
    Of pollen, now has gone away –
    She woos the moth with her sweet, low word;
And when above her his moth-wings hover
Then her bright breast she will uncover
And yield her honey-drop to her lover.

Into the yellow, evening glow
Saunters a man from the farm below;
Leans, and looks in at the low-built shed
Where the swallow has hung her marriage bed.
   The bird lies warm against the wall.
   She glances quick her startled eyes
   Towards him, then she turns away
   Her small head, making warm display
   Of red upon the throat. Her terrors sway
   Her out of the nest's warm, busy ball,
   Whose plaintive cry is heard as she flies
   In one blue stoop from out the sties
   Into the twilight's empty hall.

Oh, water-hen, beside the rushes
Hide your quaintly scarlet blushes,
Still your quick tail, lie still as dead,
Till the distance folds over his ominous tread!

The rabbit presses back her ears,
Turns back her liquid, anguished eyes
And crouches low; then with wild spring
Spurts from the terror of *his* oncoming;
To be choked back, the wire ring
Her frantic effort throttling:
   Piteous brown ball of quivering fears!
Ah, soon in his large, hard hands she dies,
And swings all loose from the swing of his walk!
Yet calm and kindly are his eyes
And ready to open in brown surprise
Should I not answer to his talk
Or should he my tears surmise.

I hear his hand on the latch, and rise from my chair
Watching the door open; he flashes bare
His strong teeth in a smile, and flashes his eyes
In a smile like triumph upon me; then careless-wise
He flings the rabbit soft on the table board
And comes towards me: ah! the uplifted sword
Of his hand against my bosom! and oh, the broad

Blade of his glance that asks me to applaud
His coming! With his hand he turns my face to him
And caresses me with his fingers that still smell grim
Of the rabbit's fur! God, I am caught in a snare!
I know not what fine wire is round my throat;
I only know I let him finger there
My pulse of life, and let him nose like a stoat
Who sniffs with joy before he drinks the blood.

And down his mouth comes to my mouth! and down
His bright dark eyes come over me, like a hood
Upon my mind! his lips meet mine, and a flood
Of sweet fire sweeps across me, so I drown
Against him, die, and find death good.

Gipsy

I, the man with the red scarf,
    Will give thee what I have, this last week's earnings.
Take them and buy thee a silver ring
    And wed me, to ease my yearnings.

For the rest, when thou art wedded
    I'll wet my brow for thee
With sweat, I'll enter a house for thy sake,
    Thou shalt shut doors on me.

The Collier's Wife

Somebody's knockin' at th' door
    Mother, come down an' see!
– I's think it's nobbut a beggar;
    Say I'm busy.

It's not a beggar, mother: hark
    How 'ard 'e knocks!
– Eh, tha'rt a mard-arsed kid,
    'E'll gie thee socks![2]

Shout an' ax what 'e wants,
    I canna come down.
– 'E says, is it Arthur Holliday's?
     – Say Yes, tha clown.

'E says: Tell your mother as 'er mester's
    Got hurt i' th' pit –
What? Oh my Sirs, 'e never says that,
    That's not it!

Come out o' th' way an' let me see!
    Eh, there's no peace!
An' stop thy scraightin',³ childt,
    Do shut thy face!

'Your mester's 'ad a accident
    An' they ta'ein' 'im i' th' ambulance
Ter Nottingham.' – Eh dear o' me,
    If 'e's not a man for mischance!

Wheer's 'e hurt this time, lad?
    – I dunna know,
They on'y towd me it wor bad –
    It would be so!

Out o' my way, childt! dear o' me, wheer
    'Ave I put 'is clean stockin's an' shirt?
Goodness knows if they'll be able
    To take off 'is pit-dirt!

An' what a moan 'e'll make! there niver
    Was such a man for a fuss
If anything ailed 'im; at any rate
    I shan't 'ave 'im to nuss.

I do 'ope as it's not so very bad!
    Eh, what a shame it seems
As some should ha'e hardly a smite o' trouble
    An' others 'as reams!

It's a shame as 'e should be knocked about
　　　Like this, I'm sure it is!
'E's 'ad twenty accidents, if 'e's 'ad one;
　　　Owt bad, an' it's his!

There's one thing, we s'll 'ave a peaceful 'ouse f'r a
　　　　　bit,
　　　Thank heaven for a peaceful house!
An' there's compensation, sin' it's accident.
　　　An' club-money – I won't growse.

An' a fork an' a spoon 'e'll want – an' what else?
　　　I s'll never catch that train!
What a traipse it is, if a man gets hurt!
　　　I sh'd think 'e'll get right again.

Flapper

Love has crept out of her sealèd heart
　　　As a field-bee, black and amber,
　　　Breaks from the winter-cell, to clamber
Up the warm grass where the sunbeams start.

Mischief has come in her dawning eyes,
　　　And a glint of coloured iris brings
　　　Such as lies along the folded wings
Of the bee before he flies.

Who, with a ruffling, careful breath,
　　　Has opened the wings of the wild young sprite?
　　　Has fluttered her spirit to stumbling flight
In her eyes, as a young bee stumbleth?

Love makes the burden of her voice.
　　　The hum of his heavy, staggering wings
　　　Sets quivering with wisdom the common things
That she says, and her words rejoice.

Thief in the Night

Last night a thief came to me
    And struck at me with something dark.
I cried, but no one heard me,
    I lay dumb and stark.

When I awoke this morning
    I could find no trace;
Perhaps 'twas a dream of warning,
    For I've lost my peace.

Monologue of a Mother

This is the last of all, then, this is the last!
I must fold my hands, and turn my face to the fire,
And watch my dead days fusing together in dross,
Shape after shape, and scene after scene of my past
Clotting to one dead mass in the sinking fire
Where ash on the dying coals grows swiftly, like heavy moss.

Strange he is, my son, for whom I have waited like a lover;
Strange to me, like a captive in a foreign country, haunting
The confines, gazing out beyond, where the winds go free;
White and gaunt, with wistful eyes that hover
Always on the distance, as if his soul were chaunting
A monotonous weird[4] of departure away from me.

Like a thin white bird blown out of the northern seas,
Like a bird from the far north blown with a broken wing
Into our sooty garden, he drags and beats
Along the fence perpetually, seeking release
From me, from the hand of my love which creeps up, needing
His happiness, whilst he in displeasure retreats.

I must look away from him, for my faded eyes
Like a cringing dog at his heels offend him now,
Like a toothless hound pursuing him with my will;
Till he chafes at my crouching persistence, and a sharp spark flies
In my soul from under the sudden frown of his brow
As he blenches and turns away, and my heart stands still.

This is the last, it will not be any more.
All my life I have borne the burden of myself,
All the long years of sitting in my husband's house;
Never have I said to myself as he closed the door:
'Now I am caught! You are hopelessly lost, O Self!
You are frightened with joy, my heart, like a frightened mouse.'

Three times have I offered myself, three times rejected.
It will not be any more. No more, my son, my son! –
Never to know the glad freedom of obedience, since long ago
The angel of childhood kissed me and went! I expected
This last one to claim me; – and now, my son, O my son,
I must sit alone and wait, and never know
The loss of myself, till death comes, who cannot fail.

Death, in whose service is nothing of gladness, takes me;
For the lips and the eyes of God are behind a veil.
And the thought of the lipless voice of the Father shakes me
With dread, and fills my heart with the tears of desire,
And my heart rebels with anguish, as night draws nigher.

The Little Town at Evening

The chime of the bells, and the church clock striking eight
Solemnly and distinctly cries down the babel of children still
      playing in the hay.
The church draws nearer upon us, gentle and great
In shadow, covering us up with her grey.

Like drowsy creatures the houses fall asleep
Under the fleece of shadow, as in between
Tall and dark the church moves, anxious to keep
Their sleeping, cover them soft unseen.

Hardly a murmur comes from the sleeping brood;
I wish the church had covered me up with the rest
In the home-place. Why is it she should exclude
Me so distinctly from sleeping the sleep I'd love best?

In a Boat

See the stars, love,
In the water much clearer and brighter
Than those above us, and whiter,
Like nenuphars!

Star-shadows shine, love:
How many stars in your bowl?
How many shadows in your soul?
Only mine, love, mine?

When I move the oars, see
How the stars are tossed,
Distorted, even lost!
Even yours, do you see?

The poor waters spill
The stars, waters troubled, forsaken! –
The heavens are not shaken, you say, love;
Its stars stand still.

There! did you see
That spark fly up at us? even
Stars are not safe in heaven!
What of me then, love, me?

What then, love, if soon
Your star be tossed over a wave?
Would the darkness look like a grave?
Would you swoon, love, swoon?

Last Hours

The cool of an oak's unchequered shade
Falls on me as I lie in deep grass
Which rushes upward, blade beyond blade,
While higher the darting grass-flowers pass
Piercing the blue with their crocketed spires
And waving flags, and the ragged fires
Of the sorrel's cresset – a green, brave town
Vegetable, new in renown.

Over the tree's edge, as over a mountain
Surges the white of the moon,
A cloud comes up like the surge of a fountain,
Pressing round and low at first, but soon
Heaving and piling a round white dome.
How lovely it is to be at home
Like an insect in the grass
Letting life pass!

There's a scent of clover crept through my hair
From the full resource of some purple dome
Where that lumbering bee, who can hardly bear
His burden above me, never has clomb.
But not even the scent of insouciant flowers
Makes pause the hours.

Down the valley roars a townward train.
I hear it through the grass
Dragging the links of my shortening chain
Southwards, alas!

Flat Suburbs SW, in the Morning

The new red houses spring like plants
    In level rows
Of reddish herbage that bristles and slants
    Its square shadows.

The pink young houses show one side bright
    Flatly assuming the sun,
And one side shadow, half in sight,
    Half-hiding the pavement-run;

Where hastening creatures pass intent
    On their level way,
Threading like ants that can never relent
    And have nothing to say.

Bare stems of street lamps stiffly stand
    At random, desolate twigs,
To testify to a blight on the land
    That has stripped their sprigs.

The Best of School

The blinds are drawn because of the sun,
And the boys and the room in a colourless gloom
Of underwater float: bright ripples run
Across the walls as the blinds are blown
To let the sunlight in; and I,
As I sit on the shores of the class, alone,
Watch the boys in their summer blouses
As they write, their round heads busily bowed:
And one after another rouses
His face to look at me,
To ponder very quietly,
As seeing, he does not see.

And then he turns again, with a little, glad
Thrill of his work he turns again from me,
Having found what he wanted, having got what was to be had.

And very sweet it is, while the sunlight waves
In the ripening morning, to sit alone with the class
And feel the stream of awakening ripple and pass
From me to the boys, whose brightening souls it laves
For this little hour.

                    This morning, sweet it is
To feel the lads' looks light on me,
Then back in a swift, bright flutter to work;
Each one darting away with his
Discovery, like birds that steal and flee.

Touch after touch I feel on me
As their eyes glance at me for the grain
Of rigour they taste delightedly.

As tendrils reach out yearningly,
Slowly rotate till they touch the tree
That they cleave unto, and up which they climb
Up to their lives – so they to me.

I feel them cling and cleave to me
As vines going eagerly up; they twine
My life with other leaves, my time
Is hidden in theirs, their thrills are mine.

Dreams Old and Nascent

OLD

I have opened the windows to warm my hands on the sill
Where the sunlight soaks in the stone: the afternoon
Is full of dreams, my love; the boys are all still
In a wistful dream of Lorna Doone.

The clink of the shunting engines is sharp and fine
Like savage music striking far off; and there
On the great blue palace at Sydenham, lights stir and shine
Where the glass is domed on the silent air.

There lies the world, my darling, full of wonder and wistfulness,
    and strange
Recognitions and greetings of half-acquaint things, as I greet
    the cloud
Of glass palace aloft there, among misty, indefinite things that
    range
At the back of my life's experience, where dreams from the old lives
    crowd.

Over the nearness of Norwood Hill, through the mellow veil
Of the afternoon glows still the old romance of David and Dora,[5]
With the old, sweet, soothing tears, and laughter that shakes the
    sail
Of the ship of the soul over seas where dreamed dreams lure the
    unoceaned explorer.

All the bygone, hushèd years
Streaming back where the mists distil
To forgetfulness: soft-sailing waters where fears
No longer hurt, where the silk sails fill

With that unfelt breeze that ebbs over the seas where the storm
Of living has passed, ebbing on
Through the stirred iridescence that swims in the warm
Wake of a tumult now spent and gone,
Drifts my boat, wistfully lapsing after
The silence of vanishing tears, and the echoes of laughter.

Suburbs on a Hazy Day

O stiffly shapen houses that change not,
    What conjurer's cloth was thrown across you, and
      raised
To show you thus transfigured, changed,
    Your stuff all gone, your menace almost rased?

Such resolute shapes so harshly set
    In hollow blocks and cubes deformed, and heaped
In void and null profusion, how is this?
    In what strong aqua regia[6] now are you steeped?

That you lose the brick-stuff out of you
    And hover like a presentment, fading faint
And vanquished, evaporate away
    To leave but only the merest possible taint!

Weeknight Service

The five old bells
Are hurrying and stridently calling,
Insisting, protesting
They are right, yet clamorously falling
Into gabbling confusion, without resting,
Like spattering shouts of an orator endlessly dropping
From the tower on the town, but endlessly, never stopping.

The silver moon
That somebody has spun so high
To settle the question, heads or tails? has caught

In the net of the night's balloon,
And sits with a smooth, bland smile up there in the sky
Serenely smiling at naught,
Unless the little star that keeps her company
Makes tittering jests at the bells' obscenity;
As if *he* knew aught!

While patient Night
Sits indifferent, hugged in her rags;
She neither knows nor cares
Why the old church bellows and brags;
The noise distresses her ears, and tears
At her tattered silence, as she crouches and covers her face,
Bent, if we did but know it, on a weary and bitter grimace.

The wise old trees
Drop their leaves with a faint, sharp hiss of contempt;
A car at the end of the street goes by with a laugh.
As by degrees
The damned bells cease, and we are exempt,
And the stars can chaff
The cool high moon at their ease; while the droning church
Is peopled with shadows and wailing, and last ghosts lurch
Towards its cenotaph.

A Man Who Died

Ah, stern, cold man,
How can you lie so relentless hard
While I wash you with weeping water!
Do you set your face against the daughter
Of life? Can you never discard
Your curt pride's ban?

You masquerader!
How can you shame to act this part
Of unswerving indifference to me?
You want at last, ah me!
To break my heart,
Evader!

You know your mouth
Was always sooner to soften
Even than your eyes.
Now shut it lies
Relentless, however often
I kiss it in drouth.

It has no breath
Nor any relaxing. Where,
Where are you, what have you done?
What is this mouth of stone?
How did you dare
Take cover in death!

Once you could see,
The white moon show like a breast revealed
By the slipping shawl of stars.
Could see the small stars tremble
As the heart beneath did wield
Systole, diastole.

All the lovely macrocosm
Was woman once to you,
Bride to your groom.
No tree in bloom
But it leaned you a new
White bosom.

And always and ever
Soft as a summering tree
Unfolds from the sky, for your good,
Unfolded womanhood:
Shedding you down as a tree
Sheds its flowers on a river.

I saw your brows
Set like rocks beside a sea of gloom,
And I shed my very soul down into your thought;
Like flowers I fell, to be caught
On the comforted pool, like bloom
That leaves the boughs.

Oh, masquerader,
With a hard face white-enamelled,
What are you now?
Do you care no longer how
My heart is trammelled,
Evader?

Is this you, after all,
Metallic, obdurate,
With bowels of steel?
Did you *never* feel? –
Cold, insensate,
Mechanical!

Ah, no! – you multiform,
You that I loved, you wonderful,
You who darkened and shone,
You were many men in one;
But never this null
This never-warm!

Is this the sum of you?
Is it all naught?
Cold, metal-cold?
Are you all told
Here, iron-wrought?
Is this what's become of you?

Letter from Town: On a Grey
Morning in March

The clouds are pushing in grey reluctance slowly northward to you,
    While north of them all, at the farthest ends, stands one bright
        bosomed, aglance
With fire as it guards the wild north-coasts, red-fire seas running
        through
    The rocks where ravens flying to windward melt as a well-shot
        lance.

You should be out by the orchard, where violets secretly darken the
    earth,
    Or there in the woods of the twilight, with northern wind-flowers
        shaken astir.
Think of me here in the library, trying and trying a song that is
    worth
    Tears and swords to my heart, arrows no armour will turn or
        deter.

You tell me the lambs have come, they lie like daisies white in the
    grass
    Of the dark-green hills; new calves in shed; peewits turn after the
        plough –
It is well for you. For me the navvies work in the road where I pass
    And I want to smite in anger the barren rock of each waterless
        brow.

Like the sough of a wind that is caught up high in the mesh of the
    budding trees,
    A sudden car goes sweeping past, and I strain my soul to hear
The voice of the furtive triumphant engine as it rushes past like a
    breeze,
    To hear on its mocking triumphance unwitting the after-echo of
        fear.

Letter from Town: The Almond Tree

You promised to send me some violets. Did you forget?
    White ones and blue ones from under the orchard hedge?
    Sweet dark purple, and white ones mixed for a pledge
Of our early love that hardly has opened yet.

Here there's an almond tree – you have never seen
    Such a one in the north – it flowers on the street, and I stand
    Every day by the fence to look up at the flowers that expand
At rest in the blue, and wonder at what they mean.

Under the almond tree, the happy lands
    Provence, Japan, and Italy repose;
    And passing feet are chatter and clapping of those
Who play around us, country girls clapping their hands.

You, my love, the foremost, in a flowered gown,
   All your unbearable tenderness, you with the laughter
   Startled upon your eyes now so wide with hereafter,
You with loose hands of abandonment hanging down.

Wedding Morn

The morning breaks like a pomegranate
   In a shining crack of red;
Ah, when to-morrow the dawn comes late
   Whitening across the bed
It will find me watching at the marriage gate
   And waiting while light is shed
On him who is sleeping satiate
   With a sunk, unconscious head.

And when the dawn comes creeping in,
   Cautiously I shall raise
Myself to watch the daylight win
   On my first of days,
As it shows him sleeping a sleep he got
   With me, as under my gaze
He grows distinct, and I see his hot
   Face freed of the wavering blaze.

Then I shall know which image of God
   My man is made toward;
And I shall see my sleeping rod
   Or my life's reward;
And I shall count the stamp and worth
   Of the man I've accepted as mine,
Shall see an image of heaven or of earth
   On his minted metal shine.

Oh, and I long to see him sleep
   In my power utterly;
So I shall know what I have to keep . . .
   I long to see
My love, that spinning coin, laid still

And plain at the side of me
For me to reckon – for surely he will
    Be wealth of life to me.

And then he will be mine, he will lie
    Revealed to me;
Patent and open beneath my eye
    He will sleep of me;
He will lie negligent, resign
    His truth to me, and I
Shall watch the dawn light up for me
    This fate of mine.

And as I watch the wan light shine
    On his sleep that is filled of me,
On his brow where the curved wisps clot and twine
    Carelessly,
On his lips where the light breaths come and go
    Unconsciously,
On his limbs in sleep at last laid low
    Helplessly,
I shall weep, oh, I shall weep, I know
    For joy or for misery.

Violets

Sister, tha knows while we was on th' planks
    Aside o' t' grave, an' th' coffin set
On th' yaller clay, wi' th' white flowers top of it
    Waitin' ter be buried out o' th' wet?

An' t' parson makin' haste, an' a' t' black
    Huddlin' up i' t' rain,
Did t' 'appen ter notice a bit of a lass way back
    Hoverin', lookin' poor an' plain?

       – How should I be lookin' round!
          An' me standin' there on th' plank,
         An' our Ted's coffin set on th' ground,
          Waitin' to be sank!

I'd as much as I could do, to think
  Of 'im bein' gone
That young, an' a' the fault of drink
  An' carryin's on! –

Let that be; 'appen it worna th' drink, neither,
Nor th' carryin' on as killed 'im.
       – No,'appen not,
My sirs! But I say 'twas! For a blither
Lad never stepped, till 'e got in with your lot. –

All right, all right, it's my fault! But let
Me tell about that lass. When you'd all gone
Ah stopped behind on t' pad, i' t' pourin' wet
An' watched what 'er 'ad on.

Tha should ha' seed 'er slive[7] up when yer'd gone!
Tha should ha' seed 'er kneel an' look in
At th' sloppy grave! an' 'er little neck shone
That white, an' 'er cried that much, I'd like to begin

Scraightin' mysen as well. 'Er undid 'er black
Jacket at th' bosom, an' took out
Over a double 'andful o' violets, a' in a pack
An' white an' blue in a ravel, like a clout.[8]

An' warm, for th' smell come waftin' to me. 'Er put 'er face
Right in 'em, an' scraighted a bit again,
Then after a bit 'er dropped 'em down that place,
An' I come away, acause o' th' teemin' rain.

But I thowt ter mysen, as that wor th' only bit
O' warmth as 'e got down theer; th' rest wor stone cold.
From that bit of a wench's bosom; 'e'd be glad of it,
Gladder nor of thy lilies, if tha maun be told.

Lightning

I felt the lurch and halt of her heart
      Next my breast, where my own heart was beating;
And I laughed to feel it plunge and bound,
And strange in my blood-swept ears was the sound
      Of the words I kept repeating,
Repeating with tightened arms, and the hot blood's blindfold art.

Her breath flew warm against my neck,
      Warm as a flame in the close night air;
And the sense of her clinging flesh was sweet
Where her arms and my neck's thick pulse could meet.
      Holding her thus, could I care
That the black night hid her from me, blotted out every speck?

I leaned in the darkness to find her lips
      And claim her utterly in a kiss,
When the lightning flew across her face
And I saw her for the flaring space
      Of a second, like snow that slips
From a roof, inert with death, weeping 'Not this! Not this!'

A moment there, like snow in the dark
      Her face lay pale against my breast,
Pale love lost in a thaw of fear
And melted in an icy tear,
      And open lips, distressed;
A moment; then darkness shut the lid of the sacred ark.

And I heard the thunder, and felt the rain,
      And my arms fell loose, and I was dumb.
Almost I hated her, sacrificed;
Hated myself, and the place, and the iced
      Rain that burnt on my rage; saying: Come
Home, come home, the lightning has made it too plain!

End of Another Home Holiday

When shall I see the half-moon sink again
Behind the black sycamore at the end of the garden?
When will the scent of the dim white phlox
Creep up the wall to me, and in at my open window?

Why is it, the long, slow stroke of the midnight bell
      (Will it never finish the twelve?)
Falls again and again on my heart with a heavy reproach?

The moon-mist is over the village, out of the mist speaks the bell,
And all the little roofs of the village bow low, pitiful, beseeching,
    resigned.
– Speak, you my home! what is it I don't do well?

Ah home, suddenly I love you
As I hear the sharp clean trot of a pony down the road,
Succeeding sharp little sounds dropping into silence
Clear upon the long-drawn hoarseness of a train across the valley.

            *

The light has gone out, from under my mother's door.
      That she should love me so! –
      She, so lonely, greying now!
      And I leaving her,
      Bent on my pursuits!

        Love is the great Asker.
        The sun and the rain do not ask the secret
        Of the time when the grain struggles down in the
          dark.
        The moon walks her lonely way without anguish,
        Because no-one grieves over her departure.

Forever, ever by my shoulder pitiful love will linger,
Crouching as little houses crouch under the mist when I turn.
Forever, out of the mist, the church lifts up a reproachful finger,
Pointing my eyes in wretched defiance where love hides her face to
    mourn.

Oh! but the rain creeps down to wet the grain
That struggles alone in the dark,
And asking nothing, patiently steals back again!
The moon sets forth o' nights
To walk the lonely, dusky heights
Serenely, with steps unswerving;
Pursued by no sign of bereavement
No tears of love unnerving
Her constant tread:
While ever at my side
Frail and sad, with grey, bowed head,
The beggar-woman, the yearning-eyed
Inexorable love goes lagging.

The wild young heifer, glancing distraught,
With a strange new knocking of life at her side
      Runs seeking a loneliness.
The little grain draws down the earth, to hide.
Nay, even the slumberous egg, as it labours under the shell
      Patiently to divide and self-divide,
Asks to be hidden, and wishes nothing to tell.

But when I draw the scanty cloak of silence over my eyes
Piteous love comes peering under the hood;
Touches the clasp with trembling fingers, and tries
To put her ear to the painful sob of my blood;
While her tears soak through to my breast,
      Where they burn and cauterise.

*

The moon lies back and reddens.
In the valley a corncrake calls
      Monotonously,
With a plaintive, unalterable voice, that deadens
      My confident activity;
With a hoarse, insistent request that falls
      Unweariedly, unweariedly,
      Asking something more of me,
            Yet more of me.

Baby Running Barefoot

When the white feet of the baby beat across the grass
The little white feet nod like white flowers in a wind,
They poise and run like puffs of wind that pass
Over water where the weeds are thinned.

And the sight of their white playing in the grass
Is winsome as a robin's song, so fluttering;
Or like two butterflies that settle on a glass
Cup for a moment, soft little wing-beats uttering.

And I wish that the baby would tack across here to me
Like a wind-shadow running on a pond, so she could stand
With two little bare white feet upon my knee
And I could feel her feet in either hand

Cool as syringa buds in morning hours,
Or firm and silken as young peony flowers.

Sigh No More

The cuckoo and the coo-dove's ceaseless calling,
               Calling,
Of a meaningless monotony is palling
All my morning's pleasure in the sun-fleck-scattered wood.

May-blossom and blue bird's-eye flowers falling,
               Falling
In a litter through the elm tree shade are scrawling
Messages of true-love down the dust of the highroad.

I do not like to hear the gentle grieving,
               Grieving
Of the she-dove in the blossom, still believing
Love will yet again return to her and make all good.

When I know that there must ever be deceiving,
               Deceiving
Of the mournful constant heart, that while she's weaving
Her woes, her lover woos and sings within another wood.

Oh, boisterous the cuckoo shouts, forestalling,
                    Stalling
A progress down the intricate enthralling
By-paths where the wanton-headed flowers doff their hood.

And like a laughter leads me onward, heaving,
                    Heaving
A sigh among the shadows, thus retrieving
A decent short regret for that which once was very good.

Guards

A REVIEW IN HYDE PARK, 1910: THE CROWD WATCHES

Where the trees rise like cliffs, proud and blue-tinted in the
        distance,
Between the cliffs of the trees, on the grey-green park
Rests a still line of soldiers, red, motionless range of guards
Smouldering with darkened busbies beneath the bayonets'
        slant rain.

Colossal in nearness a blue police sits still on his horse
Guarding the path; his hand relaxed at his thigh,
And skywards his face is immobile, eyelids aslant
In tedium, and mouth relaxed as if smiling – ineffable tedium!

So! So! Gaily a general canters across the space,
With white plumes blinking under the evening grey sky.
And suddenly, as if the ground moved,
The red range heaves in slow, magnetic reply.

EVOLUTIONS OF SOLDIERS

The red range heaves and compulsory sways, ah see! in the flush of
        a march.
Softly-impulsive advancing as water towards a weir from the arch
Of shadow emerging as blood emerges from inward shades
        of our night
Encroaching towards a crisis, a meeting, a spasm and throb of
        delight.

The wave of soldiers, the coming wave, the throbbing red breast of
    approach
Upon us; dark eyes as here beneath the busbies glittering, dark threats
    that broach
Our beached vessel; darkened rencontre inhuman, and closed warm
    lips, and dark
Mouth-hair of soldiers passing above us, over the wreck of our bark.

And so, it is ebb time, they turn, the eyes beneath the busbies are
    gone.
But the blood has suspended its timbre, the heart from out of oblivion
Knows but the retreat of the burning shoulders, the red-swift
    waves of the sweet
Fire horizontal declining and ebbing, the twilit ebb of retreat.

Aware

Slowly the moon is rising out of the ruddy haze,
Divesting herself of her golden shift, and so
Emerging white and exquisite; and I in amaze
See in the sky before me, a woman I did not know
I loved, but there she goes, and her beauty hurts my heart;
I follow her down the night, begging her not to depart.

A Pang of Reminiscence

High and smaller goes the moon, she is small and very far
    from me,
Wistful and candid, watching me wistfully from her distance,
    and I see
Trembling blue in her pallor a tear that surely I have seen
    before,
A tear which I had hoped that even hell held not again in
    store.

A White Blossom

A tiny moon as small and white as a single jasmine flower
Leans all alone above my window, on night's wintry bower,
Liquid as lime tree blossom, soft as brilliant water or rain
She shines, the first white love of my youth, passionless and in vain.

Corot

The trees rise taller and taller, lifted
On a subtle rush of cool grey flame
That issuing out of the east has sifted
    The spirit from each leaf's frame.

For the trailing, leisurely rapture of life
Drifts dimly forward, easily hidden
By bright leaves uttered aloud; and strife
    Of shapes by a hard wind ridden.

The grey, plasm-limpid, pellucid advance
Of the luminous purpose of Life shines out
Where lofty trees athwart-stream chance
    To shake flakes of its shadow about.

The subtle, steady rush of the whole
Grey foam-mist of advancing Time
As it silently sweeps to its somewhere, its goal,
    Is seen in the gossamer's rime.

Is heard in the windless whisper of leaves,
In the silent labours of men in the field,
In the downward-dropping of flimsy sheaves
    Of cloud the rain-skies yield.

In the tapping haste of a fallen leaf,
In the flapping of red-roof smoke, and the small
Footstepping tap of men beneath
    Dim trees so huge and tall.

For what can all sharp-rimmed substance but catch
In a backward ripple, the wave-length, reveal
For a moment the mighty direction, snatch
    A spark beneath the wheel!

Since Life sweeps whirling, dim and vast,
Creating the channelled vein of man
And leaf for its passage; a shadow cast
    And gone before we can scan.

Ah listen, for silence is not lonely!
Imitate the magnificent trees
That speak no word of their rapture, but only
    Breathe largely the luminous breeze.

Michael Angelo

Who shook thy roundness in his finger's cup?
Who sunk his hands in firmness down thy sides
And drew the circle of his grasp, O man,
Along thy limbs delighted as a bride's?

How wert thou so strange-shapen? What warm finger
Curved thy mouth for thee? and what strong shoulder
Planted thee upright? art proud to see
In the curves of thy form the trace of the unknown moulder?

Who took a handful of light and rolled a ball,
Compressed it till its beam grew wondrous dark,
Then gave thee thy dark eyes, O man! that all
The rest had doorway to thee through that spark?

Who, crouching, put his mouth down in a kiss
And kissed thee to a passion of life, and left
Life in thy mouth, and dim breath's hastening hiss?
Whence cometh this, that thou must guard from theft?

Whence cometh, whither goeth? still the same
Old question without answer! Strange and fain
Life comes to thee, on which thou hast no claim;
Then leaves thee, and thou canst not but complain!

Hyde Park at Night, Before the War

CLERKS

We have shut the doors behind us, and the velvet flowers of night
Lean about us scattering their pollen grains of golden light.

Now at last we lift our faces, and our faces come aflower
To the night that takes us willing, liberates us to the hour.

Now at last the ink and dudgeon passes from our fervent eyes
And out of the chambered wilderness wanders a spirit abroad on its
   enterprise.

> Not too near and not too far
> Out of the stress of the crowd
> Music screams as elephants scream
> When they lift their trunks and scream aloud
> For joy of the night when masters are
>   Asleep and adream.

> So here I hide in the Shalimar[9]
> With a wanton princess slender and proud,
> And we swoon with kisses, swoon till we seem
> Two streaming peacocks gone in a cloud
> Of golden dust, with star after star
>   On our stream.

Piccadilly Circus at Night

STREET-WALKERS

When into the night the yellow light is roused like dust above the
   towns,
Or like a mist the moon has kissed from off a pool in the midst of the
   downs,

Our faces flower for a little hour pale and uncertain along the street,
Daisies that waken all mistaken white-spread in expectancy to
   meet

The luminous mist which the poor things wist was dawn arriving
      across the sky,
When dawn is far behind the star the dust-lit town has driven so high.

All the birds are folded in a silent ball of sleep,
   All the flowers are faded from the asphalt isle in the sea,
Only we hard-faced creatures go round and round, and keep
   The shores of this innermost ocean alive and illusory.

Wanton sparrows that twittered when morning looked in at their eyes
   And the Cyprian's pavement-roses are gone, and now it is we
Flowers of illusion who shine in our gauds, make a Paradise
   On the shores of this ceaseless ocean, gay birds of the town-dark
      sea.

After the Opera

Down the stone stairs
Girls with their large eyes wide with tragedy
Lift looks of shocked and momentous emotion up at me.
And I smile.

Ladies
Stepping like birds with their bright and pointed feet
Peer anxiously forth, as if for a boat to carry them out of the
   wreckage;
And among the wreck of the theatre crowd
I stand and smile.
They take tragedy so becomingly;
Which pleases me.

But when I meet the weary eyes
The reddened, aching eyes of the bar-man with thin arms,
I am glad to go back to where I came from.

Morning Work

A gang of labourers on the piled wet timber
That shines blood-red beside the railway siding
Seem to be making out of the blue of the morning
Something faery and fine, the shuttles sliding,

The red-gold spools of their hands and their faces swinging
Hither and thither across the high crystalline frame
Of day: trolls at the cave of ringing cerulean mining
And laughing with labour, living their work like a game.

Transformations

I THE TOWN

Oh you stiff shapes, swift transformation seethes
About you; only last night you were
A Sodom smouldering in the dense, soiled air:
To-day a thicket of sunshine with blue smoke-wreaths.

To-morrow swimming in evening's vague, dim vapour
Like a weeded city in shadow under the sea,
Below the ocean of shimmering light you will be:
Then a group of toadstools waiting the moon's white taper.

And when I awake in the morning, after rain,
To find the new houses a cluster of lilies glittering
In scarlet, alive with the birds' bright twittering,
I'll say your bond of ugliness is vain.

II THE EARTH

Oh Earth, you spinning clod of earth.
And then you lamp, you lemon-coloured beauty!
Oh Earth, you rotten apple rolling downward;
Then brilliant Earth, from the burr of night in beauty
As a jewel-brown horse-chestnut newly issued!

You are all these, and on me lies the duty
To see you all, sordid or radiant-tissued.

III MEN

Oh labourers, oh shuttles across the blue frame of morning!
You feet of the rainbow balancing the sky!
Oh you who flash your arms like rockets to heaven,
Who in lassitude lean as yachts on the sea-wind lie!

Who crowd in crowds like rhododendrons in blossom,
Who stand alone in despair like a guttering light;
Who grappling down with work or hate or passion
Take writhing forms of all beasts that sweat and that fight;
You who are twisted in grief like crumpling beech-leaves,
Who curl in sleep like kittens, who mass as a swarm
Of bees that vibrate with revolt; who fall to earth
And rot like a bean-pod; what are you, oh multiform?

A Baby Asleep After Pain

As a drenched, drowned bee
Hangs numb and heavy from a bending flower,
    So clings to me
My baby, her brown hair brushed with wet tears
    And laid against her cheek;
Her soft white legs hanging heavily over my arm
    Swing to my walking movement, weak
With after-pain. My sleeping baby hangs upon my life
    Like a burden she hangs on me;
She who has always seemed so light,
    Now wet with tears and pain hangs heavily,
    Even her floating hair sinks heavily
        Reaching downwards;
As the wings of a drenched, drowned bee
    Are a heaviness, and a weariness.

Last Lesson of the Afternoon

When will the bell ring, and end this weariness?
How long have they tugged the leash, and strained apart,
My pack of unruly hounds! I cannot start
Them again on a quarry of knowledge they hate to hunt,
I can haul them and urge them no more.

No longer now can I endure the brunt
Of the books that lie out on the desks; a full threescore
Of several insults of blotted pages, and scrawl
Of slovenly work that they have offered me.
I am sick, and what on earth is the good of it all?
What good to them or me, I cannot see!

                    So, shall I take
My last dear fuel of life to heap on my soul
And kindle my will to a flame that shall consume
Their dross of indifference; and take the toll
Of their insults in punishment? – I will not! –

I will not waste my soul and my strength for this.
What do I care for all that they do amiss!
What is the point of this teaching of mine, and of this
Learning of theirs? It all goes down the same abyss.

What does it matter to me, if they can write
A description of a dog, or if they can't?
What is the point? To us both, it is all my aunt!
And yet I'm supposed to care, with all my might.

I do not, and will not; they won't and they don't; and that's all!
I shall keep my strength for myself; they can keep theirs as well.
Why should we beat our heads against the wall
Of each other? I shall sit and wait for the bell.

School on the Outskirts

How different, in the midst of snow, the great school rises red!
  A red rock silent and shadowless, clung round with clusters of
    shouting lads,
Some few dark-cleaving the doorway, souls that cling as the souls
  of the dead
  In stupor persist at the gates of life, obstinate dark monads.

This new red rock in a waste of white rises against the day
  With shelter now, and with blandishment, since the winds have had
    their way
And laid the desert horrific of silence and snow on the world of
  mankind,
  School now is the rock in this weary land the winter burns and
    makes blind.

A Snowy Day in School

All the long school-hours, round the irregular hum of the class
Have pressed immeasurable spaces of hoarse silence
Muffling my mind, as snow muffles the sounds that pass
Down the soiled street. We have pattered the lessons ceaselessly –

But the faces of the boys, in the brooding, yellow light
Have been for me like a dazed constellation of stars,
Like half-blown flowers dimly shaking at the night,
Like half-seen froth on an ebbing shore in the moon.

Out of each face, strange, dark beams that disquiet;
In the open depths of each flower, dark, restless drops;
Twin-bubbling challenge and mystery, in the foam's whispering riot.
– How can I answer the challenge of so many eyes?

The thick snow is crumpled on the roof, it plunges down
Awfully! – Must I call back a hundred eyes? – A voice
Falters a statement about an abstract noun –
What was my question? – My God, must I break this hoarse

Silence that rustles beyond the stars? – There! –
I have startled a hundred eyes, and now I must look
Them an answer back; it is more than I can bear.

The snow descends as if the slow sky shook
In flakes of shadow down; while through the gap
Between the schools sweeps one black rook.

In the playground, a shaggy snowball stands huge and still
With fair flakes lighting down on it. Beyond, the town
Is lost in this shadowed silence the skies distil.

And all things are in silence, they can brood
Alone within the dim and hoarse silence.
Only I and the class must wrangle; this work is a bitter rood!

Whether or Not

I

Dunna thee tell me it's his'n, mother,
    Dunna thee, dunna thee!
– Oh ay, he'll come an' tell thee his-sèn,
    Wench, wunna he?

Tha doesna mean ter say ter me, mother,
    He's gone wi' that –
– My gel, owt'll do for a man i' th' dark;
    Tha's got it flat!

But 'er's old, mother, 'er's twenty year
    Older nor him –
– Ay, an' yaller as a crowflower; an' yet i' th' dark
    Er'd do for Tim.

Tha niver believes it, does ter, mother?
    It's somebody's lies.
– Ax 'im thy-sèn, wench; a widder's lodger!
    It's no surprise.

II

A widow o' forty-five
Wi' a bitter, dirty skin,
To ha' 'ticed a lad o' twenty-five,
An' 'im to 'ave been took in!

A widow of forty-five
As 'as sludged like a horse all 'er life
Till 'er's tough as whit-leather, to slive
Atween a lad an' 'is wife!

A widow of forty-five!
A glum old otchel,[10] wi' long
Witch teeth, an' 'er black hawk-eyes, as I've
Mistrusted all along!

An' me as 'as kep' my-sèn
Shut like a daisy bud,
Clean an' new an' nice, so's when
He wed he'd ha'e summat good!

An' 'im as nice an' fresh
As any man i' th' force,
To ha' gone an' given his clean young flesh
To a woman that coarse!

III

You're stout to brave this snow, Miss Stainwright,
    Are you makin' Brinsley way?
– I'm off up th' line to Underwood
    Wi' a dress as is wanted to-day.

Oh, are you goin' to Underwood?
    'Appen then you've 'eered!
– What's that as 'appen I've 'eered on, Missis?
    Speak up, you nedn't be feared.

Why, your young man an' Widow Naylor,
    'Er as 'e lodges wi'!
They say he's got 'er wi' childt; but there
    It's nothing to do wi' me!

Though if it's true, they'll turn 'im out
    O' th' p'lice force, without fail;
An' if it's *not* true, you may back your life
    They'll listen to *her* tale.

– Well, I'm believin' no tale, Missis,
    I'm seein' for my-sèn.
An' when I know for sure, Missis,
    I'll talk *then*.

IV

Nay, robin red-breast, tha nedna
    Sit noddin' thy head at me!
My breast's as red as thine, I reckon,
    Flayed red, if tha could but see.

Nay, yo' blessed pee-whips,
    Yo' nedna scraight at me!
I'm scraightin' my-sèn, but arena goin'
    Ter let iv'rybody see.

Tha *art* smock-ravelled,[11] bunny,
    Larropin[12] neck an' crop
I' th' snow! but I's warrant thee
    I'm further ower th' top.

V

Now sithee theer at th' reelroad crossin'
Warmin' 'is-sèn at the stool o' fire
Under th' tank as fills th' ingines,
If there isn't my dearly-beloved liar!

My constable, wi' 'is buttoned breast
As stout as the truth, my Sirs! an' 'is face
As bold as a robin! it's much he cares
For this nice old shame an' disgrace.

Oh, but 'e drops 'is flag when 'e sees me!
Yi, an' 'is face goes white! Oh yes,
Tha can stare at me wi' thy fierce blue eyes;
Tha won't stare me out, I guess.

VI

Whativer brings thee out so far
    In a' this depth o' snow?
– I'm takin' 'ome a weddin'-dress,
    If yer mun know.

Why, is there a weddin' at Underwood
    As tha ne'd trudge up 'ere?
– It's Widder Naylor's weddin'-dress,
    'Er'll be wantin' it, I 'ear.

'Er doesna want no weddin'-dress –
    Why – ? but what dost mean?
– Doesn't ter know what I mean, Timmy?
    Yi, tha must ha' bin 'ard ter wean!

Tha'rt a good-un at suckin'-in yet, Timmy!
    But tell me, isn't it true
As 'er'll be wantin' my weddin'-dress
    In a wik or two?

– Tha's no 'casions ter ha'e me on,
    Lizzie; what's done is done.
– Done, I should think so! An' might I ask
    When tha begun?

It's thee as 'as done it, as much as me,
    So there, an' I tell thee flat.
– Me gotten a childt ter thy landlady?
    – Tha's gotten thy answer pat.

As tha allus 'ast; but let me tell thee
    Hasna ter sent me whoam, when I
Was a'most burstin' mad o' my-sèn,
    An' walkin' in agony?

After I'd kissed thee at night, Lizzie,
    An' tha's laid against me, an' melted
Into me, melted right into me, Lizzie,
    Till I was verily swelted.[13]

An' if my landlady seed me like it.
    An' if 'er clawkin'[14] eyes
Went through me as the light went out,
    Is it any cause for surprise?

– No cause for surprise at all, my lad;
    After kissin' an' cuddlin' wi' me, tha could
Turn thy mouth on a woman like that!
    I hope it did thee good.

– Ay, it did; but afterwards
    I could ha' killed 'er.
– Afterwards! how many times afterwards
    Could ter ha' killed 'er?

Say no more, Liz, dunna thee;
    'Er's as good as thee.
– Then I'll say goodbye to thee, Timothy;
    Take 'er i'stead o' me.

I'll ta'e thy word goodbye, Liz,
    Though I shonna marry 'er.
Nor 'er nor nub'dy. – It is
    Very brave of you, Sir!

– T' childt maun ta'e its luck, it mun,
    An' 'er maun ta'e 'er luck.
F'r I tell yer I h'arena marryin' none
    On yer; yo'n got what yer took!

– That's spoken like a man, Timmy,
    That's spoken like a man!
' 'E up an' fired 'is pistol,
    An' then away 'e ran!'

– I damn well shanna marry 'er,
    Nor yo', so chew it no more!
I'll chuck the flamin' lot o' you –
    – Yer nedn't 'ave swore!

VII

There's 'is collar round th' candlestick,
An' there's the dark-blue tie I bought 'im!
An' these is the woman's kids 'e's so fond on,
An' 'ere comes the cat as caught 'im!

I dunno wheer 'is eyes was – a gret
Round-shouldered hag! My Sirs, to think
Of 'im stoopin' to 'er! You'd wonder 'e could
Throw 'imself down *that* sink!

I expect yer know who I am, Mrs Naylor?
    – Who y'are? yis, you're Lizzie Stainwright.
An' 'appen you'd guess then what I've come for?
    – 'Appen I mightn't, 'appen I might.

Yer knowed as I was courtin' Tim Merfin?
    – Yis, I knowed 'e wor courtin' thee.
An' yet yer've bin carryin' on wi' 'im!
    – Ay, an' 'im wi' me.

Well, now yer've got ter pay for it.
    – If I han, what's that ter thee?
'E isn't goin' ter marry yer.
    – Tha wants 'im thy-sèn, I see.

It 'asn't nothin' to do with me.
    – Then what art colleyfoglin'[15] for?
I'm not 'avin' your orts an' slarts.
    – Which on us said you wor?

But I want you to know 'e's not *marryin'* you.
    – Tha wants 'im thy-sèn too bad.
Though I'll see as 'e pays you, an' does what's right.
    – Tha'rt for doin' a lot wi' t' lad!

VIII

To think I should 'ave ter 'affle an' caffle[16]
    Wi' a woman, an' name 'er a price
For lettin' me marry the lad as I thought
    Ter marry wi' cabs an' rice!

But we'll go unbeknown ter th' registrar,
    An' give *'er* the money there is;
For I won't be beholden to such as 'er,
    I won't, or my name's not Liz.

IX

Ta'e off thy duty stripes, Tim,
    An' come in 'ere wi' me;
Ta'e off thy p'liceman's helmet
    An' look at me.

I wish tha hadna done it, Tim,
    I do, an' that I do!
For whenever I look thee i' th' face, I s'll see
    Her face too.

I wish I could wesh 'er off'n thee;
    'Appen I can, if I try.
But tha'll ha'e ter promise ter be true ter me
    Till I die . . .

X

Twenty pound o' thy own tha hast, an' fifty pound ha'e I;
Thine shall go ter pay the woman, an' wi' my bit we'll buy
All as we s'll want for furniture when tha leaves this place;
An' we'll be married at th' registrar – now lift thy face!

Lift thy face an' look at me, man! canna ter look at me?
Sorry I am for this business, an' sorry if ever I've driven thee
To do such a thing; though it's a poor tale, it is, that I'm
    bound to say,
Afore I can ta'e thee I've got a widder o' forty-five ter pay!

Dunnat thee think but what I've loved thee; I've loved thee
    too well.
An' 'deed an' I wish as this tale o' thine wor niver my tale to tell!
Deed an' I wish I c'd 'a' stood at th' altar wi' thee an' bin
    proud o' thee!
That I could 'a' bin first woman ter thee, as tha'rt first man
    ter me!

But we maun ma'e the best on't. So now rouse up an' look
    at me.
Look up an' say tha'rt sorry tha did it; say tha'rt sorry for
    me.
They'll turn thee out o' th' force, I doubt me; if they do, we
    can see
If my father can get thee a job on t' bank. Say tha'rt sorry, Timmy!

XI

Ay, I'm sorry, I'm sorry,
    But what o' that!
Ay, I'm sorry! Tha nedna worry
    Nor fret thy fat.

I'm sorry for thee, I'm sorry f'r 'er,
    I'm sorry f'r us a'.
But what then? Tha wants me, does ter
    After a'?

Ah'n put my-sèn i' th' wrong, Liz,
    An' 'er as well.
An' tha'rt that right, tha knows; 'tis
    Other folks in hell.

Tha *art* so sure tha'rt right, Liz!
    That damned sure!
But 'ark thee 'ere, that widder woman
    's less graspin', if 'er's poor.

What 'er gen, 'er gen[17] me
    Beout a thought.
'Er gen me summat; I shanna
    Say it wor nought.

I'm sorry for th' trouble, ay
    As comes on us a'.
But sorry for what I had? why
    I'm not, that's a'.

As for marryin', I shanna marry
    Neither on yer.
Ah've 'ad a' as I can carry
    From you an' from 'er.

So I s'll go an' leave yer,
    Both on yer.
I don't like yer, Liz, I want ter
    Get away from yer.

An' I really like 'er neither,
    Even though I've 'ad
More from 'er than from you; but either
    Of yer's too much for this lad.

Let me go! what's good o' talkin'?
    Let's a' ha' done.
Talk about love o' women!
    Ter me it's no fun.

What bit o' cunt I had wi' 'er
    's all I got out of it.
An' 's not good enough, it isn't
    For a permanent fit.

I'll say goodbye, Liz, to yer,
    Yer too much i' th' right for me.
An' wi' 'er somehow it isn't right.
    So goodbye, an' let's let be!

A Winter's Tale

Yesterday the fields were only grey with scattered snow,
And now the longest grass-leaves hardly emerge;
Yet her deep footsteps mark the snow, and go
On towards the pines at the hill's white verge.

I cannot see her, since the mist's pale scarf
Obscures the dark wood and the dull orange sky;
But she's waiting, I know, impatient and cold, half
Sobs struggling into her frosty sigh.

Why does she come so promptly, when she must know
She's only the nearer to the inevitable farewell?
The hill is steep, on the snow my steps are slow –
Why does she come, when she knows what I have to tell?

Return

Now I am come again, to you who have so desired
My coming, why do you look away from me?
Why burns your cheek against me? how have I inspired
Such anger as sets your mouth unwontedly?

Now here I sit while you break the music beneath
Your bow; for broken it is, and hurting to hear.
Cease then from music! Does anguish of absence bequeath
But barbed aloofness when I would draw near?

The Appeal

You, Helen, who see the stars
As mistletoe berries burning in a black tree,
You surely, seeing I am a bowl of kisses
Should put your mouth to mine and drink of me.

Helen, you let my kisses steam
Wasteful into the night's black nostrils; drink
Me up, I pray; oh you, who are Night's bacchante,
How can you from my bowl of kisses shrink?

Lilies in the Fire

I

Ah, you stack of white lilies, all white and gold!
I am adrift as a moonbeam, and without form
Or substance, save I light on you to warm
Your pallor into radiance, flush your cold

White petals incandescent: so that you
Are not a stack of white lilies now, but a white
And clustered star called down to me to-night,
Lighting these autumn leaves like a star dropped through

The slender bare arms of the branches, your tire-maidens
Who lift swart arms to fend me off; but I come
Upon you as an autumn wind on some
Stray whitebeam, and her white fire all unladens.

So now you're a glistening toadstool shining here
Among the crumpled beech-leaves, phosphorescent,
My stack of lilies once white incandescent,
My fallen star among the leaves, my dear!

II

Is it with pain, my dear, that you shudder so?
Is it because I hurt you with pain, my dear?

> Did I shiver? Nay, truly I do not know.
> Some dewdrop maybe splashed my face down here.

Why even now you speak through close-shut teeth.
Was this too much for you?

>   Nay, dear, be still!
> The earth perhaps is chilly underneath
> The leaves – and, dear, you have had your will.

You hold yourself all hard, as if my kisses
Hurt as I gave them; you put me away –

> Nay, never, I put you away: yet each kiss hisses
> Like soft hot ashes on my helpless clay.

III

I am ashamed, you wanted me not to-night.
And it is always so, you sigh against me.
Your brightness dims when I draw too near, and my free
Fire enters you like frost, like a cruel blight.

And now I know, so I must be ashamed;
You love me while I hover tenderly
Like moonbeams kissing you; but the body of me
Closing upon you in the lightning-flamed

Moment, destroys you, you are just destroyed.
Humiliation deep to me, that all my best
Soul's naked lightning, which should sure attest
God stepping through our loins in one bright stride

Means but to you a burden of dead flesh
Heavy to bear, even heavy to uprear
Again from earth, like lilies flagged and sere
Upon the floor, that erst stood up so fresh.

Red Moon-Rise

The train, in running across the weald, has fallen into a steadier stroke,
So even, it beats like silence, and sky and earth in one unbroke
Embrace of darkness lie around, and crushed between them, all
    the loose
And littered lettering of trees and hills and houses closed, and
    we can use
The open book of landscape no more, for the covers of darkness have
    shut upon
Its figured pages, and sky and earth and all between are closed
    in one.

And we are crushed between the covers, we close our eyes and
    say 'Hush!' We try
To escape in sleep the terror of this great bivalve darkness, and
    we lie

Rounded like pearls, for sleep. – And then, from between shut
    lips of the darkness, red
As if from the womb the slow moon rises, as if the twin-walled
    darkness had bled
In a new night-spasm of birth, and given us this new red moon-rise
Which lies on the knees of the night-time ruddy, and makes us hide
    our eyes.

The train beats frantic in haste, and struggles away
From this rosy terror of birth that has slid down
From out of the loins of night, to glow in our way
Like a portent; but, Lord, I am glad, so glad, I drown
My fear in accepting the portent. The train can now
Not pass the red moon risen, and I am glad,

Glad as the Magi were when they saw the brow
Of the hot-born infant bless the folly which had
Led them thither to peace;
               for now I know
The world within worlds is a womb, whence issues all
The shapeliness that decks us here-below:
And the same fire that boils within this ball
Of earth, and quickens all herself with flowers,
Is womb-fire in the stiffened clay of us:

And every flash of thought that we and ours
Send suddenly out, and every gesture, does
Fly like a spark into the womb of passion,
To start a birth, from joy of the begetting.

World within worlds a womb, that gives and takes;
Gives us all forth, that we may give again
The seed of life incarnate, that falls and wakes
Within the womb, new shapes, and then, new men.

    And pangs of birth, and joy of the begetting,
    And sweat of labour, and the meanest fashion
    Of fretting or of gladness, shows the jetting
    Of a trail of our small fire on the darkened sky
    Where we can see it, our fire to the innermost fire
    Leaping like spray, in the return of passion.

And even in the watery shells that lie
Alive within the oozy under-mire,
A grain of this same fire we can descry
Spurting to soothe the womb's unslaked desire.

And so, from out the screaming birds that fly
Across the heavens when the storm leaps higher,
And from the swirling, angry folk that try
To come at last to that which they require,

And from the men that dance, and the girls that laugh,
And the flower that puts its tongue out, and fern that puffs
Dust as the puff-ball does, and birds that chaff
And chitter, and wind that shakes and cuffs
The branches, invisible seed of experience blows
Into the womb of the worlds, that nothing knows.

And though it be love's wet blue eyes that cry
To the other love, to relinquish his desire,
Even there I see a blue spark that will fly
Into the womb, to kindle an unknown fire.

Scent of Irises

A faint, sickening scent of irises
Persists all morning. Here in a jar on the table
A fine proud spike of purple irises
Rising up in the class-room litter, makes me unable
To see the class's lifted and bended faces
Save in a broken pattern, amid purple and gold and sable.

I can smell the bog-end, gorgeous in its breathless
Dazzle of may-blobs, where the marigold glare overcast you
With fire on your cheeks and your brow and your chin as you
    dipped
Your face in the marigold bunch, to touch and contrast you,
Your own dark mouth with the bridal faint lady-smocks,
And the kingcups' glisten, that shall long outlast you.

You amid the bog-end's yellow incantation,
You sitting in the cowslips of the meadow above,
Me, your shadow on the bog-flame flowery may-blobs,
Me full length in the cowslips, muttering you love;
You, your soul like a lady-smock, lost, evanescent,
You with your face all rich, like the sheen on a dove!

You are always asking, do I remember, remember
The buttercup bog-end where the flowers rose up
And glazed you over with a sheen of gold?
You ask me, do the healing days close up
The gulf that came between us, and drew us in?
Do they wipe away the gloom the gulf throws up?

You upon the dry, dead beech-leaves, once more, only once
Taken like a sacrifice, in the night invisible;
Only the darkness, and the scent of you! –
And yes, thank God, it still is possible
The healing days shall close the dark gulf up
Wherein we fainted like a smoke or dew!

Like vapour, dew, or poison! Now, thank God
The last year's fire is gone, and your face is ash;
And the gulf that came between you, woman, and me, man,
That day, is half grown over, it need not abash
Either of us any more; henceforth we can
Forget each other and the bruise of our bodies' clash.

Forecast

Patience, little Heart!
One day a heavy-breasted, June-hot woman
Will enter and shut the door, to stay.

And when your stifling soul would summon
Cool, lonely night, her breasts will keep the night at bay,
Leaning in your room like two tiger-lilies, curving
Their pale-gold petals back with steady will,
Killing the blue dusk with harsh scent, unnerving
Your body with their nipple-thrust, until
You thirst for coolness with a husky thirst.

And then you will remember, for the first
Time with true longing, what I was to you.
Like a wild daffodil down-dreaming,
And waiting through the blue
Chill dusk for you, and gladly gleaming
Like a little light at your feet.

Patience, little Heart! I shall be sweet
In after years, in memory, to you.

Prophet

Ah, my darling, when over the purple horizon shall loom
The shrouded mother of a new idea, men hide their faces,
Cry out and fend her off, as she seeks her procreant groom,
Wounding themselves against her, denying her fecund embraces.

Discipline

It is stormy, and raindrops cling like silver bees to the panes,
The thin sycamore in the playground is swinging with flattened leaves;
The heads of the boys move dimly through a yellow gloom that stains
The class; over them all the dark net of my discipline weaves.

It is no good, dear, gentleness and forbearance; I endured too long.
I have pushed my hands in the dark soil, under the flower of my soul
And the gentle leaves, and have felt where the roots are strong
Fixed in the darkness, grappling for the deep soil's crowded control.

And there in the dark, my darling, where the roots are entangled and
    fight
Each one for its hold on the concrete darkness, I know that there
In the night where we first have being, before we rise on the light,
We are not lovers, my darling, we fight and we do not spare.

And in the original dark the roots cannot keep, cannot know
Any communion whatever, but they bind themselves on to the dark,
And drawing the darkness together, crush from it a twilight, a slow
Dim self that rises slowly to leaves and the flower's gay spark.

I came to the boys with love, dear, and only they turned on me;
With gentleness came I, with my heart 'twixt my hands like a bowl,
Like a loving-cup, like a grail, but they spilt it triumphantly
And tried to break the vessel, and violate my soul.

And perhaps they were right, for the young are busy deep down at the
    roots,
And love would only weaken their under-earth grip, make shallow
Their hold on reality, enfeeble their rising shoots
With too much tincture of me, instead of the dark's deep fallow.

I thought that love would do all things, but now I know I am wrong.
There are depths below depths, my darling, where love does not
    belong.
Where the fight that is fight for being is fought throughout the long
Young years, and the old must not win, not even if they love and are
    strong.

I must not win their souls, no never, I only must win
The brief material control of the hour, leave them free of me.
Learn they must to obey, for all harmony is discipline,
And only in harmony with others the single soul can be free.

Let them live, the boys, and learn not to trespass; I had to learn
Not to trespass on them with love, they must learn not to trespass in
    the young
Cruel self; the fight is not for existence, the fight is to burn
At last into blossom of being, each one his own flower outflung.

They are here to learn but one lesson, that they shall not thwart each
    other
Nor be thwarted, in life's slow struggle to unfold the flower of the self.
They draw their sap from the Godhead, not from me, but they
    must not smother
The sun from their neighbour either, nor be smothered in turn by pelf.

I will teach them the beginning of the lesson at the roots, and
    then no more.
I throw from out of the darkness myself like a flower into sight
Of the day, but it's nothing to do with the boys, so let them ignore
What's beyond them, and fight with me in discipline's little fight.

But whoever would pluck apart my flowering will burn their hands,
For flowers are tender folk, and roots can only hide.
But sometimes the opening petals are fire, and the scarlet brands
Of the blossom are roses to look at, but flames when they're tried.

But now I am trodden to earth, and my fires are low;
Now I am broken down like a plant in winter, and all
Myself but a knowledge of roots, of roots in the dark, that throw
A net on the undersoil, that lies passive, and quickened with gall.

Yet wait awhile, for henceforth I will love when a blossom calls
To my blossom in perfume and seed-dust, and only then; I will give
My love where it is wanted. Yet wait awhile! My fall
Is complete for the moment, yet wait, and you'll see that my
    flower will live.

The Punisher

I have fetched the tears up out of the little wells,
Scooped them up with small, iron words,
          Dripping over the runnels.

The harsh, cold wind of my words drove on, and still
I watched the tears on the guilty cheeks of the boys
          Glitter and spill.

Cringing Pity, and Love, white-handed, came
Hovering about the Judgment that stood in my eyes
          Whirling a flame.

                              *

The tears are dry, and the cheek's young fruits are fresh
With laughter, and clear the exonerated eyes, since pain
          Beat through the flesh.

The Angel of Judgment has departed again to the Nearness.
Desolate I am as a church whose lights are put out
          And doubt enters in drearness.

The fire rose up in the bush and blazed apace,
The thorn-leaves crackled and twisted and sweated in anguish;
     Then God left the place.

Like a flower that the frost has hugged and let go, my head
Is heavy, and my heart beats slowly, laboriously,
          My spirit is dead.

Tease

I will give you all my keys,
    You shall be my châtelaine,
You shall enter as you please,
    As you please shall go again.

When I hear you jingling through
    All the chambers of my soul,
How I sit and laugh at you
    In your close housekeeping rôle!

Jealous of the smallest cover,
    Angry at the simplest door;
Well, you anxious, inquisitive lover,
    Are you pleased with what's in store?

You have fingered all my treasures,
    Have you not, most curiously
Handled all my tools and measures
    And masculine machinery?

Over every single beauty
    You have had your little rapture;
You have slain, as was your duty,
    Every sin-mouse you could capture.

Still you are not satisfied!
    Still you tremble faint reproach!
Challenge me I keep aside
    Secrets that you may not broach.

Maybe yes, and maybe no;
    Maybe there *are* secret places,
Altars barbarous below,
    Elsewhere halls of high disgraces.

Maybe yes, and maybe no,
    You may have it as you please;
Since you are so keen to know
    Everything, Miss Ill-at-ease!

Mystery

Now I am all
One bowl of kisses,
Such as the tall
Slim votaresses
Of Egypt filled
For divine excesses.

I lift to you
My bowl of kisses,
And through the temple's
Blue recesses
Cry out to you
In wild caresses.

As to my lips'
Bright crimson rim
The passion slips;
And down my slim
White body drips
The moving hymn.

And still before
The altar, I
Exalt the bowl
Brimful, and cry
To you to stoop
And drink, Most High.

Ah, drink me up
That I may be
Within your cup
Like a mystery,
Like wine that is still
In ecstasy.

Glimmering still
In ecstasy
Commingled wines
Of you and me
In one fulfil
The mystery.

Repulsed

The last silk-floating thought has gone from the dandelion stem,
And the flesh of the stalk holds up for nothing a blank diadem.

So night's flood-winds have lifted my last desire from me,
And my hollow flesh stands up in the night like vanity.

As I stand on this hill, with the whitening cave of the city in front
And this Helen beside me, I am blank; being nothing, I bear the brunt

Of the nightly heavens overhead, like an immense, open eye,
Like a cat's distended pupil, that sparkles with little stars
As with thoughts that flash and crackle in far-off malignancy,
So distant, they cannot touch me, whom now nothing mars.

In front of me, yes, up the darkness, goes the gush of the lights of two
    towns,
As the breath which rushes upwards from the nostrils of an immense
Beast crouched across the globe, ready, if need be, to pounce
Across the space on the cat in heaven's hostile eminence.

All round me, above and below, the night's twin consciousness roars
With sounds that endlessly swell and sink like the storm of
    thought in the brain,
Lifting and falling, long gasps through the sluices, like silence
    that pours
Through invisible pulses, slowly, filling the night's dark vein.

The night is immense and awful, yet to me it is nothing at all.
Or rather 'tis I am nothing, here in the fur of the heather
Like an empty dandelion stalk, bereft of connection, small
And nakedly nothing 'twixt world and heaven, two creatures
    hostile together.

I in the fur of the world, alone; but this Helen close by!
How we hate one another to-night, hate, she and I
To numbness and nothingness; I dead, she refusing to die.
The female whose venom can more than kill, can numb and then
    nullify.

Coldness in Love

And you remember, in the afternoon
The sea and the sky went grey, as if there had sunk
A flocculent dust on the floor of the world: the festoon
Of the sky sagged dusty as spider cloth,
And coldness clogged the sea, till it ceased to croon.

A dank, sickening scent came up from the grime
Of weed that blackened the shore, so that I recoiled
Feeling the raw cold dun me: and all the time
You leapt about on the slippery rocks, and threw
Me words that rang with a brassy, shallow chime.

And all day long, that raw and ancient cold
Deadened me through, till the grey downs dulled to sleep.
Then I longed for you with your mantle of love to fold
Me over, and drive from out of my body the deep
Cold that had sunk to my soul, and there kept hold.

But still to me all evening long you were cold,
And I was numb with a bitter, deathly ache;
Till old days drew me back into their fold,
And dim hopes crowded me warm with companionship,
And memories clustered me close, and sleep was cajoled.

And I slept till dawn at the window blew in like dust,
Like a linty, raw-cold dust disturbed from the floor
Of the unswept sea; a grey pale light like must
That settled upon my face and hands till it seemed
To flourish there, as pale mould blooms on a crust.

And I rose in fear, needing you fearfully.
For I thought you were warm as a sudden jet of blood.
I thought I could plunge in your living hotness, and be
Clean of the cold and the must. With my hand on the latch
I heard you in your sleep speak strangely to me.

And I dared not enter, feeling suddenly dismayed.
So I went and washed my deadened flesh in the sea

And came back tingling clean, but worn and frayed
With cold, like the shell of the moon; and strange it seems
That my love can dawn in warmth again, unafraid.

Suspense

The wind comes from the north
Blowing little flocks of birds
Like spray across the town,
And a train roaring forth
Rushes stampeding down
South, with flying curds
Of steam, from the darkening north.

Whither I turn and set
Like a needle steadfastly,
Waiting ever to get
The news that she is free;
But ever fixed, as yet,
To the lode of her agony.

Endless Anxiety

The hoar-frost crumbles in the sun,
    The crisping steam of a train
Melts in the air, while two black birds
    Sweep past the window again.

Along the vacant road a red
    Telegram-bicycle approaches; I wait
In a thaw of anxiety, for the boy
    To leap down at our gate.

He has passed us by; but is it
    Relief that starts in my breast?
Or a deeper bruise of knowing that still
    She has no rest.

The End

If I could have put you in my heart,
If but I could have wrapped you in myself
How glad I should have been!
And now the chart
Of memory unrolls again to me
The course of our journey here, here where we part.

And oh, that you had never, never been
Some of your selves, my love; that some
Of your several faces I had never seen!
And still they come before me, and they go;
And I cry aloud in the moments that intervene.

And oh, my love, as I rock for you to-night
And have not any longer any hope
To heal the suffering, or to make requite
For all your life of asking and despair,
I own that some of me is dead to-night.

The Bride

My love looks like a girl tonight,
        But she is old.
The plaits that lie along her pillow
        Are not gold,
But threaded with filigree silver,
        And uncanny cold.

She looks like a young maiden, since her brow
        Is smooth and fair;
Her cheeks are very smooth, her eyes are closed,
        She sleeps a rare,
Still, winsome sleep, so still, and so composed.

Nay, but she sleeps like a bride, and dreams her dreams
        Of perfect things.
She lies at last, the darling, in the shape of her dream;
        And her dead mouth sings
By its shape, like thrushes in clear evenings.

The Virgin Mother

My little love, my darling,
You were a doorway to me;
You let me out of the confines
Into this strange countrie
Where people are crowded like thistles,
Yet are shapely and comely to see.

My little love, my dearest,
Twice you have issued me,
Once from your womb, sweet mother,
Once from your soul, to be
Free of all hearts, my darling,
Of each heart's entrance free.

And so, my love, my mother,
I shall always be true to you.
Twice I am born, my dearest:
To life, and to death, in you;
And this is the life hereafter
Wherein I am true.

I kiss you goodbye, my darling,
Our ways are different now;
You are a seed in the night-time,
I am a man, to plough
The difficult glebe of the future
For seed to endow.

I kiss you goodbye, my dearest,
It is finished between us here.
Oh, if I were calm as you are,
Sweet and still on your bier!
Oh God, if I had not to leave you
Alone, my dear!

Is the last word now uttered?
Is the farewell said?
Spare me the strength to leave you
Now you are dead.
I must go, but my soul lies helpless
Beside your bed.

At the Window

The pine trees bend to listen to the autumn wind as it mutters
Something which sets the black poplars ashake with hysterical
    laughter;
As slowly the house of day is closing its eastern shutters.

Farther down the valley the clustered tombstones recede,
Winding about their dimness the mist's grey cerements, after
The street lamps in the twilight have suddenly started to bleed.

The leaves fly over the window, and utter a word as they pass
To the face that gazes outwards, watching for night to waft a
Meaning or a message over the window glass.

Reminder

Do you remember
How night after night swept level and low
Overhead, at home, and had not one star
Nor one narrow gate for the moon to go
    Forth to her fields, that November?

And you remember
How towards the north a red blotch on the sky
Burns like a blot of anxiety
Over the forges, and small flames ply
    Like ghosts on the glowing of the ember?

Those were the days
When it was awful autumn to me;
When only there glowed on the dark of the sky
The red reflection of her agony,
    My beloved, smelting down in the blaze

Of death; my dearest
Love who had borne, and now was leaving me.
And I at the foot of her cross did suffer
    My own gethsemane.

So I came to you;
And twice, after wild kisses, I saw
The rim of the moon divinely rise
And strive to detach herself from the raw
    Blackened edge of the skies.

Strive to escape;
With her whiteness revealing my sunken world
Tall and loftily shadowed. But the moon
Never magnolia-like unfurled
    Her white, her lamp-like shape.

For you told me no.
Begged me to ask not for the dour
Communion, offering 'a better thing.'
So I lay on your breast for an obscure hour
    Feeling your fingers go

Like a rhythmic breeze
Over my hair, and tracing my brows,
Till I knew you not from a little wind.
– I wonder if God allows
    Us only one moment his keys!

If only then
You could have unlocked the moon on the night?
And I baptized myself in the well
Of your love? we both have entered then the right
    Rare passion, and never again?

I wonder if only
You had taken me then, how different
Life would have been? should I have spent
Myself in anger, and you have bent
    Your head, through being lonely?

Drunk

Too far away, O love, I know,
To save me from this haunted road
Whose lofty roses break and blow
On a night-sky bent with a load

Of lights; each solitary rose,
Each arc-lamp golden does expose
Ghost beyond ghost of blossom, shows
Might blenched with a thousand snows

Of hawthorn and of lilac trees,
White lilac; shows discoloured night
Dripping with all the golden lees
Laburnum gives back to light.

And shows the red of hawthorn set
On high to the fuming sky of night
Like flags in pale blood newly wet,
Blood shed in the silent fight

Of life with love and love with life,
Of battling for a little food
Of kisses, long seeking for a wife
Long ago, long ago wooed.

Too far away you are, my love,
To steady my brain in this phantom show
That passes the nightly road above
And returns again below.

*

The enormous cliff of horse-chestnut trees
    Has poised on each of its ledges
An erect small girl looking down at me;
White-nightgowned little chits I see
    And they peep at me over the edges
Of the leaves as though they would leap, should I call
    Them down to my arms:
– But, child, you're too small for me; too small
    Your little charms! –

White little sheaves of nightgowned maids
        Some other will thresh you out! –
But I see leaning from the shades
A lilac there, like a lady who braids
        Her white mantilla about
Her face, and forward leans to catch the sight
        Of a lover's face;
Gracefully sighing through the white
        Flowery mantilla of lace.

And another lilac in purple veiled
        Discreetly, yet recklessly calls
In a low, shocking perfume, to know who has hailed
Her forth from the dark: my strength has failed
        In her voice, and a weak tear falls –
Oh, and see the laburnum shimmering
                Her draperies down
As if she would slip the gold, and glimmering
                White stand naked of gown.

                        *

The pageant of flowery trees above
        The street pale-passionate goes.
And down below on the pavement, love
        In a meaner pageant flows.

Two and two are the folk that walk,
        They pass in a half embrace
Of linking elbows, and they talk
        With dull face leaning to face.

        But I am alone, and wavering home
                Along this haunted road;
        And never a blossoming woman will roam
                To my arms with her welcome load.

        And never a girl like a chestnut flower
                Will tiptoe into my room.
        I shall get no answer in any hour.
                To live alone is my doom.

Sorrow

Why does the thin grey strand
Floating up from the forgotten
Cigarette between my fingers,
Why does it trouble me?

Ah, you will understand;
When I carried my mother downstairs,
A few times only, at the beginning
Of her soft-foot malady,

I should find, for a reprimand
To my gaiety, a few long grey hairs
On the breast of my coat; and one by one
I watched them float up the dark chimney.

Dolour of Autumn

The acrid scents of autumn,
Reminiscent of slinking beasts, make me fear
Everything, tear-trembling stars of autumn
And the snore of the night in my ear.

For suddenly, flush-fallen,
All my life, in a rush
Of shedding away, has left me
Naked exposed on the bush.

I on the bush of the globe
Like a newly-naked berry shrink
Disclosed; but 'tis I who am prowling
As well in the scents that slink

Abroad: I in this naked berry
Of flesh that stands dismayed on the bush!
And I in the stealthy, brindled odours
Prowling about the lush

And acrid night of autumn!
My soul, along with the rout
Rank and treacherous, prowling
Disseminated out.

For the night, with a great breath taken
Has drawn my spirit outside
Me, till I reel with disseminated consciousness
Like a man who has died.

At the same time stand exposed
Here on the bush of the globe,
A newly-naked berry of flesh
For the stars to probe.

The Inheritance

Since you did depart
Out of my reach, my darling,
Into the hidden,
I see each shadow start
With recognition, and I
Am wonder-ridden.

I am dazed with the farewell
But I scarcely feel your loss.
You left me a gift
Of tongues, so the shadows tell
Me things, and the silences toss
Me their drift.

You sent me a cloven fire
Out of death, and it burns in the draught
Of the breathing hosts,
Kindles the darkening pyre
Of the mournful, till people waft
Like candid ghosts.

Form after form, in the streets
Waves like a ghost along
Kindled to me;
The star above the house-tops greets
Me every eve with a long
Song fierily.

And all day long, the town
Glimmers with subtle ghosts
Going up and down
In the common, prison-like dress,
Yet their daunted looking flickers
To me, that I answer Yes!

So I am not lonely nor sad
Although bereaved of you,
My love.
I move among a townfolk clad
With words, but the night shows through
Their words as they move.

Silence

Since I lost you, I am silence-haunted;
        Sounds wave their little wings
A moment, then in weariness settle
        On the flood that soundless swings.

Whether the people in the street
        Like pattering ripples go by,
Or whether the theatre sighs and sighs
        With a loud, hoarse sigh:

Or the wind shakes a ravel of light
        Over the dead-black river,
Or last night's echoings
        Make the daybreak shiver:

I feel the silence waiting
    To sip them all up again,
In its last completeness drinking
    Down the noise of men.

Listening

I listen to the stillness of you,
    My dear, among it all;
I feel your silence touch my words as I talk
    And hold them in thrall.

My words fly off a forge
    The length of a spark;
I see the silence easily sip them
    Up in the dark.

The lark sings loud and glad,
    Yet I am not loth
That silence should take the song and the bird
    And lose them both.

A train goes roaring south,
    The steam-flag flowing;
I see the stealthy shadow of silence
    Alongside going.

And off the forge of the world
    Whirling in the draught of life
Go myriad sparks of people, filling
    The night with strife.

Yet they never change the darkness
    Nor blench it with noise;
Alone on the perfect silence
    The stars are buoys.

Brooding Grief

A yellow leaf, from the darkness
Hops like a frog before me;
Why should I start and stand still?

I was watching the woman that bore me
Stretched in the brindled darkness
Of the sick-room, rigid with will
To die: and the quick leaf tore me
Back to this rainy swill
Of leaves and lamps and the city street mingled before me.

Last Words to Miriam

Yours is the sullen sorrow,
    The disgrace is also mine;
Your love was intense and thorough,
Mine was the love of a growing flower
    For the sunshine.

You had the power to explore me,
    Blossom me stalk by stalk;
You woke my spirit, you bore me
To consciousness, you gave me the dour
    Awareness – then I suffered a balk.

Body to body I could not
    Love you, although I would.
We kissed, we kissed though we should not.
You yielded, we threw the last cast,
    And it was no good.

You only endured, and it broke
    My craftsman's nerve.
No flesh responded to my stroke;
So I failed to give you the last
    Fine torture you did deserve.

You are shapely, you are adorned
  But opaque and null in the flesh;
Who, had I but pierced with the thorned
Full anguish, perhaps had been cast
  In a lovely illumined mesh

Like a painted window; the best
  Fire passed through your flesh,
Undrossed it, and left it blest
In clean new awareness. But now
  Who shall take you afresh?

Now who will burn you free
  From your body's deadness and dross?
Since the fire has failed in me,
What man will stoop in your flesh to plough
  The shrieking cross?

A mute, nearly beautiful thing
  Is your face, that fills me with shame
As I see it hardening;
I should have been cruel enough to bring
  You through the flame.

Malade

The sick grapes on the chair by the bed lie prone; at the window
The tassel of the blind swings constantly, tapping the pane
As the air moves in.

The room is the hollow rind of a fruit, a gourd
Scooped out and bare, where a spider,
Folded in its legs as in a bed,
Lies on the dust, watching where there is nothing to see but dusky
  walls.

And if the day outside were mine! What is the day
But a grey cave, with great grey spider-cloths hanging

Low from the roof, and the wet dust falling softly from them
Over the wet dark rocks, the houses, and over
The spiders with white faces, that scuttle on the floor of the cave!

Ah, but I am ill, and it is still raining, coldly raining!

Lotus and Frost

How many times, like lotus lilies risen
    Upon the surface of the waters, there
    Have risen floating on my blood the rare
Soft glimmers of desire escaped from prison!

So I am clothed all over with the light
    And sensitive, bud-like blossoming of passion;
    Till, naked for her in the finest fashion,
The flowers of all my mud swim into sight.

And then I offer all myself unto
    This woman who likes to love me; but she turns
    A look of hatred on the flower that burns
To break and pour her out its precious dew.

And slowly all the blossom shuts in pain,
    And all the lotus buds of love sink over
    To die unopened; when this moon-faced lover
Kind on the weight of suffering smiles again.

The Yew Tree on the Downs

A gibbous moon hangs out of the twilight,
    Star-spiders, spinning their thread,
Drop a little lower, withouten respite
    Watching us overhead.

Come then under this tree, where the tent-cloths
    Curtain us in so dark
That here we're safe from even the ermine moth's
    Twitching remark.

Here in this swarthy, secret tent,
 Whose black boughs flap the ground,
Come, draw the thorn from my discontent,
 And bless the wound.

This rare, ancient night! For in here
 Under the yew tree tent
The darkness is secret, and I could sear
 You like frankincense into scent.

Here not even the stars can spy us,
 Not even the moths can alight
On our mystery; nought can descry us
 Nor put us to flight.

Put trust then now in the black-boughed tree,
 Lie down, and open to me
The inner dark of the mystery,
 Be penetrate, like the tree.

Waste not the yew tree's waiting, waste
 Not this inner night!
Open the core of gloaming, taste
 The last dark delight.

Troth with the Dead

The moon is broken in twain, and half a moon
Beyond me lies on the low, still floor of the sky;
The other half of the broken coin of troth
Is buried away in the dark, where the dead all lie.

They buried her half in the grave when they laid her away;
Pushed gently away and hidden in the thick of her hair
Where it gathered towards the plait, on that very last day;
And like a moon unshowing it must still shine there.

So half lies on the sky, for a general sign
Of the troth with the dead that we are pledged to keep;
Turning its broken edge to the dark, its shine
Ends like a broken love, that turns to the dark of sleep.

And half lies there in the dark where the dead all lie
Lost and yet still connected; and between the two
Strange beams must travel still, for I feel that I
Am lit beneath my heart with a half-moon, weird and blue.

At a Loose End

Many years have I still to burn, detained
Like a candle-flame on this body; but I enclose
Blue shadow within me, a presence which lives contained
In my flame of living, the invisible heart of the rose.

So through these days, while I burn on the fuel of life,
What matter the stuff I lick up in my daily flame;
Seeing the core is a shadow inviolate,
A darkness that dreams my dream for me, ever the same.

Submergence

When along the pavement,
Palpitating flames of life,
People flicker round me,
I forget my bereavement,
The gap in my life's constellation,
The place where a star used to be.

Nay, though the pole-star
Is blown out like a candle,
And all the heavens are wandering in disarray,
Yet when pleiads of people are
Deployed around me, and I see
The street's long, outstretched milky-way!

When people flicker down the pavement
I forget my bereavement.

The Enkindled Spring

This spring as it comes bursts up in bonfires green,
Wild puffing of green-fire trees, and flame-green bushes,
Thorn-blossom lifting in wreaths of smoke between
Where the wood fumes up, and the flickering, watery rushes.

I am amazed at this spring, this conflagration
Of green fires lit on the soil of earth, this blaze
Of growing, these smoke-puffs that puff in wild gyration,
Faces of people blowing across my gaze!

And us what sort of fire am I among
This conflagration of spring? the gap in it all – !
Not even palish smoke like the rest of the throng.
Less than the wind that runs to the flamy call!

Excursion Train

I wonder, can the night go by,
Can this shot arrow of travel fly
Shaft-golden with light, sheer into the sky
        Of a dawned to-morrow,
Without ever sleep delivering us
From each other, or loosing the dolorous
        And turgid sorrow!

What is it then that you can see,
That at the window endlessly
You watch the red sparks whirl and flee
        And the night look through?
Your presence peering lonelily there
Oppresses me so, I can hardly bear
        To share the night with you.

You hurt my heart-beat's privacy:
I wish I could put you away from me:
I suffocate in this intimacy
        In which I half love you;

How I have longed for this night in the train!
Yet now every fibre of me cries in pain
    To God to remove you!

Though surely my soul's best dream is still
That a new night pouring down shall swill
Us away in an utter sleep, until
    We are one, smooth-rounded!
Yet closely bitten in to me
Is this armour of stiff reluctancy,
    And my dream is ill-founded.

So, Helen, when another night
Comes on us, lift your fingers white
And strip me naked, touch me light
    Light, light all over.
For I ache most earnestly for your touch,
Yet I cannot move, however much
    I would be your lover.

Night after night with a blemish of day
Unblown and unblossomed has withered away;
Come another night, come a new night, say
    Will you pluck it apart?
Will you open the amorous, aching bud
Of my body, and loose the essential flood
    That would pour to you from my heart?

Release

Helen, had I known yesterday
That you could discharge the ache
    Out of the wound,
Had I known yesterday you could take
The turgid electric ache away,
    Drink it up in the ground
Of your soft white body, as lightning
Is drunk from an agonised sky by the earth,
    I should have hated you, Helen.

But since my limbs gushed full of fire,
Since from out of my blood and bone
            Poured a heavy flame
To you, earth of my atmosphere, stone
Of my steel, lovely white flint of desire,
            You have no name.
Earth of my swaying atmosphere,
Substance of my inconstant breath,
            I cannot but cleave to you, Helen.

Since you have drunken up the drear
Death-darkened storm, and death
            Is washed from the blue
Of my eyes, I see you beautiful, and dear.
Beautiful, passive and strong, as the breath
            Of my yearning blows over you.
I see myself as the winds that hover
Half substanceless, and without grave worth.
            But you
            Are the earth I hover over.

These Clever Women

Close your eyes, my love, let me make you blind!
            They have taught you to see
Only problems writ on the face of things,
And algebra in the eyes of desirous men,
            And God like geometry
Tangling his circles, to baffle you and me.

I would kiss you over the eyes till I kissed you blind;
            If I could – if anyone could!
Then perhaps in the dark you'd get what you want to find:
The solution that ever is much too deep for the mind;
            Dissolved in the blood . . .
That I am the hart, and you are the gentle hind.

Now stop carping at me! Do you want me to hate you?
            Am I a kaleidoscope

For you to shake and shake, and it won't come right?
Am I doomed in a long coition of words to mate you?
            Unsatisfied! Is there no hope
Between your thighs, far, far from your peering sight?

Ballad of Another Ophelia

O the green glimmer of apples in the orchard,
Lamps in a wash of rain!
O the wet walk of my brown hen through the stackyard!
O tears on the window-pane!

Nothing now will ripen the bright green apples
Full of disappointment and of rain;
Brackish they will taste, of tears, when the yellow dapples
Of autumn tell the withered tale again.

All round the yard it is cluck! my brown hen.
Cluck! and the rain-wet wings;
Cluck! my marigold bird, and again
Cluck! for your yellow darlings.

For a grey rat found the gold thirteen
Huddled away in the dark.
Flutter for a moment, oh, the beast is quick and keen,
Extinct one yellow-fluffy spark!

Once I had a lover bright like running water,
Once his face was open like the sky,
Open like the sky looking down in all its laughter
On the buttercups, and the buttercups was I.

What then is there hidden in the skirts of all the blossom?
What is peeping from your skirts, O mother hen?
'Tis the sun that asks the question, in a lovely haste for wisdom;
What a lovely haste for wisdom is in men!

Yea, but it is cruel when undressed is all the blossom
And her shift is lying white upon the floor,
That a grey one, like a shadow, like a rat, a thief, a rainstorm
Creeps upon her then and ravishes her store!

O the grey garner that is full of half-grown apples!
O the golden sparkles laid extinct!
And O, behind the cloud-leaves, like yellow autumn dapples,
Did you see the wicked sun that winked?

Kisses in the Train

I saw the midlands
    Revolve through her hair;
The fields of autumn
    Stretching bare,
And sheep on the pasture
    Tossed back in a scare.

And still as ever
    The world went round,
My mouth on her pulsing
    Throat was found,
And my breast to her beating
    Breast was bound.

But my heart at the centre
    Of all, in a swound
Was still as a pivot,
    As all the ground
On its prowling orbit
    Shifted round.

And still in my nostrils
    The scent of her flesh;
And still my blind face
    Sought her afresh;
And still one pulse
    Through the world did thresh.

And the world all whirling
     Round in joy
Like the dance of a dervish
     Did destroy
My sense – and reason
     Spun like a toy.

But firm at the centre
     My heart was found;
My own to her perfect
     Heartbeat bound,
Like a magnet's keeper
     Closing the round.

Turned Down

Hollow rang the house when I knocked at the door,
And I lingered on the threshold with my hand
Upraised to knock and knock once more;
Listening for the sound of her feet across the floor
Hollow re-echoed my heart.

The low-hung lamps stretched down the street
With people passing underneath,
With a rhythm of tapping, coming feet
To quicken my hope as I hastened to greet
The waking smile of her eyes.

The tired lights down the street went out,
The last car trailed the night behind;
And I in the darkness wandered about
With a flutter of hope and a quenching doubt
In the dying lamp of my love.

Two brown ponies trotting slowly
Stopped at a dim-lit trough to drink;
The dark van drummed down the distance lowly;
And city stars, so dim and holy,
Came nearer, to search through the streets.

A hastening car swept shameful past,
I saw her hid in the shadow;
I saw her step to the kerb, and fast
Run to the silent door, where last
I had stood with my hand uplifted.
She clung to the door in her haste to enter,
Entered, and quickly cast
It shut behind her, leaving the street aghast.

After Many Days

I wonder if with you, as it is with me,
If under your slipping words, that easily flow
About you as a garment, easily,
    Your violent heart beats to and fro!

Long have I waited, never once confessed,
Even to myself, how bitter the separation;
Now, being come again, how make the best
    Reparation?

If I could cast this clothing off from me,
If I could lift my naked self to you,
Or if only you would repulse me, a wound would be
    Good, it would let the ache come through.

But that you hold me still so kindly cold
Aloof, my flaming heart will not allow;
Yea, but I loathe you that you should withhold
    Your greeting now!

Snap-Dragon

She bade me follow to her garden, where
The mellow sunlight stood as in a cup
Between the old grey walls; I did not dare
To raise my face, I did not dare look up,
Lest her bright eyes like sparrows should fly in
My windows of discovery, and shrill 'Sin!'

So with a downcast mien and laughing voice
I followed, followed the swing of her white dress
That rocked in a lilt along; I watched the poise
Of her feet as they flew for a space, then paused to press
The grass deep down with the royal burden of her;
And gladly I'd offered my breast to the tread of her.

'I like to see,' she said, and she crouched her down,
She sunk into my sight like a settling bird;
And her bosom couched in the confines of her gown
Like heavy birds at rest there, softly stirred
By her measured breaths: 'I like to see,' said she,
'The snap-dragon put out his tongue at me.'

She laughed, she reached her hand out to the flower,
Closing its crimson throat. My own throat in her power
Strangled, my heart swelled up so full
As if it would burst its wine-skin in my throat,
Choke me in my own crimson. I watched her pull
The gorge of the gaping flower, till the blood did float

> Over my eyes, and I was blind –
> Her large brown hand stretched over
> The windows of my mind;
> And there in the dark I did discover
> Things I was out to find:

My Grail, a brown bowl twined
With swollen veins that met in the wrist,
Under whose brown the amethyst
I longed to taste! I longed to turn
My heart's red measure in her cup;
I longed to feel my hot blood burn
With the amethyst in her cup.

Then suddenly she looked up,
And I was blind in a tawny-gold day.
Till she took her eyes away.

So she came down from above
And emptied my heart of love.
So I held my heart aloft
To the cuckoo that hung like a dove,
And she settled soft.

It seemed that I and the morning world
Were pressed cup-shape to take this reiver
Bird who was weary to have furled
Her wings in us,
As we were weary to receive her.

> *This bird, this rich,*
> *Sumptuous central grain;*
> *This mutable witch,*
> *This one refrain,*
> *This laugh in the fight,*
> *This clot of night,*
> *This field of delight.*

She spoke, and I closed my eyes
To shut hallucinations out.
I echoed with surprise
Hearing my mere lips shout
The answer they did devise.

> Again I saw a brown bird hover
> Over the flowers at my feet;
> I felt a brown bird hover
> Over my heart, and sweet
> Its shadow lay on my heart.
> I thought I saw on the clover
> A brown bee pulling apart
> The closed flesh of the clover
> And burrowing in its heart.

> She moved her hand, and again
> I felt the brown bird cover
> My heart; and then
> The bird came down on my heart,
> As on a nest the rover
> Cuckoo comes, and shoves over
> The brim each careful part
> Of love, takes possession, and settles her down,
> With her wings and her feathers to drown
> The nest in a heat of love.

She turned her flushed face to me for the glint
Of a moment. – 'See,' she laughed, 'if you also
Can make them yawn!' – I put my hand to the dint
In the flower's throat, and the flower gaped wide with woe.
She watched, she went of a sudden intensely still,
She watched my hand, to see what it would fulfil.

I pressed the wretched, throttled flower between
My fingers, till its head lay back, its fangs
Poised at her. Like a weapon my hand was white and keen,
And I held the choked flower-serpent in its pangs
Of mordant anguish, till she ceased to laugh,
Until her pride's flag, smitten, cleaved down to the staff.

She hid her face, she murmured between her lips
The low word 'Don't!' – I let the flower fall,
But held my hand afloat towards the slips
Of blossom she fingered, and my fingers all
Put forth to her: she did not move, nor I,
For my hand like a snake watched hers, that could not fly.

Then I laughed in the dark of my heart, I did exult
Like a sudden chuckling of music. I bade her eyes
Meet mine, I opened her helpless eyes to consult
Their fear, their shame, their joy that underlies
Defeat in such a battle. In the dark of her eyes
My heart was fierce to make her laughter rise.

Till her dark deeps shook with convulsive thrills, and the dark
Of her spirit wavered like water thrilled with light;
And my heart leaped up in longing to plunge its stark
Fervour within the pool of her twilight,
Within her spacious soul, to find delight.

And I do not care, though the large hands of revenge
Shall get my throat at last, shall get it soon,
If the joy that they are lifted to avenge
Have risen red on my night as a harvest moon,
Which even death can only put out for me;
And death, I know, is better than not-to-be.

Come Spring, Come Sorrow

Round clouds roll in the arms of the wind,
The round earth rolls like a germ in the sky,
And see, where the budding hazels are thinned
     The wild anemones lie
In undulating shivers beneath the wind!

Over the blue of the duck-pond ply
White ducks, a quacking flotilla of cloud;
And look you, floating just thereby
     The blue-gleamed drake stems proud
As Abraham, whose seed shall multiply.

In the lustrous gleam of the water, there
Scramble seven toads, across silk, obscure leaves,
Seven toads that move in the dusk to share
     Dim spring that interweaves
The hidden bodies mating everywhere.

Look now, through the woods where the beech-green spurts
Like a storm of emerald snow, now see!
A great bay stallion dances, skirts
     The bushes sumptuously,
Going out in spring to the round of his tame deserts.

And you, my lass, with your rich warm face aglow,
What sudden expectation opens you
So wide as you watch the catkins blow
     Their dust from the birch on the blue
Lift of the pulsing wind? ah, say that you know!

Yes, say it! For, sure from the golden sun
A quickening, masculine gleam floats in to all
Us creatures, people and flowers undone
     And opened under his thrall
As he plants his new germ in us. What is there to shun?

Why, I should think that from the earth there fly
Fine thrills to the neighbour stars, fine hidden beams

Thrown lustily off from our full-sappy, high
   And fecund globe of dreams,
To quicken the spheres spring-virgin again in the sky.

Do you not hear each morsel thrill
With joy at travelling to plant itself within
The expectant one, and therein to instil
   Newness, new shape to win,
From the drowse of life wake up another will?

Surely, ah not in words alone I'd spill
The vivid, ah, the fiery surplus of life
From off my measure, to touch you deep, and fill
   You flush and rife
With this year's newness! – And is that evil?

The Hands of the Betrothed

Her tawny eyes are onyx of thoughtlessness,
Hardened they are like gems in time-long prudery;
Yea, and her mouth's prudent and crude caress
Means even less than her many words to me.

Except her kiss betrays me this, this only
Consolation, that in her lips her blood at climax clips
Two hard, crude paws in hunger on the lonely
Flesh of my heart, ere down, rebuked, it slips.

I know from her hardened lips that still her heart is
Hungry for love, yet if I lay my hand in her breast
She puts me away, like a saleswoman whose mart is
Endangered by the pilferer on his quest.

Though her hands are still the woman, her large, strong hands
Heavier than mine, yet like leverets caught in steel
When I hold them; my spent soul understands
Their dumb confession of what her blood must feel.

For never her hands come nigh me but they lift
Like heavy birds from the morning stubble, to settle

Upon me like sleeping birds, like birds that shift
Uneasily in their sleep, disturbing my mettle.

How caressingly she lays her hand on my knee!
How strangely she tries to disown it, as it sinks
In my flesh and my bone, and forages into me!
How it stirs like a subtle stoat, whatever she thinks!

And often I see her clench her fingers tight
And thrust her fists suppressed in the folds of her skirt;
And sometimes, how she grasps her arms with her bright
Big hands, as if surely her arms did hurt.

And I have seen her stand all unaware
Pressing her spread hands over her breasts, as she
Would crush their mounds on her heart, to kill in there
The pain that is her simple ache for me.

She makes her hands take my part, the part of the man
To her; she crushes them into her bosom deep
Where I should be, and with her own strong span
Closes her arms, that should fold on me in sleep.

Ah, and she puts her hands upon the wall,
Presses them there, and kisses her big dark hands,
Then lets her black hair loose, the darkness fall
About her from her maiden-folded bands.

And sits in her own dark night of her bitter hair
Dreaming – God knows of what, for to me she's the same
Betrothed young lady who loves me, and takes good care
Of her maidenly virtue and of my good name.

A Love Song

Reject me not if I should say to you
I do forget the sounding of your voice,
I do forget your eyes, that searching through
The days perceive our marriage, and rejoice.

But, when the apple-blossom opens wide
Under the pallid moonlight's fingering,
I see your blanched face at my breast, and hide
My eyes from duteous work, malingering.

Ah, then upon the bedroom I do draw
The blind to hide the garden, where the moon
Enjoys the open blossoms as they straw
Their beauty for his taking, boon for boon.

And I do lift my aching arms to you,
And I do lift my anguished, avid breast,
And I do weep for very pain of you,
And fling myself at the doors of sleep, for rest.

And I do toss through the troubled night for you,
Dreaming your yielded mouth is given to mine,
Feeling your strong breast carry me on into
The sleep no dream nor doubt can undermine.

Twofold

How gorgeous that shock of red lilies, and larkspur cleaving
All with a flash of blue! – when will she be leaving
Her room, where the night still hangs like a half-folded bat,
And passion unbearable seethes in the darkness, like must in a vat.

Tarantella

Sad as he sits on the white sea-stone
And the suave sea chuckles, and turns to the moon,
And the moon significant smiles at the cliffs and the boulders.
He sits like a shade by the flood alone
While I dance a tarantella on the rocks, and the croon
Of my mockery mocks at him over the waves' bright shoulders.

What can I do but dance alone,
Dance to the sliding sea and the moon,
For the moon on my breast and the air on my limbs and
    the foam on my feet?
For surely this earnest man has none
Of the night in his soul, and none of the tune
Of the waters within him; only the world's old wisdom to bleat.

I wish a wild sea-fellow would come down the glittering
    shingle,
A soulless neckar,[18] with winking seas in his eyes
And falling waves in his arms, and the lost soul's kiss
On his lips: I long to be soulless, I tingle
To touch the sea in the last surprise
Of fiery coldness, to be gone in a lost soul's bliss.

Under the Oak

You, if you were sensible,
When I tell you the stars flash signals, each one dreadful,
You would not turn and answer me
'The night is wonderful.'

Even you, if you knew
How this darkness soaks me through and through, and infuses
Unholy fear in my essence, you would pause to distinguish
What hurts from what amuses.

For I tell you
Beneath this powerful tree, my whole soul's fluid

Oozes away from me as a sacrifice steam
At the knife of a Druid.

Again I tell you, I bleed, I am bound with withies,
My life runs out.
I tell you my blood runs out on the floor of this oak.
Gout upon gout.

Above me springs the blood-born mistletoe
In the shady smoke.
But who are you, twittering to and fro
Beneath the oak?

What thing better are you, what worse?
What have you to do with the mysteries
Of this ancient place, of my ancient curse?
What place have you in my histories?

Brother and Sister

The shorn moon trembling indistinct on her path,
Frail as a scar upon the pale blue sky,
Draws towards the downward slope; some sorrow hath
Worn her away to the quick, so she faintly fares
Along her foot-searched way without knowing why
She creeps persistent down the sky's long stairs.

Some say they see, though I have never seen,
The dead moon heaped within the new moon's arms;
For surely the fragile, fine young thing had been
Too heavily burdened to mount the heavens so!
But my heart stands still, as a new, strong dread alarms
Me; might a young girl be heaped with such shadow of woe?

Since Death from the mother moon has pared us down to the
     quick,
And cast us forth like thin, shorn moons, to travel
An uncharted way among the myriad thick
Strewn stars of unknown people, and luminous litter
Of lives which sorrows like mischievous dark mice chavel
To nought, diminishing each star's glitter;

Since Death has delivered us utterly, stripped and white,
Since the month of childhood is over, and we stand alone,
Since the beloved, faded mother that set us alight
Is delivered out and pays no heed though we moan
In sorrow; since we stand in bewilderment, strange
And fearful to sally forth down the sky's long range:

Let us not cry to her still to sustain us here,
Let us not hold her shadow back from the dark!
Oh, let us here forget, let us take the sheer
Unknown that lies before us, bearing the ark
Of the covenant onwards where she cannot go!
Let us rise and leave her now, she will never know.

The Shadow of Death

The earth again like a ship steams out of the dark sea over
The edge of the blue, and the sun stands up to see us glide
Slowly into another day; slowly the rover
Vessel of darkness takes the rising tide.

I, on the deck, am startled by this dawn confronting
Me who am issued amazed from the darkness, stripped
And quailing here in the sunshine, betrayed from haunting
The soundless night whereon our days are shipped.

Feeling myself undawning, the day's light playing upon me,
I who am substance of shadow, I all compact
Of the stuff of the night, finding myself all wrongly
Among crowds of things in the sunshine jostled and racked.

I with the night on my lips, I sigh with the silence of death;
And what do I care though the very stones should cry me unreal,
     though the clouds
Shine in conceit of substance upon me, who am less than the rain!
Do I not know the darkness within them? What are they but
     shrouds?

The clouds go down the sky with a wealthy ease,
Casting a shadow of scorn upon me for my share in death; but I
Hold my own in the midst of them, darkling defy
The whole of the day to extinguish the shadow I lift on the breeze.

Yea, though the very clouds have vantage over me
Enjoying their glancing flight, though love is dead,
I still am not homeless here, I've a tent by day
Of darkness whereon she sleeps on her perfect bed.

Birdcage Walk

When the wind blows her veil
    And uncovers her laughter
I cease, I turn pale.
When the wind blows her veil
From the woes I bewail
    Of love and hereafter:
When the wind blows her veil
I cease, I turn pale.

In Trouble and Shame

I look at the swaling sunset
    And wish I could go also
Through the red doors beyond the black-purple bar.

I wish that I could go
Through the red doors where I could put off
    My shame like shoes in the porch,
    My pain like garments,
And leave my flesh discarded lying
Like luggage of some departed traveller
    Gone one knows not whither.

Then I would turn round,
And seeing my cast-off body lying like lumber,
    I would laugh with joy.

Call into Death

Since I lost you, my darling, the sky has come near,
And I am of it, the small sharp stars are quite near,
The white moon going among them like a white bird among snow-
    berries,
And the sound of her gently rustling in heaven like a bird I hear.

And I am willing to come to you now, my dear,
As a pigeon lets itself off from a cathedral dome
To be lost in the haze of the sky; I would like to come
And be lost out of sight with you, like a melting foam.

For I am tired, my dear, and if I could lift my feet,
My tenacious feet, from off the dome of the earth
To fall like a breath within the breathing wind
Where you are lost, what rest, my love, what rest!

Grey Evening

When you went, how was it you carried with you
My missal book of fine, flamboyant Hours?
My book of turrets and of red-thorn bowers,
And skies of gold, and ladies in bright tissue?

Now underneath a blue-grey twilight, heaped
Beyond the withering snow of the shorn fields
Stands rubble of stunted houses; all is reaped
And trodden that the happy summer yields.

Now lamps like yellow echoes glimmer among
The shadowy stubble of the under-dusk;
As farther off the scythe of night is swung
Ripe little stars come rolling from their husk.

And all the earth is gone into a dust
Of greyness mingled with a fume of gold,
Timeless as branching lichens, pale as must,
Since all the sky has withered and gone cold.

And so I sit and scan the book of grey,
Feeling the shadows like a blind man reading,
All fearful lest I find the last words bleeding:
Nay, take this weary Book of Hours away.

Firelight and Nightfall

The darkness steals the forms of all the queens,
But oh, the palms of his two black hands are red
Inflamed with binding up the sheaves of the dead
Hours that were once all glory and all queens.

And I remember still the sunny hours
Of queens in hyacinth and skies of gold,
And morning singing where the woods are scrolled
And diapered above the chaunting flowers.

Here lamps are white like snowdrops in the grass;
The town is like a churchyard, all so still
And grey now night is here; nor will
Another torn red sunset come to pass.

Blueness

Out of the darkness, fretted sometimes in its sleeping,
Jets of sparks in fountains of blue come leaping
To sight, revealing a secret, numberless secrets keeping.

Sometimes the darkness trapped within a wheel
Runs into speed like a dream, the blue of the steel
Showing the rocking darkness now a-reel.

And out of the invisible, streams of bright blue drops
Rain from the showery heavens, and bright blue crops
Of flowers surge from below to their ladder-tops.

And all the manifold blue, amazing eyes,
The rainbow arching over in the skies,
New sparks of wonder opening in surprise:

All these pure things come foam and spray of the sea
Of Darkness abundant, which shaken mysteriously
Breaks into dazzle of living, as dolphins leap from the sea
Of midnight and shake it to fire, till the flame of the
    shadow we see.

A Passing-Bell

Mournfully to and fro, to and fro the trees are waving,
    What did you say, my dear?
The rain-bruised leaves are suddenly shaken, as a child
Asleep still shakes in the clutch of a sob –
    Yes, my love, I hear.

One lonely bell, one only, the storm-tossed afternoon is braving,
    Why not let it ring?
The roses lean down when they hear it, the tender, mild
Flowers of the bleeding-heart fall to the throb –
    'Tis a little thing!

A wet bird walks on the lawn, call to the boy to come and look,
    Yes, it is over now.
Call to him out of the silence, call him to see
The starling shaking its head as it walks in the grass –
    Ah, who knows how?

He cannot see it, I can never show it him, how it shook
    Don't disturb it, darling! –
Its head as it walked: I can never call him to me,
Never, he *is* not, whatever shall come to pass.
    No, look at the wet starling!

The Drained Cup

    T' snow is witherin' off'n th' gress –
        Lad, should I tell thee summat?
    T' snow is witherin' off'n th' gress
    An' mist is suckin' at th' spots o' snow,

An' ower a' the thaw an' mess
There's a moon, full blow.
    Lad, but I'm tellin' thee summat!

Tha's bin snowed up i' this cottage wi' me –
    'Ark, tha'rt for hearin' summat!
Tha's bin snowed up i' this cottage wi' me
While t' clocks 'as a' run down an' stopped,
An' t' short days goin' unknown ter thee
Unbeknown has dropped.
    Yi, but I'm tellin' thee summat.

How, many days dost think has gone?
    Now, lad, I'm axin' thee summat.
How many days dost think has gone?
How many times has t' candle-light shone
On thy face as tha got more white an' wan?
    – Seven days, my lad, or none!
    Aren't ter hearin' summat?

Tha come ter say goodbye ter me,
    Tha wert frit o' summat.
Tha come ter ha' finished an' done wi' me
An' off to a gel as wor younger than me,
An' fresh an' more nicer for marryin' wi' –
    Yi, but tha'rt frit o' summat.

Ah wunna kiss thee, tha trembles so!
    Tha'rt daunted, or summat.
Tha arena very flig[19] ter go.
Dost want me ter want thee again? Nay though,
There's hardly owt left o' thee; get up an' go!
    Or dear o' me, say summat.

Tha wanted ter leave me that bad, tha knows!
    Doesn't ter know it?
But tha wanted me more ter want thee, so's
Tha could let thy very soul out. A man
Like thee can't rest till his last spunk goes
Out of 'im into a woman as can
    Draw it out of 'im. Did ter know it?

Tha thought tha wanted a little wench,
    Ay, lad, I'll tell thee thy mind.
Tha thought tha wanted a little wench
As 'ud make thee a wife an' look up ter thee.
As 'ud wince when tha touched 'er close, an' blench
An' lie frightened ter death under thee.
    She worn't hard ter find.

Tha thought tha wanted ter be rid o' me.
    'Appen tha did, an' a'.
Tha thought tha wanted ter marry an' see
If ter couldna be master an' th' woman's boss.
Tha'd need a woman different from me,
An' tha knowed it; ay, yet tha comes across
    Ter say goodbye! an' a'.

I tell thee tha won't be satisfied,
    Tha might as well listen, tha knows.
I tell thee tha won't be satisfied
Till a woman has drawn the last last drop
O' thy spunk, an' tha'rt empty an' mortified.
Empty an' empty from bottom to top.
    It's true, tha knows.

Tha'rt one o' th' men as has got to drain
    – An' I've loved thee for it,
Their blood in a woman, to the very last vein.
Tha *must*, though tha tries ter get away.
Tha wants it, and everything else is in vain.
    An' a woman like me loves thee for it.

Maun tha cling to the wa' as tha stan's?
    Ay, an' tha maun.
An' tha looks at me, an' tha understan's.
Yi, tha can go. Tha hates me now.
But tha'lt come again. Because when a man's
Not finished, he hasn't, no matter how.
    Go then, sin' tha maun.

Tha come ter say goodbye ter me.
    Now go then, now then go.
It's ta'en thee seven days ter say it ter me.

Now go an' marry that wench, an' see
How long it'll be afore tha'lt be
Weary an' sick o' the likes o' she,
        An' hankerin' for me. But go!

A woman's man tha art, ma lad,
        But it's my sort o' woman.
Go then, tha'lt ha'e no peace till ter's had
A go at t'other, for I'm a bad
Sort o' woman for any lad.
        – Ay, it's a rum un!

Late at Night

Rigid sleeps the house in darkness, I alone
Like a thing unwarrantable cross the hall
And climb the stairs to find the group of doors
Standing angel-stern and tall.

I want my own room's shelter. But what is this
Throng of startled beings suddenly thrown
In confusion against my entry? Is it only the trees'
Large shadows from the outside street-lamp blown?

Phantom to phantom leaning; strange women weep
Aloud, suddenly on my mind
Startling a fear unspeakable, as the shuddering wind
Breaks and sobs in the blind.

So like to women, tall strange women weeping!
Why continually do they cross the bed?
Why does my soul contract with unnatural fear?
I am listening! Is anything said?

Ever the long black figures swoop by the bed;
They seem to be beckoning, rushing away, and beckoning.
Whither then, whither? what is it? say
What is the reckoning?

Tall black Bacchae of midnight, why then, why
Do you rush to assail me?
Do I intrude on your rites nocturnal?
What should it avail me?

Is there some great Iacchos[20] of these slopes
Suburban dismal?
Have I profaned some female mystery, orgies
Black and phantasmal?

Next Morning

How have I wandered here to this vaulted room
In the house of life? – the floor was ruffled with gold
Last evening, and she who was softly in bloom
Glimmered as flowers that in perfume at twilight unfold

For the flush of the night; whereas now the gloom
Of every dirty, must-besprinkled mould
And damp old web of misery's heirloom
Deadens this day's grey-dropping arras-fold.

And what is this that floats on the undermist
Of the mirror towards the dusty grate, as if feeling
Unsightly its way to the warmth? – this thing with a list
To the left? – this ghost like a candle swealing?

Pale-blurred, with two round black drops, as if it missed
Itself among everything else, here hungrily stealing
Upon me! – my own reflection! explicit gist
Of my presence there in the mirror that leans from the ceiling!

Then will somebody square this shade with the being I know
I was last night, when my soul rang clear as a bell
And happy as rain in summer? Why should it be so?
What is there gone against me, why am I in hell?

Winter in the Boulevard

The frost has settled down upon the trees
And ruthlessly strangled off the fantasies
Of leaves that have gone unnoticed, swept like old
Romantic stories now no more to be told.

The trees down the boulevard stand naked in thought
Their abundant summer wordage silenced, caught
In the grim undertow; naked the trees confront
Implacable winter's long, cross-questioning brunt.

Has some hand balanced more leaves in the depths of the twigs?
Some dim little efforts placed in the threads of the birch? –
It is only the sparrows, like dead black leaves on the sprigs,
Sitting huddled against the cerulean, one flesh with their perch.

The clear, cold sky coldly bethinks itself.
Like vivid thought the air spins bright, and all
Trees, birds, and earth, arrested in the after-thought,
Awaiting the sentence out from the welkin brought.

Parliament Hill in the Evening

The houses fade in a melt of mist
   Blotching the thick, soiled air
With reddish places that still resist
   The Night's slow care.

The hopeless, wintry twilight fades,
   The city corrodes out of sight
As the body corrodes when death invades
   That citadel of delight.

Now verdigris smoulderings softly spread
   Through the shroud of the town, as slow
Night-lights hither and thither shed
   Their ghastly glow.

Embankment at Night, Before the War

CHARITY

By the river
In the black wet night as the furtive rain slinks down,
Dropping and starting from sleep
Alone on a seat
A woman crouches.

I must go back to her.

I want to give her
Some money. Her hand slips out of the breast of her gown
Asleep. My fingers creep
Carefully over the sweet
Thumb-mound, into the palm's deep pouches.

So the gift!

God, how she starts!
And looks at me, and looks in the palm of her hand
And again at me! –
I turn and run
Down the Embankment, run for my life.

But why? – why?

Because of my heart's
Beating like sobs, I come to myself, and stand
In the street spilled over splendidly
With wet, flat lights. What I've done
I know not, my soul is in strife.

The touch was on the quick. I want to forget.

Embankment at Night, Before the War

OUTCASTS

The night rain, dripping unseen,
Comes endlessly kissing my face and my hands.

The river slipping between
Lamps, is rayed with golden bands
Half way down its heaving sides;
Revealed where it hides.

Under the bridge
Great electric cars
Sing through, and each with a floor-light racing along at
    its side.
Far off, oh, midge after midge
Drifts over the gulf that bars
The night with silence, crossing the lamp-touched tide.

At Charing Cross, here, beneath the bridge
Sleep in a row the outcasts,
Packed in a line with their heads against the wall.
Their feet in a broken ridge
Stretched out on the way, and a lout casts
A look as he stands on the edge of this naked stall.

Beasts that sleep will cover
Their face in their flank; so these
Have huddled rags or limbs on the naked sleep.
Save, as the tram-cars hover
Past with the noise of a breeze
And gleam as of sunshine crossing the low black heap,

Two naked faces are seen
Bare and asleep,
Two pale clots swept by the light of the cars.
Foam-clots showing between
The long, low tidal-heap,
The mud-weed opening two pale, shadowless stars.

Over the pallor of only two faces
Passes the gallivant beam of the trams;
Shows in only two sad places
The white bare bone of our shams.

A little, bearded man, peaked in sleeping,
With a face like a chickweed flower.
And a heavy woman, sleeping still keeping
Callous and dour.

Over the pallor of only two places
Tossed on the low, black, ruffled heap
Passes the light of the tram as it races
Out of the deep.

Eloquent limbs
In disarray,
Sleep-suave limbs of a youth with long, smooth thighs
Hutched up for warmth; the muddy rims
Of trousers fray
On the thin bare shins of a man who uneasily lies.

The balls of five red toes
As red and dirty, bare
Young birds forsaken and left in a nest of mud –
Newspaper sheets enclose
Some limbs like parcels, and tear
When the sleeper stirs or turns on the ebb of the flood –

One heaped mound
Of a woman's knees
As she thrusts them upward under the ruffled skirt –
And a curious dearth of sound
In the presence of these
Wastrels that sleep on the flagstones without any hurt.

Over two shadowless, shameless faces
Stark on the heap
Travels the light as it tilts in its paces
Gone in one leap.

At the feet of the sleepers, watching,
Stand those that wait
For a place to lie down; and still as they stand, they sleep;
Wearily catching
The flood's slow gait
Like men who are drowned, but float erect in the deep.

Oh, the singing mansions,
Golden-lighted tall
Trams that pass, blown ruddily down the night!
The bridge on its stanchions
Stoops like a pall
To this human blight.

On the outer pavement, slowly,
Theatre people pass,
Holding aloft their umbrellas that flash and are bright
Like flowers of infernal moly
Over nocturnal grass
Wetly bobbing and drifting away on our sight.

And still by the rotten row of shattered feet,
Outcasts keep guard.
Forgotten,
Forgetting, till fate shall delete
One from the ward.

The factories on the Surrey side
Are beautifully laid in black on a gold-grey sky.
The river's invisible tide
Threads and thrills like ore that is wealth to the eye.

And great gold midges
Cross the chasm
At the bridges
Above intertwined plasm.

Sickness

Waving slowly before me, pushed into the dark,
Unseen my hands explore the silence, drawing the bark
Of my body slowly behind.

Nothing to meet my fingers but the fleece of night
Invisible blinding my face and my eyes! What if in their flight
My hands should touch the door!

What if I suddenly stumble, and push the door
Open, and a great grey dawn swirls over my feet, before
I can draw back!

What if unwitting I set the door of eternity wide
And am swept away in the horrible dawn, am gone down the
    tide
Of eternal hereafter!

Catch my hands, my darling, between your breasts.
Take them away from their venture, before fate wrests
The meaning out of them.

In Church

In the choir the boys are singing the hymn.
        The morning light on their lips
Moves in silver-moist flashes, in musical trim.

Sudden outside the high window, one crow
        Hangs in the air
And lights on a withered oak tree's top of woe.

One bird, one blot, folded and still at the top
        Of the withered tree! – in the grail
Of crystal heaven falls one full black drop.

Like a soft full drop of darkness it seems to sway
        In the tender wine
Of our Sabbath, suffusing our sacred day.

Piano

Softly, in the dusk, a woman is singing to me;
Taking me back down the vista of years, till I see
A child sitting under the piano, in the boom of the tingling strings
And pressing the small, poised feet of a mother who smiles as she
    sings.

In spite of myself, the insidious mastery of song
Betrays me back, till the heart of me weeps to belong
To the old Sunday evenings at home, with winter outside
And hymns in the cosy parlour, the tinkling piano our guide.

So now it is vain for the singer to burst into clamour
With the great black piano appassionato. The glamour
Of childish days is upon me, my manhood is cast
Down in the flood of remembrance, I weep like a child for the past.

The North Country

In another country, black poplars shake themselves over a pond,
And rooks and the rising smoke-waves scatter and wheel from the
    works beyond:
The air is dark with north and with sulphur, the grass is a darker green,
And people darkly invested with purple move palpable through
    the scene.

Soundlessly down across the counties, out of the resonant gloom
That wraps the north in stupor and purple travels the deep, slow boom
Of the man-life north imprisoned, shut in the hum of the purpled steel
As it spins to sleep on its motion, drugged dense in the sleep of
    the wheel.

Out of the sleep, from the gloom of motion, soundlessly, somnambule
Moans and booms the soul of a people imprisoned, asleep in
    the rule
Of the strong machine that runs mesmeric, booming the spell of
    its word
Upon them and moving them helpless, mechanic, their will to its will
    deferred.

Yet all the while comes the droning inaudible, out of the violet air,
The moaning of sleep-bound beings in travail that toil and are
    will-less there
In the spellbound north, convulsive now with a dream near morning,
    strong
With violent achings heaving to burst the sleep that is now not long.

Love Storm

     Many roses in the wind
     Are tapping at the window-sash.
     A hawk is in the sky; his wings
     Slowly begin to plash.

     The roses with the west wind rapping
     Are torn away, and a splash
     Of red goes down the billowing air.

     Still hangs the hawk, with the whole sky moving
     Past him – only a wing-beat proving
     The will that holds him there.

     The daisies in the grass are bending,
     The hawk has dropped, the wind is spending
     All the roses, and unending
     Rustle of leaves washes out the rending
     Cry of a bird.

     A red rose goes on the wind. – Ascending
     The hawk his windswept way is wending
     Easily down the sky. The daisies, sending
     Strange white signals, seem intending
     To show the place whence the scream was heard.

     But, oh, my heart, what birds are piping!
     A silver wind is hastily wiping
     The face of the youngest rose.

And oh, my heart, cease apprehending!
The hawk is gone, a rose is tapping
The window-sash as the west wind blows.

Knock, knock, 'tis no more than a red rose rapping,
And fear is a plash of wings.
What, then, if a scarlet rose goes flapping
Down the bright-grey ruin of things!

Passing Visit to Helen

Returning, I find her just the same,
At just the same old delicate game.

Still she says: 'Nay, loose no flame
To lick me up and do me harm!
Be all yourself! – for oh, the charm
Of your heart of fire in which I look!
Oh, better there than in any book
Glow and enact the dramas and dreams
I love for ever! – there it seems
You are lovelier than life itself, till desire
Comes licking through the bars of your lips,
And over my face the stray fire slips,
Leaving a burn and an ugly smart
That will have the oil of illusion. Oh, heart
Of fire and beauty, loose no more
Your reptile flames of lust; ah, store
Your passion in the basket of your soul,
Be all yourself, one bonny, burning coal
That stays with steady joy of its own fire!
For in the firing all my porcelain
Of flesh does crackle and shiver and break in pain,
My ivory and marble black with stain,
My veil of sensitive mystery rent in twain,
My altars sullied, I bereft, remain
A priestess execrable, taken in vain – '

So the refrain
Sings itself over, and so the game
Restarts itself wherein I am kept
Like a glowing brazier faintly blue of flame,
So that the delicate love-adept
Can warm her hands and invite her soul,
Sprinkling incense and salt of words
And kisses pale, and sipping the toll
Of incense-smoke that rises like birds.

Yet I've forgotten in playing this game,
Things I have known that shall have no name;
Forgetting the place from which I came
I watch her ward away the flame
Yet warm herself at the fire – then blame
Me that I flicker in the basket;
Me that I glow not with content
To have my substance so subtly spent;
Me that I interrupt her game . . .
I ought to be proud that she should ask it
Of me to be her fire-opal . . .

It is well
Since I am here for so short a spell
Not to interrupt her? – Why should I
Break in by making any reply!

Twenty Years Ago

Round the house were lilacs and strawberries
      And foal-foots spangling the paths,
And far away on the sand-hills, dewberries
      Caught dust from the sea's long swaths.

Up the wolds the woods were walking,
      And nuts fell out of their hair.
At the gate the nets hung, balking
      The star-lit rush of a hare.

In the autumn fields, the stubble
      Tinkled the music of gleaning.
At a mother's knees, the trouble
      Lost all its meaning.

Yea, what good beginnings
      To this sad end!
Have we had our innings?
      God forfend!

Reading a Letter

She sits on the recreation ground
      Under an oak whose yellow buds dot the pale blue sky.
The young grass twinkles in the wind, and the sound
      Of the wind in the knotted buds makes a canopy.

So sitting under the knotted canopy
      Of the wind, she is lifted and carried away as in a balloon
Across the insensible void, till she stoops to see
      The sandy desert beneath her, the dreary platoon.

She knows the waste all dry beneath her, in one place
      Stirring with earth-coloured life, ever turning and stirring.
But never the motion has a human face
      Nor sound, only intermittent machinery whirring.

And so again, on the recreation ground
      She alights a stranger, wondering, unused to the scene;
Suffering at sight of the children playing around,
      Hurt at the chalk-coloured tulips, and the evening-green.

Seven Seals

Since this is the last night I keep you home,
Come, I will consecrate you for the journey.

Rather I had you would not go. Nay come,
I will not again reproach you. Lie back
And let me love you a long time ere you go.
For you are sullen-hearted still, and lack
The will to love me. But even so
I will set a seal upon you from my lip,
Will set a guard of honour at each door,
Seal up each channel out of which might slip
Your love for me.

                  I kiss your mouth. Ah, love,
Could I but seal its ruddy, shining spring
Of passion, parch it up, destroy, remove
Its softly-stirring crimson welling-up
Of kisses! Oh, help me, God! Here at the source
I'd lie for ever drinking and drawing in
Your fountains, as heaven drinks from out their course
The floods.

                I close your ears with kisses
And seal your nostrils; and round your neck you'll wear –
Nay, let me work – a delicate chain of kisses.
Like beads they go around, and not one misses
To touch its fellow on either side.

                      And there
Full mid-between the champaign of your breast
I place a great and burning seal of love
Like a dark rose, a mystery of rest
On the slow bubbling of your rhythmic heart.
Nay, I persist, and very faith shall keep
You integral to me. Each door, each mystic port
Of egress from you I will seal and steep
In perfect chrism.

                    Now it is done. The mort

Will sound in heaven before it is undone.
But let me finish what I have begun
And shirt you now invulnerable in the mail
Of iron kisses, kisses linked like steel.
Put greaves upon your thighs and knees, and frail
Webbing of steel on your feet. So you shall feel
Ensheathed invulnerable with me, with seven
Great seals upon your outgoings, and woven
Chain of my mystic will wrapped perfectly
Upon you, wrapped in indomitable me.

Two Wives

I

Into the shadow-white chamber silts the white
Flux of another dawn. The wind that all night
Long has waited restless, suddenly wafts
A whirl like snow from the plum trees and the pear,
Till petals heaped between the window-shafts
      In a drift die there.

A nurse in white, at the dawning, flower-foamed pane
Draws down the blinds, whose shadows scarcely stain
The white rugs on the floor, nor the silent bed
That rides the room like a frozen berg, its crest
Finally ridged with the austere line of the dead
      Stretched out at rest.

Less than a year the fourfold feet had pressed
The peaceful floor, when fell the sword on their rest.
Yet soon, too soon, she had him home again
With wounds between them, and suffering like a guest
That will not go. Now suddenly going, the pain
      Leaves an empty breast.

II

A tall woman, with her long white gown aflow
As she strode her limbs amongst it, once more
She hastened towards the room. Did she know
As she listened in silence outside the silent door?
Entering, she saw him in outline, raised on a pyre
       Awaiting the fire.

Upraised on the bed, with feet erect as a bow,
Like the prow of a boat, his head laid back like the stern
Of a ship that stands in a shadowy sea of snow
With frozen rigging, she saw him; she drooped like a fern
Refolding, she slipped to the floor as a ghost-white peony slips
       When the thread clips.

Soft she lay as a shed flower fallen, nor heard
The ominous entry, nor saw the other love,
The dark, the grave-eyed mistress who thus dared
At such an hour to lay her claim, above
A stricken wife, so sunk in oblivion, bowed
       With misery, no more proud.

III

The stranger's hair was shorn like a lad's dark poll
And pale her ivory face: her eyes would fail
In silence when she looked: for all the whole
Darkness of failure was in them, without avail.
Dark in indomitable failure, she who had lost
       Now claimed the host.

She softly passed the sorrowful flower shed
In blonde and white on the floor, nor even turned
Her head aside, but straight towards the bed
Moved with slow feet, and her eyes' flame steadily burned.
She looked at him as he lay with banded cheek,
       And she started to speak

Softly: 'I knew it would come to this,' she said,
'I knew that some day, soon, I should find you thus.
So I did not fight you. You went your way instead
Of coming mine – and of the two of us
I died the first, I in the after-life
      Am now your wife.'

IV

' 'Twas I whose fingers did draw up the young
Plant of your body: to me you looked ere sprung
The secret of the moon within your eyes!
My mouth you met before your fine red mouth
Was set to song – and never your song denies
      My love, till you went south.'

' 'Twas I who placed the bloom of manhood on
Your youthful smoothness: I fleeced where fleece was none
Your fervent limbs with flickers and tendrils of new
Knowledge; I set your heart to its stronger beat;
I put my strength upon you, and I threw
      My life at your feet.'

'But I whom the years had reared to be your bride,
Who for years was sun for your shivering, shade for your sweat,
Who for one strange year was as a bride to you – you set me aside
With the old, sweet things of our youth; – and never yet
Have I ceased to grieve that I was not great enough
      To defeat your baser stuff.'

V

'But you are given back again to me
Who have kept intact for you your virginity.
Who for the rest of life walk out of care,
Indifferent here of myself, since I am gone
Where you are gone, and you and I out there
      Walk now as one.'

'Your widow am I, and only I. I dream
God bows His head and grants me this supreme
Pure look of your last dead face, whence now is gone
The mobility, the panther's gambolling,
And all your being is given to me, so none
      Can mock my struggling.'

'And now at last I kiss your perfect face,
Perfecting now our unfinished, first embrace.
Your young hushed look that then saw God ablaze
In every bush, is given you back, and we
Are met at length to finish our rest of days
      In a unity.'

VI

The other woman rose, and swiftly said:
'So! you have come to get him now he's dead!
Now you can triumph, now he is no more
Than a dream of yours! 'twas all you ever could
See in him, your self's dream in his sore
      Heart's blood.'

'How did you love him, you who only roused
His mind until it burnt his heart away!
'Twas you who killed him, when you both caroused
In words and things well said. But the other way
He never loved you, never with desire
      Touched you to fire.'

'Take what you've got, your memory of words
Between you, but his touch you never knew.
Caresses never flew to you like birds.
You never bore his children, never drew
His body down in weight to rest in you
      The night through.'

VII

'Take then eternity, for what is that
But another word, conceit and vanity!
But do not touch this man who never yet
Took pleasure in touching you. Mortality
Is not for you, and he is mortal still
          Against his will.'

'Even dead, he still is mortal, and his hair
Is soft though it is cold. Do not dare
To touch him while he still is lying there!
Stand a way off, and if you like commune
With his wan spirit somewhere in the air
          Like a lost tune.'

'But do not touch him, for he hated you
To touch him, and he said so, and you knew.
Why are you here? What is his corpse to you?
Stand you far off and triumph like a Jew
That he is dead and you are not. But stand
          Back, you understand!'

Noise of Battle

And all hours long, the town
   Roars like a beast in a cave
That is wounded there
And like to drown;
   While days rush, wave after wave
On its lair.

An invisible woe unseals
   The flood. so it passes beyond
All bounds: the great old city
Recumbent roars as it feels
   The foamy paw of the pond
Reach from immensity.

But all that it can do
    Now, as the tide rises,
Is to listen and hear the grim
Waves crash like thunder through
    The splintered streets, hear noises
Roll hollow in the interim.

At the Front

Far-off the lily-statues stand white-ranked in the garden at home.
Would God they were shattered quickly, the cattle would tread them
    out in the loam.
I wish the elder trees in flower could suddenly heave, and burst
The walls of the house, and nettles puff out from the hearth at which I
    was nursed.

It stands so still in the hush composed of trees and inviolate peace,
The home of my fathers, the place that is mine, my fate and my old
    increase,
And now that the skies are falling, the world is spouting in fountains of
    dirt,
I would give my soul for the homestead to fall with me, go with
    me, both in one hurt.

Reality of Peace, 1916

The trees in trouble because of autumn,
    And scarlet berries falling from the bush,
And all the myriad houseless seeds
    Loosing hold in the wind's insistent push

Moan softly with autumnal parturition,
    Poor, obscure fruits extruded out of light
Into the world of shadow, carried down
    Between the bitter knees of the after-night.

Bushed in an uncouth ardour, coiled at core
    With a knot of life that only bliss can unravel,
Fall all the fruits most bitterly into earth,
    Bitterly into corrosion bitterly travel.

What is it internecine that is locked
  By very fierceness into a quiescence
Within the rage? We shall not know till it burst
  Out of corrosion into new florescence.

Nay, but how tortured is the frightful seed,
  The spark intense within it, all without
Mordant corrosion gnashing and champing hard
  For ruin on the naked small redoubt.

Bitter to fold the issue, and make no sally!
  To have the mystery, but not go forth!
To bear, but retaliate nothing, given to save
  The spark from storms of corrosion, as seeds
    from the north.

The sharper, more horrid the pressure, the harder
    the heart
  That saves the blue grain of eternal fire
Within its quick, committed to hold and wait
  And suffer unheeding, only forbidden to expire.

Narcissus

Where the minnows trace
A glinting web quick hid in the gloom of the brook,
When I think of the place
And remember the small lad lying intent to look
Through the shadowy face
At the little fish thread-threading the watery nook –

It seems to me
The woman you are should be nixie, there is a pool
Where we ought to be.
You undine-clear and pearly, soullessly cool
And waterly,
The pool for my limbs to fathom, my soul's last school.

Narcissus
Ventured so long ago in the deeps of reflection.
Illyssus
Broke the bounds and beyond! – Dim recollection
Of fishes
Soundlessly moving in heaven's other direction!

Be
Undine towards the waters, moving back;
For me
A pool! Put off the soul you've got, oh, lack
Your human self immortal; take the watery track!

Tommies in the Train

The sun shines,
The coltsfoot flowers along the railway banks
Shine like flat coin which Jove in thanks
Strews each side the lines.

A steeple
In purple elms, daffodils
Sparkle beneath; luminous hills
Beyond – and no people.

England, O Danaë
To this spring of cosmic gold
That falls on your lap of mould! –
What then are we?

What are we
Clay-coloured, who roll in fatigue
As the train falls league after league
From our destiny?

A hand is over my face,
A cold hand. – I peep between the fingers
To watch the world that lingers
Behind, yet keeps pace.

Always there, as I peep
Between the fingers that cover my face!
Which then is it that falls from its place
And rolls down the steep?

Is it the train
That falls like a meteorite
Backward into space, to alight
Never again?

Or is it the illusory world
That falls from reality
As we look? Or are we
Like a thunderbolt hurled?

One or another
Is lost, since we fall apart
Endlessly, in one motion depart
From each other.

On the March

We are out on the open road.
Through the low west window a cold light flows
On the floor where never my numb feet trode
Before; onward the strange road goes.

Soon the spaces of the western sky
With shutters of sombre cloud will close.
But we'll still be together, this road and I,
Together, wherever the long road goes.

The wind chases by us, and over the corn
Pale shadows flee from us as if from their foes.
Like a snake we thresh on the long, forlorn
Land, as onward the long road goes.

From the sky, the low, tired moon fades out;
Through the poplars the night-wind blows;
Pale, sleepy phantoms are tossed about
As the wind asks whither the wan road goes.

Away in the distance wakes a lamp.
Inscrutable small lights glitter in rows.
They come no nearer, and still we tramp
Onwards, wherever the strange road goes.

Beat after beat falls sombre and dull.
The wind is unchanging, not one of us knows
What will be in the final lull
When we find the place where this dead road goes.

For something must come, since we pass and pass
Along in the coiled, convulsive throes
Of this marching, along with the invisible grass
That goes wherever this old road goes.

Perhaps we shall come to oblivion.
Perhaps we shall march till our tired toes
Tread over the edge of the pit, and we're gone
Down the endless slope where the last road goes.

If so, let us forge ahead, straight on,
If we're going to sleep the sleep with those
That fall for ever, knowing none
Of this land whereon the wrong road goes.

Ruination

The sun is bleeding its fires upon the mist
That huddles in grey heaps coiling and holding back.
Like cliffs abutting in shadow a dead grey sea
Some street-ends thrust forward their stack.

On the misty waste lands, away from the flushing grey
Of the morning, the elms are loftily dimmed, and tall
As if moving in air towards us, tall angels
Of darkness advancing steadily over us all.

The Attack

When we came out of the wood
Was a great light!
The night uprisen stood
In white.

I wondered, I looked around
It was so fair. The bright
Stubble upon the ground
Shone white

Like any field of snow;
Yet warm the chase
Of faint night-breaths did go
Across my face!

White-bodied and warm the night was,
Sweet-scented to hold in the throat;
White and alight the night was;
A pale stroke smote

The pulse through the whole bland being
Which was This and me;
A pulse that still went fleeing,
Yet did not flee.

In front of the terrible rage, the death,
This wonder stood glistening!
All shapes of wonder, with suspended breath,
Arrested listening

In ecstatic reverie;
The whole, white Night! –
With wonder, every black tree
Blossomed outright.

I saw the transfiguration
And the present Host.
Transubstantiation
Of the Luminous Ghost.

Winter-Lull

Because of the silent snow, we are all hushed
    Into awe.
No sound of guns nor overhead no rushed
    Vibration to draw
Our attention out of the void wherein we are crushed.

A crow floats past on level wings
    Noiselessly.
Uninterrupted silence swings
    Invisibly, inaudibly
To and fro in our misgivings.

We do not look at each other, we hide
    Our daunted eyes.
White earth, and ruins, ourselves, and nothing beside . . .
    It all belies
Our existence; we wait, and are still denied.

We are folded together, men and the snowy ground
    Into nullity.
There is silence, only the silence, never a sound
    Nor a verity
To assist us; disastrously silence-bound!

Bombardment

The Town has opened to the sun.
Like a flat red lily with a million petals
She unfolds, she comes undone.

A sharp sky brushes upon
The myriad glittering chimney-tips
As she gently exhales to the sun.

Hurrying creatures run
Down the labyrinth of the sinister flower.
What is it they shun?

A dark bird falls from the sun.
It curves in a rush to the heart of the vast
Flower: the day has begun.

Rondeau of a Conscientious Objector

The hours have tumbled their leaden, monotonous sands
And piled them up in a dull grey heap in the west.
I carry my patience sullenly through the waste lands;
To morrow will pour them all back, the dull hours I detest.

I force my cart through the sodden filth that is pressed
Into ooze, and the sombre dirt spouts up at my hands
As I make my way in twilight now to rest.
The hours have tumbled their leaden, monotonous sands.

A twisted thorn tree still in the evening stands
Defending the memory of leaves and the happy round nest.
But mud has flooded the homes of these weary lands
And piled them up in a dull grey heap in the west.

All day has the clank of iron on iron distressed
The nerve-bare place. Now a little silence expands
And a gasp of relief. But the soul is still compressed;
I carry my patience sullenly through the waste lands.

The hours have ceased to fall, and a star commands
Shadows to cover our stricken manhood, and blest
Sleep to make us forget: but he understands:
To-morrow will pour them all back, the dull hours I detest.

Obsequial Ode

Surely you've trodden straight
    To the very door!
Surely you took your fate
Faultlessly! Now it's too late
    To say more.

    It is evident you were right,
    That man has a course to go,
A voyage to sail beyond the charted seas.
You have passed from out of sight
    And my questions blow
Back from the straight horizon that ends all one sees.

Now like a vessel in port
You unlade your riches into death;
And glad are the eager dead to receive you there.
Let the dead sort
Your cargo out, breath from breath
Let them disencumber your bounty, let them all share.

I imagine dead hands are brighter,
Their fingers in sunset shine
With jewels of passion once broken through you as a prism
Breaks light into gems; and dead breasts whiter
For your wrath; and yes, I opine
They anoint their brows with your pain, as a perfect chrism.

On your body, the beaten anvil,
Was hammered out
That moon-like sword the ascendant dead unsheathe
Against us; sword that no man will
Put to rout;
Sword that severs the question from us who breathe.

Surely you've trodden straight
To the very door!
You have surely achieved your fate;
And the perfect dead are elate
To have won once more.

Now to the dead you are giving
Your last allegiance.
But what of us who are living,
And fearful yet of believing
In your pitiless legions?

Going Back

The night turns slowly round,
Swift trains go by in a rush of light;
Slow trains steal past.
This train beats anxiously, outward bound.

But I am not here.
I am away, beyond the scope of this turning;
There, where the pivot is, the axis
Of all this gear.

I, who sit in tears,
I, whose heart is torn with parting;
Who cannot bear to think back to the departure platform; –
My spirit hears

Voices of men,
Sound of artillery, aeroplanes, presences,
And more than all, the dead-sure silence,
The pivot again . . .

There, at the axis
Pain, or love, or grief
Sleep on speed; in dead certainty;
Pure relief.

There, at the pivot
Time sleeps again.
No has-been, no hereafter; only the perfected
Presence of men.

Shades

Shall I tell you, then, how it is? –
There came a cloven gleam
Like a tongue of darkened flame
To flicker in me.

And so I seem
To have you still the same
In one world with me.

In the flicker of a flower,
In a worm that is blind, yet strives,
In a mouse that pauses to listen

Glimmers our
Shadow; yet it deprives
Them none of the glisten.

In every shaken morsel
I see our shadow tremble
As if it rippled from out of us hand in hand.

As if it were part and parcel,
One shadow, and we need not dissemble
Our darkness: do you understand?

For I have told you plainly how it is.

Town in 1917

London
Used to wear her lights splendidly,
Flinging her shawl-fringe over the River,
Tassels in abandon.

And up in the sky
A two-eyed clock, like an owl
Solemnly used to approve, chime, chiming
Approval, goggle-eyed fowl!

There are no gleams on the River,
No goggling clock;
No sound from St Stephen's;
No lamp-fringed frock.

Instead
Darkness, and skin-wrapped
Fleet, hurrying limbs,
Soft-footed dead.

London
Original, wolf-wrapped
In pelts of wolves, all her luminous
Garments gone.

London, with hair
Like a forest darkness, like a marsh
Of rushes, ere the Romans
Broke in her lair.

It is well
That London, lair of sudden
Male and female darknesses,
Has broken her spell.

Bread upon the Waters

So you are lost to me!
Ah you, you ear of corn straight lying,
What food is this for the darkly flying
Fowls of the Afterwards!

White bread afloat on the waters,
Cast out by the hand that scatters
Food untowards;

Will you come back when the tide turns?
After many days? My heart yearns
To know!

Will you return after many days
To say your say as a traveller says,
More marvel than woe? –

Drift then, for the sightless birds
And the fish in shadow-waved herds
To approach you!

For you are lost to me.

War-Baby

The child like mustard seed
Rolls out of the husk of death
    Into the woman's fertile, fathomless lap.

Look, it has taken root!
See how it flourisheth!
    See how it rises with magical, rosy sap!

As for our faith, it was there
When we did not know, did not care;
    It fell from our husk in a little hasty seed.

Say, is it all we need?
Is it true that the little weed
    Will flourish its branches in heaven when we slumber
        beneath?

Nostalgia

The waning moon looks upward; this grey night
Slopes round the heavens in one smooth curve
Of easy sailing; odd red wicks serve
To show where the ships at sea move out of sight.

The place is palpable me, for here I was born
Of this self-same darkness. Yet the shadowy house below
Is out of bounds, and only the old ghosts know
I have come, I feel them whimper in welcome, and mourn.

My father suddenly died in the harvesting corn
And the place is no longer ours. Watching, I hear
No sound from the strangers, the place is dark, and fear
Opens my eyes till the roots of my vision seem torn.

Can I go no nearer, never towards the door?
The ghosts and I we mourn together, and shrink
In the shadow of the cart-shed. Must we hover on the brink
For ever, and never enter the homestead any more?

Is it irrevocable? Can I really not go
Through the open yard-way? Can I not go past the sheds
And through to the mowie?[21] – Only the dead in their beds
Can know the fearful anguish that this is so.

I kiss the stones, I kiss the moss on the wall,
And wish I could pass impregnate into the place.
I wish I could take it all in a last embrace.
I wish with my breast I here could annihilate it all.

Dreams Old and Nascent

NASCENT

The world is a painted memory, where coloured shapes
Of old, spent lives linger blurred and warm;
An endless tapestry the past has woven, drapes
The halls of my mind, compelling my life to conform.

I have lived delighted in the halls of the past
Where dead men's lives glow gently, and iron hurts
No more, and money stinks not, and death at last
Is only sad men taking off their shirts.

But now I think I have seen it all, and now
I feel thick walls of stone behind the arras.
I am shut in, a prisoner, I know not how.
And past lives hamper me, clog and embarrass.

They have no hands, they have no bodies, all
These shapes that now are dreams and once were men.
And so my heart begins to cry and call
But to get out from this dim, dreadful den.

*

The surface of dreams is broken, the arras is torn,
There's a breach in the walls of the past, lets the daylight through.
Fluent figures of men go down the upborne
Track of the railway, alive, and with something to do.

Along the railway, active figures of men!
Each with a secret which stirs in his limbs, as they move
Out of the distance nearer, coming to prove
With a touch the dead and the living, while time counts ten.

In the subtle lift of the thighs as they come unmarching
Beats the new fresh air of life. They come for strife,
For the ripping of arras, and smashing of walls, and the fight
   for life;
With axe in hand, and the hammer, and the pick-axe over-arching.

Oh come, and break this prison, this house of yesterday!
The arras is all illusion, oh come and tear it away!
The walls are thick, and the inner rooms are such, they dismay
The heart, all crowded with slaves, most working, some few at play.

                              *

The old dreams are beautiful, beloved, soft-toned and sure,
But worn out, they hide no more the walls they stand before.
Walled in, walled in, the whole world is a vast impure
Interior, a house of dreams where the dreamers writhe and snore.

Oh come, and wake us up from the ghastly dream of to-day.
We asphyxiate in a sleep of dreams, rebreathing the impure air.
For the house is shut and sealed, and the breath of the hosts is grey
As they dream corrupted dreams, all poisoned with care.

The ghastly dream of labour, and the stench of steel and of oil.
The writhing of myriads of workmen, all dreaming they are going to
   be rich
And giving off dreadful effluvia in a ghastly effort of toil
Unfinished for ever, but gasping for money, as they dream
   and they itch.

The ghastly dream of riches, of masses of money to spend,
Of walking over the faces of men, like cobble-stones!
Of riding, and being envied, such envy as has no end!
Of making a triumph of envy, the rich and successful ones.

                              *

The whole wide world is interior now, and we're all shut up.
The air is all close and poisonous, it has drugged our souls, so we sleep
A sleep that is writhing stupor, weighed down, so we can't
     wake up.
The rich and the poor alike dreaming and writhing, all in one heap.

Oh come, oh, men along the railway! Oh come as men
And break the walls of possession of all the wide world!
Give us air, we cry. Oh, let us but breathe again!
Let us breathe fresh air and wake from foul dreams in which
     we are furled.

To feel fresh air in our throats, to have fresh breath in our breasts,
To make new words with our lips, to escape the foul dream
Of having and getting and owning, the struggle which wrests
Money from out of the earth or the beast or the man, as they labour in
     steam.

*

Oh, men with the axe and the pick-axe, break the walls of the
     filthy dream
And release us, poor ones and rich ones, let us breathe and touch
One another in wonder of wakening, let us wake to the gleam
Of real daylight upon us, released from the foul dream's hutch.

For the proper dream-stuff is molten, and moving mysteriously,
And the bodies of men and women are molten matter of dreams
That stirs with a stir which is cosmic, as ever, invisibly
The heart of the live world pulses, and the blood of the live world
     teems.

And what is life, but the swelling and shaping the dream in the flesh!
And our bodies molten drops of dream-blood that swirl and swell
In a tissue, as all the molten cells in the living mesh
Of a rose tree move to roses and thorns and a delicate smell.

On That Day

On that day
I shall put roses on roses, and cover your grave
With multitude of white roses: and, since you were brave,
One bright red ray.

So people, passing under
The ash trees of the valley-road, will raise
Their eyes and look at the grave on the hill, in wonder,
Wondering mount, and put the flowers asunder:

To see whose praise
Is blazoned here so white and so bloodily red.
Then they will say: ' 'Tis long since she is dead,
Who has remembered her after many days?'

And standing there
They will consider how you went your ways
Unnoticed among them, a still queen lost in the maze
Of this earthly affair.

A queen, they'll say,
Has slept unnoticed on a forgotten hill.
Sleeps on unknown, unnoticed there, until
Dawns my insurgent day.

Autumn Sunshine

The sun sets out the autumn crocuses
And fills them up a pouring measure
Of death-producing wine, till treasure
Runs waste down their chalices.

All, all Persephone's pale cups of mould
Are on the board, are over-filled;
The portion to the gods is spilled;
Now, mortals all, take hold!

The time is now, the wine-cup full and full
  Of lambent heaven, a pledging-cup;
  Let now all mortal men take up
The drink, and a long, strong pull!

Out of the hell-queen's cup, the heaven's pale wine!
  Drink then, invisible heroes, drink!
  Lips to the vessels, never shrink,
Throats to the heavens incline.

And take within the wine the god's great oath
  By heaven and earth and hellish stream,
  To break this sick and nauseous dream
We writhe and lust in, both.

Swear, in the pale wine poured from the cups of the queen
  Of hell, to wake and be free
  From this nightmare we writhe in,
Break out of this foul has-been.

UNRHYMING POEMS

Look! We have come through!

Argument

After much struggling and loss in love and in the world of man, the protagonist throws in his lot with a woman who is already married. Together they go into another country, she perforce leaving her children behind. The conflict of love and hate goes on between the man and the woman, and between these two and the world around them, till it reaches some sort of conclusion.

Moonrise

And who has seen the moon, who has not seen
Her rise from out the chamber of the deep,
Flushed and grand and naked, as from the chamber
Of finished bridegroom, seen her rise and throw
Confession of delight upon the wave,
Littering the waves with her own superscription
Of bliss, till all her lambent beauty shakes towards us
Spread out and known at last, and we are sure
That beauty is a thing beyond the grave,
That perfect, bright experience never falls
To nothingness, and time will dim the moon
Sooner than our full consummation here
In this odd life will tarnish or pass away.

Elegy

The sun immense and rosy
Must have sunk and become extinct
The night you closed your eyes for ever against me.

Grey days, and wan, dree dawnings
Since then, with fritter of flowers –
Day wearies me with its ostentation and fawnings.

Still, you left me the nights,
The great dark glittery window,
The bubble hemming this empty existence with lights.

Still in the vast hollow
Like a breath in a bubble spinning
Brushing the stars, goes my soul, that skims the bounds
    like a swallow!

I can look through
The film of the bubble night, to where you are.
Through the film I can almost touch you.

                                        Eastwood.

Nonentity

The stars that open and shut
Fall on my shallow breast
Like stars on a pool.

The soft wind, blowing cool,
Laps little crest after crest
Of ripples across my breast.

And dark grass under my feet
Seems to dabble in me
Like grass in a brook.

Oh, and it is sweet
To be all these things, not to be
Any more myself.

For look,
I am weary of myself!

Martyr à la Mode

Ah God, life, law, so many names you keep,
You great, you patient Effort, and you Sleep
That does inform this various dream of living,
You sleep stretched out for ever, ever giving
Us out as dreams, you august Sleep
Coursed round by rhythmic movement of all time,
The constellations, your great heart, the sun
Fierily pulsing, unable to refrain;
Since you, vast, outstretched, wordless Sleep
Permit of no beyond, ah you, whose dreams
We are, and body of sleep, let it never be said
I quailed at my appointed function, turned poltroon.

For when at night, from out the full surcharge
Of a day's experience, sleep does slowly draw
The harvest, the spent action to itself;

Leaves me unburdened to begin again;
At night, I say, when I am gone in sleep,
Does my slow heart rebel, do my dead hands
Complain of what the day has had them do?

Never let it be said I was poltroon
At this my task of living, this my dream,
This me which rises from the dark of sleep
In white flesh robed to drape another dream,
As lightning comes all white and trembling
From out the cloud of sleep, looks round about
One moment, sees, and swift its dream is over,
In one rich drip it sinks to another sleep,
And sleep thereby is one more dream enrichened.

If so the Vast, the God, the Sleep that still grows richer
Have said that I, this mote in the body of sleep,
Must in my transiency pass all through pain,
Must be a dream of grief, must like a crude
Dull meteorite flash only into light
When tearing through the anguish of this life,
Still in full flight extinct, shall I then turn
Poltroon, and beg the silent, outspread God
To alter my one speck of doom, when round me burns
The whole great conflagration of all life,
Lapped like a body close upon a sleep,
Hiding and covering in the eternal Sleep
Within the immense and toilsome life-time, heaved
With ache of dreams that body forth the Sleep?

Shall I, less than the least red grain of flesh
Within my body, cry out to the dreaming soul
That slowly labours in a vast travail,
To halt the heart, divert the streaming flow
That carries moons along, and spare the stress
That crushes me to an unseen atom of fire?

When pain and all
And grief are but the same last wonder, Sleep
Rising to dream in me a small keen dream
Of sudden anguish, sudden over and spent –

Croydon

Don Juan

It is Isis the mystery
Must be in love with me.

Here this round ball of earth
Where all the mountains sit
Solemn in groups,
And the bright rivers flit
Round them for girth.

Here the trees and troops
Darken the shining grass,
And many people pass
Plundered from heaven,
Many bright people pass,
Plunder from heaven.

What of the mistresses,
What the beloved seven?
– They were but witnesses,
I was just driven.

Where is there peace for me?
Isis the mystery
Must be in love with me.

The Sea

You, you are all unloving, loveless, you;
Restless and lonely, shaken by your own moods,
You are celibate and single, scorning a comrade even,
Threshing your own passions with no woman for the threshing-
    floor,
Finishing your dreams for your own sake only,
Playing your great game around the world, alone,
Without playmate, or helpmate, having no one to cherish,
No one to comfort, and refusing any comforter.

Not like the earth, the spouse all full of increase
Moiled over with the rearing of her many-mouthed young;
You are single, you are fruitless, phosphorescent, cold and
    callous,
Naked of worship, of love or of adornment,
Scorning the panacea even of labour,
Sworn to a high and splendid purposelessness
Of brooding and delighting in the secret of life's goings,
Sea, only you are free, sophisticated.

You who toil not, you who spin not,
Surely but for you and your like, toiling
Were not worth while, nor spinning worth the effort!

You who take the moon as in a sieve, and sift
Her flake by flake and spread her meaning out;
You who roll the stars like jewels in your palm,
So that they seem to utter themselves aloud;
You who steep from out the days their colour,
Reveal the universal tint that dyes
Their web; who shadow the sun's great gestures and pressions
So that he seems a stranger in his passing;
Who voice the dumb night fittingly;
Sea, you shadow of all things, now mock us to death
    with your shadowing.

                              Bournemouth

Hymn to Priapus

    My love lies underground
    With her face upturned to mine,
    And her mouth unclosed in a last long kiss
    That ended her life and mine.

    I dance at the Christmas party
    Under the mistletoe
    Along with a ripe, slack country lass
    Jostling to and fro.

The big, soft country lass,
Like a loose sheaf of wheat
Slipped through my arms on the threshing floor
At my feet.

The warm, soft country lass,
Sweet as an armful of wheat
At threshing-time broken, was broken
For me, and ah, it was sweet!

Now I am going home
Fulfilled and alone,
I see the great Orion standing
Looking down.

He's the star of my first beloved
Love-making.
The witness of all that bitter-sweet
Heart-aching.

Now he sees this as well,
This last commission.
Nor do I get any look
Of admonition.

He can add the reckoning up
I suppose, between now and then,
Having walked himself in the thorny, difficult
Ways of men.

He has done as I have done
No doubt:
Remembered and forgotten
Turn and about.

My love lies underground
With her face upturned to mine;
And her mouth unclosed in the last long kiss
That ended her life and mine.

She fares in the stark immortal
Fields of death;
I in these goodly, frozen
Fields beneath.

Something in me remembers
And will not forget.
The stream of my life in the darkness
Deathward set!

And something in me has forgotten,
Has ceased to care.
Desire comes up, and contentment
Is debonair.

I, who am worn and careful,
How much do I care?
How is it I grin then, and chuckle
Over despair?

Grief, grief, I suppose and sufficient
Grief makes us free
To be faithless and faithful together
As we have to be.

Ballad of a Wilful Woman

FIRST PART

Upon her plodding palfrey
With a heavy child at her breast
And Joseph holding the bridle
They mount to the last hill-crest.

Dissatisfied and weary
She sees the blade of the sea
Dividing earth and heaven
In a glitter of ecstasy.

Sudden a dark-faced stranger,
With his back to the sun, holds out
His arms; so she lights from her palfrey
And turns her round about.

She has given the child to Joseph,
Gone down to the flashing shore;
And Joseph, shading his eyes with his hand,
Stands watching evermore.

SECOND PART

The sea in the stones is singing,
A woman binds her hair
With yellow, frail sea-poppies,
That shine as her fingers stir.

While a naked man comes swiftly
Like a spurt of white foam rent
From the crest of a falling breaker,
Over the poppies sent.

He puts his surf-wet fingers
Over her startled eyes,
And asks if she sees the land, the land,
The land of her glad surmise.

THIRD PART

Again in her blue, blue mantle
Riding at Joseph's side,
She says, 'I went to Cythera,
And woe betide!'

Her heart is a swinging cradle
That holds the perfect child,
But the shade on her forehead ill becomes
A mother mild.

So on with the slow, mean journey
In the pride of humility;
Till they halt at a cliff on the edge of the land
Over a sullen sea.

While Joseph pitches the sleep-tent
She goes far down to the shore
To where a man in a heaving boat
Waits with a lifted oar.

FOURTH PART

They dwelt in a huge, hoarse sea-cave
And looked far down the dark
Where an archway torn and glittering
Shone like a huge sea-spark.

He said: 'Do you see the spirits
Crowding the bright doorway?'
He said: 'Do you hear them whispering?'
He said: 'Do you catch what they say?'

FIFTH PART

Then Joseph, grey with waiting,
His dark eyes full of pain,
Heard: 'I have been to Patmos;
Give me the child again.'

Now on with the hopeless journey
Looking bleak ahead she rode,
And the man and the child of no more account
Than the earth the palfrey trode.

Till a beggar spoke to Joseph,
But looked into her eyes;
So she turned, and said to her husband:
'I give, whoever denies.'

SIXTH PART

She gave on the open heather
Beneath bare judgment stars,
And she dreamed of her children and Joseph,
And the isles, and her men, and her scars.

And she woke to distil the berries
The beggar had gathered at night,
Whence he drew the curious liquors
He held in delight.

He gave her no crown of flowers,
No child and no palfrey slow,
Only led her through harsh, hard places
Where strange winds blow.

She follows his restless wanderings
Till night when, by the fire's red stain,
Her face is bent in the bitter steam
That comes from the flowers of pain.

Then merciless and ruthless
He takes the flame-wild drops
To the town, and tries to sell them
With the market-crops.

So she follows the cruel journey
That ends not anywhere,
And dreams, as she stirs the mixing-pot,
She is brewing hope from despair.

Trier

Bei Hennef [22]

The little river twittering in the twilight,
The wan, wondering look of the pale sky,
    This is almost bliss.

And everything shut up and gone to sleep,
All the troubles and anxieties and pain
    Gone under the twilight.

Only the twilight now, and the soft 'Sh!' of the river
    That will last for ever.

And at last I know my love for you is here;
I can see it all, it is whole like the twilight,
It is large, so large, I could not see it before,
Because of the little lights and flickers and interruptions,
>Troubles, anxieties and pains.

>You are the call and I am the answer,
>You are the wish, and I the fulfilment,
>You are the night, and I the day.
>>What else? it is perfect enough.
>>It is perfectly complete,
>>You and us
>>What more – ?

Strange, how we suffer in spite of this!

Hennef am Rhein

First Morning

The night was a failure
>but why not – ?

In the darkness
>with the pale dawn seething at the window
>through the black frame
>I could not be free,
>not free myself from the past, those others –
>and our love was a confusion,
>there was a horror,
>you recoiled away from me.

Now, in the morning
As we sit in the sunshine on the seat by the little shrine,
And look at the mountain-walls,
Walls of blue shadow,
And see so near at our feet in the meadow
Myriads of dandelion pappus
Bubbles ravelled in the dark green grass
Held still beneath the sunshine –

It is enough, you are near –
The mountains are balanced,
The dandelion seeds stay half-submerged in the grass;
You and I together
We hold them proud and blithe
On our love.
They stand upright on our love,
Everything starts from us,
We are the source.

Beuerberg

'And Oh – That the Man I am
Might Cease to be – '

No, now I wish the sunshine would stop,
and the white shining houses, and the gay red flowers on the
    balconies
and the bluish mountains beyond, would be crushed out
between two valves of darkness;
the darkness falling, the darkness rising, with muffled sound
obliterating everything.

I wish that whatever props up the walls of light
would fall, and darkness would come hurling heavily down,
and it would be thick black dark for ever.
Not sleep, which is grey with dreams,
nor death, which quivers with birth,
but heavy, sealing darkness, silence, all immovable.

What is sleep?
It goes over me, like a shadow over a hill,
but it does not alter me, nor help me.
And death would ache still, I am sure;
it would be lambent, uneasy.
I wish it would be completely dark everywhere,
inside me, and out, heavily dark
utterly.

Wolfratshausen

She Looks Back

The pale bubbles,
The lovely pale-gold bubbles of the globe-flowers,
In a great swarm clotted and single
Went rolling in the dusk towards the river
To where the sunset hung its wan gold cloths;
And you stood alone, watching them go,
And that mother-love like a demon drew you from me
Towards England.

Along the road, after nightfall,
Along the glamorous birch tree avenue
Across the river levels
We went in silence, and you staring to England.

So then there shone within the jungle darkness
Of the long, lush under-grass, a glow-worm's sudden
Green lantern of pure light, a little, intense, fusing triumph,
White and haloed with fire-mist, down in the tangled darkness.
Then you put your hand in mine again, kissed me, and we
    struggled to be together.
And the little electric flashes went with us, in the grass,
Tiny lighthouses, little souls of lanterns, courage burst into an
    explosion of green light
Everywhere down in the grass, where darkness was ravelled in
    darkness.

Still, the kiss was a touch of bitterness on my mouth
Like salt, burning in.
And my hand withered in your hand.
For you were straining with a wild heart, back, back again,
Back to those children you had left behind, to all the aeons of the
    past.
And I was here in the under-dusk of the Isar.

At home, we leaned in the bedroom window
Of the old Bavarian Gasthaus,
And the frogs in the pool beyond thrilled with exuberance,
Like a boiling pot the pond crackled with happiness,

Like a rattle a child spins round for joy, the night rattled
With the extravagance of the frogs,
And you leaned your cheek on mine,
And I suffered it, wanting to sympathise.

At last, as you stood, your white gown falling from your breasts,
You looked into my eyes, and said: 'But this is joy!'
I acquiesced again.
But the shadow of lying was in your eyes,
The mother in you, fierce as a murderess, glaring to England,
Yearning towards England, towards your young children,
Insisting upon your motherhood, devastating.

Still, the joy was there also, you spoke truly,
The joy was not to be driven off so easily;
Stronger than fear or destructive mother-love, it stood flickering;
The frogs helped also, whirring away.
Yet how I have learned to know that look in your eyes
Of horrid sorrow!
How I know that glitter of salt, – dry, sterile, sharp, corrosive salt!
Not tears, but white sharp brine
Making hideous your eyes.

I have seen it, felt it in my mouth, my throat, my chest, my belly,
Burning of powerful salt, burning, eating through my defenceless
    nakedness.
I have been thrust into white, sharp crystals,
Writhing, twisting, superpenetrated.
Ah, Lot's Wife, Lot's Wife!
The pillar of salt, the whirling, horrible column of salt, like a
    waterspout
That has enveloped me!
Snow of salt, white, burning, eating salt
In which I have writhed.

Lot's Wife! – Not Wife, but Mother.
I have learned to curse your motherhood,
You pillar of salt accursed.
I have cursed motherhood because of you,
Accursed, base motherhood!

I long for the time to come, when the curse against you will have
    gone out of my heart.
But it has not gone yet.
Nevertheless, once, the frogs, the globe-flowers of Bavaria, the
    glow-worms
Gave me sweet lymph against the salt-burns,
There is a kindness in the very rain.

Therefore, even in the hour of my deepest, passionate malediction
I try to remember it is also well between us.
That you are with me in the end.
That you never look quite back; nine-tenths, ah, more
You look round over your shoulder;
But never quite back.

Nevertheless the curse against you is still in my heart
Like a deep, deep burn.
The curse against all mothers.
All mothers who fortify themselves in motherhood, devastating the
    vision.
They are accursed, and the curse is not taken off;
It burns within me like a deep, old burn,
And oh, I wish it was better.

Beuerberg

On the Balcony

In front of the sombre mountains, a faint, lost ribbon of rainbow;
And between us and it, the thunder;
And down below in the green wheat, the labourers
Stand like dark stumps, still in the green wheat.

You are near to me, and your naked feet in their sandals,
And through the scent of the balcony's naked timber
I distinguish the scent of your hair: so now the limber
Lightning falls from heaven.

Adown the pale-green glacier river floats
A dark boat through the gloom – and whither?
The thunder roars. But still we have each other!
The naked lightnings in the heavens dither
And disappear – what have we but each other?
The boat has gone.

Icking

Frohnleichnam [23]

You have come your way, I have come my way;
You have stepped across your people, carelessly, hurting them all;
I have stepped across my people, and hurt them in spite of my
    care.

But steadily, surely, and notwithstanding
We have come our ways and met at last
Here in this upper room.

Here the balcony
Overhangs the street where the bullock-wagons slowly
Go by with their loads of green and silver birch trees
For the feast of Corpus Christi.

Here from the balcony
We look over the growing wheat, where the jade-green river
Goes between the pine-woods,
Over and beyond to where the many mountains
Stand in their blueness, flashing with snow and the morning.

I have done; a quiver of exultation goes through me, like the first
Breeze of the morning through a narrow white birch.
You glow at last like the mountain tops when they catch
Day and make magic in heaven.

At last I can throw away world without end, and meet you
Unsheathed and naked and narrow and white;
At last you can throw immortality off, and I see you
Glistening with all the moment and all your beauty.

Shameless and callous I love you;
Out of indifference I love you;
Out of mockery we dance together,
Out of the sunshine into the shadow,
Passing across the shadow into the sunlight,
Out of sunlight to shadow.

As we dance
Your eyes take all of me in as a communication;
As we dance
I see you, ah, in full!
Only to dance together in triumph of being together
Two white ones, sharp, vindicated,
Shining and touching,
Is heaven of our own, sheer with repudiation.

In the Dark

A blotch of pallor stirs beneath the high
Square picture-dusk, the window of dark sky.

A sound subdued in the darkness: tears!
As if a bird in difficulty up the valley steers.

'Why have you gone to the window? Why don't you sleep?
How you have wakened me! – But why, why do you weep?'

'I am afraid of you, I am afraid, afraid!
There is something in you destroys me – !'

'You have dreamed and are not awake, come here to me.'
'No, I have wakened. It is you, you are cruel to me!'

'My dear!' – *'Yes, yes, you are cruel to me. You cast*
A shadow over my breasts that will kill me at last.'

'Come!' – *'No, I'm a thing of life. I give*
You armfuls of sunshine, and you won't let me live.'

'Nay, I'm too sleepy!' – *'Ah, you are horrible;*
You stand before me like ghosts, like a darkness upright.'

'I!' – '*How can you treat me so, and love me?*
My feet have no hold, you take the sky from above me.'

'My dear, the night is soft and eternal, no doubt
You love it!' – '*It is dark, it kills me, I am put out.*'

'My dear, when you cross the street in the sunshine, surely
Your own small night goes with you. Why treat it so poorly?'

'*No, no, I dance in the sun, I'm a thing of life –* '
'Even then it is dark behind you. Turn round, my wife.'

'*No, how cruel you are, you people the sunshine*
With shadows!' – 'With yours I people the sunshine, yours and
    mine –

'In the darkness we all are gone, we are gone with the trees
And the restless river; – we are lost and gone with all these.'

'*But I am myself, I have nothing to do with these.*'
'Come back to bed, let us sleep on our mysteries.

'Come to me here, and lay your body by mine,
And I will be all the shadow, you the shine.

'Come, you are cold, the night has frightened you.
Hark at the river! It pants as it hurries through

'The pine-woods. How I love them so, in their mystery of not-to-
    be.'
' – *But let me be myself, not a river or a tree.*'

'Kiss me! How cold you are! – Your little breasts
Are bubbles of ice. Kiss me! – You know how it rests

'One to be quenched, to be given up, to be gone in the dark;
To be blown out, to let night dowse the spark.

'But never mind, my love. Nothing matters, save sleep;
Save you, and me, and sleep; all the rest will keep.'

Mutilation

A thick mist-sheet lies over the broken wheat.
I walk up to my neck in mist, holding my mouth up.
Across there, a discoloured moon burns itself out.

I hold the night in horror;
I dare not turn round.

To-night I have left her alone.
They would have it I have left her for ever.

Oh my God, how it aches
Where she is cut off from me!

Perhaps she will go back to England.
Perhaps she will go back,
Perhaps we are parted for ever.

If I go on walking through the whole breadth of Germany
I come to the North Sea, or to the Baltic.

Over there is Russia – Austria, Switzerland, France, in a circle!
I here in the undermist on the Bavarian road.

It aches in me.
What is England or France, far off,
But a name she might take?
I don't mind this continent stretching, the sea far away;
It aches in me for her
Like the agony of limbs cut off and aching;
Not even longing,
It is only agony.

A cripple!
Oh God, to be mutilated!
To be a cripple!

And if I never see her again?

I think, if they told me so
I could convulse the heavens with my horror.
I think I could alter the frame of things in my agony.
I think I could break the System with my heart.
I think, in my convulsion, the skies would break.

She too suffers.
But who could compel her, if she chose me against them all?
She has not chosen me finally, she suspends her choice.
Night folk, Tuatha De Danaan,[24] dark Gods, govern her sleep,
Magnificent ghosts of the darkness, carry off her decision in sleep,
Leave her no choice, make her lapse me-ward, make her,
Oh Gods of the living Darkness, powers of Night.

Wolfratshausen

Humiliation

I have been so innerly proud, and so long alone,
Do not leave me, or I shall break.
Do not leave me.

What should I do if you were gone again
So soon?
What should I look for?
Where should I go?
What should I be, I myself,
'I'?
What would it mean, this
I?

Do not leave me.

What should I think of death?
If I died, it would not be you:
It would be simply the same
Lack of you.
The same want, life or death,
Unfulfilment,
The same insanity of space,
You not there for me.

Think, I daren't die
For fear of the lack in death.
And I daren't live.

Unless there were a morphine or a drug.

I would bear the pain.
But always, strong, unremitting
It would make me not me.
The thing with my body that would go on living
Would not be me.
Neither life nor death could help.

Think, I couldn't look towards death
Nor towards the future:
Only not look.
Only myself
Stand still and bind and blind myself.

God, that I have no choice!
That my own fulfilment is up against me
Timelessly!
The burden of self-accomplishment!
The charge of fulfilment!
And God, that she is *necessary*!
Necessary, and I have no choice!

Do not leave me.

A Young Wife

The pain of loving you
Is almost more than I can bear.

I walk in fear of you.
The darkness starts up where
You stand, and the night comes through
Your eyes when you look at me.

Ah never before did I see
The shadows that live in the sun!

Now every tall glad tree
Turns round its back to the sun
And looks down on the ground, to see
The shadow it used to shun.

At the foot of each glowing thing
A night lies looking up.

Oh, and I want to sing
And dance, but I can't lift up
My eyes from the shadows: dark
They lie spilt round the cup.

What is it? – Hark
The faint fine seethe in the air!

Like the seething sound in a shell!
It is death still seething where
The wild-flower shakes its bell
And the skylark twinkles blue –

The pain of loving you
Is almost more than I can bear.

Green

The dawn was apple-green,
The sky was green wine held up in the sun,
The moon was a golden petal between.

She opened her eyes, and green
They shone, clear like flowers undone
For the first time, now for the first time seen.

Icking

River Roses

By the Isar, in the twilight
We were wandering and singing,
By the Isar, in the evening
We climbed the huntsman's ladder and sat swinging
In the fir tree overlooking the marshes,
While river met with river, and the ringing
Of their pale-green glacier water filled the evening.

By the Isar, in the twilight
We found the dark wild roses
Hanging red at the river; and simmering
Frogs were singing, and over the river closes
Was savour of ice and of roses; and glimmering
Fear was abroad. We whispered: 'No one knows us.
Let it be as the snake disposes
Here in this simmering marsh.'

Kloster Schaeftlarn

Gloire de Dijon

When she rises in the morning
I linger to watch her;
She spreads the bath-cloth underneath the window
And the sunbeams catch her
Glistening white on the shoulders,
While down her sides the mellow
Golden shadow glows as
She stoops to the sponge, and her swung breasts
Sway like full-blown yellow
Gloire de Dijon roses.

She drips herself with water, and her shoulders
Glisten as silver, they crumple up
Like wet and falling roses, and I listen
For the sluicing of their rain-dishevelled petals.
In the window full of sunlight
Concentrates her golden shadow
Fold on fold, until it glows as
Mellow as the glory roses.

Icking

Roses on the Breakfast Table

Just a few of the roses we gathered from the Isar
Are fallen, and their mauve-red petals on the cloth
Float like boats on a river, while other
Roses are ready to fall, reluctant and loth.

She laughs at me across the table, saying
I am beautiful. I look at the rumpled young roses
And suddenly realize, in them as in me,
How lovely is the self this day discloses.

I am like a Rose

I am myself at last; now I achieve
My very self. I with the wonder mellow,
Full of fine warmth, I issue forth in clear
And single me, perfected from my fellow.

Here I am all myself. No rose-bush heaving
Its limpid sap to culmination has brought
Itself more sheer and naked out of the green
In stark-clear roses, than I to myself am brought.

Rose of all the World

I am here myself; as though this heave of effort
At starting other life, fulfilled my own:
Rose-leaves that whirl in colour round a core
Of seed-specks kindled lately and softly blown

By all the blood of the rose-bush into being –
Strange, that the urgent will in me, to set
My mouth on hers in kisses, and so softly
To bring together two strange sparks, beget

Another life from our lives, so should send
The innermost fire of my own dim soul out-spinning
And whirling in blossom of flame and being upon me!
That my completion of manhood should be the beginning

Another life from mine! For so it looks.
The seed is purpose, blossom accident.
The seed is all in all, the blossom lent
To crown the triumph of this new descent.

Is that it, woman? Does it strike you so?
The Great Breath blowing a tiny seed of fire
Fans out your petals for excess of flame,
Till all your being smokes with fine desire?

Or are we kindled, you and I, to be
One rose of wonderment upon the tree
Of perfect life, and is our possible seed
But the residuum of the ecstasy?

How will you have it? – the rose is all in all,
Or the ripe rose-fruits of the luscious fall?
The sharp begetting, or the child begot?
Our consummation matters, or does it not?

To me it seems the seed is just left over
From the red rose-flowers' fiery transience;
Just orts and slarts;[25] berries that smoulder in the bush
Which burnt just now with marvellous immanence.

Blossom, my darling, blossom, be a rose
Of roses unchidden and purposeless; a rose
For rosiness only, without an ulterior motive;
For me it is more than enough if the flower unclose.

A Youth Mowing

There are four men mowing down by the Isar;
I can hear the swish of the scythe-strokes, four
Sharp breaths taken: yea, and I
Am sorry for what's in store.

The first man out of the four that's mowing
Is mine, I claim him once and for all;
Though it's sorry I am, on his young feet, knowing
None of the trouble he's led to stall.

As he sees me bringing the dinner, he lifts
His head as proud as a deer that looks
Shoulder-deep out of the corn; and wipes
His scythe-blade bright, unhooks

The scythe-stone and over the stubble to me.
Lad, thou hast gotten a child in me,
Laddie, a man thou'lt ha'e to be,
Yea, though I'm sorry for thee.

Quite Forsaken

What pain, to wake and miss you!
　　To wake with a tightened heart,
And mouth reaching forward to kiss you!

This then at last is the dawn, and the bell
　　Clanging at the farm! Such bewilderment
Comes with the sight of the room, I cannot tell.

It is raining. Down the half-obscure road
　　Four labourers pass with their scythes
Dejectedly; – a huntsman goes by with his load:

A gun, and a bunched-up deer, its four little feet
　　Clustered dead. – And this is the dawn
For which I wanted the night to retreat!

Forsaken and Forlorn

The house is silent, it is late at night, I am alone.
　　　　　　From the balcony
　　　　　I can hear the Isar moan
　　　　　Can see the white
Rift of the river eerily, between the pines, under a sky of stone.

Some fireflies drift through the middle air
　　　　　　Tinily.
　　　　　I wonder where
Ends this darkness that annihilates me.

Fireflies in the Corn

SHE SPEAKS.

Look at the little darlings in the corn!
    The rye is taller than you, who think yourself
So high and mighty: look how the heads are borne
    Dark and proud on the sky, like a number of knights
Passing with spears and pennants and manly scorn.

Knights indeed! – much knight I know will ride
    With his head held high-serene against the sky!
Limping and following rather at my side
    Moaning for me to love him! – O darling rye
How I adore you for your simple pride!

And the dear, dear fireflies wafting in between
    And over the swaying corn-stalks, just above
All the dark-feathered helmets, like little green
    Stars come low and wandering here for love
Of these dark knights, shedding their delicate sheen!

I thank you I do, you happy creatures, you dears,
    Riding the air, and carrying all the time
Your little lanterns behind you! Ah, it cheers
    My soul to see you settling and trying to climb
The corn-stalks, tipping with fire the spears.

All over the dim corn's motion, against the blue
    Dark sky of night, a wandering glitter, a swarm
Of questing brilliant souls going out with their true
    Proud knights to battle! Sweet, how I warm
My poor, my perished soul with the sight of you!

A Doe at Evening

As I went through the marshes
a doe sprang out of the corn
and flashed up the hill-side
leaving her fawn.

On the sky-line
she moved round to watch,
she pricked a fine black blotch
on the sky.

I looked at her
and felt her watching;
I became a strange being.
Still, I had my right to be there with her.

Her nimble shadow trotting
along the sky-line, she
put back her fine, level-balanced head.
And I knew her.

Ah yes, being male, is not my head hard-balanced, antlered?
Are not my haunches light?
Has she not fled on the same wind with me?
Does not my fear cover her fear?

Irschenhausen

Song of a Man Who is Not Loved

The space of the world is immense, before me and around me;
If I turn quickly, I am terrified, feeling space surround me;
Like a man in a boat on very clear, deep water, space frightens and
    confounds me.

I see myself isolated in the universe, and wonder
What effect I can have. My hands wave under
The heavens like specks of dust that are floating asunder.

I hold myself up, and feel a big wind blowing
Me like a gadfly into the dusk, without my knowing
Whither or why or even how I am going.

So much there is outside me, so infinitely
Small am I, what matter if minutely
I beat my way, to be lost immediately?

How shall I flatter myself that I can do
Anything in such immensity? I am too
Little to count in the wind that drifts me through.

Glashütte

Sinners

The big mountains sit still in the afternoon light,
    Shadows in their lap;
The bees roll round in the wild-thyme with delight.

We sitting here among the cranberries
    So still in the gap
Of rock, distilling our memories,

Are sinners! Strange! The bee that blunders
    Against me goes off with a laugh.
A squirrel cocks his head on the fence, and wonders

What about sin? – For, it seems
    The mountains have
No shadow of us on their snowy forehead of dreams

As they ought to have. They rise above us
    Dreaming
For ever. One even might think that they love us.

    Little red cranberries cheek to cheek,
    Two great dragon-flies wrestling;
    You, with your forehead nestling
    Against me, and bright peak shining to peak –

There's a love-song for you! – Ah, if only
    There were no teeming
Swarms of mankind in the world, and we were less lonely!

Mayrhofen

Misery

Out of this oubliette between the mountains
five valleys go, five passes like gates;
three of them black in shadow, two of them bright
with distant sunshine;
and sunshine fills one high valley bed,
green grass shining, and little white houses
like quartz crystals,
little, but distinct a way off.

Why don't I go?
Why do I crawl about this pot, this oubliette,
stupidly?
Why don't I go?

But where?
If I come to a pine-wood, I can't say:
Now I am arrived!
What are so many straight trees to me!

Sterzing

Everlasting Flowers

FOR A DEAD MOTHER

Who do you think stands watching
    The snow-tops shining rosy
In heaven, now that the darkness
    Takes all but the tallest posy?

Who then sees the two-winged
    Boat down there, all alone
And asleep on the snow's last shadow,
    Like a moth on a stone?

The olive-leaves, light as gad-flies,
    Have all gone dark, gone black.
And now in the dark my soul to you
    Turns back.

To you, my little darling,
>   To you, out of Italy.
For what is loveliness, my love,
>   Save you have it with me!

So, there's an oxen wagon
>   Comes darkly into sight:
A man with a lantern, swinging
>   A little light.

What does he see, my darling,
>   Here by the darkened lake?
Here, in the sloping shadow
>   The mountains make?

He says not a word, but passes,
>   Staring at what he sees.
What ghost of us both do you think he saw
>   Under the olive trees?

All the things that are lovely –
>   The things you never knew –
I wanted to gather them one by one
>   And bring them to you.

But never now, my darling,
>   Can I gather the mountain-tips
From the twilight like half-shut lilies
>   To hold to your lips.

And never the two-winged vessel
>   That sleeps below on the lake
Can I catch like a moth between my hands
>   For you to take.

But hush, I am not regretting:
>   It is far more·perfect now.
I'll whisper the ghostly truth to you
>   And tell you how

I know you here in the darkness,
>   How you sit in the throne of my eyes
At peace, and look out of the windows
>   In glad surprise.

Lago di Garda

Sunday Afternoon in Italy

The man and the maid go side by side
With an interval of space between;
And his hands are awkward and want to hide,
She braves it out since she must be seen.

When some one passes he drops his head,
Shading his face in his black felt hat,
While the hard girl hardens; nothing is said,
There is nothing to wonder or cavil at.

Alone on the open road again,
With the mountain snows across the lake
Flushing the afternoon, they are uncomfortable,
The loneliness daunts them, their stiff throats ache.

And he sighs with relief when she parts from him;
Her proud head held in its black silk scarf
Gone under the archway, home, he can join
The men that lounge in a group on the wharf.

His evening is a flame of wine
Among the eager, cordial men.
And she with her women hot and hard
Moves at her ease again.

She is marked, she is singled out
  For the fire:
The brand is upon him, look you!
  Of desire.

They are chosen, ah, they are fated
  For the fight!
Champion her, all you women! Men, menfolk,
  Hold him your light!

Nourish her, train her, harden her,
  Women all!
Fold him, be good to him, cherish him,
  Men, ere he fall.

Women, another champion!
  This, men, is yours!
Wreathe and enlap and anoint them
  Behind separate doors.

         Gargnano

Winter Dawn

Green star Sirius
Dribbling over the lake;
The stars have gone so far on their road,
Yet we're awake!

Without a sound
The new young year comes in
And is half-way over the lake.
We must begin

Again. This love so full
Of hate has hurt us so,
We lie side by side
Moored – but no,

Let me get up
And wash quite clean
Of this hate. –
So green

The great star goes!
I am washed quite clean,
Quite clean of it all.
But e'en

So cold, so cold and clean
Now the hate is gone!
It is all no good,
I am chilled to the bone

Now the hate is gone;
There is nothing left;
I am pure like bone,
Of all feeling bereft.

A Bad Beginning

The yellow sun steps over the mountain-top
And falters a few short steps across the lake –
Are you awake?

See, glittering on the milk-blue, morning lake
They are laying the golden racing-track of the sun;
The day has begun.

The sun is in my eyes, I must get up.
I want to go, there's a gold road blazes before
My breast – which is so sore.

What? – your throat is bruised, bruised with my kisses?
Ah, but if I am cruel what then are you?
I am bruised right through.

What if I love you! – This misery
Of your dissatisfaction and misprision
Stupefies me.

Ah yes, your open arms! Ah yes, ah yes,
You would take me to your breast! – But no,
You should come to mine,
It were better so.

Here I am – get up and come to me!
Not as a visitor either, nor a sweet
And winsome child of innocence; nor
As an insolent mistress telling my pulse's beat.

Come to me like a woman coming home
To the man who is her husband, all the rest
Subordinate to this, that he and she
Are joined together for ever, as is best.

Behind me on the lake I hear the steamer drumming
From Austria. There lies the world, and here
Am I. Which way are you coming?

Why Does She Weep?

Hush then
why do you cry?
It's you and me
the same as before.

If you hear a rustle
it's only a rabbit
gone back to his hole
in a bustle.

If something stirs in the branches
overhead, it will be a squirrel moving
uneasily, disturbed by the stress
of our loving.

Why should you cry then?
Are you afraid of God
in the dark?

I'm not afraid of God.
Let him come forth.
If he is hiding in the cover
let him come forth.

Now in the cool of the day
it is we who walk in the trees
and call to God 'Where art thou?'
And it is he who hides.

Why do you cry?
My heart is bitter.
Let God come forth to justify
himself now.

Why do you cry?
Is it Wehmut, ist dir weh?[26]
Weep then, yea
for the abomination of our old righteousness.

We have done wrong
many times;
but this time we begin to do right.

Weep then, weep
for the abomination of our past righteousness.
God will keep
hidden, he won't come forth.

Giorno dei Morti

Along the avenue of cypresses,
All in their scarlet cloaks and surplices
Of linen, go the chanting choristers,
The priests in gold and black, the villagers . . .

And all along the path to the cemetery
The round dark heads of men crowd silently,
And black-scarved faces of womenfolk, wistfully
Watch at the banner of death, and the mystery.

And at the foot of a grave a father stands
With sunken head, and forgotten, folded hands;
And at the foot of a grave a mother kneels
With pale shut face, nor either hears nor feels

The coming of the chanting choristers
Between the avenue of cypresses,
The silence of the many villagers,
The candle-flames beside the surplices.

All Souls

They are chanting now the service of All the Dead
And the village folk outside in the burying-ground
Listen – except those who strive with their dead,
Reaching out in anguish, yet unable quite to touch them:
Those villagers isolated at the grave

Where the candles burn in the daylight, and the painted
   wreaths
Are propped on end, there, where the mystery starts.

The naked candles burn on every grave.
On your grave, in England, the weeds grow.

But I am your naked candle burning,
And that is not your grave, in England,
The world is your grave.
And my naked body standing on your grave
Upright towards heaven is burning off to you
Its flame of life, now and always, till the end.

It is my offering to you; every day is All Souls' Day.

I forget you, have forgotten you.
I am busy only at my burning,
I am busy only at my life.
But my feet are on your grave, planted.
And when I lift my face, it is a flame that goes up
To the other world, where you are now.
But I am not concerned with you.
     I have forgotten you.

I am a naked candle burning on your grave.

Lady Wife

Ah yes, I know you well, a sojourner
   At the hearth;
I know right well the marriage ring you wear,
   And what it's worth.

The angels came to Abraham, and they stayed
   In his house awhile;
So you to mine, I imagine; yes, happily
   Condescend to be vile.

I see you all the time, you bird-blithe, lovely
    Angel in disguise.
I see right well how I ought to be grateful,
    Smitten with reverent surprise.

Listen, I have no use
    For so rare a visit;
Mine is a common devil's
    Requisite.

Rise up and go, I have no use for you
    And your blithe, glad mien.
No angels here, for me no goddesses,
    Nor any Queen.

Put ashes on your head, put sackcloth on
    And learn to serve.
You have fed me with your sweetness, now I am sick,
    As I deserve.

Queens, ladies, angels, women rare,
    I have had enough.
Put sackcloth on, be crowned with powdery ash,
    Be common stuff.

And serve now, woman, serve, as a woman should,
    Implicitly.
Since I must serve and struggle with the imminent
    Mystery.

Serve then, I tell you, add your strength to mine,
    Take on this doom.
What are you by yourself, do you think, and what
    The mere fruit of your womb?

What is the fruit of your womb then, you mother, you queen,
    When it falls to the ground?
Is it more than the apples of Sodom you scorn so, the men
    Who abound?

Bring forth the sons of your womb then, and put them
    Into the fire
Of Sodom that covers the earth; bring them forth
    From the womb of your precious desire.

You woman most holy, you mother, you being beyond
    Question or diminution,
Add yourself up, and your seed, to the nought
    Of your last solution.

Both Sides of the Medal

And because you love me,
think you you do not hate me?
Ha, since you love me
to ecstasy
it follows you hate me to ecstasy.

Because when you hear me
go down the road outside the house
you must come to the window to watch me go,
do you think it is pure worship?

Because, when I sit in the room,
here, in my own house,
and you want to enlarge yourself with this friend of mine,
such a friend as he is,
yet you cannot get beyond your awareness of me,
you are held back by my being in the same world with you,
do you think it is bliss alone?
sheer harmony?

No doubt if I were dead, you must
reach into death after me,
but would not your hate reach even more madly than your love?
your impassioned, unfinished hate?

Since you have a passion for me,
as I for you,
does not that passion stand in your way like a Balaam's ass?
and am I not Balaam's ass
golden-mouthed occasionally?
But mostly, do you not detest my bray?

Since you are confined in the orbit of me
do you not loathe the confinement?
Is not even the beauty and peace of an orbit
an intolerable prison to you,
as it is to everybody?

But we will learn to submit
each of us to the balanced, eternal orbit
wherein we circle on our fate
in strange conjunction.

What is chaos, my love?
It is not freedom.
A disarray of falling stars coming to nought.

Loggerheads

Please yourself how you have it.
Take my words, and fling
Them down on the counter roundly;
See if they ring.

Sift my looks and expressions,
And see what proportion there is
Of sand in my doubtful sugar
Of verities.

Have a real stock-taking
Of my manly breast;
Find out if I'm sound or bankrupt,
Or a poor thing at best.

For I am quite indifferent
To your dubious state,
As to whether you've found a fortune
In me, or a flea-bitten fate.

Make a good investigation
Of all that is there,
And then, if it's worth it, be grateful –
If not, then despair.

If despair is our portion
Then let us despair.
Let us make for the weeping willow.
I don't care.

December Night

Take off your cloak and your hat
And your shoes, and draw up at my hearth
Where never woman sat.

I have made the fire up bright;
Let us leave the rest in the dark
And sit by firelight.

The wine is warm in the hearth;
The flickers come and go.
I will warm your limbs with kisses
Until they glow.

New Year's Eve

There are only two things now,
The great black night scooped out
And this fireglow.

This fireglow, the core,
And we the two ripe pips
That are held in store.

Listen, the darkness rings
As it circulates round our fire.
Take off your things.

Your shoulders, your bruised throat!
Your breasts, your nakedness!
This fiery coat!

As the darkness flickers and dips,
As the firelight falls and leaps
From your feet to your lips!

New Year's Night

Now you are mine, tonight at last I say it;
You're a dove I have bought for sacrifice,
And to-night I slay it.

Here in my arms my naked sacrifice!
Death, do you hear, in my arms I am bringing
My offering, bought at great price.

She's a silvery dove worth more than all I've got.
Now I offer her up to the ancient, inexorable God,
Who knows me not.

Look, she's a wonderful dove, without blemish or spot!
I sacrifice all in her, my last of the world,
Pride, strength, all the lot.

All, all on the altar! And death swooping down
Like a falcon. 'Tis God has taken the victim;
I have won my renown.

Valentine's Night

You shadow and flame,
You interchange,
You death in the game!

Now I gather you up,
Now I put you back
Like a poppy in its cup.

And so, you are a maid
Again, my darling, but new,
Unafraid.

My love, my blossom, a child
Almost! The flower in the bud
Again, undefiled.

And yet, a woman, knowing
All, good, evil, both
In one blossom blowing.

Birth Night

This fireglow is a red womb
In the night, where you're folded up
On your doom.

And the ugly, brutal years
Are dissolving out of you,
And the stagnant tears.

I the great vein that leads
From the night to the source of you
Which the sweet blood feeds.

New phase in the germ of you;
New sunny streams of blood
Washing you through.

You are born again of me.
I, Adam, from the veins of me
The Eve that is to be.

What has been long ago
Grows dimmer, we both forget,
We no longer know.

You are lovely, your face is soft
Like a flower in bud
On a mountain croft.

This is Noël for me.
To-night is a woman born
Of the man in me.

Rabbit Snared in the Night

Why do you spurt and sprottle
like that, bunny?
Why should I want to throttle
you, bunny?

Yes, bunch yourself between
my knees and lie still.
Lie on me with a hot, plumb, live weight,
heavy as a stone, passive,
yet hot, waiting.

What are you waiting for?
What are you waiting for?
What is the hot, plumb weight of your desire on me?
You have a hot, unthinkable desire of me, bunny.

What is that spark
glittering at me on the unutterable darkness
of your eye, bunny?
The finest splinter of a spark
that you throw off, straight on the tinder of my nerves!

It sets up a strange fire,
a soft, most unwarrantable burning,
a bale-fire mounting, mounting up in me.

'Tis not of me, bunny.
It was you engendered it,
with that fine, demoniacal spark
you jetted off your eye at me.

I did not want it,
this furnace, this draught-maddened fire
which mounts up my arms
making them swell with turgid, ungovernable strength.

'Twas not *I* that wished it,
that my fingers should turn into these flames
avid and terrible
that they are at this moment.

It must have been *your* inbreathing, gaping desire
that drew this red gush in me;
I must be reciprocating *your* vacuous, hideous passion.

It must be the want in you
that has drawn this terrible draught of white fire
up my veins as up a chimney.

It must be you who desire
this intermingling of the black and monstrous fingers of Moloch
in the blood-jets of your throat.

Come, you shall have your desire,
since already I am implicated with you
in your strange lust.

Paradise Re-entered

Through the strait gate of passion,
Between the bickering fire
Where flames of fierce love tremble
On the body of fierce desire:

To the intoxication,
The mind, fused down like a bead,
Flees in its agitation
The flames' stiff speed:

At last to calm incandescence,
Burned clean by remorseless hate,
Now, at the day's renascence
We approach the gate.

Now, from the darkened spaces
Of fear, and of frightened faces,
Death, in our awed embraces
Approached and passed by;

We near the flame-burnt porches
Where the brands of the angels, like torches,
Whirl, – in these perilous marches
Pausing to sigh;

We look back on the withering roses,
The stars, in their sun-dimmed closes,
Where 'twas given us to repose us
Sure on our sanctity;

Beautiful, candid lovers,
Burnt out of our earthly covers,
We might have nestled like plovers
In the fields of eternity.

There, sure in sinless being,
All-seen, and then all-seeing,
In us life unto death agreeing,
We might have lain.

But we storm the angel-guarded
Gates of the long-discarded
Garden, which God has hoarded
Against our pain.

The Lord of Hosts and the Devil
Are left on Eternity's level
Field, and as victors we travel
To Eden home.

Back beyond good and evil
Return we. Eve dishevel
Your hair for the bliss-drenched revel
On our primal loam.

Coming Awake

When I woke, the lake-lights were quivering on the wall,
    The sunshine swam in a shoal across and across,
And a hairy, big bee hung over the primulas
    In the window, his body black fur, and the sound of him
        cross.

There was something I ought to remember: and yet
    I did not remember. Why should I? The running lights
And the airy primulas, oblivious
    Of the impending bee – they were fair enough sights.

Spring Morning

Ah, through the open door
Is there an almond tree
Aflame with blossom!
    – Let us fight no more.

Among the pink and blue
Of the sky and the almond flowers
A sparrow flutters.
    – We have come through,

It is really spring! – See,
When he thinks himself alone
How he bullies the flowers.
    – Ah, you and me

How happy we'll be! – See him?
He clouts the tufts of flowers
In his impudence.
    – But, did you dream

It would be so bitter? Never mind,
It is finished, the spring is here.
And we're going to be summer-happy
    And summer-kind.

We have died, we have slain and been slain,
We are not our old selves any more.
I feel new and eager
    To start again.

It is gorgeous to live and forget.
And to feel quite new.
See the bird in the flowers? – he's making
    A rare to-do!

He thinks the whole blue sky
Is much less than the bit of blue egg
He's got in his nest – we'll be happy,
    You and I, I and you.

With nothing to fight any more –
In each other, at least.
See, how gorgeous the world is
    Outside the door!

San Gaudenzio

Wedlock

I

Come, my little one, closer up against me,
Creep right up, with your round head pushed in my breast.

How I love all of you! Do you feel me wrap you
Up with myself and my warmth, like a flame round the wick?

And how I am not at all, except a flame that mounts off you.
Where I touch you, I flame into being; – but is it me, or you?

That round head pushed in my chest, like a nut in its socket,
And I the swift bracts that sheathe it: those breasts, those
    thighs and knees,

Those shoulders so warm and smooth: I feel that I
Am a sunlight upon them, that shines them into being.

But how lovely to be you! Creep closer in, that I am more.
I spread over you! How lovely, your round head, your arms,

Your breasts, your knees and feet! I feel that we
Are a bonfire of oneness, me flame flung leaping round you,
You the core of the fire, crept into me.

II

And oh, my little one, you whom I enfold,
How quaveringly I depend on you, to keep me alive
Like a flame on a wick!

I, the man who enfolds you and holds you close,
How my soul cleaves to your bosom as I clasp you,
The very quick of my being!

Suppose you didn't want me! I should sink down
Like a light that has no sustenance
And sinks low.

Cherish me, my tiny one, cherish me who enfold you.
Nourish me, and endue me, I am only of you,
I am your issue.

How full and big like a robust, happy flame
When I enfold you, and you creep into me,
And my life is fierce at its quick
Where it comes off you!

III

My little one, my big one,
My bird, my brown sparrow in my breast.
My squirrel clutching in to me;
My pigeon, my little one, so warm,
So close, breathing so still.

My little one, my big one,
I, who am so fierce and strong, enfolding you,
If you start away from my breast, and leave me,
How suddenly I shall go down into nothing
Like a flame that falls of a sudden.

And you will be before me, tall and towering,
And I shall be wavering uncertain
Like a sunken flame that grasps for support.

IV

But now I am full and strong and certain
With you there firm at the core of me
Keeping me.

How sure I feel, how warm and strong and happy
For the future! How sure the future is within me
I am like a seed with a perfect flower enclosed.

I wonder what it will be,
What will come forth of us.
What flower, my love?

No matter, I am so happy,
I feel like a firm, rich, healthy root,
Rejoicing in what is to come.

How I depend on you utterly,
My little one, my big one!
How everything that will be, will not be of me,
Nor of either of us,
But of both of us.

V

And think, there will something come forth from us,
We two, folded so small together,
There will something come forth from us.
Children, acts, utterance,
Perhaps only happiness.

Perhaps only happiness will come forth from us.
Old sorrow, and new happiness.
Only that one newness.

But that is all I want.
And I am sure of that.
We are sure of that.

VI

And yet all the while you are you, you are not me.
And I am I, I am never you.
How awfully distinct and far off from each other's being we are!

Yet I am glad.
I am so glad there is always you beyond my scope,
Something that stands over,
Something I shall never be,
That I shall always wonder over, and wait for,
Look for like the breath of life as long as I live,
Still waiting for you, however old you are, and I am,
I shall always wonder over you, and look for you.

And you will always be with me.
I shall never cease to be filled with newness,
Having you near me.

History

The listless beauty of the hour
When snow fell on the apple trees
And the wood-ash gathered in the fire
And we faced our first miseries.

Then the sweeping sunshine of noon
When the mountains like chariot cars
Were ranked to blue battle – and you and I
Counted our scars.

And then in a strange, grey hour
We lay mouth to mouth, with your face
Under mine like a star on the lake,
And I covered the earth, and all space.

The silent, drifting hours
Of morn after morn
And night drifting up to the night
Yet no pathway worn.

Your life, and mine, my love
Passing on and on, the hate
Fusing closer and closer with love
Till at length they mate.

The Cearne

Song of a Man Who is Loved

Between her breasts is my home, between her breasts.
Three sides set on me space and fear, but the fourth side rests
Sure and a tower of strength, 'twixt the walls of her breasts.

Having known the world so long, I have never confessed
How it impresses me, how hard and compressed
Rocks seem, and earth, and air uneasy, and waters still ebbing
    west.

All things on the move, going their own little ways, and all
Jostling, people touching and talking and making small
Contacts and bouncing off again, bounce! bounce like a ball!

My flesh is weary with bounce and gone again! –
My ears are weary with words that bounce on them, and then
Bounce off again, meaning nothing. Assertions! Assertions! stones,
    women and men!

Between her breasts is my home, between her breasts.
Three sides set on me chaos and bounce, but the fourth side rests
Sure on a haven of peace, between the mounds of her breasts.

I am that I am, and no more than that: but so much
I am, nor will I be bounced out of it. So at last I touch
All that I am-not in softness, sweet softness, for she is such.

And the chaos that bounces and rattles like shrapnel, at least
Has for me a door into peace, warm dawn in the east
Where her bosom softens towards me, and the turmoil has ceased.

So I hope I shall spend eternity
With my face down buried between her breasts;
And my still heart full of security,
And my still hands full of her breasts.

Song of a Man Who has Come Through

Not I, not I, but the wind that blows through me!
A fine wind is blowing the new direction of Time.
If only I let it bear me, carry me, if only it carry me!
If only I am sensitive, subtle, oh, delicate, a winged gift!
If only, most lovely of all, I yield myself and am borrowed
By the fine, fine wind that takes its course through the chaos
      of the world
Like a fine, an exquisite chisel, a wedge-blade inserted;
If only I am keen and hard like the sheer tip of a wedge
Driven by invisible blows,
The rock will split, we shall come at the wonder, we shall find the
      Hesperides.

Oh, for the wonder that bubbles into my soul,
I would be a good fountain, a good well-head,
Would blur no whisper, spoil no expression.

What is the knocking?
What is the knocking at the door in the night?
It is somebody wants to do us harm.

No, no, it is the three strange angels.
Admit them, admit them.

One Woman to all Women

I don't care whether I am beautiful to you,
         You other women.
Nothing of me that you see is my own;
A man balances, bone unto bone
Balances, everything thrown
         In the scale, you other women.

You may look and say to yourselves, I do
         Not show like the rest.
My face may not please you, nor my stature; yet if you knew
How happy I am, how my heart in the wind rings true
Like a bell that is chiming, each stroke as a stroke falls due,
         You other women:

You would draw your mirror towards you, you would wish
         To be different.
There's the beauty you cannot see, myself and him
Balanced in glorious equilibrium,
The swinging beauty of equilibrium,
         You other women.

There's this other beauty, the way of the stars,
         You straggling women.
If you knew how I swerve in peace, in the equipoise
With the man, if you knew how my flesh enjoys
The swinging bliss no shattering ever destroys,
         You other women:

You would envy me, you would think me wonderful
         Beyond compare;
You would weep to be lapsing on such harmony
As carries me, you would wonder aloud that he
Who is so strange should correspond with me
         Everywhere.

You see he is different, he is dangerous,
         Without pity or love.
And yet how his separate being liberates me
And gives me peace! You cannot see
How the stars are moving in surety
         Exquisite, high above.

We move without knowing, we sleep, and we travel on,
      You other women.
And this is beauty to me, to be lifted and gone
In a motion human inhuman, two and one
Encompassed, and many reduced to none,
      You other women.

                              Kensington

People

The great gold apples of night
Hang from the street's long bough
      Dripping their light
On the faces that drift below,
On the faces that drift and blow
Down the night-time, out of sight
      In the wind's sad sough.

The ripeness of these apples of night
Distilling over me
      Makes sickening the white
Ghost-flux of faces that hie
Them endlessly, endlessly by
Without meaning or reason why
      They ever should be.

Street Lamps

Gold, with an innermost speck
Of silver, singing afloat
      Beneath the night,
Like balls of thistledown
Wandering up and down
Over the whispering town
      Seeking where to alight!

Slowly, above the street,
Above the ebb of feet
      Drifting in flight;

Still, in the purple distance
The gold of their strange persistence
        As they cross and part and meet
            And pass out of sight!

The seed-ball of the sun
Is broken at last, and done
            Is the orb of day.
Now to their separate ends
Seed after day-seed wends
            A separate way.

No sun will ever rise
Again on the wonted skies
            In the midst of the spheres.
The globe of the day, over-ripe,
Is shattered at last beneath the stripe
Of the wind, and its oneness veers
            Out myriad-wise.

Seed after seed after seed
Drifts over the town, in its need
            To sink and have done;
To settle at last in the dark,
To bury its weary spark
            Where the end is begun.

Darkness, and depth of sleep,
Nothing to know or to weep
            Where the seed sinks in
To the earth of the under-night
Where all is silent, quite
Still, and the darknesses steep
            Out all the sin.

'She Said as Well to Me'

She said as well to me: 'Why are you ashamed?
That little bit of your chest that shows between
the gap of your shirt, why cover it up?
Why shouldn't your legs and your good strong thighs

be rough and hairy? – I'm glad they are like that.
You are shy, you silly, you silly shy thing.
Men are the shyest creatures, they never will come
out of their covers. Like any snake
slipping into its bed of dead leaves, you hurry into your clothes.
And I love you so! Straight and clean and all of a piece is the body
    of a man,
such an instrument, a spade, like a spear, or an oar,
such a joy to me – '
So she laid her hands and pressed them down my sides,
so that I began to wonder over myself, and what I was.

She said to me: 'What an instrument, your body!
single and perfectly distinct from everything else!
What a tool in the hands of the Lord!
Only God could have brought it to its shape.
It feels as if his handgrasp, wearing you
had polished you and hollowed you,
hollowed this groove in your sides, grasped you under the breasts
and brought you to the very quick of your form,
subtler than an old, soft-worn fiddle-bow.

'When I was a child, I loved my father's riding-whip
that he used so often.
I loved to handle it, it seemed like a near part of him.
So I did his pens, and the jasper seal on his desk.
Something seemed to surge through me when I touched them.

'So it is with you, but here
The joy I feel!
God knows what I feel, but it is joy!
Look, you are clean and fine and singled out!
I admire you so, you are beautiful: this clean sweep of your sides,
    this firmness, this hard mould!
I would die rather than have it injured with one scar.
I wish I could grip you like the fist of the Lord,
and have you – '

So she said, and I wondered,
feeling trammelled and hurt.
It did not make me free.

Now I say to her: 'No tool, no instrument, no God!
Don't touch me and appreciate me.
It is an infamy.
You would think twice before you touched a weasel on a fence
as it lifts its straight white throat.
Your hand would not be so flig and easy.
Nor the adder we saw asleep with her head on her shoulder,
curled up in the sunshine like a princess;
when she lifted her head in delicate, startled wonder
you did not stretch forward to caress her
though she looked rarely beautiful
and a miracle as she glided delicately away, with such dignity.
And the young bull in the field, with his wrinkled, sad face,
you are afraid if he rises to his feet,
though he is all wistful and pathetic, like a monolith, arrested,
        static.

'Is there nothing in me to make you hesitate?
I tell you there is all these.
And why should you overlook them in me? – '

New Heaven and Earth

I

And so I cross into another world
shyly and in homage linger for an invitation
from this unknown that I would trespass on.

I am very glad, and all alone in the world,
all alone, and very glad, in a new world
where I am disembarked at last.

I could cry with joy, because I am in the new world, just ventured
        in.
I could cry with joy, and quite freely, there is nobody to know.

And whosoever the unknown people of this unknown world may
        be
they will never understand my weeping for joy to be adventuring
        among them

because it will still be a gesture of the old world I am making
which they will not understand, because it is quite, quite foreign to
    them.

II

I was so weary of the world,
I was so sick of it,
everything was tainted with myself,
skies, trees, flowers, birds, water,
people, houses, streets, vehicles, machines,
nations, armies, war, peace-talking,
work, recreation, governing, anarchy,
it was all tainted with myself, I knew it all to start with
because it was all myself.

When I gathered flowers, I knew it was myself plucking my own
    flowering.
When I went in a train, I knew it was myself travelling by my own
    invention.
When I heard the cannon of the war, I listened with my own ears
    to my own destruction.
When I saw the torn dead, I knew it was my own torn dead body.
It was all me, I had done it all in my own flesh.

III

I shall never forget the maniacal horror of it all in the end
when everything was me, I knew it all already, I anticipated
    it all in my soul
because I was the author and the result
I was the God and the creation at once;
creator, I looked at my creation;
created, I looked at myself, the creator:
it was a maniacal horror in the end.

I was a lover, I kissed the woman I loved,
and God of horror, I was kissing also myself.
I was a father and a begetter of children,
and oh, oh horror, I was begetting and conceiving in my own body.

IV

At last came death, sufficiency of death,
and that at last relieved me, I died.
I buried my beloved; it was good, I buried myself and was gone.
War came, and every hand raised to murder;
very good, very good, every hand raised to murder!
Very good, very good, I am a murderer!
It is good, I can murder and murder, and see them fall,
the mutilated, horror-struck youths, a multitude
one on another, and then in clusters together
smashed, all oozing with blood, and burned in heaps
going up in a foetid smoke to get rid of them,
the murdered bodies of youths and men in heaps
and heaps and heaps and horrible reeking heaps
till it is almost enough, till I am reduced perhaps;
thousands and thousands of gaping, hideous foul dead
that are youths and men and me
being burned with oil, and consumed in corrupt thick smoke, that
    rolls
and taints and blackens the sky, till at last it is dark, dark as night,
    or death, or hell
and I am dead, and trodden to nought in the smoke-sodden tomb;
dead and trodden to nought in the sour black earth
of the tomb; dead and trodden to nought, trodden to nought.

V

God, but it is good to have died and been trodden out,
trodden to nought in sour, dead earth,
quite to nought,
absolutely to nothing
nothing
nothing
nothing.

For when it is quite, quite nothing, then it is everything.
When I am trodden quite out, quite, quite out,
every vestige gone, then I am here

risen and setting my foot on another world
risen, accomplishing a resurrection
risen, not born again, but risen, body the same as before,
new beyond knowledge of newness, alive beyond life,
proud beyond inkling or furthest conception of pride,
living where life was never yet dreamed of, nor hinted at,
here, in the other world, still terrestrial
myself, the same as before, yet unaccountably new.

VI

I, in the sour black tomb, trodden to absolute death
I put out my hand in the night, one night, and my hand
touched that which was verily not me,
verily it was not me.
Where I had been was a sudden blaze,
a sudden flaring blaze!
So I put my hand out further, a little further
and I felt that which was not I,
it verily was not I,
it was the unknown.

Ha, I was a blaze leaping up!
I was a tiger bursting into sunlight.
I was greedy, I was mad for the unknown.
I, new-risen, resurrected, starved from the tomb,
starved from a life of devouring always myself,
now here was I, new-awakened, with my hand stretching out
and touching the unknown, the real unknown, the unknown
     unknown.

My God, but I can only say
I touch, I feel the unknown!
I am the first comer!
Cortes, Pisarro, Columbus, Cabot, they are nothing, nothing!
I am the first comer!
I am the discoverer!
I have found the other world!

The unknown, the unknown!
I am thrown upon the shore.
I am covering myself with the sand.
I am filling my mouth with the earth.
I am burrowing my body into the soil.
The unknown, the new world!

VII

It was the flank of my wife
I touched with my hand, I clutched with my hand,
rising, new-awakened from the tomb!
It was the flank of my wife
whom I married years ago
at whose side I have lain for over a thousand nights
and all that previous while, she was I, she was I;
I touched her, it was I who touched and I who was touched.

Yet rising from the tomb, from the black oblivion
stretching out my hand, my hand flung like a drowned man's hand
    on a rock,
I touched her flank and knew I was carried by the current in death
over to the new world, and was climbing out on the shore,
risen, not to the old world, the old, changeless I, the old life,
wakened not to the old knowledge
but to a new earth, a new I, a new knowledge, a new world of time.

Ah no, I cannot tell you what it is, the new world.
I cannot tell you the mad, astounded rapture of its discovery.
I shall be mad with delight before I have done,
and whosoever comes after will find me in the new world
a madman in rapture.

VIII

Green streams that flow from the innermost continent of the new
    world,
what are they?
Green and illumined and travelling for ever
dissolved with the mystery of the innermost heart of the continent,

mystery beyond knowledge or endurance, so sumptuous
out of the well-heads of the new world. –

The other, she too has strange green eyes!
White sands and fruits unknown and perfumes that never
can blow across the dark seas to our usual world!
And land that beats with a pulse!
And valleys that draw close in love!
And strange ways where I fall into oblivion of uttermost living! –
Also she who is the other has strange-mounded breasts and strange
     sheer slopes, and white levels.

Sightless and strong oblivion in utter life takes possession of me!
The unknown, strong current of life supreme
drowns me and sweeps me away and holds me down
to the sources of mystery, in the depths,
extinguishes there my risen resurrected life
and kindles it further at the core of utter mystery.

Greatham

Elysium

I have found a place of loneliness
Lonelier than Lyonesse,
Lovelier than Paradise;

Full of sweet stillness
That no noise can transgress,
Never a lamp distress.

The full moon sank in state.
I saw her stand and wait
For her watchers to shut the gate.

Then I found myself in a wonderland
All of shadow and of bland
Silence hard to understand.

I waited therefore; then I knew
The presence of the flowers that grew
Noiseless, their wonder noiseless blew.

And flashing kingfishers that flew
In sightless beauty, and the few
Shadows the passing wild-beast threw.

And Eve approaching over the ground
Unheard and subtle, never a sound
To let me know that I was found.

Invisible the hands of Eve
Upon me travelling to reeve
Me from the matrix, to relieve

Me from the rest! Ah, terribly
Between the body of life and me
Her hands slid in and set me free.

Ah, with a fearful, strange detection
She found the source of my subjection
To the All, and severed the connection.

Delivered helpless and amazed
From the womb of the All, I am waiting, dazed
For memory to be erased.

Then I shall know the Elysium
That lies outside the monstrous womb
Of time from out of which I come.

Manifesto

I

A woman has given me strength and affluence.
Admitted!

All the rocking wheat of Canada, ripening now,
has not so much of strength as the body of one woman
sweet in ear, nor so much to give
though it feed nations.

Hunger is the very Satan.
The fear of hunger is Moloch, Belial, the horrible God.
It is a fearful thing to be dominated by the fear of hunger.

Not bread alone, not the belly nor the thirsty throat.
I have never yet been smitten through the belly, with the lack
    of bread,
no, nor even milk and honey.

The fear of the want of these things seems to be quite left out
    of me.
For so much, I thank the good generations of mankind.

II

And the sweet, constant, balanced heat
of the suave sensitive body, the hunger for this
has never seized me and terrified me.
Here again, man has been good in his legacy to us, in these
    two primary instances.

III

Then the dumb, aching, bitter, helpless need,
the pining to be initiated,
to have access to the knowledge that the great dead
have opened up for us, to know, to satisfy
the great and dominant hunger of the mind;
man's sweetest harvest of the centuries, sweet, printed books,
bright, glancing, exquisite corn of many a stubborn
glebe in the upturned darkness;
I thank mankind with passionate heart
that I just escaped the hunger for these,
that they were given when I needed them,
because I am the son of man.

I have eaten, and drunk, and warmed and clothed my body,
I have been taught the language of understanding,
I have chosen among the bright and marvellous books,
like any prince, such stores of the world's supply
were open to me, in the wisdom and goodness of man.
So far, so good.
Wise, good provision that makes the heart swell with love!

IV

But then came another hunger
very deep, and ravening;
the very body's body crying out
with a hunger more frightening, more profound
than stomach or throat or even the mind;
redder than death, more clamorous.

The hunger for the woman. Alas,
it is so deep a Moloch, ruthless and strong,
'tis like the unutterable name of the dread Lord,
not to be spoken aloud.
Yet there it is, the hunger which comes upon us,
which we must learn to satisfy with pure, real satisfaction;
or perish, there is no alternative.

I thought it was woman, indiscriminate woman,
mere female adjunct of what I was.
Ah, that was torment hard enough
and a thing to be afraid of,
a threatening, torturing, phallic Moloch.

A woman fed that hunger in me at last.
What many women cannot give, one woman can;
so I have known it.

She stood before me like riches that were mine.
Even then, in the dark, I was tortured, ravening, unfree,
Ashamed, and shameful, and vicious.
A man is so terrified of strong hunger;
and this terror is the root of all cruelty.
She loved me, and stood before me, looking to me.
How could I look, when I was mad? I looked sideways, furtively,
being mad with voracious desire.

V

This comes right at last.
When a man is rich, he loses at last the hunger fear.
I lost at last the fierceness that fears it will starve.
I could put my face at last between her breasts
and know that they were given for ever

that I should never starve,
never perish;
I had eaten of the bread that satisfies
and my body's body was appeased,
there was peace and richness,
fulfilment.

Let them praise desire who will,
but only fulfilment will do,
real fulfilment, nothing short.
It is our ratification,
our heaven, as a matter of fact.
Immortality, the heaven, is only a projection of this strange
    but actual fulfilment,
here in the flesh.

So, another hunger was supplied,
and for this I have to thank one woman,
not mankind, for mankind would have prevented me;
but one woman,
and these are my red-letter thanksgivings.

VI

To be, or not to be, is still the question.
This ache for being is the ultimate hunger.
And for myself, I can say 'almost, almost, oh, very nearly.'
Yet something remains.
Something shall not always remain.
For the main already is fulfilment.

What remains in me, is to be known even as I know.
I know her now: or perhaps, I know my own limitation against her.

Plunging as I have done, over, over the brink
I have dropped at last headlong into nought, plunging upon sheer
    hard extinction;
I have come, as it were, not to know,
died, as it were; ceased from knowing; surpassed myself.
What can I say more, except that I know what it is to surpass
    myself?

It is a kind of death which is not death.
It is going a little beyond the bounds.
How can one speak, where there is a dumbness on one's mouth?
I suppose, ultimately she is all beyond me,
she is all not-me, ultimately.

It is that that one comes to.
A curious agony, and a relief, when I touch that which is not
    me in any sense,
it wounds me to death with my own not-being; definite, inviolable
    limitation,
and something beyond, quite beyond, if you understand what that
    means.
It is the major part of being, this having surpassed oneself,
this having touched the edge of the beyond, and perished, yet not
    perished.

VII

I want her though, to take the same from me.
She touches me as if I were herself, her own.
She has not realised yet, that fearful thing, that I am the other,
she thinks we are all of one piece.
It is painfully untrue.

I want her to touch me at last, ah, on the root and quick of my
    darkness
and perish on me, as I have perished on her.

Then, we shall be two and distinct, we shall have each our separate
    being.
And that will be pure existence, real liberty.
Till then, we are confused, a mixture, unresolved, unextricated one
    from the other.
It is in pure, unutterable resolvedness, distinction of being, that
    one is free,
not in mixing, merging, not in similarity.
When she has put her hand on my secret, darkest sources, the
    darkest outgoings,
when it has struck home to her, like a death, 'this is *him*!'
she has no part in it, no part whatever,

it is the terrible *other*,
when she knows the fearful *other flesh*, ah, darkness unfathomable
    and fearful, contiguous and concrete,
when she is slain against me, and lies in a heap like one
    outside the house,
when she passes away as I have passed away,
being pressed up against the *other*,
then I shall be glad, I shall not be confused with her,
I shall be cleared, distinct, single as if burnished in silver,
having no adherence, no adhesion anywhere,
one clear, burnished, isolated being, unique,
and she also, pure, isolated, complete,
two of us, unutterably distinguished, and in unutterable
    conjunction.

Then we shall be free, freer than angels, ah, perfect.

VIII

After that, there will only remain that all men detach
    themselves and become unique,
that we are all detached, moving in freedom more than the angels,
conditioned only by our own pure single being,
having no laws but the laws of our own being.

Every human being will then be like a flower, untrammelled.
Every movement will be direct.
Only to be will be such delight, we cover our faces when we think
    of it
lest our faces betray us to some untimely fiend.

Every man himself, and therefore, a surpassing singleness of
    mankind.
The blazing tiger will spring upon the deer, undimmed,
the hen will nestle over her chickens,
we shall love, we shall hate,
but it will be like music, sheer utterance,
issuing straight out of the unknown,
the lightning and the rainbow appearing in us unbidden,
    unchecked,
like ambassadors.

We shall not look before and after.
We shall *be, now*.
We shall know in full.
We, the mystic NOW.

Zennor

Autumn Rain

The plane leaves
fall black and wet
on the lawn;

the cloud sheaves
in heaven's fields set
droop and are drawn

in falling seeds of rain;
the seed of heaven
on my face

falling – I hear again
like echoes even
that softly pace

heaven's muffled floor,
the winds that tread
out all the grain

of tears, the store
harvested
in the sheaves of pain

caught up aloft:
the sheaves of dead
men that are slain

now winnowed soft
on the floor of heaven;
manna invisible

of all the pain
here to us given;
finely divisible
falling as rain.

Frost Flowers

It is not long since, here among all these folk
in London, I should have held myself
of no account whatever,
but should have stood aside and made them way
thinking that they, perhaps,
had more right than I – for who was I?

Now I see them just the same, and watch them.
But of what account do I hold them?

Especially the young women. I look at them
as they dart and flash
before the shops, like wagtails on the edge of a pool.

If I pass them close, or any man,
like sharp, slim wagtails they flash a little aside
pretending to avoid us; yet all the time
calculating.

They think that we adore them – alas, would it were true!
Probably they think all men adore them,
howsoever they pass by.

What is it, that, from their faces fresh as spring,
such fair, fresh, alert, first-flower faces,
like lavender crocuses, snowdrops, like Roman hyacinths,
scyllas and yellow-haired hellebore, jonquils, dim anemones,
even the sulphur auriculas,
flowers that come first from the darkness, and feel cold to the
    touch,
flowers scentless or pungent, ammoniacal almost;
what is it, that, from the faces of the fair young women
comes like a pungent scent, a vibration beneath
that startles me, alarms me, stirs up a repulsion?

They are the issue of acrid winter, these first-flower young women;
their scent is lacerating and repellent,
it smells of burning snow, of hot-ache,

of earth, winter-pressed, strangled in corruption;
it is the scent of the fiery-cold dregs of corruption,
when destruction soaks through the mortified, decomposing earth,
and the last fires of dissolution burn in the bosom of the ground.

They are the flowers of ice-vivid mortification,
thaw-cold, ice-corrupt blossoms,
with a loveliness I loathe;
for what kind of ice-rotten, hot-aching heart must they need
    to root in!

Craving for Spring

I wish it were spring in the world.

Let it be spring!
Come, bubbling, surging tide of sap!
Come, rush of creation!
Come, life! surge through this mass of mortification!
Come, sweep away these exquisite, ghastly first-flowers,
which are rather last-flowers!
Come, thaw down their cool portentousness, dissolve them:
snowdrops, straight, death-veined exhalations of white and purple
    crocuses,
flowers of the penumbra, issue of corruption, nourished in
    mortification,
jets of exquisite finality;
Come, spring, make havoc of them!

I trample on the snowdrops, it gives me pleasure to tread down the
    jonquils,
to destroy the chill Lent lilies;
for I am sick of them, their faint-bloodedness,
slow-blooded, icy-fleshed, portentous.

I want the fine, kindling wine-sap of spring,
gold, and of inconceivably fine, quintessential brightness,
rare almost as beams, yet overwhelmingly potent,
strong like the greatest force of world-balancing.

This is the same that picks up the harvest of wheat
and rocks it, tons of grain, on the ripening wind;
the same that dangles the globe-shaped pleiads of fruit
temptingly in mid-air, between a playful thumb and finger;
oh, and suddenly, from out of nowhere, whirls the pear-bloom,
upon us, and apple- and almond- and apricot- and quince-blossom,
storms and cumulus clouds of all imaginable blossom
about our bewildered faces,
though we do not worship.

I wish it were spring
cunningly blowing on the fallen sparks, odds and ends of the old,
    scattered fire,
and kindling shapely little conflagrations
curious long-legged foals, and wide-eared calves, and naked
    sparrow-bubs.

I wish that spring
would start the thundering traffic of feet
new feet on the earth, beating with impatience.

I wish it were spring, thundering
delicate, tender spring.
I wish these brittle, frost-lovely flowers of passionate, mysterious
    corruption
were not yet to come still more from the still-flickering discontent.

Oh, in the spring, the bluebell bows him down for very exuberance,
exulting with secret warm excess,
bowed down with his inner magnificence!

Oh, yes, the gush of spring is strong enough
to toss the globe of earth like a ball on a water-jet
dancing sportfully;
as you see a tiny celluloid ball tossing on a squirt of water
for men to shoot at, penny-a-time, in a booth at a fair.

The gush of spring is strong enough
to play with the globe of earth like a ball on a fountain;
At the same time it opens the tiny hands of the hazel

with such infinite patience.
The power of the rising, golden, all-creative sap could take the
    earth
and heave it off among the stars, into the invisible;
the same sets the throstle at sunset on a bough
singing against the blackbird;
comes out in the hesitating tremor of the primrose,
and betrays its candour in the round white strawberry flower,
is dignified in the foxglove, like a Red-Indian brave.

Ah come, come quickly, spring!
Come and lift us towards our culmination, we myriads;
we who have never flowered, like patient cactuses.
Come and lift us to our end, to blossom, bring us to our summer,
we who are winter-weary in the winter of the world.
Come making the chaffinch nests hollow and cosy,
come and soften the willow buds till they are puffed and furred,
then blow them over with gold.
Come and cajole the gawky colt's-foot flowers.

Come quickly, and vindicate us
against too much death.
Come quickly, and stir the rotten globe of the world from within,
burst it with germination, with world anew.
Come now, to us, your adherents, who cannot flower from
    the ice.
All the world gleams with the lilies of Death the Unconquerable,
but come, give us our turn.
Enough of the virgins and lilies, of passionate, suffocating perfume
    of corruption,
no more narcissus perfume, lily harlots, the blades of sensation
piercing the flesh to blossom of death.
Have done, have done with this shuddering, delicious business
of thrilling ruin in the flesh, of pungent passion, of rare,
    death-edged ecstasy.
Give us our turn, give us a chance, let our hour strike,
O soon, soon!
Let the darkness turn violet with rich dawn.
Let the darkness be warmed, warmed through to a ruddy violet,
incipient purpling towards summer in the world of the heart
    of man.

Are the violets already here!
Show me! I tremble so much to hear it, that even now
on the threshold of spring, I fear I shall die.
Show me the violets that are out.

Oh, if it be true, and the living darkness of the blood of man
    is purpling with violets,
if the violets are coming out from under the rack of men, winter-
    rotten and fallen,
we shall have spring.
Pray not to die on this Pisgah blossoming with violets.
Pray to live through.

If you catch a whiff of violets from the darkness of the shadow of
    man
it will be spring in the world,
it will be spring in the world of the living;
wonderment organising itself, heralding itself with the violets,
stirring of new seasons.

Ah, do not let me die on the brink of such anticipation!
Worse, let me not deceive myself.

                                                                    Zennor

FRUITS

Pomegranate

You tell me I am wrong.
Who are you, who is anybody to tell me I am wrong?
I am not wrong.

In Syracuse, rock left bare by the viciousness of Greek women,[27]
No doubt you have forgotten the pomegranate trees in flower,
Oh so red, and such a lot of them.

Whereas at Venice,
Abhorrent, green, slippery city
Whose Doges were old, and had ancient eyes,
In the dense foliage of the inner garden
Pomegranates like bright green stone,
And barbed, barbed with a crown.
Oh, crown of spiked green metal
Actually growing!

Now in Tuscany,
Pomegranates to warm your hands at;
And crowns, kingly, generous, tilting crowns
Over the left eyebrow.

And, if you dare, the fissure!

Do you mean to tell me you will see no fissure?
Do you prefer to look on the plain side?

For all that, the setting suns are open.
The end cracks open with the beginning:
Rosy, tender, glittering within the fissure.

Do you mean to tell me there should be no fissure?
No glittering, compact drops of dawn?
Do you mean it is wrong, the gold-filmed skin, integument,
    shown ruptured?

For my part, I prefer my heart to be broken.
It is so lovely, dawn-kaleidoscopic within the crack.

San Gervasio in Tuscany

Peach

Would you like to throw a stone at me?
Here, take all that's left of my peach.

Blood-red, deep;
Heaven knows how it came to pass.
Somebody's pound of flesh rendered up.

Wrinkled with secrets
And hard with the intention to keep them.

Why, from silvery peach-bloom,
From that shallow-silvery wine-glass on a short stem
This rolling, dropping, heavy globule?

I am thinking, of course, of the peach before I ate it.

Why so velvety, why so voluptuous heavy?
Why hanging with such inordinate weight?
Why so indented?

Why the groove?
Why the lovely, bivalve roundnesses?
Why the ripple down the sphere?
Why the suggestion of incision?

Why was not my peach round and finished like a
    billiard ball?
It would have been if man had made it.
Though I've eaten it now.

But it wasn't round and finished like a billiard ball.
And because I say so, you would like to throw something
    at me.

Here, you can have my peach stone.

San Gervasio

Medlars and Sorb-Apples

I love you, rotten,
Delicious rottenness.

I love to suck you out from your skins
So brown and soft and coming suave,
So morbid, as the Italians say.[28]

What a rare, powerful, reminiscent flavour
Comes out of your falling through the stages of decay:
Stream within stream.

Something of the same flavour as Syracusan muscat wine
Or vulgar Marsala.

Though even the word Marsala will smack of preciosity
Soon in the pussyfoot West.

What is it?
What is it, in the grape turning raisin,
In the medlar, in the sorb-apple,
Wineskins of brown morbidity,
Autumnal excrementa;
What is it that reminds us of white gods?

Gods nude as blanched nut-kernels,
Strangely, half-sinisterly flesh-fragrant
As if with sweat,
And drenched with mystery.

Sorb-apples, medlars with dead crowns.
I say, wonderful are the hellish experiences,
Orphic, delicate
Dionysos of the Underworld.

A kiss, and a spasm of farewell, a moment's orgasm of rupture,
Then along the damp road alone, till the next turning.
And there, a new partner, a new parting, a new unfusing into
     twain,
A new gasp of further isolation,
A new intoxication of loneliness, among decaying,
     frost-cold leaves.

Going down the strange lanes of hell, more and more intensely
    alone,
The fibres of the heart parting one after the other
And yet the soul continuing, naked-footed, ever more
    vividly embodied
Like a flame blown whiter and whiter
In a deeper and deeper darkness
Ever more exquisite, distilled in separation.

So, in the strange retorts of medlars and sorb-apples
The distilled essence of hell.
The exquisite odour of leave-taking.
     Jamque vale!
Orpheus, and the winding, leaf-clogged, silent lanes of hell.

Each soul departing with its own isolation,
Strangest of all strange companions,
And best.

Medlars, sorb-apples,
More than sweet
Flux of autumn
Sucked out of your empty bladders

And sipped down, perhaps, with a sip of Marsala
So that the rambling, sky-dropped grape can add its savour to
    yours,
Orphic farewell, and farewell, and farewell
And the *ego sum* of Dionysos
The *sono io*[29] of perfect drunkenness
Intoxication of final loneliness.

                      San Gervasio

Figs

The proper way to eat a fig, in society,
Is to split it in four, holding it by the stump,
And open it, so that it is a glittering, rosy, moist, honied, heavy-
    petalled four-petalled flower.

Then you throw away the skin
Which is just like a four-sepalled calyx,
After you have taken off the blossom with your lips.

But the vulgar way
Is just to put your mouth to the crack, and take out the
    flesh in one bite.

Every fruit has its secret.

The fig is a very secretive fruit.
As you see it standing growing, you feel at once it is symbolic:
And it seems male.
But when you come to know it better, you agree with the
    Romans, it is female.

The Italians vulgarly say, it stands for the female part; the fig-
    fruit:
The fissure, the yoni,
The wonderful moist conductivity towards the centre.

Involved,
Inturned,
The flowering all inward and womb-fibrilled;
And but one orifice.

The fig, the horse-shoe, the squash-blossom.
Symbols.

There was a flower that flowered inward, womb-ward;
Now there is a fruit like a ripe womb.

It was always a secret.
That's how it should be, the female should always be secret.

There never was any standing aloft and unfolded on
    a bough
Like other flowers, in a revelation of petals;
Silver-pink peach, venetian green glass of medlars and
    sorb-apples,

Shallow wine-cups on short, bulging stems
Openly pledging heaven:
Here's to the thorn in flower! Here is to Utterance!
The brave, adventurous rosaceae.

Folded upon itself, and secret unutterable,
And milky-sapped, sap that curdles milk and makes *ricotta,*
Sap that smells strange on your fingers, that even goats
    won't taste it;
Folded upon itself, enclosed like any Mohammedan woman,
Its nakedness all within-walls, its flowering forever unseen,
One small way of access only, and this close-curtained from
    the light;
Fig, fruit of the female mystery, covert and inward,
Mediterranean fruit, with your covert nakedness,
Where everything happens invisible, flowering and fertilisation, and
    fruiting
In the inwardness of your you, that eye will never see
Till it's finished, and you're over-ripe, and you burst to give
    up your ghost.

Till the drop of ripeness exudes,
And the year is over.

And then the fig has kept her secret long enough.
So it explodes, and you see through the fissure the scarlet.
And the fig is finished, the year is over.

That's how the fig dies, showing her crimson through the purple
    slit
Like a wound, the exposure of her secret, on the open day.
Like a prostitute, the bursten fig, making a show of her secret.

That's how women die too.

The year is fallen over-ripe,
The year of our women.
The year of our women is fallen over-ripe.
The secret is laid bare.
And rottenness soon sets in.
The year of our women is fallen over-ripe.

When Eve once knew *in her mind* that she was naked
She quickly sewed fig-leaves, and sewed the same for the man.
She'd been naked all her days before,
But till then, till that apple of knowledge, she hadn't had the fact
    on her mind.

She got the fact on her mind, and quickly sewed fig-leaves.
And women have been sewing ever since.
But now they stitch to adorn the bursten fig, not to cover it.
They have their nakedness more than ever on their mind,
And they won't let us forget it.

Now, the secret
Becomes an affirmation through moist, scarlet lips
That laugh at the Lord's indignation.

What then, good Lord! cry the women.
We have kept our secret long enough.
We are a ripe fig.
Let us burst into affirmation.

They forget, ripe figs won't keep.
Ripe figs won't keep.

Honey-white figs of the north, black figs with scarlet inside, of the
    south.
Ripe figs won't keep, won't keep in any clime.
What then, when women the world over have all bursten into self-
    assertion?
And bursten figs won't keep?

                                                        San Gervasio

Grapes

So many fruits come from roses,
From the rose of all roses,
From the unfolded rose,
Rose of all the world.

Admit that apples and strawberries and peaches and pears
        and blackberries
Are all Rosaceae,
Issue of the explicit rose,
The open-countenanced, skyward-smiling rose.

What then of the vine?
Oh, what of the tendrilled vine?

Ours is the universe of the unfolded rose,
The explicit
The candid revelation.

But long ago, oh, long ago
Before the rose began to simper supreme,
Before the rose of all roses, rose of all the world, was even in bud,
Before the glaciers were gathered up in a bunch out of the
        unsettled seas and winds,
Or else before they had been let down again, in Noah's flood,
There was another world, a dusky, flowerless, tendrilled world
And creatures webbed and marshy,
And on the margin, men soft-footed and pristine,
Still, and sensitive, and active,
Audile, tactile sensitiveness as of a tendril which orientates
        and reaches out,
Reaching out and grasping by an instinct more delicate than
        the moon's as she feels for the tides.

Of which world, the vine was the invisible rose,
Before petals spread, before colour made its disturbance,
        before eyes saw too much.

In a green, muddy, web-foot, unutterably songless world
The vine was rose of all roses.

There were no poppies or carnations,
Hardly a greenish lily, watery faint.
Green, dim, invisible flourishing of vines
Royally gesticulate.

Look now even now, how it keeps its power of invisibility!
Look how black, how blue-black, how globed in Egyptian darkness
Dropping among his leaves, hangs the dark grape!
See him there, the swart, so palpably invisible:
Whom shall we ask about him?

The negro might know a little.
When the vine was rose, Gods were dark-skinned.
Bacchus is a dream's dream.
Once God was all negroid, as now he is fair.
But it's so long ago, the ancient Bushman has forgotten more
    utterly than we, who have never known.

For we are on the brink of re-remembrance.
Which, I suppose, is why America has gone dry.
Our pale day is sinking into twilight,
And if we sip the wine, we find dreams coming upon us
Out of the imminent night.
Nay, we find ourselves crossing the fern-scented frontiers
Of the world before the floods, where man was dark and evasive
And the tiny vine-flower rose of all roses, perfumed,
And all in naked communion communicating as now our clothed
    vision can never communicate.
Vistas, down dark avenues,
As we sip the wine.

The grape is swart, the avenues dusky and tendrilled, subtly
    prehensile,
But we, as we start awake, clutch at our vistas democratic,
    boulevards, tram-cars, policemen.
Give us our own back,
Let us go to the soda-fountain, to get sober.

Soberness, sobriety.
It is like the agonised perverseness of a child heavy with sleep, yet
    fighting, fighting to keep awake;
Soberness, sobriety, with heavy eyes propped open.

Dusky are the avenues of wine,
And we must cross the frontiers, though we will not,

Of the lost, fern-scented world:
Take the fern-seed on our lips,
Close the eyes, and go
Down the tendrilled avenues of wine and the otherworld.

San Gervasio

The Revolutionary

Look at them standing there in authority,
The pale-faces,
As if it could have any effect any more.

Pale-face authority,
Caryatids,
Pillars of white bronze standing rigid, lest the skies fall.

What a job they've got to keep it up.
Their poor, idealist foreheads naked capitals
To the entablature of clouded heaven.

When the skies are going to fall, fall they will
In a great chute and rush of débâcle downwards.

Oh and I wish the high and super-gothic heavens would come
    down now,
The heavens above, that we yearn to and aspire to.

I do not yearn, nor aspire, for I am a blind Samson.
And what is daylight to me that I should look skyward?
Only I grope among you, pale-faces, caryatids, as among a
    forest of pillars that hold up the dome of high ideal heaven
Which is my prison,
And all these human pillars of loftiness, going stiff, metallic-
    stunned with the weight of their responsibility
I stumble against them.
Stumbling-blocks, painful ones.

To keep on holding up this ideal civilisation
Must be excruciating: unless you stiffen into metal, when it is
    easier to stand stock rigid than to move.

This is why I tug at them, individually, with my arm round
     their waist,
The human pillars.
They are not stronger than I am, blind Samson.
The house sways.

I shall be so glad when it comes down.
I am so tired of the limitations of their Infinite.
I am so sick of the pretensions of the Spirit.
I am so weary of pale-face importance.

Am I not blind, at the round-turning mill?
Then why should I fear their pale faces?
Or love the effulgence of their holy light,
The sun of their righteousness?

To me, all faces are dark,
All lips are dusky and valved.

Save your lips, O pale-faces,
Which are slips of metal,
Like slits in an automatic-machine, you columns of give-and-take.

To me, the earth rolls ponderously, superbly
Coming my way without forethought or afterthought.
To me, men's footfalls fall with a dull, soft rumble, ominous and
     lovely,
Coming my way.

But not your foot-falls, pale-faces,
They are a clicketing of bits of disjointed metal
Working in motion.

To me, men are palpable, invisible nearnesses in the dark
Sending out magnetic vibrations of warning, pitch-dark throbs of
     invitation.
But you, pale-faces,
You are painful, harsh-surfaced pillars that give off nothing except
     rigidity,
And I jut against you if I try to move, for you are everywhere, and I
     am blind,
Sightless among all your visuality,
You staring caryatids.

See if I don't bring you down, and all your high opinion
And all your ponderous roofed-in erection of right and wrong,
Your particular heavens,
With a smash.

See if your skies aren't falling!
And my head, at least, is thick enough to stand it, the smash.

See if I don't move under a dark and nude, vast heaven
When your world is in ruins, under your fallen skies.
Caryatids, pale-faces.
See if I am not Lord of the dark and moving hosts
Before I die.

Florence

The Evening Land

Oh, America,
The sun sets in you.
Are you the grave of our day?

Shall I come to you, the open tomb of my race?

I would come, if I felt my hour had struck.
I would rather you came to me.

For that matter
Mahomet never went to any mountain
Save it had first approached him and cajoled his soul.

You have cajoled the souls of millions of us,
America,
Why won't you cajole my soul?
I wish you would.

I confess I am afraid of you.

The catastrophe of your exaggerate love,
You who never find yourself in love
But only lose yourself further, decomposing.

You who never recover from out of the orgasm of loving
Your pristine, isolate integrity, lost aeons ago.
Your singleness within the universe.

You who in loving break down
And break further and further down
Your bounds of isolation,
But who never rise, resurrected, from this grave of
    mingling,
In a new proud singleness, America.

Your more-than-European idealism,
Like a be-aureoled bleached skeleton hovering
Its cage-ribs in the social heaven, beneficent.

And then your single resurrection
Into machine-uprisen perfect man.

Even the winged skeleton of your bleached ideal
Is not so frightening as that clean smooth
Automaton of your uprisen self,
Machine American.

Do you wonder that I am afraid to come
And answer the first machine-cut question from the lips
    of your iron men?
Put the first cents into metallic fingers of your officers
And sit beside the steel-straight arms of your fair women,
American?

This may be a withering tree, this Europe,
But here, even a customs-official is still vulnerable.

I am so terrified, America,
Of the iron click of your human contact.
And after this
The winding-sheet of your self-less ideal love.
Boundless love
Like a poison gas.

Does no one realise that love should be intense, individual,
Not boundless.
This boundless love is like the bad smell
Of something gone wrong in the middle.
All this philanthropy and benevolence on other people's behalf
Just a bad smell.

Yet, America,
Your elvishness,
Your New England uncanniness,
Your western brutal faery quality.

My soul is half-cajoled, half-cajoled.

Something in you which carries me beyond,
Yankee, Yankee,
What we call human.
Carries me where I want to be carried . . .
Or don't I?

What does it matter
What we call human, and what we don't call human?
The rose would smell as sweet.
And to be limited by a mere word is to be less than a hopping
    flea, which hops over such an obstruction at first jump.

Your horrible, skeleton, aureoled ideal,
Your weird bright motor-productive mechanism,
Two spectres.

But moreover
A dark, unfathomed will, that is not un-Jewish;
A set, stoic endurance, non-European;
An ultimate desperateness, un-African;
A deliberate generosity, non-Oriental.

The strange, unaccustomed geste of your demonish New World
    nature
Glimpsed now and then.

Nobody knows you.
You don't know yourself.
And I, who am half in love with you,

What am I in love with?
My own imaginings?
Say it is not so.

Say, through the branches
America, America
Of all your machines,
Say, in the deep sockets of your idealistic skull,
Dark, aboriginal eyes
Stoic, able to wait through ages
Glancing.

Say, in the sound of all your machines
And white words, white-wash American,
Deep pulsing of a strange heart
New throb, like a stirring under the false dawn that
    precedes the real.

Nascent American
Demonish, lurking among the undergrowth
Of many-stemmed machines and chimneys that smoke
    like pine trees.

Dark, elvish,
Modern, unissued, uncanny America,
Your nascent demon people
Lurking among the deeps of your industrial thicket
Allure me till I am beside myself,
A nympholepht,

'These States!' as Whitman said,
Whatever he meant.

                                              Baden-Baden

Peace

Peace is written on the doorstep
In lava.

Peace, black peace congealed.
My heart will know no peace
Till the hill bursts.

Brilliant, intolerable lava,
Brilliant as a powerful burning-glass,
Walking like a royal snake down the mountain towards
    the sea.

Forests, cities, bridges
Gone again in the bright trail of lava.
Naxos thousands of feet below the olive-roots,
And now the olive leaves thousands of feet below the lava fire.

Peace congealed in black lava on the doorstep.
Within, white-hot lava, never at peace
Till it burst forth blinding, withering the earth;
To set again into rock,
Grey-black rock.

Call it Peace?

Taormina

TREES

Cypresses

Tuscan cypresses,
What is it?

Folded in like a dark thought
For which the language is lost,
Tuscan cypresses,
Is there a great secret?
Are our words no good?

The undeliverable secret,
Dead with a dead race and a dead speech, and yet
Darkly monumental in you,
Etruscan cypresses.

Ah, how I admire your fidelity,
Dark cypresses!

Is it the secret of the long-nosed Etruscans?
The long-nosed, sensitive-footed, subtly-smiling
    Etruscans,
Who made so little noise outside the cypress groves?

Among the sinuous, flame-tall cypresses
That swayed their length of darkness all around
Etruscan-dusky, wavering men of old Etruria:
Naked except for fanciful long shoes,
Going with insidious, half-smiling quietness
And some of Africa's imperturbable sang-froid
About a forgotten business.

What business, then?
Nay, tongues are dead, and words are hollow as hollow seed-
    pods,
Having shed their sound and finished all their echoing

Etruscan syllables,
That had the telling.

Yet more I see you darkly concentrate,
Tuscan cypresses,
On one old thought:
On one old slim imperishable thought, while you remain
Etruscan cypresses;
Dusky, slim marrow-thought of slender, flickering men
   of Etruria,
Whom Rome called vicious.

Vicious, dark cypresses:
Vicious, you supple, brooding, softly-swaying pillars
   of dark flame.
Monumental to a dead, dead race
Embowered in you!

Were they then vicious, the slender, tender-footed
Long-nosed men of Etruria?
Or was their way only evasive and different, dark, like cypress
   trees in a wind?

They are dead, with all their vices,
And all that is left
Is the shadowy monomania of some cypresses
And tombs.

The smile, the subtle Etruscan smile still lurking
Within the tombs,
Etruscan cypresses.
He laughs longest who laughs last;
Nay, Leonardo only bungled the pure Etruscan smile.

What would I not give
To bring back the rare and orchid-like
Evil-yclept Etruscan?
For as to the evil
We have only Roman word for it,
Which I, being a little weary of Roman virtue,
Don't hang much weight on.

For oh, I know, in the dust where we have buried
The silenced races and all their abominations,
We have buried so much of the delicate magic of life.

There in the deeps
That churn the frankincense and ooze the myrrh,
Cypress shadowy,
Such an aroma of lost human life!

They say the fit survive,
But I invoke the spirits of the lost.
Those that have not survived, the darkly lost,
To bring their meaning back into life again,
Which they have taken away
And wrapt inviolable in soft cypress trees,
Etruscan cypresses.

Evil, what is evil?
There is only one evil, to deny life
As Rome denied Etruria
And mechanical America Montezuma still.

Fiesole

Bare Fig Trees

Fig trees, weird fig trees
Made of thick smooth silver,
Made of sweet, untarnished silver in the sea-southern air –
I say untarnished, but I mean opaque –
Thick, smooth-fleshed silver, dull only as human limbs are dull
With the life-lustre,
Nude with the dim light of full, healthy life
That is always half-dark,
And suave like passion-flower petals,
Like passion-flowers,
With the half-secret gleam of a passion-flower hanging from
     the rock,
Great, complicated, nude fig tree, stemless flower-mesh,
Flowerily naked in flesh, and giving off hues of life.

Rather like an octopus, but strange and sweet-myriad-limbed
    octopus;
Like a nude, like a rock-living, sweet-fleshed sea-anemone,
Flourishing from the rock in a mysterious arrogance.

Let me sit down beneath the many-branching candelabrum
That lives upon this rock
And laugh at Time, and laugh at dull Eternity,
And make a joke of stale Infinity,
Within the flesh-scent of this wicked tree,
That has kept so many secrets up its sleeve,
And has been laughing through so many ages
At man and his uncomfortablenesses,
And his attempt to assure himself that what is so is not so,
Up its sleeve.

Let me sit down beneath this many-branching candelabrum,
The Jewish seven-branched, tallow-stinking candlestick kicked over
    the cliff
And all its tallow righteousness got rid of,
And let me notice it behave itself.

And watch it putting forth each time to heaven,
Each time straight to heaven,
With marvellous naked assurance each single twig,
Each one setting off straight to the sky
As if it were the leader, the main-stem, the forerunner,
Intent to hold the candle of the sun upon its socket-tip,
It alone.

Every young twig
No sooner issued sideways from the thigh of his predecessor
Than off he starts without a qualm
To hold the one and only lighted candle of the sun in his socket-
    tip.
He casually gives birth to another young bud from his thigh,
Which at once sets off to be the one and only,
And hold the lighted candle of the sun.

Oh many-branching candelabrum, oh strange up-starting fig tree,
Oh weird Demos, where every twig is the arch twig,
Each imperiously over-equal to each, equality over-reaching itself
Like the snakes on Medusa's head,
Oh naked fig tree!

Still, no doubt every one of you can be the sun-socket as well
        as every other of you.
Demos, Demos, Demos!
Demon, too,
Wicked fig tree, equality puzzle, with your self-conscious
        secret fruits.

Taormina

Bare Almond Trees

Wet almond trees, in the rain,
Like iron sticking grimly out of earth;
Black almond trunks, in the rain,
Like iron implements twisted, hideous, out of the earth,
Out of the deep, soft fledge of Sicilian winter-green,
Earth-grass uneatable,
Almond trunks curving blackly, iron-dark, climbing the slopes.

Almond tree, beneath the terrace rail,
Black, rusted, iron trunk,
You have welded your thin stems finer,
Like steel, like sensitive steel in the air,
Grey, lavender, sensitive steel, curving thinly and brittly
        up in a parabola.

What are you doing in the December rain?
Have you a strange electric sensitiveness in your steel tips?
Do you feel the air for electric influences
Like some strange magnetic apparatus?
Do you take in messages, in some strange code,
From heaven's wolfish, wandering electricity, that prowls
        so constantly round Etna?
Do you take the whisper of sulphur from the air?

Do you hear the chemical accents of the sun?
Do you telephone the roar of the waters over the earth?
And from all this, do you make calculations?

Sicily, December's Sicily in a mass of rain
With iron branching blackly, rusted like old, twisted
     implements
And brandishing and stooping over earth's wintry fledge,
     climbing the slopes
Of uneatable soft green!

                                                    Taormina

Tropic

Sun, dark sun,
Sun of black void heat,
Sun of the torrid mid-day's horrific darkness:

Behold my hair twisting and going black.
Behold my eyes turn tawny yellow
Negroid;
See the milk of northern spume
Coagulating and going black in my veins
Aromatic as frankincense.

Columns dark and soft,
Sunblack men,
Soft shafts, sunbreathing mouths,
Eyes of yellow, golden sand
As frictional, as perilous, explosive as brimstone.

Rock, waves of dark heat;
Waves of dark heat, rock, sway upwards,
Waver perpendicular.

What is the horizontal rolling of water
Compared to the flood of black heat that rolls upwards
     past my eyes?

                                                    Taormina

Southern Night

Come up, thou red thing.
Come up, and be called a moon.

The mosquitoes are biting to-night
Like memories.

Memories, northern memories,
Bitter-stinging white world that bore us
Subsiding into this night.

Call it moonrise
This red anathema?

Rise, thou red thing,
Unfold slowly upwards, blood-dark;
Burst the night's membrane of tranquil stars
Finally.

Maculate
The red Macula.

Taormina

FLOWERS

Almond Blossom

Even iron can put forth,
Even iron.

This is the iron age,
But let us take heart
Seeing iron break and bud,
Seeing rusty iron puff with clouds of blossom.

The almond tree,
December's bare iron hooks sticking out of earth.

The almond tree,
That knows the deadliest poison, like a snake
In supreme bitterness.

Upon the iron, and upon the steel,
Odd flakes as if of snow, odd bits of snow,
Odd crumbs of melting snow.

But you mistake, it is not from the sky;
From out the iron, and from out the steel,
Flying not down from heaven, but storming up,
Strange storming up from the dense under-earth
Along the iron, to the living steel
In rose-hot tips, and flakes of rose-pale snow
Setting supreme annunciation to the world.

Nay, what a heart of delicate super-faith,
Iron-breaking,
The rusty swords of almond trees.

Trees suffer, like races, down the long ages.
They wander and are exiled, they live in exile through
    long ages
Like drawn blades never sheathed, hacked and gone black,

The alien trees in alien lands: and yet
The heart of blossom,
The unquenchable heart of blossom!

Look at the many-cicatrised frail vine, none more scarred and frail,
Yet see him fling himself abroad in fresh abandon
From the small wound-stump.

Even the wilful, obstinate, gummy fig tree
Can be kept down, but he'll burst like a polyp into prolixity.

And the almond tree, in exile, in the iron age!

This is the ancient southern earth whence the vases were baked,
    amphoras, craters, cantharus, oenochoe, and open-hearted
    cylix,
Bristling now with the iron of almond trees

Iron, but unforgotten.
Iron, dawn-hearted,
Ever-beating dawn-heart, enveloped in iron against
    the exile, against the ages.

See it come forth in blossom
From the snow-remembering heart
In long-nighted January,
In the long dark nights of the evening star, and Sirius,
    and the Etna snow-wind through the long night.

Sweating his drops of blood through the long-nighted Gethsemane
Into blossom, into pride, into honey-triumph, into most exquisite
    splendour.
Oh, give me the tree of life in blossom
And the Cross sprouting its superb and fearless flowers!

Something must be reassuring to the almond, in the evening star,
    and the snow-wind, and the long, long nights,
Some memory of far, sun-gentler lands,
So that the faith in his heart smiles again
And his blood ripples with that untellable delight of
    once-more-vindicated faith,
And the Gethsemane blood at the iron pores unfolds, unfolds,
Pearls itself into tenderness of bud
And in a great and sacred forthcoming steps forth, steps
    out in one stride

A naked tree of blossom, like a bridegroom bathing in dew,
    divested of cover,
Frail-naked, utterly uncovered
To the green night-baying of the dog-star, Etna's snow-edged wind
And January's loud-seeming sun.

Think of it, from the iron fastness
Suddenly to dare to come out naked, in perfection of blossom,
    beyond the sword-rust.
Think, to stand there in full unfolded nudity, smiling,
With all the snow-wind, and the sun-glare, and the
    dog-star baying epithalamion.

Oh, honey-bodied beautiful one
Come forth from iron,
Red your heart is.
Fragile-tender, fragile-tender life-body,
More fearless than iron all the time,
And so much prouder, so disdainful of reluctances.

In the distance like hoar-frost, like silvery ghosts communing
    on a green hill,
Hoar-frost-like and mysterious.
In the garden raying out
With a body like spray, dawn-tender, and looking about
With such insuperable, subtly-smiling assurance,
Sword-blade-born.

Unpromised,
No bounds being set.
Flaked out and come unpromised,
The tree being life-divine,
Fearing nothing, life-blissful at the core
Within iron and earth.

Knots of pink, fish-silvery
In heaven, in blue, blue heaven,
Soundless, bliss-full, wide-rayed, honey-bodied,
Red at the core,
Red at the core,
Knotted in heaven upon the fine light.

Open,
Open,
Five times wide open,
Six times wide open,
And given, and perfect;
And red at the core with the last sore-heartedness,
Sore-hearted-looking.

                                        Fontana Vecchia

Purple Anemones

Who gave us flowers?
Heaven? The white God?

Nonsense!
Up out of hell,
From Hades;
Infernal Dis!

Jesus the god of flowers – ?
Not he.
Or sun-bright Apollo, him so musical?
Him neither.

Who then?
Say who.
Say it – and it is Pluto,
Dis,
The dark one.
Proserpine's master.

Who contradicts – ?

When she broke forth from below,
Flowers came, hell-hounds on her heels.
Dis, the dark, the jealous god, the husband,
Flower-sumptuous-blooded.

Go then, he said.
And in Sicily, on the meadows of Enna,

She thought she had left him;
But opened around her purple anemones,

Caverns,
Little hells of colour, caves of darkness,
Hell, risen in pursuit of her; royal, sumptuous
Pit-falls.

All at her feet
Hell opening;
At her white ankles
Hell rearing its husband-splendid, serpent heads,
Hell-purple, to get at her –
Why did he let her go?
So he could track her down again, white victim.

Ah mastery!
Hell's husband-blossoms
Out on earth again.

Look out, Persephone!
You, Madame Ceres, mind yourself, the enemy is
      upon you.
About your feet spontaneous aconite,
Hell-glamorous, and purple husband-tyranny
Enveloping your late-enfranchised plains.

You thought your daughter had escaped?
No more stockings to darn for the flower-roots, down
      in hell?
But ah, my dear!
Aha, the stripe-cheeked whelps, whippet-slim crocuses,
At 'em, boys, at 'em!
Ho, golden-spaniel, sweet alert narcissus,
Smell 'em, smell 'em out!

      Those two enfranchised women.

      Somebody is coming
      Oho there!
      Dark blue anemones!
      Hell is up!
      Hell on earth, and Dis within the depths!

Run, Persephone, he is after you already.

Why did he let her go?
To track her down;
All the sport of summer and spring, and flowers
    snapping at her ankles and catching her by the
    hair!
Poor Persephone and her rights for women.

Husband-snared hell-queen,
It is spring.

It is spring,
And pomp of husband-strategy on earth.

Ceres, kiss your girl, you think you've got her back.
The bit of husband-tilth she is,
Persephone!

Poor mothers-in-law!
They are always sold.

It is spring.

                                        Taormina

Sicilian Cyclamens

When he pushed his bush of black hair off his brow:
When she lifted her mop from her eyes, and screwed it in a knob
    behind
        – O act of fearful temerity!
When they felt their foreheads bare, naked to heaven, their
    eyes revealed:
When they felt the light of heaven brandished like a knife at their
    defenceless eyes,
And the sea like a blade at their face,
Mediterranean savages:
When they came out, face-revealed, under heaven, from the shaggy
    undergrowth of their own hair
For the first time,
They saw tiny rose cyclamens between their toes, growing
Where the slow toads sat brooding on the past.

Slow toads, and cyclamen leaves
Stickily glistening with eternal shadow
Keeping to earth.
Cyclamen leaves
Toad-filmy, earth-iridescent
Beautiful
Frost-filigreed
Spumed with mud
Snail-nacreous
Low down.

The shaking aspect of the sea
And man's defenceless bare face
And cyclamens putting their ears back.
Long, pensive, slim-muzzled greyhound buds
Dreamy, not yet present,
Drawn out of earth
At his toes.

Dawn-rose
Sub-delighted, stone-engendered
Cyclamens, young cyclamens

Arching
Waking, pricking their ears
Like delicate very-young greyhound bitches
Half-yawning at the open, inexperienced
Vista of day,
Folding back their soundless petalled ears.

Greyhound bitches
Bending their rosy muzzles pensive down,
And breathing soft, unwilling to wake to the new day
Yet sub-delighted.

Ah Mediterranean morning, when our world began!
Far-off Mediterranean mornings,
Pelasgic faces uncovered,
And unbudding cyclamens.

The hare suddenly goes uphill
Laying back her long ears with unwinking bliss.

And up the pallid, sea-blenched Mediterranean stone-slopes
Rose cyclamen, ecstatic fore-runner!
Cyclamens, ruddy-muzzled cyclamens
In little bunches like bunches of wild hares
Muzzles together, ears-aprick,
Whispering witchcraft
Like women at a well, the dawn-fountain.

Greece, and the world's morning
Where all the Parthenon marbles still fostered the roots of
    the cyclamen.
Violets
Pagan, rosy-muzzled violets
Autumnal
Dawn-pink,
Dawn-pale
Among squat toad-leaves sprinkling the unborn
Erechtheion[30] marbles.

Taormina

Hibiscus and Salvia Flowers

Hark! Hark!
The dogs do bark!
It's the socialists come to town,
None in rags and none in tags,
Swaggering up and down.

Sunday morning,
And from the Sicilian townlets skirting Etna
The socialists have gathered upon us, to look at us.

How shall we know them when we see them?
How shall we know them now they've come?

Not by their rags and not by their tags,
Nor by any distinctive gown;
The same unremarkable Sunday suit
And hats cocked up and down.

Yet there they are, youths, loutishly
Strolling in gangs and staring along the Corso
With the gang-stare
And a half-threatening envy
At every *forestière*,[31]
Every lordly tuppenny foreigner from the hotels,
    fattening on the exchange.

Hark! Hark!
The dogs do bark!
It's the socialists in the town.

Sans rags, sans tags,
Sans beards, sans bags,
Sans any distinction at all except loutish commonness.

How do we know then, that they are they?
Bolshevists.
Leninists.
Communists.
Socialists.
-Ists! -Ists!

Alas, salvia and hibiscus flowers.
Salvia and hibiscus flowers.

Listen again.
Salvia and hibiscus flowers.
Is it not so?
Salvia and hibiscus flowers.

Hark! Hark!
The dogs do bark!
Salvia and hibiscus flowers.

Who smeared their doors with blood?
Who on their breasts
Put salvias and hibiscus?

Rosy, rosy scarlet,
And flame-rage, golden-throated
Bloom along the Corso on the living, perambulating bush.

Who said they might assume these blossoms?
What god did they consult?

Rose-red, princess hibiscus, rolling her pointed Chinese petals!
Azalea and camellia, single peony
And pomegranate bloom and scarlet mallow-flower
And all the eastern, exquisite royal plants
That noble blood has brought us down the ages!
Gently nurtured, frail and splendid
Hibiscus flower –
Alas, the Sunday coats of Sicilian bolshevists!

Pure blood, and noble blood, in the fine and rose-red veins;
Small, interspersed with jewels of white gold
Frail-filigreed among the rest;
Rose of the oldest races of princesses, Polynesian
Hibiscus.

Eve, in her happy moments,
Put hibiscus in her hair,
Before she humbled herself, and knocked her knees with
      repentance.

Sicilian bolshevists,
With hibiscus flowers in the buttonholes of your Sunday suits,
Come now, speaking of rights, what right have you to this flower?

The exquisite and ageless aristocracy
Of a peerless soul,
Blessed are the pure in heart and the fathomless in bright pride;
The loveliness that knows *noblesse oblige*;
The native royalty of red hibiscus flowers;
The exquisite assertion of new delicate life
Risen from the roots:
Is this how you'll have it, red-decked socialists,
Hibiscus-breasted?

If it be so, I fly to join you,
And if it be not so, brutes to pull down hibiscus flowers!

Or salvia!
Or dragon-mouthed salvia with gold throat of wrath!
Flame-flushed, enraged, splendid salvia,
Cock-crested, crowing your orange scarlet like a tocsin
Along the Corso all this Sunday morning.

Is your wrath red as salvias,
You socialists?
You with your grudging, envious, furtive rage,
In Sunday suits and yellow boots along the Corso.
You look well with your salvia flowers, I must say.
Warrior-like, dawn-cock's-comb flaring flower
Shouting forth flame to set the world on fire,
The dust-heap of man's filthy world on fire,
And burn it down, the glutted, stuffy world,
And feed the young new fields of life with ash,
With ash I say,
Bolshevists,
Your ashes even, my friends,
Among much other ash.

If there were salvia-savage bolshevists
To burn the world back to manure-good ash,

Wouldn't I stick the salvia in my coat!
But these themselves must burn, these louts!

The dragon-faced,
The anger-reddened, golden-throated salvia
With its long antennae of rage put out
Upon the frightened air.
Ugh, how I love its fangs of perfect rage
That gnash the air;
The molten gold of its intolerable rage
Hot in the throat.

I long to be a bolshevist
And set the stinking rubbish-heap of this foul world
Afire at a myriad scarlet points,
A bolshevist, a salvia-face
To lick the world with flame that licks it clean.
I long to see its chock-full crowdedness
And glutted squirming populousness on fire
Like a field of filthy weeds
Burnt back to ash,
And then to see the new, real souls sprout up.

Not this vast rotting cabbage patch we call the world:
But from the ash-scarred fallow
New wild souls.

Nettles, and a rose sprout,
Hibiscus, and mere grass,
Salvia still in a rage
And almond honey-still,
And fig-wort stinking for the carrion wasp;
All the lot of them, and let them fight it out.

But not a trace of foul equality,
Nor sound of still more foul human perfection.
You need not clear the world like a cabbage patch for me;
Leave me my nettles,
Let me fight the wicked, obstreperous weeds myself, and put them
    in their place,

Severely in their place.
I don't at all want to annihilate them,
I like a row with them,
But I won't be put on a cabbage-idealistic level of equality
    with them.

What rot, to see the cabbage and hibiscus tree
As equals!
What rot, to say the louts along the Corso
In Sunday suits and yellow shoes
Are my equals!
I am their superior, saluting the hibiscus flower, not them.
The same I say to the profiteers from the hotels, the
    money-fat-ones,
Profiteers here being called dog-fish, stinking dog-fish, sharks.
The same I say to the pale and elegant persons,
Pale-face authorities loitering tepidly:
That I salute the red hibiscus flowers
And send mankind to its inferior blazes.
Mankind's inferior blazes,
And these along with it, all the inferior lot –
These bolshevists,
These dog-fish,
These precious and ideal ones,
All rubbish ready for fire.

And I salute hibiscus and the salvia flower
Upon the breasts of loutish bolshevists,
Damned loutish bolshevists,
Who perhaps will do the business after all,
In the long run, in spite of themselves.

Meanwhile, alas
For me no fellow-men,
No salvia-frenzied comrades, antennae
Of yellow-red, outreaching, living wrath
Upon the smouldering air,
And throat of brimstone-molten angry gold.
Red, angry men are a race extinct, alas!

Never
To be a bolshevist
With a hibiscus flower behind my ear
In sign of life, of lovely, dangerous life
And passionate disquality of men;
In sign of dauntless, silent violets,
And impudent nettles grabbing the under-earth,
And cabbages born to be cut and eat,
And salvia fierce to crow and shout for fight,
And rosy-red hibiscus wincingly
Unfolding all her coiled and lovely self
In a doubtful world.

Never, bolshevistically
To be able to stand for all these!
Alas, alas, I have got to leave it all
To the youths in Sunday suits and yellow shoes
Who have pulled down the salvia flowers
And rosy delicate hibiscus flowers
And everything else to their disgusting level,
Never, of course, to put anything up again.

But yet
If they pull all the world down,
The process will amount to the same in the end.
Instead of flame and flame-clean ash,
Slow watery rotting back to level muck
And final humus,
Whence the re-start.

And still I cannot bear it
That they take hibiscus and the salvia flower.

                                                          Taormina

THE EVANGELISTIC BEASTS

St Matthew

They are not all beasts.
One is a man, for example, and one is a bird.

I, Matthew, am a man.

'And I, if I be lifted up, will draw all men unto me' –

That is Jesus.
But then Jesus was not quite a man.
He was the Son of Man
Filius Meus, O remorseless logic
Out of His own mouth.

I, Matthew, being a man
Cannot be lifted up, the Paraclete
To draw all men unto me,
Seeing I am on a par with all men.

I, on the other hand,
Am drawn to the Uplifted, as all men are drawn,
To the Son of Man
Filius Meus.

Wilt thou lift me up, Son of Man?
How my heart beats!
I am man.

I am man, and therefore my heart beats, and throws
      the dark blood from side to side
All the time I am lifted up.
Yes, even during my uplifting.

And if it ceased?
If it ceased, I should be no longer man
As I am, if my heart in uplifting ceased to beat, to toss the dark
      blood from side to side, causing my myriad secret streams.

After the cessation
I might be a soul in bliss, an angel, approximating to the Uplifted;
But that is another matter;
I am Matthew, the man,
And I am not that other angelic matter.

So I will be lifted up, Saviour,
But put me down again in time, Master,
Before my heart stops beating, and I become what I am not.
Put me down again on the earth, Jesus, on the brown soil
Where flowers sprout in the acrid humus, and fade into humus
     again.
Where beasts drop their unlicked young, and pasture, and
     drop their droppings among the turf.
Where the adder darts horizontal.
Down on the damp, unceasing ground, where my feet belong
And even my heart, Lord, forever, after all uplifting:
The crumbling, damp, fresh land, life horizontal and ceaseless.

Matthew I am, the man.
And I take the wings of the morning, to Thee, Crucified, Glorified.
But while flowers club their petals at evening
And rabbits make pills among the short grass
And long snakes quickly glide into the dark hole in the
     wall, hearing man approach,
I must be put down, Lord, in the afternoon,
And at evening I must leave off my wings of the spirit
As I leave off my braces,
And I must resume my nakedness like a fish, sinking down
     the dark reversion of night
Like a fish seeking the bottom, Jesus,
IXΘΥΣ[34]
Face downwards
Veering slowly
Down between the steep slopes of darkness, fucus-dark, seaweed-
     fringed valleys of the waters under the sea,

Over the edge of the soundless cataract
Into the fathomless, bottomless pit
Where my soul falls in the last throes of bottomless
     convulsion, and is fallen

Utterly beyond Thee, Dove of the Spirit;
Beyond everything, except itself.

Nay, Son of Man, I have been lifted up.
To Thee I rose like a rocket ending in mid-heaven.
But even thou, Son of Man, canst not quaff out the dregs of
    terrestrial manhood!
They fall back from Thee.

They fall back, and like a dripping of quicksilver taking the
    downward track,
Break into drops, burn into drops of blood, and dropping,
    dropping take wing
Membraned, blood-veined wings.
On fans of unsuspected tissue, like bats
They thread and thrill and flicker ever downward
To the dark zenith of Thine antipodes
Jesus Uplifted.

Bat-winged heart of man,
Reversed flame
Shuddering a strange way down the bottomless pit
To the great depths of its reversèd zenith.

Afterwards, afterwards
Morning comes, and I shake the dews of night from the
    wings of my spirit
And mount like a lark, Beloved.

But remember, Saviour,
That my heart which like a lark at heaven's gate singing, hovers
    morning-bright to Thee,
Throws still the dark blood back and forth
In the avenues where the bat hangs sleeping, upside-down
And to me undeniable, Jesus.

Listen, Paraclete.
I can no more deny the bat-wings of my fathom-flickering
    spirit of darkness
Than the wings of the Morning and Thee, Thou Glorified.

I am Matthew, the Man:
It is understood.
And Thou art Jesus, Son of Man
Drawing all men unto Thee, but bound to release them when the
     hour strikes.

I have been, and I have returned.
I have mounted up on the wings of the morning, and I
     have dredged down to the zenith's reversal.
Which is my way, being man.
Gods may stay in mid-heaven, the Son of Man has climbed to the
     Whitsun zenith,
But I, Matthew, being a man
Am a traveller back and forth.

So be it.

St Mark

There was a lion in Judah
Which whelped, and was Mark.

But winged.
A lion with wings.
At least at Venice.
Even as late as Daniele Manin.

Why should he have wings?
Is he to be a bird also?
Or a spirit?
Or a winged thought?
Or a soaring consciousness?

Evidently he is all that,
The lion of the spirit.

Ah, Lamb of God,
Would a wingless lion lie down before Thee, as this winged
    lion lies?

The lion of the spirit.

Once he lay in the mouth of a cave
And sunned his whiskers,
And lashed his tail slowly, slowly
Thinking of voluptuousness
Even of blood.

But later, in the sun of the afternoon,
Having tasted all there was to taste, and having slept his fill
He fell to frowning, as he lay with his head on his paws
And the sun coming in through the narrowest fibril of a slit in his
    eyes.

So, nine-tenths asleep, motionless, bored, and statically angry,
He saw in a shaft of light a lamb on a pinnacle, balancing a flag on
    its paw,
And he was thoroughly startled.

Going out to investigate
He found the lamb beyond him, on the inaccessible pinnacle
    of light.
So he put his paw to his nose, and pondered.

'Guard my sheep,' came the silvery voice from the pinnacle,
'And I will give thee the wings of the morning.'
So the lion of the senses thought it was worth it.

Hence he became a curly sheepdog with dangerous propensities,
As Carpaccio will tell you:
Ramping round, guarding the flock of mankind,
Sharpening his teeth on the wolves,
Ramping up through the air like a kestrel
And lashing his tail above the world
And enjoying the sensation of heaven and righteousness and
    voluptuous wrath.

There is a new sweetness in his voluptuously licking his paw
Now that it is a weapon of heaven.
There is a new ecstasy in his roar of desirous love
Now that it sounds self-conscious through the unlimited sky.
He is well aware of himself
And he cherishes voluptuous delights, and thinks about them
And ceases to be a blood-thirsty king of beasts
And becomes the faithful sheep-dog of the Shepherd, thinking of
   his voluptuous pleasures of chasing the sheep to the fold
And increasing the flock, and perhaps giving a real nip here
   and there, a real pinch, but always well meant.

And somewhere there is a lioness,
The she-mate.
Whelps play between the paws of the lion,
The she-mate purrs,
Their castle is impregnable, their cave,
The sun comes in their lair, they are well-off,
A well-to-do family.

Then the proud lion stalks abroad alone,
And roars to announce himself to the wolves
And also to encourage the red-cross Lamb
And also to ensure a goodly increase in the world.

Look at him, with his paw on the world
At Venice and elsewhere.
Going blind at last.

St Luke

A wall, a bastion,
A living forehead with its slow whorl of hair
And a bull's large, sombre, glancing eye
And glistening, adhesive muzzle
With cavernous nostrils where the winds run hot
Snorting defiance
Or greedily snuffling behind the cows.

Horns,
The golden horns of power,
Power to kill, power to create
Such as Moses had, and God,
Head-power.

Shall great wings flame from his shoulder sockets
Assyrian-wise?
It would be no wonder.

Knowing the thunder of his heart,
The massive thunder of his dew-lapped chest
Deep and reverberating,
It would be no wonder if great wings, like flame, fanned
      out from the furnace-cracks of his shoulder-sockets.

Thud! Thud! Thud!
And the roar of black bull's blood in the mighty passages
      of his chest.
Ah, the dewlap swings pendulous with excess.
The great, roaring weight above
Like a furnace dripping a molten drip
The urge, the massive, burning ache
Of the bull's breast.
The open furnace-doors of his nostrils.

For what does he ache, and groan?

Is his breast a wall?

Nay, once it was also a fortress wall, and the weight of a
      vast battery.
But now it is a burning hearthstone only,
Massive old altar of his own burnt offering.

It was always an altar of burnt offering
His own black blood poured out like a sheet of flame
      over his fecundating herd
As he gave himself forth.

But also it was a fiery fortress frowning shaggily on the
world
And announcing battle ready.

Since the Lamb bewitched him with that red-struck flag
His fortress is dismantled
His fires of wrath are banked down
His horns turn away from the enemy.

He serves the Son of Man.

And hear him bellow, after many years, the bull that serves
the Son of Man.
Moaning, booing, roaring hollow
Constrained to pour forth all his fire down the narrow
sluice of procreation
Through such narrow loins, too narrow
Is he not over-charged by the dammed-up pressure of his own
massive black blood
Luke, the Bull, the father of substance, the Providence
Bull, after two thousand years?
Is he not over-full of offering, a vast, vast offer of himself
Which must be poured through so small a vent?

Too small a vent.

Let him remember his horns, then.
Seal up his forehead once more to a bastion,
Let it know nothing.
Let him charge like a mighty catapult on the red-cross flag,
let him roar out challenge on the world
And throwing himself upon it, throw off the madness of
his blood.
Let it be war.

And so it is war.
The bull of the proletariat has got his head down.

St John

John, oh John,
Thou honourable bird,
Sun-peering eagle.

Taking a bird's-eye view
Even of Calvary and Resurrection
Not to speak of Babylon's whoredom.

High over the mild effulgence of the dove
Hung all the time, did we but know it, the all-knowing
    shadow
Of John's great gold-barred eagle.

John knew all about it
Even the very beginning.

'In the beginning was the Word
And the Word was God
And the Word was with God.'

Having been to school
John knew the whole proposition.
As for innocent Jesus
He was one of Nature's phenomena, no doubt.

Oh that mind-soaring eagle of an Evangelist
Staring creation out of countenance
And telling it off
As an eagle staring down on the Sun!

The Logos, the Logos!
'In the beginning was the Word.'

Is there not a great Mind pre-ordaining?
Does not a supreme Intellect ideally procreate
    the Universe?
Is not each soul a vivid thought in the great consciousness
    stream of God?

Put salt on his tail
The sly bird of John.

Proud intellect, high-soaring Mind
Like a king eagle, bird of the most High, sweeping
    the round of heaven
And casting the cycles of creation
On two wings, like a pair of compasses;
Jesus' pale and lambent dove, cooing in the lower boughs
On sufferance.

In the beginning was the Word, of course.
And the word was the first offspring of the almighty Johannine
    mind,
Chick of the intellectual eagle.

Yet put salt on the tail of the Johannine bird
Put salt on its tail
John's eagle.

Shoo it down out of the empyrean
Of the all-seeing, all-fore-ordaining ideal.
Make it roost on bird-spattered, rocky Patmos
And let it moult there, among the stones of the bitter sea.

For the almighty eagle of the fore-ordaining Mind
Is looking rather shabby and island-bound these days:
Moulting, and rather naked about the rump, and down in the
    beak,
Rather dirty, on dung-whitened Patmos.

From which we are led to assume
That the old bird is weary, and almost willing
That a new chick should chip the extensive shell
Of the mundane egg.

The poor old golden eagle of the word-fledged spirit
Moulting and moping and waiting, willing at last
For the fire to burn it up, feathers and all,
So that a new conception of the beginning and end
Can rise from the ashes.

Ah Phoenix, Phoenix,
John's Eagle!
You are only known to us now as the badge of an insurance
    Company.

Phoenix, Phoenix,
The nest is in flames,
Feathers are singeing,
Ash flutters flocculent, like down on a blue, wan fledgeling.

San Gervasio

CREATURES

The Mosquito

When did you start your tricks,
Monsieur?

What do you stand on such high legs for?
Why this length of shredded shank,
You exaltation?

Is it so that you shall lift your centre of gravity upwards
And weigh no more than air as you alight upon me,
Stand upon me weightless, you phantom?

I heard a woman call you the Winged Victory
In sluggish Venice.
You turn your head towards your tail, and smile.

How can you put so much devilry
Into that translucent phantom shred
Of a frail corpus?

Queer, with your thin wings and your streaming legs,
How you sail like a heron, or a dull clot of air,
A nothingness.

Yet what an aura surrounds you;
Your evil little aura, prowling, and casting a numbness on my
    mind.

That is your trick, your bit of filthy magic:
Invisibility, and the anaesthetic power
To deaden my attention in your direction.

But I know your game now, streaky sorcerer.
Queer, how you stalk and prowl the air
In circles and evasions, enveloping me,
Ghoul on wings
Winged Victory.

Settle, and stand on long thin shanks
Eyeing me sideways, and cunningly conscious that I
    am aware,
You speck.

I hate the way you lurch off sideways into air
Having read my thoughts against you.

Come then, let us play at unawares,
And see who wins in this sly game of bluff.
Man or mosquito.

You don't know that I exist, and I don't know that you exist.
Now then!

It is your trump,
It is your hateful little trump,
You pointed fiend,
Which shakes my sudden blood to hatred of you:
It is your small, high, hateful bugle in my ear.

Why do you do it?
Surely it is bad policy.

They say you can't help it.

If that is so, then I believe a little in Providence protecting the
    innocent.
But it sounds so amazingly like a slogan,
A yell of triumph as you snatch my scalp.

Blood, red blood
Super-magical
Forbidden liquor.

I behold you stand
For a second enspasmed in oblivion,
Obscenely ecstasied
Sucking live blood,
My blood.

Such silence, such suspended transport,
Such gorging,
Such obscenity of trespass.

You stagger
As well as you may.
Only your accursed hairy frailty,
Your own imponderable weightlessness
Saves you, wafts you away on the very draught my anger makes
    in its snatching.

Away with a paean of derision,
You winged blood-drop.

Can I not overtake you?
Are you one too many for me,
Winged Victory?
Am I not mosquito enough to out-mosquito you?

Queer, what a big stain my sucked blood makes
Beside the infinitesimal faint smear of you!
Queer, what a dim dark smudge you have disappeared into!

                                                    Siracusa

Fish

Fish, oh Fish,
So little matters!

Whether the waters rise and cover the earth
Or whether the waters wilt in the hollow places,
All one to you.

Aqueous, subaqueous,
Submerged
And wave-thrilled.

As the waters roll
Roll you.
The waters wash,

You wash in oneness
And never emerge.

Never know,
Never grasp.

Your life a sluice of sensation along your sides,
A flush at the flails of your fins, down the whorl of your
    tail,
And water wetly on fire in the grates of your gills;
Fixed water-eyes.

Even snakes lie together.

But oh, fish, that rock in water,
You lie only with the waters;
One touch.
No fingers, no hands and feet, no lips;
No tender muzzles,
No wistful bellies,
No loins of desire,
None.

You and the naked element,
Sway-wave.
Curvetting bits of tin in the evening light.

Who is it ejects his sperm to the naked flood?
In the wave-mother?
Who swims enwombed?
Who lies with the waters of his silent passion,
    womb-element?
– Fish in the waters under the earth.

What price *his* bread upon the waters?

Himself all silvery himself
In the element,
No more.

Nothing more.

Himself,
And the element.
Food, of course!
Water-eager eyes,
Mouth-gate open
And strong spine urging, driving;
And desirous belly gulping.

Fear also!
He knows fear!
Water-eyes craning,
A rush that almost screams,
Almost fish voice
As the pike comes . . .
Then gay fear, that turns the tail sprightly, from a shadow.

Food, and fear, and joie de vivre,
Without love.

The other way about:
Joie de vivre, and fear, and food,
All without love.

Quelle joie de vivre
Dans l'eau![35]
Slowly to gape through the waters,
Alone with the element;
To sink, and rise, and go to sleep with the waters;
To speak endless inaudible wavelets into the wave;
To breathe from the flood at the gills,
Fish-blood slowly running next to the flood, extracting
     fish-fire;
To have the element under one, like a lover;
And to spring away with a curvetting click in the air,
Provocative.
Dropping back with a slap on the face of the flood.
And merging oneself!

To be a fish!

So utterly without misgiving
To be a fish
In the waters.

Loveless, and so lively!
Born before God was love,
Or life knew loving.
Beautifully beforehand with it all.

Admitted, they swarm in companies,
Fishes.
They drive in shoals.
But soundless, and out of contact.
They exchange no word, no spasm, not even anger.
Not one touch.
Many suspended together, forever apart,
Each one alone with the waters, upon one wave with
    the rest.

A magnetism in the water between them only.

I saw a water-serpent swim across the Anapo,
And I said to my heart, *look, look* at *him!*
With his head up, steering like a bird!
He's a rare one, but he belongs . . .

But sitting in a boat on the Zeller lake
And watching the fishes in the breathing waters
Lift and swim and go their way –

I said to my heart, *who are these?*
And my heart couldn't own them . . .

A slim young pike, with smart fins
And grey-striped suit, a young cub of a pike
Slouching along away below, half out of sight,
Like a lout on an obscure pavement . . .

Aha, there's somebody in the know!

But watching closer
That motionless deadly motion,
That unnatural barrel body, that long ghoul nose, . . .
I left off hailing him.

I had made a mistake,
I didn't know him,
This grey, monotonous soul in the water,
This intense individual in shadow,
Fish-alive.

I didn't know his God,
I didn't know his God.

Which is perhaps the last admission that life has to wring
          out of us.

I saw, dimly,
Once a big pike rush,
And small fish fly like splinters.
And I said to my heart, *there are limits*
To you, my heart;
And to the one God.
Fish are beyond me.

Other Gods
Beyond my range . . . gods beyond my God . . .

They are beyond me, are fishes.
I stand at the pale of my being
And look beyond, and see
Fish, in the outerwards,
As one stands on a bank and looks in.

I have waited with a long rod
And suddenly pulled a gold-and-greenish, lucent
          fish from below,
And had him fly like a halo round my head,
Lunging in the air on the line.

Unhooked his gorping, water-horny mouth,
And seen his horror-tilted eye,
His red-gold, water-precious, mirror-flat bright eye;
And felt him beat in my hand, with his mucous, leaping
   life-throb.
And my heart accused itself
Thinking: *I am not the measure of creation.*
This is beyond me, this fish.
His God stands outside my God.

And the gold-and-green pure lacquer-mucus comes off
   in my hand,
And the red-gold mirror-eye stares and dies,
And the water-suave contour dims.

But not before I have had to know
He was born in front of my sunrise,
Before my day.

He outstarts me.
And I, a many-fingered horror of daylight to him,
Have made him die.

Fishes
With their gold, red eyes, and green-pure gleam, and
   under-gold,
And their pre-world loneliness,
And more-than-lovelessness,
And white meat;
They move in other circles.

Outsiders.
Water-wayfarers.
Things of one element.
Aqueous,
Each by itself.

Cats, and the Neapolitans,
Sulphur sun-beasts,
Thirst for fish as for more-than-water;
Water-alive
To quench their over-sulphureous lusts.

But I, I only wonder
And don't know.
I don't know fishes.

In the beginning
Jesus was called The Fish . . .
And in the end.

Zell-am-See

Bat

At evening, sitting on this terrace,
When the sun from the west, beyond Pisa, beyond the
    mountains of Carrara
Departs, and the world is taken by surprise . . .

When the tired flower of Florence is in gloom beneath
    the glowing
Brown hills surrounding . . .

When under the arches of the Ponte Vecchio
A green light enters against stream, flush from the west,
Against the current of obscure Arno . . .

Look up, and you see things flying
Between the day and the night;
Swallows with spools of dark thread sewing the shadows
    together.

A circle swoop, and a quick parabola under the bridge arches
Where light pushes through;
A sudden turning upon itself of a thing in the air.
A dip to the water.

And you think:
'The swallows are flying so late!'

Swallows?

Dark air-life looping
Yet missing the pure loop . . .
A twitch, a twitter, an elastic shudder in flight
And serrated wings against the sky,
Like a glove, a black glove thrown up at the light,
And falling back.

Never swallows!
Bats!
The swallows are gone.

At a wavering instant the swallows give way to bats
By the Ponte Vecchio . . .
Changing guard.

Bats, and an uneasy creeping in one's scalp
As the bats swoop overhead!
Flying madly.

Pipistrello![36]
Black piper on an infinitesimal pipe.
Little lumps that fly in air and have voices indefinite,
     wildly vindictive;

Wings like bits of umbrella.

Bats!

Creatures that hang themselves up like an old rag, to
     sleep;
And disgustingly upside down.
Hanging upside down like rows of disgusting old rags
And grinning in their sleep.
Bats!

In China the bat is symbol of happiness.

Not for me!

Man and Bat

When I went into my room, at mid-morning,
Say ten o'clock . . .
My room, a crash-box over that great stone rattle
The Via de' Bardi . . .

When I went into my room at mid-morning,
Why? . . . a bird!

A bird
Flying round the room in insane circles.

In insane circles!
. . . A bat!

A disgusting bat
At mid-morning! . . .

Out! Go out!

Round and round and round
With a twitchy, nervous, intolerable flight,
And a neurasthenic lunge,
And an impure frenzy;
A bat, big as a swallow.

Out, out of my room!

The venetian shutters I push wide
To the free, calm upper air;
Loop back the curtains . . .

Now out, out from my room!

So to drive him out, flicking with my white handkerchief: *Go!*
But he will not.

Round and round and round
In an impure haste,

Fumbling, a beast in air,
And stumbling, lunging and touching the walls, the bell-wires
About my room!

Always refusing to go out into the air
Above that crash-gulf of the Via de' Bardi,
Yet blind with frenzy, with cluttered fear.

At last he swerved into the window bay,
But blew back, as if an incoming wind blew him in again.
A strong inrushing wind.

And round and round and round!
Blundering more insane, and leaping, in throbs, to clutch at a
    corner,
At a wire, at a bell-rope:
On and on, watched relentless by me, round and round in my
    room,
Round and round and dithering with tiredness and haste and
    increasing delirium
Flicker-splashing round my room.

I would not let him rest;
Not one instant cleave, cling like a blot with his breast to the
    wall
In an obscure corner.
Not an instant!

I flicked him on,
Trying to drive him through the window.
Again he swerved into the window bay
And I ran forward, to frighten him forth.
But he rose, and from a terror worse than me he flew past me
Back into my room, and round, round, round in my room
Clutch, cleave, stagger,
Dropping about the air
Getting tired.

Something seemed to blow him back from the window
Every time he swerved at it;

Back on a strange parabola, then round, round, dizzy in my
  room.

He *could* not go out,
I also realised . . .
It was the light of day which he could not enter,
Any more than I could enter the white-hot door of a
    blast furnace.

He could not plunge into the daylight that streamed at the
    window.
It was asking too much of his nature.

Worse even than the hideous terror of me with my
    handkerchief
Saying: *Out, go out!* . . .
Was the horror of white daylight in the window!

So I switched on the electric light, thinking: *Now
The outside will seem brown* . . .

But no.
The outside did not seem brown.
And he did not mind the yellow electric light.

Silent!
He was having a silent rest.
But never!
Not in my room.

Round and round and round
Near the ceiling as if in a web,
Staggering;
Plunging, falling out of the web,
Broken in heaviness,
Lunging blindly,
Heavier;
And clutching, clutching for one second's pause,
Always, as if for one drop of rest,
One little drop.

And I!
Never, I say . . .
Go out!

Flying slower,
Seeming to stumble, to fall in air.
Blind-weary.

Yet never able to pass the whiteness of light into freedom . . .
A bird would have dashed through, come what might.

Fall, sink, lurch, and round and round
Flicker, flicker-heavy;
Even wings heavy:
And cleave in a high corner for a second, like a clot, also a prayer.

But no.
Out, you beast.

Till he fell in a corner, palpitating, spent.
And there, a clot, he squatted and looked at me.
With sticking out, bead-berry eyes, black,
And improper derisive ears,
And shut wings,
And brown, furry body.

Brown, nut-brown, fine fur!
But it might as well have been hair on a spider; thing
With long, black-paper ears.

So, a dilemma!
He squatted there like something unclean.

No, he must not squat, nor hang, obscene, in my room!

Yet nothing on earth will give him courage to pass the sweet
    fire of day.

What then?
Hit him and kill him and throw him away?

Nay,
I didn't create him.
Let the God that created him be responsible for his death . . .
Only, in the bright day, I will not have this clot in my room.

Let the God who is maker of bats watch with them in their unclean
    corners . . .
I admit a God in every crevice,
But not bats in my room;
Nor the God of bats, while the sun shines.

So out, out, you brute! . . .
And he lunged, flight-heavy, away from me, sideways,
    a sghembo![37]
And round and round and round my room, a clot with wings,
Impure even in weariness.

Wings dark skinny and flapping the air,
Lost their flicker.
Spent.

He fell again with a little thud
Near the curtain on the floor.
And there lay.

Ah death, death
You are no solution!
Bats must be bats.

Only life has a way out.
And the human soul is fated to wide-eyed responsibility
In life.

So I picked him up in a flannel jacket,
Well covered, lest he should bite me.
For I would have had to kill him if he'd bitten me, the impure
    one . . .
And he hardly stirred in my hand, muffled up.

Hastily, I shook him out of the window.

And away he went!
Fear craven in his tail.
Great haste, and straight, almost bird straight above the
    Via de' Bardi.
Above that crash-gulf of exploding whips,
Towards the Borgo San Jacopo.

And now, at evening, as he flickers over the river
Dipping with petty triumphant flight, and tittering over
    the sun's departure,
I believe he chirps, pipistrello, seeing me here on this
    terrace writing:
There he sits, the long loud one!
But I am greater than he . . .
I escaped him . . .

                                                    Florence

REPTILES

Snake

A snake came to my water-trough
On a hot, hot day, and I in pyjamas for the heat,
To drink there.

In the deep, strange-scented shade of the great dark carob tree
I came down the steps with my pitcher
And must wait, must stand and wait, for there he was at the trough
    before me.

He reached down from a fissure in the earth-wall in the gloom
And trailed his yellow-brown slackness soft-bellied down, over the
    edge of the stone trough
And rested his throat upon the stone bottom,
And where the water had dripped from the tap, in a small
    clearness,
He sipped with his straight mouth,
Softly drank through his straight gums, into his slack long body,
Silently.

Someone was before me at my water-trough,
And I, like a second comer, waiting.

He lifted his head from his drinking, as cattle do,
And looked at me vaguely, as drinking cattle do,
And flickered his two-forked tongue from his lips, and mused a
    moment,
And stooped and drank a little more,
Being earth-brown, earth-golden from the burning bowels of the
    earth
On the day of Sicilian July, with Etna smoking.

The voice of my education said to me
He must be killed,
For in Sicily the black, black snakes are innocent, the gold are
    venomous.

And voices in me said, If you were a man
You would take a stick and break him now, and finish him off.

But must I confess how I liked him,
How glad I was he had come like a guest in quiet, to drink
    at my water-trough
And depart peaceful, pacified, and thankless,
Into the burning bowels of this earth?

Was it cowardice, that I dared not kill him?
Was it perversity, that I longed to talk to him?
Was it humility, to feel so honoured?
I felt so honoured.

And yet those voices:
If you were not afraid, you would kill him!

And truly I was afraid, I was most afraid,
But even so, honoured still more
That he should seek my hospitality
From out the dark door of the secret earth.

He drank enough
And lifted his head, dreamily, as one who has drunken,
And flickered his tongue like a forked night on the air, so black,
Seeming to lick his lips,
And looked around like a god, unseeing, into the air,
And slowly turned his head,
And slowly, very slowly, as if thrice adream,
Proceeded to draw his slow length curving round
And climb again the broken bank of my wall-face.

And as he put his head into that dreadful hole,
And as he slowly drew up, snake-easing his shoulders,
    and entered farther,
A sort of horror, a sort of protest against his withdrawing into that
    horrid black hole,
Deliberately going into the blackness, and slowly drawing himself
    after,
Overcame me now his back was turned.

I looked round, I put down my pitcher,
I picked up a clumsy log
And threw it at the water-trough with a clatter.

I think it did not hit him,
But suddenly that part of him that was left behind convulsed
    in undignified haste,
Writhed like lightning and was gone
Into the black hole, the earth-lipped fissure in the wall-front,
At which, in the intense still noon, I stared with fascination.

And immediately I regretted it.
I thought how paltry, how vulgar, what a mean act!
I despised myself and the voices of my accursed human education.

And I thought of the albatross,
And I wished he would come back, my snake.

For he seemed to me again like a king,
Like a king in exile, uncrowned in the underworld,
Now due to be crowned again.

And so, I missed my chance with one of the lords
Of life.
And I have something to expiate;
A pettiness.

                                                    Taormina

Baby Tortoise

You know what it is to be born alone,
Baby tortoise!

The first day to heave your feet little by little from the
    shell,
Not yet awake,
And remain lapsed on earth,
Not quite alive.

A tiny, fragile, half-animate bean.

To open your tiny beak-mouth, that looks as if it would never
    open,
Like some iron door;
To lift the upper hawk-beak from the lower base
And reach your skinny little neck
And take your first bite at some dim bit of herbage,
Alone, small insect,
Tiny bright-eye,
Slow one.

To take your first solitary bite
And move on your slow, solitary hunt.
Your bright, dark little eye,
Your eye of a dark disturbed night,
Under its slow lid, tiny baby tortoise,
So indomitable.

No one ever heard you complain.

You draw your head forward, slowly, from your little wimple
And set forward, slow-dragging, on your four-pinned toes,
Rowing slowly forward.
Whither away, small bird?
Rather like a baby working its limbs,
Except that you make slow, ageless progress
And a baby makes none.

The touch of sun excites you,
And the long ages, and the lingering chill
Make you pause to yawn,
Opening your impervious mouth,
Suddenly beak-shaped, and very wide, like some suddenly
    gaping pincers;
Soft red tongue, and hard thin gums,
Then close the wedge of your little mountain front,
Your face, baby tortoise.

Do you wonder at the world, as slowly you turn your
        head in its wimple
And look with laconic, black eyes?
Or is sleep coming over you again,
The non-life?

You are so hard to wake.

Are you able to wonder?
Or is it just your indomitable will and pride of the first life
Looking round
And slowly pitching itself against the inertia
Which had seemed invincible?

The vast inanimate,
And the fine brilliance of your so tiny eye,
Challenger.

Nay, tiny shell-bird,
What a huge vast inanimate it is, that you must row against,
What an incalculable inertia.

Challenger,
Little Ulysses, fore-runner,
No bigger than my thumb-nail,
Buon viaggio.[38]

All animate creation on your shoulder,
Set forth, little Titan, under your battle-shield.

The ponderous, preponderate,
Inanimate universe;
And you are slowly moving, pioneer, you alone.

How vivid your travelling seems now, in the troubled sunshine,
Stoic, Ulyssean atom;
Suddenly hasty, reckless, on high toes.

Voiceless little bird,
Resting your head half out of your wimple

In the slow dignity of your eternal pause.
Alone, with no sense of being alone,
And hence six times more solitary;
Fulfilled of the slow passion of pitching through
    immemorial ages
Your little round house in the midst of chaos.

Over the garden earth,
Small bird,
Over the edge of all things.

Traveller,
With your tail tucked a little on one side
Like a gentleman in a long-skirted coat.

All life carried on your shoulder,
Invincible fore-runner.

Tortoise Shell

The Cross, the Cross
Goes deeper in than we know,
Deeper into life;
Right into the marrow
And through the bone.

Along the back of the baby tortoise
The scales are locked in an arch like a bridge,
Scale-lapping, like a lobster's sections
Or a bee's.

Then crossways down his sides
Tiger-stripes and wasp-bands.

Five, and five again, and five again,
And round the edges twenty-five little ones,
The sections of the baby tortoise shell.

Four, and a keystone;
Four, and a keystone;
Four, and a keystone;
Then twenty-four, and a tiny little keystone.

It needed Pythagoras to see life playing with counters on the
    living back
Of the baby tortoise;
Life establishing the first eternal mathematical tablet,
Not in stone, like the Judean Lord, or bronze, but in
    life-clouded, life-rosy tortoise shell.

The first little mathematical gentleman
Stepping, wee mite, in his loose trousers
Under all the eternal dome of mathematical law.

Fives, and tens,
Threes and fours and twelves,
All the *volte face* of decimals,
The whirligig of dozens and the pinnacle of seven.

Turn him on his back,
The kicking little beetle,
And there again, on his shell-tender, earth-touching belly,
The long cleavage of division, upright of the eternal cross
And on either side count five,
On each side, two above, on each side, two below
The dark bar horizontal.

The Cross!
It goes right through him, the sprottling insect,
Through his cross-wise cloven psyche,
Through his five-fold complex-nature.

So turn him over on his toes again;
Four pin-point toes, and a problematical thumb-piece,
Four rowing limbs, and one wedge-balancing head,
Four and one makes five, which is the clue to all mathematics.

The Lord wrote it all down on the little slate
Of the baby tortoise.
Outward and visible indication of the plan within,
The complex, manifold involvedness of an individual
    creature
Plotted out
On this small bird, this rudiment,
This little dome, this pediment
Of all creation,
This slow one.

Tortoise Family Connections

On he goes, the little one,
Bud of the universe,
Pediment of life.

Setting off somewhere, apparently.
Whither away, brisk egg?

His mother deposited him on the soil as if he were no more than
    droppings,
And now he scuffles tinily past her as if she were an old rusty tin.

A mere obstacle,
He veers round the slow great mound of her –
Tortoises always foresee obstacles.

It is no use my saying to him in an emotional voice:
'This is your Mother, she laid you when you were an egg.'

He does not even trouble to answer: 'Woman, what have I to do
    with thee?'
He wearily looks the other way,
And she even more wearily looks another way still,
Each with the utmost apathy,
Incognisant,
Unaware,
Nothing.

As for papa,
He snaps when I offer him his offspring,
Just as he snaps when I poke a bit of stick at him,
Because he is irascible this morning, an irascible tortoise
Being touched with love, and devoid of fatherliness.

Father and mother,
And three little brothers,
And all rambling aimless, like little perambulating pebbles scattered
    in the garden,
Not knowing each other from bits of earth or old tins.

Except that papa and mama are old acquaintances, of course,
Though family feeling there is none, not even the beginnings.

Fatherless, motherless, brotherless, sisterless
Little tortoise.

Row on then, small pebble,
Over the clods of the autumn, wind-chilled sunshine,
Young gaiety.

Does he look for a companion?

No, no, don't think it.
He doesn't know he is alone;
Isolation is his birthright,
This atom.

To row forward, and reach himself tall on spiny toes,
To travel, to burrow into a little loose earth, afraid of the
    night,
To crop a little substance,
To move, and to be quite sure that he is moving:
Basta![39]
To be a tortoise!
Think of it, in a garden of inert clods
A brisk, brindled little tortoise, all to himself –
Adam!

In a garden of pebbles and insects
To roam, and feel the slow heart beat
Tortoise-wise, the first bell sounding
From the warm blood, in the dark-creation morning.

Moving, and being himself,
Slow, and unquestioned,
And inordinately there, O stoic!
Wandering in the slow triumph of his own existence,
Ringing the soundless bell of his presence in chaos,
And biting the frail grass arrogantly,
Decidedly arrogantly.

Lui et Elle

She is large and matronly
And rather dirty,
A little sardonic-looking, as if domesticity had driven her to it.

Though what she does, except lay four eggs at random in the
     garden once a year
And put up with her husband,
I don't know.

She likes to eat.
She hurries up, striding reared on long uncanny legs
When food is going.
Oh yes, she can make haste when she likes.

She snaps the soft bread from my hand in great mouthfuls,
Opening her rather pretty wedge of an iron, pristine face
Into an enormously wide-beaked mouth
Like sudden curved scissors,
And gulping at more than she can swallow, and working her thick,
     soft tongue,
And having the bread hanging over her chin.

O Mistress, Mistress,
Reptile mistress,
Your eye is very dark, very bright,
And it never softens
Although you watch.

She knows,
She knows well enough to come for food,
Yet she sees me not;
Her bright eye sees, but not me, not anything,
Sightful, sightless, seeing and visionless,
Reptile mistress.

Taking bread in her curved, gaping, toothless mouth,
She has no qualm when she catches my finger in her steel
        overlapping gums,
But she hangs on, and my shout and my shrinking are nothing
        to her.
She does not even know she is nipping me with her curved beak.
Snake-like she draws at my finger, while I drag it in horror away.

Mistress, reptile mistress,
You are almost too large, I am almost frightened.

He is much smaller,
Dapper beside her,
And ridiculously small.

Her laconic eye has an earthy, materialistic look,
His, poor darling, is almost fiery.

His wimple, his blunt-prowed face,
His low forehead, his skinny neck, his long, scaled, striving legs,
So striving, striving,
Are all more delicate than she,
And he has a cruel scar on his shell.

Poor darling, biting at her feet,
Running beside her like a dog, biting her earthy, splay feet,
Nipping her ankles,
Which she drags apathetic away, though without retreating into
        her shell.

Agelessly silent,
And with a grim, reptile determination,
Cold, voiceless age-after-age behind him, serpents' long obstinacy
Of horizontal persistence.

Little old man
Scuffling beside her, bending down, catching his opportunity,
Parting his steel-trap face, so suddenly, and seizing her scaly ankle,
And hanging grimly on,
Letting go at last as she drags away,
And closing his steel-trap face.

His steel-trap, stoic, ageless, handsome face.
Alas, what a fool he looks in this scuffle.

And how he feels it!
The lonely rambler, the stoic, dignified stalker through chaos,
The immune, the animate,
Enveloped in isolation,
Fore-runner.
Now look at him!

Alas, the spear is through the side of his isolation.
His adolescence saw him crucified into sex,
Doomed, in the long crucifixion of desire, to seek his
    consummation beyond himself.
Divided into passionate duality,
He, so finished and immune, now broken into desirous
    fragmentariness,
Doomed to make an intolerable fool of himself
In his effort toward completion again.

Poor little earthy house-inhabiting Osiris,
The mysterious bull tore him at adolescence into pieces,
And he must struggle after reconstruction, ignominiously.

And so behold him following the tail
Of that mud-hovel of his slowly rambling spouse,
Like some unhappy bull at the tail of a cow,
But with more than bovine, grim, earth-dank persistence.

Suddenly seizing the ugly ankle as she stretches out to walk,
Roaming over the sods,
Or, if it happen to show, at her pointed, heavy tail
Beneath the low-dropping back-board of her shell.

Their two shells like domed boats bumping,
Hers huge, his small;
Their splay feet rambling and rowing like paddles,
And stumbling mixed up in one another,
In the race of love –
Two tortoises,
She huge, he small.

She seems earthily apathetic,
And he has a reptile's awful persistence.

I heard a woman pitying her, pitying the Mère Tortue.
While I, I pity Monsieur.
'He pesters her and torments her,' said the woman.
How much more is *he* pestered and tormented, say I.

What can he do?
He is dumb, he is visionless,
Conceptionless.
His black, sad-lidded eye sees but beholds not
As her earthen mound moves on,
But he catches the folds of vulnerable, leathery skin,
Nail-studded, that shake beneath her shell,
And drags at these with his beak,
Drags and drags and bites,
While she pulls herself free, and rows her dull mound along.

Tortoise Gallantry

Making his advances
He does not look at her, nor sniff at her,
No, not even sniff at her, his nose is blank.

Only he senses the vulnerable folds of skin
That work beneath her while she sprawls along
In her ungainly pace,
Her folds of skin that work and row
Beneath the earth-soiled hovel in which she moves.

And so he strains beneath her housey walls
And catches her trouser-legs in his beak
Suddenly, or her skinny limb,
And strange and grimly drags at her
Like a dog,
Only agelessly silent, with a reptile's awful persistency.

Grim, gruesome gallantry, to which he is doomed.
Dragged out of an eternity of silent isolation
And doomed to partiality, partial being,
Ache, and want of being,
Want,
Self-exposure, hard humiliation, need to add himself on to her.

Born to walk alone,
Fore-runner,
Now suddenly distracted into this mazy side-track,
This awkward, harrowing pursuit,
This grim necessity from within.

Does she know
As she moves eternally slowly away?
Or is he driven against her with a bang, like a bird flying
    in the dark against a window,
All knowledgeless?

The awful concussion,
And the still more awful need to persist, to follow, follow,
    continue,

Driven, after aeons of pristine, fore-god-like singleness
    and oneness,
At the end of some mysterious, red-hot iron,
Driven away from himself into her tracks,
Forced to crash against her.

Stiff, gallant, irascible, crook-legged reptile,
Little gentleman,
Sorry plight,
We ought to look the other way.

Save that, having come with you so far,
We will go on to the end.

Tortoise Shout

I thought he was dumb,
I said he was dumb,
Yet I've heard him cry.

First faint scream,
Out of life's unfathomable dawn,
Far off, so far, like a madness, under the horizon's dawning
    rim,
Far, far off, far scream.

Tortoise *in extremis*.

Why were we crucified into sex?
Why were we not left rounded off, and finished in
    ourselves,
As we began,
As he certainly began, so perfectly alone?

A far, was-it-audible scream,
Or did it sound on the plasm direct?

Worse than the cry of the new-born,
A scream,
A yell,
A shout,
A paean,
A death-agony,
A birth-cry,
A submission,
All tiny, tiny, far away, reptile under the first dawn.

War-cry, triumph, acute-delight, death-scream reptilian,
Why was the veil torn?
The silken shriek of the soul's torn membrane?
The male soul's membrane
Torn with a shriek half music, half horror.

Crucifixion.
Male tortoise, cleaving behind the hovel-wall of that dense female,
Mounted and tense, spread-eagle, out-reaching out of the shell
In tortoise-nakedness,
Long neck, and long vulnerable limbs extruded, spread-eagle over
    her house-roof,
And the deep, secret, all-penetrating tail curved beneath her walls,
Reaching and gripping tense, more reaching anguish in uttermost
    tension
Till suddenly, in the spasm of coition, tupping like a jerking leap,
    and oh!
Opening its clenched face from his outstretched neck
And giving that fragile yell, that scream,
Super-audible,
From his pink, cleft, old-man's mouth,
Giving up the ghost,
Or screaming in Pentecost, receiving the ghost.

His scream, and his moment's subsidence,
The moment of eternal silence,
Yet unreleased, and after the moment, the sudden, startling
    jerk of coition, and at once
The inexpressible faint yell –
And so on, till the last plasm of my body was melted back
To the primeval rudiments of life, and the secret.

So he tups, and screams
Time after time that frail, torn scream
After each jerk, the longish interval,
The tortoise eternity,
Age-long, reptilian persistence,
Heart-throb, slow heart-throb, persistent for the next spasm.

I remember, when I was a boy,
I heard the scream of a frog, which was caught with his foot
    in the mouth of an up-starting snake;
I remember when I first heard bull-frogs break into sound in
    the spring;
I remember hearing a wild goose out of the throat of night
Cry loudly, beyond the lake of waters;

I remember the first time, out of a bush in the darkness, a
    nightingale's piercing cries and gurgles startled the depths of
    my soul;
I remember the scream of a rabbit as I went through a wood at
    midnight;
I remember the heifer in her heat, blorting and blorting through th
    hours, persistent and irrepressible;
I remember my first terror hearing the howl of weird, amorous cats
I remember the scream of a terrified, injured horse, the
    sheet-lightning,
And running away from the sound of a woman in labour,
    something like an owl whooing,
And listening inwardly to the first bleat of a lamb,
The first wail of an infant,
And my mother singing to herself,
And the first tenor singing of the passionate throat of a young
    collier, who has long since drunk himself to death,
The first elements of foreign speech
On wild dark lips.

And more than all these,
And less than all these,
This last,
Strange, faint coition yell
Of the male tortoise at extremity,
Tiny from under the very edge of the farthest far-off horizon of life.

The cross,
The wheel on which our silence first is broken,
Sex, which breaks up our integrity, our single inviolability, our
    deep silence,
Tearing a cry from us.

Sex, which breaks us into voice, sets us calling across the deeps,
    calling, calling for the complement,
Singing, and calling, and singing again, being answered, having
    found.

Torn, to become whole again, after long seeking for what is
    lost,
The same cry from the tortoise as from Christ, the Osiris-cry
    of abandonment,
That which is whole, torn asunder,
That which is in part, finding its whole again throughout the
    universe.

BIRDS

Turkey-Cock

You ruffled black blossom,
You glossy dark wind.

Your sort of gorgeousness,
Dark and lustrous
And skinny repulsive
And poppy-glossy,
Is the gorgeousness that evokes my most puzzled admiration.

Your aboriginality
Deep, unexplained,
Like a Red Indian darkly unfinished and aloof,
Seems like the black and glossy seeds of countless centuries.

Your wattles are the colour of steel-slag which has been red-hot
And is going cold,
Cooling to a powdery, pale-oxydised sky-blue.

Why do you have wattles, and a naked, wattled head?
Why do you arch your naked-set eye with a more-than-
    comprehensible arrogance?

The vulture is bald, so is the condor, obscenely,
But only you have thrown this amazing mantilla of oxydised
    sky-blue
And hot red over you.

This queer dross shawl of blue and vermilion,
Whereas the peacock has a diadem.

I wonder why.
Perhaps it is a sort of uncanny decoration, a veil of loose skin.
Perhaps it is your assertion, in all this ostentation, of raw
    contradictoriness.
Your wattles drip down like a shawl to your breast
And the point of your mantilla drops across your nose,
    unpleasantly.

Or perhaps it is something unfinished
A bit of slag still adhering, after your firing in the furnace of
    creation.

Or perhaps there is something in your wattles of a bull's dew-lap
Which slips down like a pendulum to balance the throbbing mass
    of a generous breast,

The over-drip of a great passion hanging in the balance.
Only yours would be a raw, unsmelted passion, that will not quite
    fuse from the dross.

You contract yourself,
You arch yourself as an archer's bow
Which quivers indrawn as you clench your spine
Until your veiled head almost touches backward
To the root-rising of your erected tail.
And one intense and backward-curving frisson
Seizes you as you clench yourself together
Like some fierce magnet bringing its poles together.

Burning, pale positive pole of your wattled head!
And from the darkness of that opposite one
The upstart of your round-barred, sun-round tail!

Whilst between the two, along the tense arch of your back
Blows the magnetic current in fierce blasts,
Ruffling black, shining feathers like lifted mail,
Shuddering storm wind, or a water rushing through.

Your brittle, super-sensual arrogance
Tosses the crape of red across your brow and down your breast
As you draw yourself upon yourself in insistence.

It is a declaration of such tension in will
As time has not dared to avouch, nor eternity been able to unbend
Do what it may.
A raw American will, that has never been tempered by life;
You brittle, will-tense bird with a foolish eye.

The peacock lifts his rods of bronze
And struts blue-brilliant out of the far East.
But watch a turkey prancing low on earth
Drumming his vaulted wings, as savages drum

Their rhythms on long-drawn, hollow, sinister drums.
The ponderous, sombre sound of the great drum of Huichilobos
In pyramid Mexico, during sacrifice.

Drum, and the turkey onrush
Sudden, demonic dauntlessness, full abreast,
All the bronze gloss of all his myriad petals
Each one apart and instant.
Delicate frail crescent of the gentle outline of white
At each feather-tip
So delicate:
Yet the bronze wind-bell suddenly clashing
And the eye overweening into madness.

Turkey-cock, turkey-cock,
Are you the bird of the next dawn?

Has the peacock had his day, does he call in vain, screecher,
    for the sun to rise?
The eagle, the dove, and the barnyard rooster, do they call in vain,
    trying to wake the morrow?
And do you await us, wattled father, Westward?
Will your yell do it?

Take up the trail of the vanished American
Where it disappeared at the foot of the crucifix.
Take up the primordial Indian obstinacy,
The more than human, dense insistence of will,
And disdain, and blankness, and onrush, and prise open the new
    day with them?

The East a dead letter, and Europe moribund . . . Is that so?
And those sombre, dead, feather-lustrous Aztecs, Amerindians,
In all the sinister splendour of their red blood-sacrifices,
Do they stand under the dawn, half-godly, half-demon,
    awaiting the cry of the turkey-cock?

Or must you go through the fire once more, till you're smelted
    pure,
Slag-wattled turkey-cock,
Dross-jabot?[40]

                                                        Fiesole

Humming-Bird

I can imagine, in some otherworld
Primeval-dumb, far back
In that most awful stillness, that only gasped and hummed,
Humming-birds raced down the avenues.

Before anything had a soul,
While life was a heave of Matter, half inanimate,
This little bit chipped off in brilliance
And went whizzing through the slow, vast, succulent
    stems.

I believe there were no flowers then,
In the world where the humming-bird flashed ahead of
    creation.
I believe he pierced the slow vegetable veins with his long beak.

Probably he was big
As mosses, and little lizards, they say, were once big.
Probably he was a jabbing, terrifying monster.

We look at him through the wrong end of the long telescope
    of Time,
Luckily for us.

Española

Eagle in New Mexico

Towards the sun, towards the south-west
A scorched breast.
A scorched breast, breasting the sun like an answer,
Like a retort.

An eagle at the top of a low cedar-bush
On the sage-ash desert
Reflecting the scorch of the sun from his breast;
Eagle, with the sickle dripping darkly above.

Erect, scorched-pallid out of the hair of the cedar,
Erect, with the god-thrust entering him from below,
Eagle gloved in feathers
In scorched white feathers
In burnt dark feathers
In feathers still fire-rusted;
Sickle-overswept, sickle dripping over and above.

Sun-breaster,
Staring two ways at once, to right and left;
Masked-one
Dark-visaged
Sickle-masked
With iron between your two eyes;
You feather-gloved
To the feet;
Foot-fierce;
Erect one;
The god-thrust entering you steadily from below.

You never look at the sun with your two eyes.
Only the inner eye of your scorched broad breast
Looks straight at the sun.

You are dark
Except scorch-pale-breasted;
And dark cleaves down and weapon-hard downward
    curving
At your scorched breast,
Like a sword of Damocles,
Beaked eagle.

You've dipped it in blood so many times
That dark face-weapon, to temper it well,
Blood-thirsty bird.

Why do you front the sun so obstinately,
American eagle?
As if you owed him an old, old grudge, great sun: or an old,
    old allegiance.

When you pick the red smoky heart from a rabbit or a
    light-blooded bird
Do you lift it to the sun, as the Aztec priests used to lift red hearts
    of men?

Does the sun need steam of blood do you think
In America, still,
Old eagle?

Does the sun in New Mexico sail like a fiery bird of prey in the sky
Hovering?

Does he shriek for blood?
Does he fan great wings above the prairie, like a hovering,
    blood-thirsty bird?

And are you his priest, big eagle
Whom the Indians aspire to?
Is there a bond of bloodshed between you?

Is your continent cold from the ice-age still, that the sun is so
    angry?
Is the blood of your continent somewhat reptilian still,
That the sun should be greedy for it?

I don't yield to you, big, jowl-faced eagle.
Nor you nor your blood-thirsty sun
That sucks up blood
Leaving a nervous people.

Fly off, big bird with a big black back.
Fly slowly away, with a rust of fire in your tail,
Dark as you are on your dark side, eagle of heaven.

Even the sun in heaven can be curbed and chastened at last
By the life in the hearts of men.
And you, great bird, sun-starer, heavy black beak
Can be put out of office as sacrifice bringer.

Taos

The Blue Jay

The blue jay with a crest on his head
Comes round the cabin in the snow:
He runs in the snow like a bit of blue metal,
Turning his back on everything.

From the pine tree that towers and hisses like a pillar of shaggy
    cloud
Immense above the cabin
Comes a strident laugh as we approach, this little black dog
    and I.
So halts the little black bitch on four spread paws in the snow
And looks up inquiringly into the pillar of cloud,
With a tinge of misgiving.
Ca-u-a! comes the scrape of ridicule out of the tree.

What voice of the Lord is that, from the tree of smoke?

Oh, Bibbles, little black bitch in the snow,
With a pinch of snow in the groove of your silly snub nose,
What do you look at *me* for?
What do you look at me for, with such misgiving?

It's the blue jay laughing at us.
It's the blue jay jeering at us, Bibs.

Every day since the snow is here
The blue jay paces round the cabin, very busy, picking up bits,

Turning his back on us all,
And bobbing his thick dark crest about the snow, as if darkly
    saying:
I ignore those folk who look out.

You acid-blue metallic bird,
You thick bird with a strong crest,
Who are you?
Whose boss are you, with all your bully way?
You copper-sulphate blue bird!

                                    Lobo

ANIMALS

The Ass

The long-drawn bray of the ass
In the Sicilian twilight –

All mares are dead!
All mares are dead!
Oh-h!
Oh-h-h!
Oh-h-h-h-h – h!!
I can't bear it, I can't bear it.
I can't!
Oh, I can't!
Oh –
There's one left!
There's one left!
One!
There's one . . . left . . .

So ending on a grunt of agonised relief.

This is the authentic Arabic interpretation of the braying
    of the ass.
And Arabs should know.

And yet, as his brass-resonant howling yell resounds
    through the Sicilian twilight
I am not sure –

His big, furry head,
His big, regretful eyes,
His diminished, drooping hindquarters,
His small toes.

Such a dear!
Such an ass!
With such a knot inside him!
He regrets something that he remembers.
That's obvious.

The Steppes of Tartary,
And the wind in his teeth for a bit,
And *noli me tangere*.[41]

Ah then, when he tore the wind with his teeth,
And trod wolves underfoot,
And over-rode his mares as if he were savagely leaping
    an obstacle, to set his teeth in the sun . . .

Somehow, alas, he fell in love,
And was sold into slavery.

He fell into the rut of love,
Poor ass, like man, always in rut,
The pair of them alike in that.

All his soul in his gallant member
And his head gone heavy with the knowledge of desire
And humiliation.

The ass was the first of all animals to fall finally into love,
From obstacle-leaping pride,
Mare obstacle,
Into love, mare-goal, and the knowledge of love.

Hence Jesus rode him in the Triumphant Entry.
Hence his beautiful eyes.
Hence his ponderous head, brooding over desire, and downfall,
    Jesus, and a pack-saddle,
Hence he uncovers his big ass-teeth and howls in that
    agony that is half insatiable desire and half unquenchable
    humiliation.
Hence the black cross on his shoulders.

The Arabs were only half right, though they hinted the whole;
Everlasting lament in everlasting desire.

See him standing with his head down, near the Porta
    Cappuccini,
Asinello, Ciuco,

Somaro;
With the half-veiled, beautiful eyes, and the pensive face
        not asleep,
Motionless, like a bit of rock.

Has he seen the Gorgon's head, and turned to stone?
Alas, Love did it.
Now he's a jackass, a pack-ass, a donkey, somaro, burro,[42] with
        a boss piling loads on his back.
Tied by the nose at the Porta Cappuccini.
And tied in a knot, inside, dead-locked between two desires:
To overleap like a male all mares as obstacles
In a leap at the sun;
And to leap in one last heart-bursting leap like a male at
        the goal of a mare.
And there end.
Well, you can't have it both roads.

Hee! Hee! Ehee! Ehow! Ehaw!! Oh! Oh! Oh-h-h!!
The wave of agony bursts in the stone that he was,
Bares his long ass's teeth, flattens his long ass's ears,
        straightens his donkey neck,
And howls his pandemonium on the indignant air.

Yes, it's a quandary.
Jesus rode on him, the first burden on the first beast of burden.
Love on a submissive ass.
So the tale began.

But the ass never forgets.

The horse, being nothing but a nag, will forget.
And men, being mostly geldings and knacker-boned
        hacks, have almost all forgot.
But the ass is a primal creature, and never forgets.

        The Steppes of Tartary,
        And Jesus on a meek ass-colt: mares: Mary
                escaping to Egypt: Joseph's cudgel.

Hee! Hee! Ehee! Ehow-ow! – ow! – aw! – aw! – aw!
All mares are dead!

Or else I am dead!
One of us, or the pair of us,
I don't know-ow! – ow!
Which!
Not sure-ure-ure
Quite which!
Which!

Taormina

He-Goat

See his black nose snubbed back, pressed over like a whale's blow-
    holes,
As if his nostrils were going to curve back to the root of his tail.

As he charges slow among the herd
And rows among the females like a ship pertinaciously,
Heavy with a rancid cargo, through the lesser ships –
Old father
Sniffing forever ahead of him, at the rear of the goats, that they lift
    the little door,
And rowing on, unarrived, no matter how often he enter:
Like a big ship pushing her bowsprit over the little ships
Then swerving and steering afresh
And never, never arriving at journey's end, at the rear of the female
    ships.

Yellow eyes incomprehensible with thin slits
To round-eyed us.

Yet if you had whorled horns of bronze in a frontal dark wall
At the end of a back-bone ridge, like a straight *sierra roqueña*,[43]
And nerves urging forward to the wall, you'd have eyes like his,
Especially if, being given a needle's eye of egress elsewhere
You tried to look back to it, and couldn't.

Sometimes he turns with a start, to fight, to challenge, to suddenly
    butt.
Arid then you see the God that he is, in a cloud of black hair
And storm-lightning-slitted eye.
Splendidly planting his feet, one rocky foot striking the
    ground with a sudden rock-hammer announcement.

I am here!
And suddenly lowering his head, the whorls of bone and of horn
Slowly revolving towards unexploded explosion,
As from the stem of his bristling, lightning-conductor tail
In a rush up the shrieking duct of his vertebral way
Runs a rage drawn in from the ether divinely through him
Towards a shock and a crash and a smiting of horns ahead.

That is a grand old lust of his, to gather the great
Rage of the sullen-stagnating atmosphere of goats
And bring it hurtling to a head, with crash of horns against the
    horns
Of the opposite enemy goat,
Thus hammering the mettle of goats into proof, and smiting out
The godhead of goats from the shock.

Things of iron are beaten on the anvil,
And he-goat is anvil to he-goat, and hammer to he-goat
In the business of beating the mettle of goats to a godhead.

But they've taken his enemy from him
And left him only his libidinousness,
His nostrils turning back, to sniff at even himself
And his slitted eyes seeking the needle's eye,
His own, unthreaded, forever.

So it is, when they take the enemy from us,
And we can't fight.

He is not fatherly, like the bull, massive Providence of hot blood;
The goat is an egoist, aware of himself, devilish aware of himself,
And full of malice prepense, and overweening, determined to stand
    on the highest peak
Like the devil, and look on the world as his own.

And as for love:
With a needle of long red flint he stabs in the dark
At the living rock he is up against;
While she with her goaty mouth stands smiling the while as
    he strikes, since sure
He will never *quite* strike home, on the target-quick, for her quick
Is just beyond range of the arrow he shoots
From his leap at the zenith in her, so it falls just short of the mark,
    far enough.
It is over before it is finished.
She, smiling with goaty munch-mouth, Mona Lisa, arranges it so.

Orgasm after orgasm after orgasm
And he smells so rank and his nose goes back,
And never an enemy brow-metalled to thresh it out with in
    the open field;
Never a mountain peak, to be king of the castle.
Only those eternal females to overleap and surpass, and never
    succeed.

The involved voluptuousness of the soft-footed cat
Who is like a fur folding a fur,
The cat who laps blood, and knows
The soft welling of blood invincible even beyond bone or metal
    of bone.

The soft, the secret, the unfathomable blood
The cat has lapped;
And known it subtler than frisson-shaken nerves,
Stronger than multiplicity of bone on bone,
And darker than even the arrows of violentest will
Can pierce, for that is where will gives out, like a sinking stone
    that can sink no further.

But he-goat,
Black procreant male of the selfish will and libidinous desire,
God in black cloud with curving horns of bronze,
Find an enemy, Egoist, and clash the cymbals in face-to-face
    defiance,
And let the lightning out of your smothered dusk.

Forget the female herd for a bit,
And fight to be boss of the world.

Fight, old Satan with a selfish will, fight for your selfish will;
Fight to be the devil on the tip of the peak
Overlooking the world for his own.

But bah, how can he, poor domesticated beast!

Taormina

She-Goat

Goats go past the back of the house like dry leaves in the dawn,
And up the hill like a river, if you watch.

At dusk they patter back like a bough being dragged on the ground,
Raising dusk and acridity of goats, and bleating.

Our old goat we tie up at night in the shed at the back of the broken
      Greek tomb in the garden,
And when the herd goes by at dawn she begins to bleat for me to come
      down and untie her.

Merr-err-err! Merr-err-err! Mer! Mé!
— Wait, wait a bit, I'll come when I've lit the fire.
Merrr!
— Exactly.
Mé! Mer! Merrrrrrr!!!!
— Tace, tu, crapa, bestia![44]
Merr-ererr-ererrrr! Merrrr!

She is such an alert listener, with her ears wide, to know am I coming!
Such a canny listener, from a distance, looking upwards, lending first
      one ear, then another.

There she is, perched on her manger, looking over the boards into the
      day
Like a belle at her window.
And immediately she sees me she blinks, stares, doesn't know me,
      turns her head and ignores me vulgarly with a wooden blank
      on her face.

What do I care for her, the ugly female, standing up there with her
　　long tangled sides like an old rug thrown over a fence.
But she puts her nose down shrewdly enough when the knot is untied,
And jumps staccato to earth, a sharp, dry jump, still ignoring me,
Pretending to look round the stall.

Come on, you, crapa! I'm not your servant!

She turns her head away with an obtuse, female sort of deafness, bête.
And then invariably she crouches her rear and makes water.
That being her way of answer, if I speak to her. – Self-conscious!
Le bestie non parlano, poverine![45]

She was bought at Giardini fair, on the sands, for six hundred lire.

An obstinate old witch, almost jerking the rope from my hands to eat
　　the acanthus, or bite at the almond buds, and make me wait.
Yet the moment I hate her she trips mild and smug like a woman going
　　to mass.
The moment I really detest her.

Queer it is, suddenly, in the garden
To catch sight of her standing like some huge, ghoulish grey bird
　　in the air, on the bough of the leaning almond tree,
Straight as a board on the bough, looking down like some hairy horrid
　　God the Father in a William Blake imagination.
Come down, crapa, out of that almond tree!

Instead of which she strangely rears on her perch in the air, vast beast,
And strangely paws the air, delicate,
And reaches her black-striped face up like a snake, far up,
Subtly, to the twigs overhead, far up, vast beast,
And snaps them sharp, with a little twist of her anaconda head;
All her great hairy-shaggy belly open against the morning.

At seasons she curls back her tail like a green leaf in the fire,
Or like a lifted hand, hailing at her wrong end.
And having exposed the pink place of her nakedness, fixedly,
She trots on blithe toes,
And if you look at her, she looks back with a cold, sardonic stare.

Sardonic, sardonyx, rock of cold fire.
See me? She says, *That's me!*

That's her.

Then she leaps the rocks like a quick rock,
Her backbone sharp as a rock,
Sheer will.

Along which ridge of libidinous magnetism
Defiant, curling the leaf of her tail as if she were curling her lip behind
    her at all life,
Libidinous desire runs back and forth, asserting itself in that little lifted
    bare hand.

Yet she has such adorable spurty kids, like spurts of black ink.
And in a month again is as if she had never had them.

And when the billy goat mounts her
She is brittle as brimstone.
While his slitted eyes squint back to the roots of his ears.

Taormina

Elephant

You go down shade to the river, where naked men sit on flat
    brown rocks, to watch the ferry, in the sun;
And you cross the ferry with the naked people, go up the tropical lane
Through the palm trees and past hollow paddy-fields where naked men
    are threshing rice
And the monolithic water-buffaloes, like old, muddy stones with hair
    on them, are being idle;
And through the shadow of bread-fruit trees, with their dark green,
    glossy, fanged leaves
Very handsome, and some pure yellow fanged leaves;
Out into the open, where the path runs on the top of a dyke between
    paddy-fields:
And there, of course, you meet a huge and mud-grey elephant
    advancing his frontal bone, his trunk curled round a log of wood:
So you step down the bank, to make way.

Shuffle, shuffle, and his little wicked eye has seen you as he advances
    above you,
The slow beast curiously spreading his round feet for the dust.
And the slim naked man slips down, and the beast deposits the lump
    of wood, carefully.
The keeper hooks the vast knee, the creature salaams.

White man, you are saluted.
Pay a few cents.

But the best is the Pera-hera, at midnight, under the tropical stars,
With a pale little wisp of a Prince of Wales, diffident, up in a small
    pagoda on the temple side
And white people in evening dress buzzing and crowding the
    stand upon the grass below and opposite:
And at last the Pera-hera procession, flambeaux aloft in the
    tropical night, of blazing cocoa-nut,
Naked dark men beneath,
And the huge frontal of three great elephants stepping forth to the tom-
    tom's beat, in the torch-light,
Slowly sailing in gorgeous apparel through the flame-light, in front of a
    towering, grimacing white image of wood.

The elephant bells striking slow, tong-tong, tong-tong,
To music and queer chanting:
Enormous shadow-processions filing on in the flare of fire
In the fume of cocoa-nut oil, in the sweating tropical night,
In the noise of the tom-toms and singers;
Elephants after elephants curl their trunks, vast shadows, and
    some cry out
As they approach and salaam, under the dripping fire of the torches,
That pale fragment of a Prince up there, whose motto is *Ich dien*.[46]

Pale, dispirited Prince, with his chin on his hands, his nerves tired out,
Watching and hardly seeing the trunk-curl approach and clumsy, knee-
    lifting salaam
Of the hugest, oldest of beasts in the night and the fire-flare below.
He is royalty, pale and dejected fragment up aloft.
And down below huge homage of shadowy beasts; barefoot and trunk-
    lipped in the night.

Chieftains, three of them abreast, on foot
Strut like peg-tops, wound around with hundreds of yards of fine linen.
They glimmer with tissue of gold, and golden threads on a jacket
    of velvet,
And their faces are dark, and fat, and important.
They are royalty, dark-faced royalty, showing the conscious whites of
    their eyes
And stepping in homage, stubborn, to that nervous pale lad up there.

More elephants, tong, tong-tong, loom up,
Huge, more tassels swinging, more dripping fire of new cocoa-nut
    cressets
High, high flambeaux, smoking of the east;
And scarlet hot embers of torches knocked out of the sockets among
    bare feet of elephants and men on the path in the dark.
And devil-dancers luminous with sweat, dancing on to the shudder of
    drums,
Tom-toms, weird music of the devil, voices of men from the jungle
    singing;
Endless, under the Prince.

Towards the tail of the everlasting procession
In the long hot night, more dancers from insignificant villages,
And smaller, more frightened elephants.

Men-peasants from jungle villages dancing and running with sweat and
    laughing,
Naked dark men with ornaments on, on their naked arms and
    their naked breasts, the grooved loins
Gleaming like metal with running sweat as they suddenly turn, feet
    apart,
And dance, and dance, forever dance, with breath half sobbing in dark,
    · sweat-shining breasts,
And lustrous great tropical eyes unveiled now, gleaming a kind of
    laugh,
A naked, gleaming dark laugh, like a secret out in the dark,
And flare of a tropical energy, tireless, afire in the dark, slim limbs and
    breasts,
Perpetual, fire-laughing motion, among the slow shuffle
Of elephants,
The hot dark blood of itself a-laughing, wet, half-devilish, men all
    motion
Approaching under that small pavilion, and tropical eyes dilated
    look up
Inevitably look up
To the Prince
To that tired remnant of royalty up there
Whose motto is *Ich dien*.

As if the homage of the kindled blood of the east
Went up in wavelets to him, from the breasts and eyes of jungle
    torch-men,
And he couldn't take it.

What would they do, those jungle men running with sweat, with the
    strange dark laugh in their eyes, glancing up,
And the sparse-haired elephants slowly following,
If they knew that his motto was *Ich dien*?
And that he meant it.

They begin to understand.
The rickshaw boys begin to understand.

And then the devil comes into their faces
But a different sort, a cold, rebellious, jeering devil.

In elephants and the east are two devils, in all men maybe.
The mystery of the dark mountain of blood, reeking in homage, in lust,
      in rage,
And passive with everlasting patience,
Then the little, cunning pig-devil of the elephant's lurking eyes,
      the unbeliever.

We dodged, when the Pera-hera was finished, under the hanging, hairy
      pigs' tails
And the flat, flaccid mountains of the elephants' standing haunches,
Vast-blooded beasts,
Myself so little dodging rather scared against the eternal wrinkled
      pillars of their legs, as they were being dismantled;
Then I knew they were dejected, having come to hear the repeated
Royal summons: *Dient Ihr!*
Serve!
Serve, vast mountainous blood, in submission and splendour,
      serve royalty.
Instead of which, the silent, fatal emission from that pale, shattered
      boy up there:
Ich dien.

That's why the night fell in frustration.
That's why, as the elephants ponderously, with unseeming swiftness,
      galloped uphill in the night, going back to the jungle villages,
As the elephant bells sounded tong-tong-tong, bell of the temple
      of blood in the night, swift-striking,
And the crowd like a field of rice in the dark gave way like liquid
      to the dark
Looming gallop of the beasts,
It was as if the great bulks of elephants in the obscure light went over
      the hill-brow swiftly, with their tails between their legs,
      in haste to get away,
Their bells sounding frustrate and sinister.

And all the dark-faced, cotton-wrapped people, more numerous and
      whispering than grains of rice in a rice-field at night,
All the dark-faced, cotton-wrapped people, a countless host on the
      shores of the lake, like thick wild rice by the water's edge,

Waiting for the fireworks of the after-show,
As the rockets went up, and the glare passed over countless faces, dark
    as black rice growing,
Showing a glint of teeth, and glancing tropical eyes aroused in the
    night,
There was the faintest twist of mockery in every face, across the
    hiss of wonders as the rocket burst
High, high up, in flakes, shimmering flakes of blue fire, above the palm
    trees of the islet in the lake,
O faces upturned to the glare, O tropical wonder, wonder, a miracle in
    heaven!
And the shadow of a jeer, of underneath disappointment, as the rocket-
    coruscation died, and shadow was the same as before.

They were foiled, the myriad whispering dark-faced
    cotton-wrapped people.
They had come to see royalty,
To bow before royalty, in the land of elephants, bow deep, bow deep.
Bow deep, for it's good as a draught of cool water to bow very, very low
    to the royal.

And all there was to bow to, a weary, diffident boy whose motto is *Ich
    dien.*
I serve! I serve! in all the weary irony of his mien – *'Tis I who serve!*
Drudge to the public.

I wish they had given the three feathers to me;
That I had been he in the pavilion, as in a pepper-box aloft and alone
To stand and hold feathers, three feathers above the world,
And say to them: *Dient Ihr! Dient!*
Omnes, vos omnes, servite.[47]
Serve me, I am meet to be served.
Being royal of the gods.

And to the elephants:
First great beasts of the earth,
A prince has come back to you,
Blood-mountains.
Crook the knee and be glad.

                                                Kandy

Kangaroo

In the northern hemisphere
Life seems to leap at the air, or skim under the wind
Like stags on rocky ground, or pawing horses, or springy scut-tailed
    rabbits.

Or else rush horizontal to charge at the sky's horizon,
Like bulls or bisons or wild pigs.

Or slip like water slippery towards its ends,
As foxes, stoats, and wolves, and prairie dogs.

Only mice, and moles, and rats, and badgers, and beavers, and perhaps
    bears
Seem belly-plumbed to the earth's mid-navel.
Or frogs that when they leap come flop, and flop to the centre of the
    earth.

But the yellow antipodal Kangaroo, when she sits up,
Who can unseat her, like a liquid drop that is heavy, and just touches
    earth.

The downward drip
The down-urge.
So much denser than cold-blooded frogs.

Delicate mother Kangaroo
Sitting up there rabbit-wise, but huge, plumb-weighted,
And lifting her beautiful slender face, oh! so much more gently and
    finely lined than a rabbit's, or than a hare's,
Lifting her face to nibble at a round white peppermint drop, which she
    loves, sensitive mother Kangaroo.

Her sensitive, long, pure-bred face.
Her full antipodal eyes, so dark,
So big and quiet and remote, having watched so many empty dawns in
    silent Australia.

Her little loose hands, and drooping Victorian shoulders. And then her
    great weight below the waist, her vast pale belly
With a thin young yellow little paw hanging out, and straggle of a long
    thin ear, like ribbon,
Like a funny trimming to the middle of her belly, thin little dangle of
    an immature paw, and one thin ear.

Her belly, her big haunches
And, in addition, the great muscular python-stretch of her tail.

There, she shan't have any more peppermint drops.
So she wistfully, sensitively sniffs the air, and then turns, goes off
    in slow sad leaps

On the long flat skis of her legs,
Steered and propelled by that steel-strong snake of a tail.

Stops again, half turns, inquisitive to look back.
While something stirs quickly in her belly, and a lean little face comes
    out, as from a window,
Peaked and a bit dismayed,
Only to disappear again quickly away from the sight of the world, to
    snuggle down in the warmth,
Leaving the trail of a different paw hanging out.

Still she watches with eternal, cocked wistfulness!
How full her eyes are, like the full, fathomless, shining eyes of an
    Australian black-boy
Who has been lost so many centuries on the margins of existence!

She watches with insatiable wistfulness.
Untold centuries of watching for something to come,
For a new signal from life, in that silent lost land of the South.

Where nothing bites but insects and snakes and the sun, small life.
Where no bull roared, no cow ever lowed, no stag cried, no
    leopard screeched, no lion coughed, no dog barked,
But all was silent save for parrots occasionally, in the haunted blue
    bush.

Wistfully watching, with wonderful liquid eyes.
And all her weight, all her blood, dripping sack-wise down towards the
    earth's centre,
And the live little-one taking in its paw at the door of her belly.

Leap then, and come down on the line that draws to the earth's deep,
    heavy centre.

                                    Sydney

Bibbles

Bibbles,
Little black dog in New Mexico,
Little black snub-nosed bitch with a shoved-out jaw
And a wrinkled reproachful look;
Little black female pup, sort of French bull, they say,
With bits of brindle coming through, like rust, to show you're not
    pure;
Not pure, Bibbles,
Bubsey, bat-eared dog;
Not black enough!

First live thing I've 'owned' since the lop-eared rabbits when
    I was a lad,
And those over-prolific white mice, and Adolph, and Rex
    whom I didn't own.
And even now, Bibbles, little Ma'am, it's you who appropriated me,
    not I you.
As Benjamin Franklin appropriated Providence to his purposes.

Oh Bibbles, black little bitch,
I'd never have let you appropriate me, had I known.
I never dreamed, till now, of the awful time the Lord must
    have, 'owning' humanity,
Especially democratic live-by-love humanity.

Oh Bibbles, oh Pips, oh Pipsey,
You little black love-bird!
Don't you love *everybody*!

Just everybody.
You love 'em all.
Believe in the One Identity, don't you,
You little Walt-Whitmanesque bitch?
First time I lost you in Taos plaza,
And found you after endless chasing,
Came upon you prancing round the corner in exuberant, bibbling affection
After the black-green skirts of a yellow-green old Mexican woman
Who hated you, and kept looking round at you and cursing you in a mutter,
While you pranced and bounced with love of her, you indiscriminating animal,
All your wrinkled *miserere*[48] Chinese black little face beaming
And your black little body bouncing and wriggling
With indiscriminate love, Bibbles;
I had a moment's pure detestation of you.

As I rushed like an idiot round the corner after you
Yelling: *Pips! Pips! Bibbles!*

I've had moments of hatred of you since,
Loving everybody!
'To you, whoever you are, with endless embrace!' –
That's you, Pipsey,
With your imbecile bit of a tail in a love-flutter.
You omnipip.

Not that you're merely a softy, oh dear me, no.
You know which side your bread is buttered.
You don't care a rap for anybody.
But you love lying warm between warm human thighs, indiscriminate,
And you love to make somebody love you, indiscriminate,
You love to lap up affection, to wallow in it,
And then turn tail to the next comer, for a new dollop.

And start prancing and licking and cuddling again, indiscriminate.
Oh yes, I know your little game.

Yet you're so nice,
So quick, like a little black dragon.
So fierce, when the coyotes howl, barking like a whole little lion,
    and rumbling,
And starting forward in the dusk, with your little black fur all
    bristling like plush
Against those coyotes, who would swallow you like an oyster.

And in the morning, when the bedroom door is opened,
Rushing in like a little black whirlwind, leaping straight as an arrow
    on the bed at the pillow
And turning the day suddenly into a black tornado of *joie de vivre*,
    Chinese dragon.

So funny
Lobbing wildly through deep snow like a rabbit,
Hurtling like a black ball through the snow,
Champing it, tossing a mouthful,
Little black spot in the landscape!

So absurd
Pelting behind on the dusty trail when the horse sets off home at a
    gallop:
Left in the dust behind like a dust-ball tearing along,
Coming up on fierce little legs, tearing fast to catch up, a real little
    dust-pig, ears almost blown away,
And black eyes bulging bright in a dust-mask
Chinese-dragon-wrinkled, with a pink mouth grinning, under jaw
    shoved out
And white teeth showing in your dragon-grin as you race, you split-
    face,
Like a trundling projectile swiftly whirling up,
Cocking your eyes at me as you come alongside, to see if I'm
    I on the horse,
And panting with that split grin,
All your game little body dust-smooth like a little pig, poor Pips.

Plenty of game old spirit in you, Bibbles.
Plenty of game old spunk, little bitch.

How you hate being brushed with the boot-brush, to brush all that
    dust out of your wrinkled face,
Don't you?
How you hate being made to look undignified, Ma'am;
How you hate being laughed at, Miss Superb!

Blackberry face!

Plenty of conceit in you.
Unblemished belief in your own perfection
And utter lovableness, you ugly-mug;
Chinese puzzle-face,
Wrinkled underhung physiog that looks as if it had done with
    everything,
Through with everything.

Instead of which you sit there and roll your head like a canary
And show a tiny bunch of white teeth in your underhung
    blackness,
Self-conscious little bitch,
Aiming again at being loved.

Let the merest scallywag come to the door, and you leap your very
    dearest love at him,
As if now, at last, here was the one you *finally* loved,
Finally loved;
And even the dirtiest scallywag is taken in,
Thinking: *This dog sure has taken a fancy to me.*

You miserable little bitch of love-tricks,
I know your game.

Me or the Mexican who comes to chop wood
All the same,
All humanity is jam to you.

Everybody so dear, and yourself so ultra-beloved
That you have to run out at last and eat filth,
Gobble up filth, you horror, swallow utter abomination and fresh-
    dropped dung.

You stinker.
You worse than a carrion-crow.
Reeking dung-mouth.
You love-bird.

Reject nothing, sings Walt Whitman.
So you, you go out at last and eat the unmentionable,
In your appetite for affection.

And then you run in to vomit it in my house!
I get my love back.
And I have to clean up after you, filth which even blind Nature
    rejects
From the pit of your stomach;
But you, you snout-face, you reject nothing, you merge so
    much in love
You must eat even that.

Then when I dust you a bit with a juniper twig
You run straight away to live with somebody else,
Fawn before them, and love them as if they were the ones you had
    really loved all along.
And they're taken in.
They feel quite tender over you, till you play the same trick on
    them, dirty bitch.

Fidelity! Loyalty! Attachment!
Oh, these are abstractions to your nasty little belly.
You must always be a-waggle with LOVE.
Such a waggle of love you can hardly distinguish one human from
    another.

You love one after another, on one condition, that each one loves
    you most.
Democratic little bull-bitch, dirt-eating little swine.

But now, my lass, you've got Nemesis on your track,
Now you've come sex-alive, and the great ranch-dogs are all after
    you.
They're after what they can get, and don't you turn tail!

You loved 'em all so much before, didn't you, loved 'em
 indiscriminate.
You don't love 'em now.
They want something of you, so you squeak and come pelting
 indoors.

Come pelting to me, now the other folk have found you out, and
 the dogs are after you.
Oh yes, you're found out. I heard them kick you out of the ranch
 house.
Get out, you little, soft fool!!

And didn't you turn your eyes up at me then?
And didn't you cringe on the floor like any inkspot!
And crawl away like a black snail!
And doesn't everybody loathe you then!
And aren't your feelings violated, you high-bred little
 love-bitch!

For you're sensitive,
In many ways very finely bred.
But bred in conceit that the world is all for love
Of you, my bitch: till you get so far you eat filth.
Fool, in spite of your pretty ways, and quaint, know-all, wrinkled
 old aunty's face.

So now, what with great Airedale dogs,
And a kick or two,
And a few vomiting bouts,
And a juniper switch,
You look at me for discrimination, don't you?
Look up at me with misgiving in your bulging eyes,
And fear in the smoky whites of your eyes, you nigger;
And you're puzzled,
You think you'd better mind your P's and Q's for a bit,
Your sensitive love-pride being all hurt.

All right, my little bitch.
You learn loyalty rather than loving,
And I'll protect you.

          Lobo

Mountain Lion

Climbing through the January snow, into the Lobo canyon
Dark grow the spruce trees, blue is the balsam, water sounds still
    unfrozen, and the trail is still evident.

Men!
Two men!
Men! The only animal in the world to fear!

They hesitate.
We hesitate.
They have a gun.
We have no gun.

Then we all advance, to meet.

Two Mexicans, strangers, emerging out of the dark and snow and
    inwardness of the Lobo valley.
What are they doing here on this vanishing trail?

What is he carrying?
Something yellow.
A deer?

Qué tiene, amigo?
León – [49]

He smiles, foolishly, as if he were caught doing wrong.
And we smile, foolishly, as if we didn't know.
He is quite gentle and dark-faced.

It is a mountain lion,
A long, long slim cat, yellow like a lioness.
Dead.

He trapped her this morning, he says, smiling foolishly.

Lift up her face,
Her round, bright face, bright as frost.
Her round, fine-fashioned head, with two dead ears;
And stripes in the brilliant frost of her face, sharp, fine dark rays,
Dark, keen, fine rays in the brilliant frost of her face.
Beautiful dead eyes.

Hermoso es![50]

They go out towards the open;
We go on into the gloom of Lobo.
And above the trees I found her lair,
A hole in the blood-orange brilliant rocks that stick up, a little cave.
And bones, and twigs, and a perilous ascent.

So, she will never leap up that way again, with the yellow flash of a
    mountain lion's long shoot!
And her bright striped frost-face will never watch any more,
    out of the shadow of the cave in the blood-orange rock,
Above the trees of the Lobo dark valley-mouth!

Instead, I look out.
And out to the dim of the desert, like a dream, never real;
To the snow of the Sangre de Cristo mountains, the ice of the
    mountains of Picoris,
And near across at the opposite steep of snow, green trees
    motionless standing in snow, like a Christmas toy.

And I think in this empty world there was room for me and a
    mountain lion.
And I think in the world beyond, how easily we might spare a
    million or two of humans
And never miss them.
Yet what a gap in the world, the missing white frost-face of that
    slim yellow mountain lion!

Lobo

The Red Wolf

Over the heart of the west, the Taos desert,
Circles an eagle,
And it's dark between me and him.

The sun, as he waits a moment, huge and liquid
Standing without feet on the rim of the far-off mesa

Says: *Look for a last long time then! Look! Look well! I am going.*
So he pauses and is beholden, and straightway is gone.

And the Indian, in a white sheet
Wrapped to the eyes, the sheet bound close on his brows,
Stands saying: *See, I'm invisible!*
Behold how you can't behold me!
The invisible in its shroud!

Now that the sun has gone, and the aspen leaves
And the cotton-wood leaves are fallen, as good as fallen,
And the ponies are in corral,
And it's night.

Why, more has gone than all these;
And something has come.
A red wolf stands on the shadow's dark red rim.

Day has gone to dust on the sage-grey desert
Like a white Christus fallen to dust from a cross;
To dust, to ash, on the twilit floor of the desert.

And a black crucifix like a dead tree spreading wings;
Maybe a black eagle with its wings out
Left lonely in the night
In a sort of worship.

And coming down upon us, out of the dark concave
Of the eagle's wings,
And the coffin-like slit where the Indian's eyes are,
And the absence of cotton-wood leaves, or of aspen,
Even the absence of dark-crossed donkeys:
Come tall old demons, smiling
The Indian smile,
Saying: *How do you do, you pale-face?*

I am very well, old demon.
How are you?

Call me Harry if you will,
Call me Old Harry, says he.
Or the abbreviation of Nicolas,
Nick, Old Nick, maybe.

Well, you're a dark old demon,
And I'm a pale-face like a homeless dog
That has followed the sun from the dawn through the east,
Trotting east and east and east till the sun himself went home,
And left me homeless here in the dark at your door.
How do you think we'll get on,
Old demon, you and I?

You and I, you pale-face,
Pale-face you and I
Don't get on.

Mightn't we try?

Where's your God, you white one?
Where's your white God?

He fell to dust as the twilight fell,
Was fume as I trod
The last step out of the east.

Then you're a lost white dog of a pale-face,
And the day's now dead . . .

Touch me carefully, old father,
My beard is red.

Thin red wolf of a pale-face,
Thin red wolf, go home.

I have no home, old father,
That's why I come.

We take no hungry stray from the pale-face . . .

Father, you are not asked.
I am come. I am here. The red-dawn-wolf
Sniffs round your place.
Lifts up his voice and howls to the walls of the pueblo,
Announcing he's here.

The dogs of the dark pueblo
Have long fangs . . .

Has the red wolf trotted east and east and east
From the far, far other end of the day
To fear a few fangs?

Across the pueblo river
That dark old demon and I
Thus say a few words to each other

And wolf, he calls me, and red.
I call him no names.
He says, however, he is Star-Road.
I say, he can go back the same gait.

As for me . . .
Since I trotted at the tail of the sun as far as ever the
     creature went west,
And lost him here,
I'm going to sit down on my tail right here
And wait for him to come back with a new story.
I'm the red wolf, says the dark old father.
All right, the red-dawn-wolf I am.

                                             Taos

GHOSTS

Men in New Mexico

Mountains blanket-wrapped
Round a white hearth of desert –

While the sun goes round
And round and round the desert,
The mountains never get up and walk about.
They can't, they can't wake.

They camped and went to sleep
In the last twilight
Of Indian gods;
And they can't wake.

Indians dance and run and stamp –
No good.
White men make gold-mines and the mountains unmake them
In their sleep.

The Indians laugh in their sleep
From fear,
Like a man when he sleeps and his sleep is over, and he can't
     wake up,
And he lies like a log and screams and his scream is silent
Because his body can't wake up;
So he laughs from fear, pure fear, in the grip of the sleep.

A dark membrane over the will, holding a man down
Even when the mind has flickered awake;
A membrane of sleep, like a black blanket.

We walk in our sleep, in this land,
Somnambulist wide-eyed afraid.

We scream for someone to wake us
And our scream is soundless in the paralysis of sleep,
And we know it.

The Penitentes lash themselves till they run with blood
In their efforts to come awake for one moment;
To tear the membrane of this sleep . . .
No good.

The Indians thought the white man would awake them . . .
And instead, the white men scramble asleep in the mountains,
And ride on horseback asleep forever through the desert,
And shoot one another, amazed and mad with somnambulism,
Thinking death will awaken something . . .
No good.

Born with a caul,
A black membrane over the face,
And unable to tear it,
Though the mind is awake.

Mountains blanket-wrapped
Round the ash-white hearth of the desert;
And though the sun leaps like a thing unleashed in the sky
They can't get up, they are under the blanket.

Taos

Autumn at Taos

Over the rounded sides of the Rockies, the aspens of autumn,
The aspens of autumn,
Like yellow hair of a tigress brindled with pines.

Down on my hearth-rug of desert, sage of the mesa,
An ash-grey pelt
Of wolf all hairy and level, a wolf's wild pelt.

Trot-trot to the mottled foot-hills, cedar-mottled and pinon;
Did you ever see an otter?
Silvery-sided, fish-fanged, fierce-faced, whiskered, mottled.

When I trot my little pony through the aspen trees of the canyon,
Behold me trotting at ease betwixt the slopes of the golden

Great and glistening-feathered legs of the hawk of Horus;
The golden hawk of Horus
Astride above me.

But under the pines
I go slowly
As under the hairy belly of a great black bear.

Glad to emerge and look back
On the yellow, pointed aspen trees laid one on another like
    feathers,
Feather over feather on the breast of the great and golden
Hawk as I say of Horus.

Pleased to be out in the sage and the pine fish-dotted foothills,
Past the otter's whiskers,
On to the fur of the wolf-pelt that strews the plain.

And then to look back to the rounded sides of the squatting
    Rockies,
Tigress brindled with aspen,
Jaguar-splashed, puma-yellow, leopard-livid slopes of America.

Make big eyes, little pony,
At all these skins of wild beasts;
They won't hurt you.

Fangs and claws and talons and beaks and hawk-eyes
Are nerveless just now.
So be easy.

Taos

Spirits Summoned West

England seems full of graves to me,
Full of graves.

Women I loved and cherished, like my mother;
Yet I had to tell them to die.

England seems covered with graves to me,
Women's graves.

Women who were gentle
And who loved me
And whom I loved
And told to die.

Women with the beautiful eyes of the old days,
Belief in love, and sorrow of such belief.
'Hush, my love, then, hush.
Hush, and die, my dear!'

Women of the older generation, who knew
The full doom of loving and not being able to take back.
Who understood at last what it was to be told to die.

Now that the graves are made, and covered;
Now that in England pansies and such-like grow on the graves
    of women;
Now that in England is silence, where before was a moving of
    soft-skirted women,
Women with eyes that were gentle in olden belief in love;
Now then that all their yearning is hushed, and covered
    over with earth.

England seems like one grave to me.

And I, I sit on this high American desert
With dark-wrapped Rocky Mountains motionless
    squatting around in a ring,
Remembering I told them to die, to sink into the grave in
    England,
The gentle-kneed women.

So now I whisper: *Come away,*
Come away from the place of graves, come west,
Women,
Women whom I loved and told to die.

Come back to me now,
Now the divided yearning is over;
Now you are husbandless indeed, no more husband to cherish like a
  child
And wrestle with for the prize of perfect love.
No more children to launch in a world you mistrust.
Now you need know in part
No longer, or carry the burden of a man on your heart,
Or the burden of Man writ large.

Now you are disemburdened of Man and a man
Come back to me.
Now you are free of the toils of a would-be-perfect love
Come to me and be still.

Come back then, you who were wives and mothers
And always virgins
Overlooked.

Come back then, mother, my love, whom I told to die.
It was only I who saw the virgin you
That had no home.

The overlooked virgin,
My love.

You overlooked her too.

Now that the grave is made of mother and wife,
Now that the grave is made and lidded over with turf:

Come, delicate, overlooked virgin, come back to me
And be still,
Be glad.

I didn't tell you to die, for nothing.
I wanted the virgin you to be home at last
In my heart.

Inside my innermost heart,
Where the virgin in woman comes home to a man.

The homeless virgin
Who never in all her life could find the way home
To that difficult innermost place in a man.

Now come west, come home,
Women I've loved for gentleness,
For the virginal you.
Find the way now that you never could find in life,
So I told you to die.

Virginal first and last
Is woman.
Now at this last, my love, my many a love,
You whom I loved for gentleness,
Come home to me.

They are many, and I loved them, shall always love them,
And they know it,
The virgins.
And my heart is glad to have them at last.

Now that the wife and mother and mistress is buried in earth,
In English earth,
Come home to me, my love, my loves, my many loves,
Come west to me.

For virgins are not exclusive of virgins
As wives are of wives;
And motherhood is jealous,
But in virginity jealousy does not enter.

Taos

The American Eagle

The dove of Liberty sat on an egg
And hatched another eagle.

But didn't disown the bird.

Down with all eagles! cooed the Dove.
And down all eagles began to flutter, reeling from their perches:
Eagles with two heads, eagles with one, presently eagles with none
Fell from the hooks and were dead.

Till the American Eagle was the only eagle left in the world.

Then it began to fidget, shifting from one leg to the other,
Trying to look like a pelican,
And plucking out of his plumage a few loose feathers to feather the
     nests of all
The new naked little republics come into the world.

But the feathers were, comparatively, a mere flea-bite.
And the bub-eagle that Liberty had hatched was growing a startling
     big bird
On the roof of the world;
A bit awkward, and with a funny squawk in his voice,
His mother Liberty trying always to teach him to coo
And him always ending with a yawp
Coo! Coo! Coo! Coo-ark! Coo-ark! Quark!! Quark!!
YAWP!!!

So he clears his throat, the young Cock-eagle!
Now if the lilies of France lick Solomon in all his glory;
And the leopard cannot change his spots;
Nor the British lion his appetite;
Neither can a young Cock-eagle sit simpering
With an olive-sprig in his mouth.

It's not his nature.

The big bird of the Amerindian being the eagle,
Red Men still stick themselves over with bits of his fluff,
And feel absolutely IT.

So better make up your mind, American Eagle,
Whether you're a sucking dove, *Roo – coo – ooo! Quark!*
    Yawp!!
Or a pelican
Handing out a few loose golden breast-feathers, at moulting time;
Or a sort of prosperity-gander
Fathering endless ten-dollar golden eggs.

Or whether it actually is an eagle you are,
With a Roman nose
And claws not made to shake hands with,
And a Me-Almighty eye.

The new Proud Republic
Based on the mystery of pride.
Overweening men, full of power of life, commanding a teeming
    obedience.

Eagle of the Rockies, bird of men that are masters,
Lifting the rabbit-blood of the myriads up into something splendid,
Leaving a few bones;
Opening great wings in the face of the sheep-faced ewe
Who is losing her lamb,
Drinking a little blood, and loosing another royalty unto the world.

Is that you, American Eagle?

Or are you the goose that lays the golden egg?
Which is just a stone to anyone asking for meat.
And are you going to go on for ever
Laying that golden egg,
That addled golden egg?

Lobo

PANSIES

Our Day is Over

Our day is over, night comes up
shadows steal out of the earth.
Shadows, shadows
wash over our knees and splash between our thighs,
our day is done;
we wade, we wade, we stagger, darkness rushes between
    our stones,
we shall drown.

Our day is over
night comes up.

Hark in the Dusk!

Hark! in the dusk
voices, gurgling like water
wreathe strong weed round the knees, as the darkness
lifts us off our feet.

As the current
thrusts warm through the loins, so the little one
wildly floats, swirls,
and the flood strikes the belly, and we are gone.

Elephants in the Circus

Elephants in the circus
have aeons of weariness round their eyes.
Yet they sit up
and show vast bellies to the children.

Elephants Plodding

Plod! Plod!
And what ages of time
the worn arches of their spines support!

On the Drum

The huge old female on the drum
shuffles gingerly round
and smiles; the vastness of her elephant antiquity
is amused.

Two Performing Elephants

He stands with his forefeet on the drum
and the other, the old one, the pallid hoary female
must creep her great bulk beneath the bridge of him.

On her knees, in utmost caution
all agog, and curling up her trunk
she edges through without upsetting him.
Triumph! the ancient, pig-tailed monster!

When her trick is to climb over him
with what shadow-like slow carefulness
she skims him, sensitive
as shadows from the ages gone and perished
in touching him, and planting her round feet.

While the wispy, modern children, half-afraid
watch silent. The looming of the hoary, far-gone ages
is too much for them.

Twilight

Twilight
thick underdusk
and a hidden voice like water clucking
callously continuous.
While darkness submerges the stones
and splashes warm between the buttocks.

Cups

Cups, let them be dark
like globules of night about to plash.
I want to drink out of dark cups that drip down on their feet.

Bowls

Take away all this crystal and silver
and give me soft-skinned wood
that lives erect through long nights, physically
to put to my lips.

You

You, you don't know me.
When have your knees ever nipped me
like fire-tongs a live coal
for a minute?

After Dark

Can you, after dark, become a darkie?
Could one, at night, run up against the standing flesh of you
with a shock, as against the blackness of a negro,
and catch flesh like the night in one's arms.

Destiny

O destiny, destiny,
do you exist, and can a man touch her hand?

O destiny
if I could see your hand, and it were thumbs down,
I would be willing to give way, like the pterodactyl,
and accept obliteration.
I would not even ask to leave a fossil claw extant,
nor a thumb mark like a clue,
I would be willing to vanish completely, completely.

But if it is thumbs up, and mankind must go on being mankind,
then I am willing to fight, I will roll my sleeves up and start in.

Only, O destiny
I wish you'd show your hand.

To Let Go or to Hold On – ?

Shall we let go,
and allow the soul to find its level
downwards, ebbing downwards, ebbing downwards to the flood?
till the head floats tilted like a bottle forward tilted
on the sea, with no message in it; and the body is submerged
heavy and swaying like a whale recovering
from wounds, below the deep black wave?
like a whale recovering its velocity and strength
under the cold black wave.

Or else, or else
shall a man brace himself up
and lift his face and set his breast
and go forth to change the world?
gather his will and his energy together
and fling himself in effort after effort
upon the world, to bring a change to pass?

Tell me first, O tell me,
will the dark flood of our day's annihilation
swim deeper, deeper, till it leaves no peak emerging?

Shall we be lost, all of us
and gone like weed, like weed, like eggs of fishes,
like sperm of whales, like germs of the great dead past
into which the creative future shall blow strange, unknown forms?

Are we nothing, already, but the lapsing of a great dead past?

Is the best that we are but sperm, loose sperm, like the sperm of
    fishes
that drifts upon time and chaos, till some unknown future takes it up
and is fecund with a new Day of new creatures? different from us.

Or is our shattered Argosy, our leaking ark
at this moment scraping tardy Ararat?
Have we got to get down and clear away the debris
of a swamped civilisation, and start a new world for man
that will blossom forth the whole of human nature?

Must we hold on, hold on
and go ahead with what is human nature
and make a new job of the human world?

Or can we let it go?
O, can we let it go,
and leave it to some nature that is more than human
to use the sperm of what's worth while in us
and thus eliminate us?
Is the time come for humans
now to begin to disappear,
leaving it to the vast revolutions of creative chaos
to bring forth creatures that are an improvement on humans,
as the horse was an improvement on the ichthyosaurus?

Must we hold on?
Or can we now let go?

Or is it even possible we must do both?

How Beastly the Bourgeois is

How beastly the bourgeois is
especially the male of the species –

Presentable, eminently presentable –
shall I make you a present of him?

Isn't he handsome? Isn't he healthy? Isn't he a fine specimen?
Doesn't he look the fresh clean Englishman, outside?
Isn't it God's own image? tramping his thirty miles a day
after partridges, or a little rubber ball?
wouldn't you like to be like that, well off, and quite the thing?

Oh, but wait!
Let him meet a new emotion, let him be faced with another
          man's need,
let him come home to a bit of moral difficulty, let life face him
          with a new demand on his understanding
and then watch him go soggy, like a wet meringue.

Watch him turn into a mess, either a fool or a bully.

Just watch the display of him, confronted with a new demand
          on his intelligence,
a new life-demand.

How beastly the bourgeois is
especially the male of the species –

Nicely groomed, like a mushroom
standing there so sleek and erect and eyeable –
and like a fungus, living on the remains of bygone life
sucking his life out of the dead leaves of greater life than his
          own.

And even so, he's stale, he's been there too long.
Touch him, and you'll find he's all gone inside
Just like an old mushroom, all wormy inside, and hollow
under a smooth skin and an upright appearance.

Full of seething, wormy, hollow feelings
rather nasty –
How beastly the bourgeois is!

Standing in their thousands, these appearances, in damp
    England
what a pity they can't all be kicked over
like sickening toadstools, and left to melt back, swiftly
into the soil of England.

Worm Either Way

If you live along with all the other people
and are just like them and conform, and are nice
you're just a worm –

and if you live with all the other people
and you don't like them and won't be like them and won't
    conform
then you're just the worm that has turned,
in either case, a worm.

The conforming worm stays just inside the skin
respectably unseen, and cheerfully gnaws away at the heart of
    life,
making it all rotten inside.

The unconforming worm – that is, the worm that has turned –
gnaws just the same, gnawing the substance out of life,
but he insists on gnawing a little hole in the social epidermis
and poking his head out and waving himself
and saying: Look at me, I am *not* respectable,
I do all the things the bourgeois daren't do,
I booze and fornicate and use foul language and despise your
    honest man –

But why should the worm that has turned protest so much?
The bonnie, bonnie bourgeois goes a-whoring up back streets
just the same.

The busy, busy bourgeois pinks his language just as pink
if not pinker
and in private boasts his exploits even louder, if you ask me,
than the other.
While as to honesty, Oh, look where the money lies!

So I can't see where the worm that has turned puts anything
over
the worm that is too cunning to turn.

On the contrary, he merely gives himself away.
The turned worm shouts: I bravely booze!
The other says: What? cat-piss?
The turned worm boasts: I copulate!
the unturned says: You look it.

You're a d— b— b— p— bb—, says the worm that's turned.
Quite! says the other. Cuckoo!

Leda

Come not with kisses
not with caresses
of hands and lips and murmurings;
come with a hiss of wings
and sea-touch tip of a beak
and treading of wet, webbed, wave-working feet
into the marsh-soft belly.

Natural Complexion

But, you see, said the handsome young man with the chamois
gloves
to the woman rather older than himself,
if you don't use rouge and a lipstick, in Paris,
they'll take you for a woman of the people.

So spoke the British gentleman
pulling on his chamois gloves
and using his most melodious would-be-Oxford voice.

And the woman said: Dear me!
how rough that would be on you, darling!
Only, if you insist on pulling on those chamois gloves
I swear I'll pull off my knickers, right in the Rue de la Paix.

The Oxford Voice

When you hear it languishing
and hooing and cooing and sidling through the front teeth,
      the Oxford voice
      or worse still
      the would-be-Oxford voice
you don't even laugh any more, you can't.
For every blooming bird is an Oxford cuckoo nowadays,
you can't sit on a bus nor in the tube
but it breathes gently and languishingly in the back of your neck.

And oh, so seductively superior, so seductively
      self-effacingly
      deprecatingly
      superior. –

We wouldn't insist on it for a moment
      but we are
      we are
      you admit we are
      superior. –

To be Superior

How nice it is to be superior!
Because really, it's not use pretending, one *is* superior, isn't one?
I mean people like you and me. –

Quite! I quite agree.
The trouble is, everybody thinks they're just as superior
as we are; just as superior. –

That's what's so boring! people are so boring.
But they can't really think it, do you think?
At the bottom, they must *know* we are really superior, don't you think?
don't you think, *really,* they *know* we're their superiors? –

I couldn't say.
I've never got to the bottom of superiority.
I should like to.

True Democracy

I wish I was a gentleman
as full of wet as a watering-can
to pee in the eye of a policeman –

But my dear fellow, my dear fellow
can it be that you still don't know
that every man, whether high or low
is a gentleman if he thinks himself so? –

He is an' all, you bet 'e is!
I bet I am. – You can 'old yer phiz
abaht it. – Yes, I'm a gent, an' Liz
'ere, she's a lidy, aren't yer, old quizz? –

Of course, I'm a lidy, what d'yer think?
You mind who yer sayin' isn't lidies!
All the Hinglish is gentlemen and lidies,
like the King an' Queen, though they're up just a wink. –

– Of course you are, but let me say
I'm American from New Orleans,
and in my country, just over the way,
we are *all* kings and queens! –

Swan

Far-off
at the core of space
at the quick of time
beats
and goes still
the great swan upon the waters of all endings
the swan within vast chaos, within the electron.

For us
no longer he swims calmly
nor clacks the forces furrowing a great gay trail,
of happy energy,
nor is he nesting passive upon the atoms,
nor flying north desolative icewards
to the sleep of ice,
nor feeding in the marshes,
nor honking horn-like into the twilight. –

But he stoops, now
in the dark
upon us;
he is treading our women
and we men are put out
as the vast white bird
furrows our featherless women
with unknown shocks
and stamps his black marsh-feet on their white and
    marshy flesh.

Give Us Gods

Give us gods, Oh give them us!
Give us gods.
We are so tired of men
and motor-power. –

But not gods grey-bearded and dictatorial,
nor yet that pale young man afraid of fatherhood
shelving substance on to the woman, Madonna mia! shabby virgin!
nor gusty Jove, with his eye on immortal tarts,
nor even the musical, suave young fellow
wooing boys and beauty.

Give us gods
give us something else –

Beyond the great bull that bellowed through space, and got his
    throat cut.
Beyond even that eagle, that phoenix, hanging over the gold egg of
    all things,
further still, before the curled horns of the ram stepped forth
or the stout swart beetle rolled the globe of dung in which man
    should hatch,
or even the sly gold serpent fatherly lifted his head off the earth to
    think –
Give us gods before these –
Thou shalt have other gods before these.

Where the waters end in marshes
swims the wild swan
sweeps the high goose above the mists
honking in the gloom the honk of procreation from such throats.

Mists
where the electron behaves and misbehaves as it will,
where the forces tie themselves up into knots of atoms
and come untied;

mists
of mistiness complicated into knots and clots that barge about
and bump on one another and explode into more mist, or don't
mist of energy most scientific –
But give us gods!

Look then
where the father of all things swims in a mist of atoms
electrons and energies, quantums and relativities
mists, wreathing mists,
like a wild swan, or a goose, whose honk goes through my bladder.

And in the dark unscientific I feel the drum-winds of his wings
and the drip of his cold, webbed feet, mud-black
brush over my face as he goes
to seek the women in the dark, our women, our weird women
     whom he treads
with dreams and thrusts that make them cry in their sleep.

Gods, do you ask for gods?
Where there is woman there is swan.

Do you think, scientific man, you'll be father of your own babies?
Don't imagine it.
There'll be babies born that are cygnets, O my soul!
young wild swans!
And babies of women will come out young wild geese, O my heart!
the geese that saved Rome, and will lose London.

Won't It be Strange – ?

Won't it be strange, when the nurse brings the new-born infant
to the proud father, and shows its little, webbed greenish feet

made to smite the waters behind it?
or the round, wild vivid eye of a wild-goose staring
out of fathomless skies and seas?
or when it utters that undaunted little bird-cry
of one who will settle on icebergs, and honk across the Nile? –

And when the father says: This is none of mine!
Woman, where got you this little beast? –
will there be a whistle of wings in the air, and an icy draught?
will the singing of swans, high up, high up, invisible
break the drums of his ears
and leave him forever listening for the answer?

Spiral Flame

There have been so many gods
that now there are none.
When the One God made a monopoly of it
He wore us out, so now we are godless and unbelieving.

Yet, O my young men, there is a vivifier.
There is that which makes us eager.
While we are eager, we think nothing of it.
Sum, ergo non cogito.[51]
But when our eagerness leaves us, we are godless and full of
    thought.

We have worn out the gods, and they us.
That pale one, filled with renunciation and pain and white love
has worn us weary of renunciation and love and even pain.
That strong one, ruling the universe with a rod of iron
has sickened us thoroughly with rods of iron and rulers and
    strong men.

The All-wise has tired us of wisdom.
The weeping mother of god, inconsolable over her son
makes us prefer to be womanless, rather than be wept over.
And that poor makeshift, Aphrodite emerging in a bathing suit
    from our modern seaside foam
has successfully killed all desire in us whatsoever.

Yet, O my young men, there is a vivifier.
There is a swan-like flame that curls round the centre of space
and flutters at the core of the atom,
there is a spiral flame-tip that can lick our little atoms into fusion
so we roar up like bonfires of vitality
and fuse in a broad hard flame of many men in a oneness.

O pillars of flame by night, O my young men
spinning and dancing like flamy fire-sprouts in the dark ahead of
    the multitude!
O ruddy god in our veins, O fiery god in our genitals!
O rippling hard fire of courage, O fusing of hot trust
when the fire reaches us, O my young men!

And the same flame that fills us with life, it will dance and burn
    the house down
all the fittings and elaborate furnishings
and all the people that go with the fittings and the furnishings,
the upholstered dead that sit in deep armchairs.

Let the Dead Bury Their Dead

Let the dead go bury their dead
don't help them.
Let the dead look after the dead
leave them to one another,
don't serve them.

The dead in their nasty dead hands
have heaps of money,
don't take it.

The dead in their seething minds
have phosphorescent teeming white words
of putrescent wisdom and sapience that subtly stinks;
don't ever believe them.

The dead are in myriads, they seem mighty.
They make trains chuff, motor-cars titter, ships lurch,
mills grind on and on,
and keep you in millions at the mills, sightless pale slaves,
pretending these are the mills of God.

It is the great lie of the dead.
The mills of industry are not the mills of God.
And the mills of God grind otherwise, with the winds of life for
    the mill-stones.
Trust the mills of God, though they grind exceedingly small.
But as for the mills of men
don't be harnessed to them.

The dead give ships and engines, cinema, radio and
    gramophone,
they send aeroplanes across the sky,
and they say: Now, behold, you are living the great life!
While you listen in, while you watch the film, while you drive
    the car,
While you read about the airship crossing the wild Atlantic
behold, you are living the great life, the stupendous life!

As you know, it is a complete lie.
You are all going dead and corpse-pale
listening in to the lie.
Spit it out.

O cease to listen to the living dead
they are only greedy for your life!
O cease to labour for the gold-toothed dead,
they are so greedy, yet so helpless if not worked for,
Don't ever be kind to the smiling, tooth-mouthed dead
don't ever be kind to the dead
it is pandering to corpses,
the repulsive, living fat dead.

Bury a man gently if he has lain down and died.
But with the walking and talking and conventionally
        persuasive dead
with bank accounts and insurance policies
don't sympathise, or you taint the unborn babes.

When Wilt Thou Teach the People – ?

When wilt thou teach the people
God of justice, to save themselves – ?
They have been saved so often
and sold.

O God of justice, send no more saviours
of the people!

When a saviour has saved a people
they find he has sold them to his father.
They say: We are saved but we are starving.
He says: The sooner will you eat imaginary cake in the
        mansions of my father.
They say: Can't we have a loaf of common bread?
He says: No, you must go to heaven, and eat the most
        marvellous cake. –

Or Napoleon says: Since I have saved you from the ci-devants,
you are my property, be prepared to die for me, and to work for
    me. –

Or later republicans say: You are saved,
therefore you are savings, our capital
with which we shall do big business. –

Or Lenin says: You are saved, but you are saved wholesale.
You are no longer men, that is bourgeois;
you are items in the soviet state,
and each item will get its ration,
but it is the soviet state alone which counts
the items are of small importance,
the state having saved them all. –

And so it goes on, with the saving of the people.
God of justice, when wilt thou teach them to save themselves?

A Living

A man should never earn his living
if he earns his life he'll be lovely.

A bird picks up its seeds or little snails
between heedless earth and heaven
in heedlessness.

But, the plucky little sport, it gives to life
song, and chirruping, gay feathers, fluff-shadowed warmth
and all the unspeakable charm of birds hopping and fluttering
    and being birds.
And we, we get it all from them for nothing.

When I Went to the Film

When I went to the film, and saw all the black-and-white
    feelings that nobody felt,
and heard the audience sighing and sobbing with all the
    emotions they none of them felt,
and saw them cuddling with rising passions they none of them
    for a moment felt,
and caught them moaning from close-up kisses, black-and-
    white kisses that could not be felt,
it was like being in heaven, which I am sure has a white
    atmosphere
upon which shadows of people, pure personalities
are cast in black and white, and move
in flat ecstasy, supremely unfelt,
and heavenly.

When I Went to the Circus

When I went to the circus that had pitched on the waste lot
it was full of uneasy people
frightened of the bare earth and the temporary canvas
and the smell of horses and other beasts
instead of merely the smell of man.

Monkeys rode rather grey and wizened
on curly plump piebald ponies
and the children uttered a little cry –
and dogs jumped through hoops and turned somersaults
and then the geese scuttled in in a little flock
and round the ring they went to the sound of the whip
then doubled, and back, with a funny up-flutter of wings
and the children suddenly shouted out.

Then came the hush again, like a hush of fear.

The tight-rope lady, pink and blonde and nude-looking with a few
 gold spangles
footed cautiously out on the rope, turned prettily, spun round
bowed, and lifted her foot in her hand, smiled, swung her parasol
to another balance, tripped round, poised, and slowly sank
her handsome thighs down, down, till she slept her splendid body
 on the rope.
When she rose, tilting her parasol, and smiled at the cautious
 people
they cheered, but nervously.

The trapeze man, slim and beautiful and like a fish in the air
swung great curves through the upper space, and came down
 like a star.
– And the people applauded, with hollow, frightened applause.

The elephants, huge and grey, loomed their curved bulk through
 the dusk
and sat up, taking strange postures, showing the pink soles of
 their feet
and curling their precious live trunks like ammonites
and moving always with soft slow precision
as when a great ship moves to anchor.
The people watched and wondered, and seemed to resent the
 mystery that lies in beasts.

Horses, gay horses, swirling round and plaiting
in a long line, their heads laid over each other's necks;
they were happy, they enjoyed it;
all the creatures seemed to enjoy the game
in the circus, with their circus people.

But the audience, compelled to wonder
compelled to admire the bright rhythms of moving bodies
flesh flamey and a little heroic, even in a tumbling clown,
they were not really happy.
There was no gushing response, as there is at the film.

When modern people see the carnal body dauntless and
 flickering gay

playing among the elements neatly, beyond competition
and displaying no personality,
modern people are depressed.

Modern people feel themselves at a disadvantage.
They know they have no bodies that could play among the
    elements.
They have only their personalities, that are best seen flat, on the
    film,
flat personalities in two dimensions, imponderable and touchless.

And they grudge the circus people the swooping gay weight of limbs
that flower in mere movement,
and they grudge them the immediate, physical understanding they
    have with their circus beasts,
and they grudge them their circus life altogether.

Yet the strange, almost frightened shout of delight that comes now
    and then from the children
shows that the children vaguely know how cheated they are of
    their birthright
in the bright wild circus flesh.

The Noble Englishman

I know a noble Englishman
who is sure he is a gentleman,
that sort –

This moderately young gentleman
is very normal, as becomes an Englishman,
rather proud of being a bit of a Don Juan
you know –

But one of his beloveds, looking a little peaked
towards the end of her particular affair with him
said: Ronald, you know, is like most Englishmen,
by instinct he's a sodomist
but he's frightened to know it
so he takes it out on women.

Oh come! said I. That Don Juan of a Ronald! –
Exactly, she said. Don Juan was another of them, in love with
    himself
and taking it out on women. –

Even that isn't sodomitical, said I.
But if a man is in love with himself, isn't that the meanest form
    of homosexuality? she said.

You've no idea, when men are in love with themselves, how they
    wreak all their spite on women,
pretending to love them.
Ronald, she resumed, doesn't like women, just acutely dislikes
    them.
He might possibly like men, if he weren't too frightened and
    egoistic.
So he very cleverly tortures women, with his sort of love.
He's instinctively frightfully clever.
He can be so gentle, so gentle
so delicate in his love-making.
Even now, the thought of it bewilders me: such gentleness!
Yet I know he does it deliberately, as cautiously and deliberately
    as when he shaves himself.
Then more than that, he makes a woman feel he is *serving* her
really living in her service, and serving her
as no man ever served before.

And then, suddenly, when she's feeling all lovely about it
suddenly the ground goes from under her feet, and she clutches
    in mid-air,
but horrible, as if your heart would wrench out; –
while he stands aside watching with a superior little grin
like some malicious indecent little boy.
– No, don't talk to me about the love of Englishmen!

Things Men Have Made

Things men have made with wakened hands, and put soft life into
are awake through years with transferred touch, and go on glowing
for long years.

And for this reason, some old things are lovely
warm still with the life of forgotten men who made them.

Things Made by Iron

Things made by iron and handled by steel
are born dead, they are shrouds, they soak life out of us.

Till after a long time, when they are old and have steeped in our life
they begin to be soothed and soothing; then we throw them away.

New Houses, New Clothes

New houses, new furniture, new streets, new clothes, new sheets
everything new and machine-made sucks life out of us
and makes us cold, makes us lifeless
the more we have.

Whatever Man Makes

Whatever man makes and makes it live
lives because of the life put into it.

A yard of India muslin is alive with Hindu life.

And a Navajo woman, weaving her rug in the pattern of her dream
must run the pattern out in a little break at the end
so that her soul can come out, back to her.

But in the odd pattern, like snake-marks on the sand
it leaves its trail.

We are Transmitters

As we live, we are transmitters of life.
And when we fail to transmit life, life fails to flow through us.

That is part of the mystery of sex, it is a flow onwards.
Sexless people transmit nothing.

And if, as we work, we can transmit life into our work,
life, still more life, rushes into us to compensate, to be ready
and we ripple with life through the days.

Even if it is a woman making an apple dumpling, or a man a stool,
if life goes into the pudding, good is the pudding
good is the stool,
content is the woman, with fresh life rippling in her,
content is the man.

Give, and it shall be given unto you
is still the truth about life.
But giving life is not so easy.
It doesn't mean handing it out to some mean fool, or letting the
       living dead eat you up.
It means kindling the life-quality where it was not,
even if it's only in the whiteness of a washed pocket-handkerchief. .

Let Us be Men

For God's sake, let us be men
not monkeys minding machines
or sitting with our tails curled
while the machine amuses us, the radio or film or
       gramophone.

Monkeys with a bland grin on our faces. –

All That We Have is Life

All that we have, while we live, is life;
And if you don't live during your life, you are a piece of dung.

And work is life, and life is lived in work
unless you're a wage-slave.
While a wage-slave works, he leaves life aside
and stands there a piece of dung.

Men should refuse to be lifelessly at work.
Men should refuse to be heaps of wage-earning dung.
Men should refuse to work at all, as wage-slaves.
Men should demand to work for themselves, of themselves, and
    put their life in it.

For if a man has no life in his work, he is mostly a heap of dung.

Work

There is no point in work
unless it absorbs you
like an absorbing game.

If it doesn't absorb you
if it's never any fun,
don't do it.

When a man goes out into his work
he is alive like a tree in spring
he is living, not merely working.

When the Hindus weave thin wool into long, long lengths of
    stuff
with their thin dark hands and their wide dark eyes and their
    still souls absorbed
they are like slender trees putting forth leaves, a long white web
    of living leaf,
the tissue they weave,
and they clothe themselves in white as a tree clothes itself
in its own foliage.

As with cloth, so with houses, ships, shoes, wagons or cups or
    loaves
men might put them forth as a snail its shell, as a bird that
    leans
its breast against its nest, to make it round,
as the turnip models his round root, as the bush makes flowers
    and gooseberries,
putting them forth, not manufacturing them,
and cities might be as once they were, bowers grown out from
    the busy bodies of people.

And so it will be again, men will smash the machines.

At last, for the sake of clothing himself in his own leaf-like cloth
tissued from his life,
and dwelling in his own bowery house, like a beaver's nibbled
    mansion
and drinking from cups that came off his fingers like flowers off
    their five-fold stem,
he will cancel the machines we have got.

Why – ?

Why have money?
why have a financial system to strangle us all in its octopus
    arms?
why have industry?
why have the industrial system?
why have machines, that we only have to serve?
why have a soviet, that only wants to screw us all in as parts of
    the machine?
why have working classes at all, as if men were only embodied
    jobs?
why not have men as men, and the work as merely part of the
    game of life?

True, we've got all these things
industrial and financial systems, machines and soviets, working
    classes.
But why go on having them, if they belittle us?
Why should we be belittled any longer?

Moon Memory

When the moon falls on a man's blood
white and slippery, as on the black water in a port
shaking asunder, and flicking at his ribs –

then the noisy, dirty day-world
exists no more, nor ever truly existed;
but instead
this wet white gleam
twitches, and ebbs hitting, washing inwardly, silverily against
    his ribs,
on his soul that is dark ocean within him.

And under the flicking of the white whiplash of the moon
sea-beasts immersed lean sideways and flash bright
in pure brilliance of anger, sea-immersed anger
at the thrashy, motor-driven transit of dirty day
that has left scum on the sea, even in the night.

What is He?

What is he?
– A man, of course.
Yes, but what does he do?
– He lives and is a man.
Oh, quite! But he must work. He must have a job of some sort.
– Why?
Because obviously he's not one of the leisured classes.
– I don't know. He has lots of leisure. And he makes quite
    beautiful chairs. –
There you are then! He's a cabinet maker.
– No, no!
Anyhow a carpenter and joiner.
– Not at all.
But you said so.
– What did I say?
That he made chairs, and was a joiner and carpenter.
– I said he made chairs, but I did not say he was a carpenter.

All right then, he's just an amateur.
– Perhaps! Would you say a thrush was a professional flautist
    or just an amateur? –
I'd say it was just a bird
– And I say he is just a man.
All right! You always did quibble.

O! Start a Revolution

O! start a revolution, somebody!
not to get the money
but to lose it all for ever.

O! start a revolution, somebody!
not to install the working classes
but to abolish the working classes for ever
and have a world of men.

There is Rain in Me

There is rain in me,
running down, running down, trickling
away from memory.

There is ocean in me,
swaying, swaying, O so deep
so fathomlessly black
and spurting suddenly up, snow-white, like snow-leopards
    rearing
high and clawing with rage at the cliffs of the soul
then disappearing back with a hiss
of eternal salt rage; angry is old ocean within a man.

Desire Goes Down into the Sea

I have no desire any more
towards woman or man, bird, beast or creature or thing.
All day long I feel the tide rocking, rocking

though it strikes no shore
in me.

Only mid-ocean –

The Sea, the Sea

The sea dissolves so much
and the moon makes away with so much more than we know –

Once the moon comes down
and the sea gets hold of us
cities dissolve like rock-salt
and the sugar melts out of life
iron washes away like an old blood-stain
gold goes out into a green shadow
money makes even no sediment
and only the heart
glitters in salty triumph
over all it has known, that has gone now into salty nothingness.

Old Song

The day is ending, the night descending
the heart is frozen, the spirit dead;
but the moon is wending her way, attending
to other things that are not yet said.

Good Husbands Make Unhappy Wives

Good husbands make unhappy wives
so do bad husbands, just as often;
but the unhappiness of a wife with a good husband
is much more devastating
than the unhappiness of a wife with a bad husband.

November by the Sea

Now in November nearer comes the sun
down the abandoned heaven.

As the dark closes round him, he draws nearer
as if for our company.

At the base of the lower brain
the sun in me declines to his winter solstice
and darts a few gold rays
back to the old year's sun across the sea.

A few gold rays thickening down to red
as the sun of my soul is setting
setting fierce and undaunted, wintry
but setting, setting behind the sounding sea between my ribs.

The wide sea wins, and the dark,
winter, and the great day-sun, and the sun in my soul
sinks, sinks to setting and the winter solstice
downward, they race in decline
my sun, and the great gold sun.

Fight! O My Young Men

Fight! don't you feel you're fading
into slow death?
Fight then, poor duffers degrading
your very breath.

Open your half-dead eyes
you half-alive young,
look round and realise
the muck from which you've sprung.

The money-muck, you simple flowers
of your forefathers' muck-heap;
and the money-muck-worms, the extant powers
that have got you in keep.

Old money-worms, young money-worms
money-worm professors
spinning a glamour round money, and clergymen
lifting a bank-book to bless us!

In the odour of lucrative sanctity
stand they – and god, how they stink!
Rise then, my young men, rise at them!
Or if you can't rise, just think –

Think of the world that you're stifling in,
think what a world it might be!
Think of the rubbish you're trifling in
with enfeebled vitality!

And then, if you amount to a hill o' beans
start in and bust it all;
money, hypocrisy, greed, machines
that have ground you so small.

Women Want Fighters for Their Lovers

Women don't want wistful
mushy pathetic young men
struggling in doubtful embraces
then trying again.

Mushy and treacherous, tiny
Peterlets, Georgelets, Hamlets
Tomlets, Dicklets, Harrylets, whiney
Jimlets and self-sorry Samlets.

Women are sick of consoling
inconsolable youth, dead-beat;
pouring comfort and condoling
down the sink of the male conceit.

Woman want fighters, fighters
and the fighting cock.
Can't you give it them, blighters!

The fighting cock, the fighting cock –
have you got one, little blighters?
Let it crow then, like one o'clock!

It's Either You Fight Or You Die

It's either you fight or you die
young gents, you've got no option.
No good asking the reason why
it's either to fight or you die
die, die, lily-liveredly die
or fight and make the splinters fly
bust up the holy apple-pie
you've got no option.

Don't say you can't, start in and try;
give great hypocrisy the lie
and tackle the blowsy big blow-fly
of money; do it or die!
You've got no option.

Don'ts

Fight your little fight, my boy
fight and be a man.
Don't be a good little, good little boy
being as good as you can
and agreeing with all the mealy-mouthed, mealy-mouthed
truths that the sly trot out
to protect themselves and their greedy-mouthed, greedy-mouthed
cowardice, every lout.

Don't live up to the dear little girl who costs
you your manhood, and makes you pay.
Nor the dear old mater who so proudly boasts
that you'll make your way.

Don't earn golden opinions, opinions golden,
or at least worth Treasury notes,
from all sorts of men; don't be beholden
to the herd inside the pen.

Don't long to have dear little, dear little boys
whom you'll have to educate
to earn their living; nor yet girls, sweet joys
who will find it so hard to mate.

Nor a dear little home, with its cost, its cost
that you have to pay,
earning your living while your life is lost
and dull death comes in a day.

Don't be sucked in by the su-superior,
don't swallow the culture bait,
don't drink, don't drink and get beerier and beerier,
do learn to discriminate.

Do hold yourself together, and fight
with a hit-hit here and a hit-hit there,
and a comfortable feeling at night
that you've let in a little air.

A little fresh air in the money sty,
knocked a little hole in the holy prison,
done your little bit, made your own little try
that the risen Christ should *be* risen.

The Risen Lord

The risen lord, the risen lord
has risen in the flesh,
and treads the earth to feel the soil
though his feet are still nesh.[52]

The risen lord, the risen lord
has opened his eyes afresh,
and sees strange looks on the faces of men
all held in leash.

And he says: I never have seen them before,
these people of flesh;
these are no spirits caught and sore
in the physical mesh.

They are substance itself, that flows in thick
flame of flesh forever travelling
like the flame of a candle, slow and quick
fluttering and softly unravelling.

It moves, it ripples, and all the time
it changes, and with it change
moods, thoughts, desires, and deeds that chime
with the rippling fleshly change.

I never saw them, how they must soften
themselves with oil, and lard
their guts with a certain fat, and often
laugh, and laugh hard.

If they didn't, if they did not soften
themselves with oil, and lard
their guts with a certain fat, and often
laugh, and laugh hard

they would not be men, and they must be men,
they are their own flesh. – I lay
in the tomb and was not; I have risen again
to look the other way.

Lo! I am flesh, and the blood that races
is me in the narrows of my wrists.
Lo, I see fear in the twisted faces
of men, they clench fear in their fists!

Lo! on the other side the grave
I have conquered the fear of death,
but the fear of life is still here; I am brave
yet I fear my own breath.

Now I must conquer the fear of life,
the knock of the blood in my wrists,
the breath that rushes through my nose, the strife
of desires in the loins' dark twists,

What do you want, wild loins? and what
do you want, warm heart? and what
wide eyes and wondering spirit? – not
death, no death for your lot!

They ask, and they must be answered; they
are, and they shall be, to the end.
Lo! there is woman, and her way is a strange way,
I must follow also her trend.

I died, and death is neuter; it speaks not, it gives
no answer; man rises again
with mouth and loins and needs, he lives
again man among men.

So it is, so it will be, for ever and ever.
And still the great needs of men
will clamour forth from the flesh, and never
can denial deny them again.

The Secret Waters

What was lost is found
what was wounded is sound,
the key of life on the body of men
unlocks the fountains of peace again.

The fountains of peace, the fountains of peace
well softly up for a new increase,
but they bubble under the heavy wall
of this house of life that encloses us all.

They bubble under the heavy wall
that was once a house, and is now a prison,
and never a one among us all
knows that the waters have risen.

None of us knows, O none of us knows
the welling of peace when it rises and flows
in secret under the sickening wall
of the prison of man that encloses us all.

And we shall not know, we shall not know
till the secret water overflow
and loosen the brick and the hard cement
of the walls within which our lives are spent.

Till the walls begin to loosen and crack,
to gape and our house is going to wrack
and ruin above us, and the crash of release
is death to us all, in the marshes of peace.

Obscenity

The body of itself is clean, but the caged mind
is a sewer inside, it pollutes, O it pollutes
the guts and the stones and the womb, rots them down, leaves a
    rind
of maquillage[53] and pose and malice that would shame the brutes.

Beware! O My Dear Young Men

Beware, O my dear young men, of going rotten.
    It's so easy to follow suit;
people in their thirties, and the older ones, have gotten
    bad inside, like fruit
that nobody eats and nobody wants, so it rots, but is not forgotten.

Rotten inside, they are, and seething
    with small obscenities;
and they whisper it out, and they titter it out, breathing
    among soft amenities,
a vapour of rottenness out of their mouths, like sewer-stench
    wreathing.

And it's funny, my dear young men, that you in your twenties
    should love the sewer scent
of obscenity, and lift your noses where the vent is
    and run towards it, bent
on smelling it all, before your bit of vitality spent is.

For obscenity, after all, my dear young men
    is only mental dirt,
the dirty mind like a urinal again
    or a dung squirt;
and I thought you wanted life and experience, dear young men!

All this obscenity is just mental, mental, mental,
    it's the village-idiot mind
playing with muck; and I thought you young gents experimental
    were out to find
new life for yourselves and your women, complemental.

But if obscene village idiots you want to be, then be it.
    But don't imagine you'll get
satisfactory experience from it; can't you see it?
    the idiot with his chin all wet
goggling obscenities! If that's you and your fate, why then, dree it.

Sex Isn't Sin

Sex isn't sin, ah no! sex isn't sin,
nor is it dirty, not until the dirty mind pokes in.

We shall do as we like, sin is obsolete, the young assert.
Sin is obsolete, sin is obsolete, but not so dirt.

And sex, alas, gets dirtier and dirtier, worked from the mind.
Sex gets dirtier and dirtier, the more it is fooled with, we find.

And dirt, if it isn't sin, is worse, so there you are!
Why don't you know what's what, young people? seems to me you're
    far
duller than your grandmothers. But leave that aside.
Let's be honest at last about sex, or show at least that we've tried.

Sex isn't sin, it's a delicate flow between women and men,
and the sin is to damage the flow, force it up or dirty it or suppress it
    again.

Sex isn't something you've got to play with; sex is *you*.
It's the flow of your life, it's your moving self, and you are due
to be true to the nature of it, its reserve, its sensitive pride
that it always has to begin with, and by which you ought to abide.

Know yourself, O know yourself, that you are mortal; and know.
the sensitive delicacy of your sex, in its ebbing to and fro,
and the mortal reserve of your sex, as it stays in your depths below.

And don't, with the nasty, prying mind, drag it out from its deeps
and finger it and force it, and shatter the rhythm it keeps
when it's left alone, as it stirs and rouses and sleeps.

O know yourself, O know your sex! You must know, there is no
    escape.
You must know sex in order to save it, your deepest self, from the rape
of the itching mind and the mental self, with its pruriency always
    agape.

Sex and Trust

If you want to have sex, you've got to trust
at the core of your heart, the other creature.
The other creature, the other creature
not merely the personal upstart;
but the creature there, that has come to meet you;
trust it you must, you must
or the experience amounts to nothing,
mere evacuation lust.

The Gazelle Calf

The gazelle calf, O my children
goes behind its mother across the desert
goes behind its mother on blithe bare foot
requiring no shoes, O my children!

The Elephant is Slow to Mate

The elephant, the huge old beast,
        is slow to mate;
he finds a female, they show no haste
        they wait
for the sympathy in their vast shy hearts
        slowly, slowly to rouse
as they loiter along the river-beds
        and drink and browse
and dash in a panic through the brake
        of forest with the herd,
and sleep in massive silence, and wake
        together without a word.

So slowly the great hot elephant hearts
        grow full of desire,
and the great beasts mate in secret at last,
        hiding their fire.

Oldest they are and the wisest of beasts
    so they know at last
how to wait for the loneliest of feasts
    for the full repast.

They do not snatch, they do not tear;
    their massive blood
moves as the moon-tides, near, more near
    till they touch in flood.

Little Fish

The tiny fish enjoy themselves
in the sea.
Quick little splinters of life,
their little lives are fun to them
in the sea.

The Mosquito Knows

The mosquito knows full well, small as he is
he's a beast of prey.
But after all
he only takes his bellyful,
he doesn't put my blood in the bank.

Self-Pity

I never saw a wild thing
sorry for itself.
A small bird will drop frozen dead from a bough
without ever having felt sorry for itself.

New Moon

The new moon, of no importance
lingers behind as the yellow sun glares and is gone beyond
      the sea's edge;
earth smokes blue;
the new moon, in cool height above the blushes,
brings a fresh fragrance of heaven to our senses.

Spray

It is a wonder foam is so beautiful.
A wave bursts in anger on a rock, broken up
in wild white sibilant spray
and falls back, drawing in its breath with rage,
with frustration how beautiful!

Seaweed

Sea-weed sways and sways and swirls
as if swaying were its form of stillness;
and if it flushes against fierce rock
it slips over it as shadows do, without hurting itself.

My Enemy

If it is a question of him or me
then down with him!

If he is not with me but against me,
if his presence and his breath are poison to me,
then, if he comes near me
down with him.

Down with him
to the pit of annihilation.
But if he stays far from me, and does not touch me,
he is no longer my concern, he ceases to be my enemy.

Touch

Since we have become so cerebral
we can't bear to touch or be touched.

Since we are so cerebral
we are humanly out of touch.

And so we must remain.
For if, cerebrally, we force ourselves into touch, into contact
physical and fleshly,
we violate ourselves,
we become vicious.

Noli Me Tangere

Noli me tangere, touch me not!
O you creatures of mind, don't touch me!
O you with mental fingers, O never put your hand on me!
O you with mental bodies, stay a little distance from me!

And let us, if you will, talk and mingle
in mental contact, gay and sad.
But only that.
O don't confuse
the body into it, let us stay apart.

Great is my need to be chaste
and apart, in this cerebral age.
Great is my need to be untouched
untouched.
Noli me tangere!

Chastity

Chastity, beloved chastity
O beloved chastity
how infinitely dear to me
chastity, beloved chastity!

That my body need not be
fingered by the mind,
or prostituted by the dree
contact of cerebral flesh –

O leave me clean from mental fingering
from the cold copulation of the will,
from all the white, self-conscious lechery
the modern mind calls love!

From all the mental poetry
of deliberate love-making,
from all the false felicity
of deliberately taking
the body of another unto mine,
O God deliver me!
leave me alone, let me be!
Chastity, dearer far to me
than any contact that can be
in this mind-mischievous age!

Let Us Talk, Let Us Laugh

Let us talk, let us laugh, let us tell
all kinds of things to one another;
men and women, let us be
gay and amusing together, and free
from airs and from false modesty.

But at the same time, don't let's think.
that this quite real intimacy
of talk and thought and me-and-thee
means anything further and physical.

Nay, on the very contrary
all this talking intimacy
is only real and right if we
keep ourselves separate physically
and quite apart.

To proceed from mental intimacy
to physical, is just messy,
and really, a nasty violation,
and the ruin of any decent relation
between us –

Touch Comes

Touch comes when the white mind sleeps
and only then.
Touch comes slowly, if ever; it seeps
slowly up in the blood of men
and women.

Soft slow sympathy
of the blood in me, of the blood in thee
rises and flushes insidiously
over the conscious personality
of each of us, and covers us
with a soft one warmth, and a generous
kindled togetherness, so we go
into each other as tides flow
under a moon they do not know.

Personalities exist apart;
and personal intimacy has no heart.
Touch is of the blood
uncontaminated, the unmental flood.

When again in us
the soft blood softly flows together
towards touch, then this delirious
day of the mental welter and blether
will be passing away, we shall cease to fuss.

Leave Sex Alone

Leave sex alone, leave sex alone, let it die right away,
let it die right away, till it rises of itself again.

Meanwhile, if we must, let us think about it, and talk about it
straight to the very end,
since the need is on us.
But while we think of it, and while we talk of it
let us leave it alone, physically, keep apart.
For while we have sex in the mind, we truly have none in the
   body.

Sex is a state of grace
and you'll have to wait.
You'll even have to repent.
And in some strange and silent way
you'll have to pray to the far-off gods
to grant it you.

At present sex is the mind's preoccupation,
and in the body we can only mentally fornicate.
Today, we've got no sex.
We have only cerebral excitations.

The mind will have to glut itself,
and the ego will have to burst like the swollen frog,
and then perhaps we shall know true sex, in ourselves.

The Mess of Love

We've made a great mess of love
since we made an ideal of it.

The moment I swear to love a woman, a certain woman, all my life
that moment I begin to hate her.

The moment I even say to a woman: I love you! –
my love dies down considerably.

The moment love is an understood thing between us, we are sure
of it,
it's a cold egg, it isn't love any more.

Love is like a flower, it must flower and fade;
if it doesn't fade, it is not a flower,
it's either an artificial rag blossom, or an immortelle, for the
cemetery.

The moment the mind interferes with love, or the will fixes on it,
or the personality assumes it as an attribute, or the ego takes
possession of it
it is not love any more, it's just a mess.
And we've made a great mess of love, mind-perverted, will-
perverted, ego-perverted love.

Climb Down, O Lordly Mind

Climb down, O lordly mind!
O eagle of the mind, alas, you are more like a buzzard.

Come down now, from your pre-eminence, O mind, O lofty spirit!
Your hour has struck
your unique day is over.
Absolutism is finished, in the human consciousness too.

A man is many things, he is not only a mind.
But in his consciousness, he is two-fold at least;
he is cerebral, intellectual, mental, spiritual,
but also he is instinctive, intuitive, and in touch.

The mind that needs to know all things
must needs at last come to know its own limits,
even its own nullity, beyond a certain point.

Know thyself, and that thou art mortal,
and therefore, that thou art forever unknowable;
the mind can never reach thee.

Thou art like the moon,
and the white mind shines on one side of thee
but the other side is dark forever,
and the dark moon draws the tides also.

Thou art like the day
but thou art also like the night,
and thy darkness is forever invisible,
for the strongest light throws also the darkest shadow.

The blood knows in darkness, and forever dark,
in touch, by intuition, instinctively,
The blood also knows religiously,
and of this, the mind is incapable,
The mind is non-religious.

To my dark heart, gods *are*.
In my dark heart, love is and is not.
But to my white mind
gods and love alike are but an idea
a kind of fiction.

Man is an alternating consciousness.
Man is an alternating consciousness.

Only that exists which exists in my own consciousness.
Cogito, ergo sum.
Only that exists which exists dynamically and unmentalised, in
    my blood.
Non cogito, ergo sum.
I am, I do not think I am.

Ego-Bound

As a plant becomes pot-bound
man becomes ego-bound
enclosed in his own limited mental consciousness.

Then he can't feel any more
or love, or rejoice or even grieve any more,
he is ego-bound,
pot-bound
in the pot of his own conceit
and he can only slowly die.

Unless he is a sturdy plant.
Then he can burst the pot,
shell off his ego
and get his roots in earth again,
raw earth.

Jealousy

The jealousy of an ego-bound woman
is hideous and fearful,
it is so much stronger than her love could ever be.

The jealousy of an ego-bound woman
is a fearful thing to behold.
The ego revealed in all its monstrous inhumanity.

Ego-Bound Women

Ego-bound women are often lesbian,
perhaps always.

Perhaps the ego-bound can only love their own kind,
if they can love at all.

And of all passions
the lesbian passion is the most appalling,

a frenzy of tortured possession
and a million frenzies of tortured jealousy.

Possessive, possessive, possessive!
gentle woman gone mad
with possessive vindictiveness.

But the real fault lies in the ego-bound condition of
    mankind
Individuals must go mad.

Fidelity

Fidelity and love are two different things, like a flower and a gem.
And love, like a flower, will fade, will change into something else
or it would not be flowery.

O flowers they fade because they are moving swiftly; a little torrent
    of life
leaps up to the summit of the stem, gleams, turns over round the
    bend
of the parabola of curved flight,
sinks, and is gone, like a comet curving into the invisible.

O flowers, they are all the time travelling
like comets, and they come into our ken
for a day, for two days, and withdraw, slowly vanish again.

And we, we must take them on the wing, and let them go.
Embalmed flowers are not flowers, immortelles are not flowers;
flowers are just a motion, a swift motion, a coloured gesture;
that is their loveliness. And that is love.

But a gem is different. It lasts so much longer than we do
so much much much much longer
that it seems to last for ever.

Yet we know it is flowing away
as flowers are, and we are, only slower.
The wonderful slow flowing of the sapphire!

All flows, and every flow is related to every other flow.
Flowers and sapphires and us, diversely streaming.

In the old days, when sapphires were breathed upon and brought
        forth
during the wild orgasms of chaos
time was much slower, when the rocks came forth.
It took aeons to make a sapphire, aeons for it to pass away.

And a flower it takes a summer.

And man and woman are like the earth, that brings forth flowers
in summer, and love, but underneath is rock.
Older than flowers, older than ferns, older than foraminiferae,[54]
older than plasm altogether is the soul of a man underneath.

And when, throughout all the wild orgasms of love
slowly a gem forms, in the ancient, once-more-molten rocks
of two human hearts, two ancient rocks, a man's heart and a
        woman's,
that is the crystal of peace, the slow hard jewel of trust,
the sapphire of fidelity.
The gem of mutual peace emerging from the wild chaos of love.

Know Deeply, Know Thyself More Deeply

Go deeper than love, for the soul has greater depths,
love is like the grass, but the heart is deep wild rock,
molten, yet dense and permanent.

Go down to your deep old heart, woman, and lose sight of yourself.
And lose sight of me, the me whom you turbulently loved.

Let us lose sight of ourselves, and break the mirrors.
For the fierce curve of our lives is moving again to the depths
out of sight, in the deep dark living heart.

But say, in the dark wild metal of your heart
is there a gem, which came into being between us?
is there a sapphire of mutual trust, a blue spark?
Is there a ruby of fused being, mine and yours, an inward glint?

If there is not, O then leave me, go away.
For I cannot be bullied back into the appearances of love,
any more than August can be bullied to look like March.

Love out of season, especially at the end of the season,
is merely ridiculous.
If you insist on it, I insist on departure.

Have you no deep old heart of wild womanhood,
self-forgetful and gemmed with experience,
and swinging in a strange unison of power
with the heart of the man you are supposed to have loved?

If you have not, go away.
If you can only sit with a mirror in your hand, an ageing woman
posing on and on as a lover,
in love with a self that now is shallow and withered,
your own self – that has passed like a last summer's flower –
then go away –

I do not want a woman whom age cannot wither.
She is a made-up lie, a dyed immortelle
of infinite staleness.

All I Ask

All I ask of a woman is that she shall feel gently towards me
when my heart feels kindly towards her,
and there shall be the soft, soft tremor as of unheard bells
    between us.

It is all I ask.
I am so tired of violent women lashing out and insisting
on being loved, when there is no love in them.

The Universe Flows

The universe flows in infinite wild streams, related
in rhythms too big and too small for us to know,
since man is just middling, and his comprehension just middling.

If once, for a second, the universe ceased to flow
of course it would cease to exist.
The thought is unthinkable, anyhow.

Only man tries not to flow,
repeats himself over and over in mechanical monotony of conceit
and hence is a mess.

If only Cleopatra had left off being so Cleopatra-ish
– she was it too long –
if only she had gone down to a deeper self in herself
as time went on,

Anthony might have made a splendid thing of the East,
she might have saved herself the asp
and him from sticking himself like a pig
and us from the dreary inheritance of Roman stupidity.

Underneath

Below what we think we are
we are something else,
we are almost anything.

Below the grass and trees
and streets and houses and even seas
is rock; and below the rock, the rock
is we know not what,
the hot wild core of the earth, heavier than we can even imagine.

Pivotal core of the soul, heavier than iron
so ponderously central;
heavier and hotter than anything known;

and also alone. –
And yet
reeling with connection
spinning with the heaviness of balance
and flowing invisibly, gasping
towards the breathing stars and the central of all sunninesses.

The earth leans its weight on the sun, and the sun on the sun of
   suns.
Back and forth goes the balance and the electric breath.

The soul of man also leans in the unconscious inclination we call
   religion
towards the sun of suns, and back and forth goes the breath
of incipient energetic life.

Out of the soul's middle to the middle-most sun, way-off, or in
   every atom.

The Primal Passions

If you will go down into yourself, under your surface personality
you will find you have a great desire to drink life direct
from the source, not out of bottles and bottled personal vessels.

What the old people call immediate contact with God.
That strange essential communication of life
not bottled in human bottles.

What even the wild witchcraft of the past was seeking
before it degenerated.

Life from the source, unadulterated
with the human taint.

Contact with the sun of suns
that shines somewhere in the atom, somewhere pivots the curved
   space,
and cares not a straw for the put-up human figments.

Communion with the Godhead, they used to say in the past.
But even that is human-tainted now,
tainted with the ego and the personality.

To feel a fine, fine breeze blowing through the navel and the knees
and have a cool sense of truth, inhuman truth at last
softly fluttering the senses, in the exquisite orgasm of coition
with the godhead of energy that cannot tell lies.

The cool, cool truth of pure vitality
pouring into the veins from the direct contact with the source.
Uncontaminated by even the beginnings of a lie.
The soul's first passion is for sheer life
entering in shocks of truth, unfouled by lies.

And the soul's next passion is to reflect
and then turn round and embrace the extant body of life
with the thrusting embrace of new justice, new justice
between men and men, men and women, and earth and stars and
    suns.
The passion of justice being profound and subtle
and changing in a flow as all passions change.

But the passion of justice is a primal embrace
between man and all his known universe.

And the passion of truth is the embrace between man and his god
in the sheer coition of the life-flow, stark and unlying.

Escape

When we get out of the glass bottles of our own ego,
and when we escape like squirrels from turning in the cages of our
    personality
and get into the forest again,
we shall shiver with cold and fright
but things will happen to us
so that we don't know ourselves.

Cool, unlying life will rush in,
and passion will make our bodies taut with power,
we shall stamp our feet with new power
and old things will fall down,
we shall laugh, and institutions will curl up like burnt paper.

The Root of Our Evil

The root of our present evil is that we buy and sell.
Ultimately, we are all busy buying and selling one another.

It began with Judas, and goes on in the wage-system.
Men sell themselves for a wage, and employers look out for a
    bargain.
And employers are bought by financiers, and financiers are sold to
    the devil.

– Get thou behind me, Satan! –
That was just what Satan wanted to do,
for then nobody would have their eye on him.

And Jesus never looked round.
That is the great reproach we have against him.
He was frightened to look round
and see Satan bargaining the world away
and men, and the bread of men
behind his back
with satanically inspired financiers.

If Jesus had kept a sharp eye on Satan,
and refused to let so many things happen behind his back
we shouldn't be where we are now.

Come, Satan, don't go dodging behind my back any longer.
If you've got the goods, come forward, boy, and let's see 'em.
I'm perfectly willing to strike a decent bargain.
But I'm not having any dodging going on behind my back.

What we want is some sort of communism
not based on wages, nor profits, nor any sort of buying and selling
but on a religion of life.

The Ignoble Procession

When I see the ignoble procession
streaming forth from little doorways
citywards, in little rivers that swell to a great stream,
of men in bowler hats, hurrying
and a mingling of wallet-carrying women
hurrying, hurrying, legs going quick, quick, quick
in ignoble haste, for fear of being late –
I am filled with humiliation.

Their haste
is so
humiliating.

No Joy in Life

Never, my young men,
you who complain you know no joy in your lives,
never will you know any joy in your lives
till you ask for lightning instead of love
till you pray for the right gods, for the thunderbolt instead of pity
till you look to the right man, to put you into touch.

Then you will hit the Flat-iron Building and flatten it out.
Then you will shatter the Bank.
Then you will settle the hash of Business finally.

Wild Things in Captivity

Wild things in captivity
while they keep their own wild purity
won't breed, they mope, they die.

All men are in captivity,
active with captive activity,
and the best won't breed, though they don't know why.

The great cage of our domesticity
kills sex in a man, the simplicity
of desire is distorted and twisted awry.

And so with bitter perversity
gritting against the great adversity,
the young ones copulate, hate it, and want to cry.

Sex is a state of grace.
In a cage it can't take place.
Break the cage, then, start in and try.

Mournful Young Man

Mournful young man in your twenties
who think the only way out of your mournfulness is
    through a woman,
yet you fail to find the woman, when there are so many
    women about.

Why don't you realise
that you're not desirable?
that no woman will ever desire you, as you are,
except, of course, for secondary motives.

The women are in the cage as much as you are.
They look at you, they see a caged monkey.
How do you expect them ever to desire you?
Anyhow they never will, except for secondary motives,
or except you change.

There is No Way Out

There is no way out, we are all caged monkeys
blue-arsed with the money-bruise
and wearing our seats out sitting on money.

There is no way out, the cage has no door, it's rusted solid.

If you copulate with the finest woman on earth
there's no relief, only a moment's sullen respite.

You're a caged monkey again in five minutes.
Therefore be prepared to tackle the cage.

Money-Madness

Money is our madness, our vast collective madness.

And, of course, if the multitude is mad
the individual carries his own grain of insanity around with him.

I doubt if any man living hands out a pound note without a pang;
and a real tremor, if he hands out a ten-pound note.

We quail, money makes us quail.
It has got us down, we grovel before it in strange terror.
And no wonder, for money has a fearful cruel power among men.

But it is not money we are so terrified of,
it is the collective money-madness of mankind.
For mankind says with one voice: How much is he worth?
Has he no money? Then let him eat dirt, and go cold.

And if I have no money, they will give me a little bread
so I do not die,
but they will make me eat dirt with it.
I shall have to eat dirt, I shall have to eat dirt
if I have no money.

It is that that I am frightened of.
And that fear can become a delirium.
It is fear of my money-mad fellow-men.

We must have some money
to save us from eating dirt.

Bread should be free,
shelter should be free,
fire should be free,
to all and anybody, all and anybody, all over the world.

We must regain our sanity about money
before we start killing one another about it.
It's one thing or the other.

Kill Money

Kill money, put money out of existence.
It is a perverted instinct, a hidden thought
which rots the brain, the blood, the bones, the stones, the soul.

Make up your mind about it:
that society must establish itself upon a different principle
from the one we've got now.

We must have the courage of mutual trust.
We must have the modesty of simple living.
And the individual must have his house, food and fire all free
    like a bird.

Men Are Not Bad

Men are not bad, when they are free.
Prison makes men bad, and the money compulsion makes men bad.

If men were free from the terror of earning a living
there would be abundance in the world
and men would work gaily.

Nottingham's New University

In Nottingham, that dismal town
where I went to school and college,
they've built a new university
for a new dispensation of knowledge.

Built it most grand and cakeily
out of the noble loot
derived from shrewd cash-chemistry
by good Sir Jesse Boot.

Little I thought, when I was a lad
and turned my modest penny
over on Boot's Cash Chemist's counter,
that Jesse, by turning many

millions of similar honest pence
over, would make a pile
that would rise at last and blossom out
in grand and cakey style

into a university
where smart men would dispense
doses of smart cash-chemistry
in language of common-sense!

That future Nottingham lads would be
cash-chemically B.Sc.
that Nottingham lights would rise and say:
– By Boots I am M.A.

From this I learn, though I knew it before,
that culture has her roots
in the deep dung of cash, and lore
is a last offshoot of Boots.

I am in a Novel

I read a novel by a friend of mine
in which one of the characters was me,
the novel it sure was mighty fine
but the funniest thing that could be

was me, or what was supposed for me,
for I had to recognise
a few of the touches, like a low-born jake,
but the rest was a real surprise.

Well damn my eyes! I said to myself.
Well damn my little eyes!
If this is what Archibald thinks I am
he sure thinks a lot of lies.

Well think o' that now, think o' that!
That's what he sees in me!
I'm about as much like a Persian cat,
or a dog with a harrowing flea.

My Lord! a man's friends' ideas of him
would stock a menagerie
with a marvellous outfit! How did Archie see
such a funny pup in me?

No! Mr Lawrence!

No, Mr Lawrence, it's not like that!
I don't mind telling you
I know a thing or two about love,
perhaps more than you do.

And what I know is that you make it
too nice, too beautiful.
It's not like that, you know; you fake it.
It's really rather dull.

Red-Herring

My father was a working man
   and a collier was he,
at six in the morning they turned him down
   and they turned him up for tea

My mother was a superior soul
   a superior soul was she,
cut out to play a superior role
   in the god-damn bourgeoisie.

We children were the in-betweens
   little nondescripts were we,
indoors we called each other *you*,
   outside, it was *tha* and *thee*.

But time has fled, our parents are dead
   we've risen in the world all three;
but still we are in-betweens, we tread
   between the devil and the deep sad sea.

I am a member of the bourgeoisie
   and a servant-maid brings me my tea –
But I'm always longing for someone to say
   'ark 'ere, lad! atween thee an' me

they're a' a b— d— lot o' —s,
   an' I reckon it's nowt but right
we should start an' kick their —ses for 'em
   an' tell 'em to —.

Our Moral Age

Of course, if you make naughtiness nasty,
　　spicily nasty, of course,
then it's quite all right; we understand
　　life's voice, even when she's hoarse.

But when you go and make naughtiness nice
　　there's no excuse;
if such things were nice, and we needn't think twice,
　　what would be the use?

My Naughty Book

They say I wrote a naughty book
With perfectly awful things in it,
putting in all the impossible words
like b— and f— and sh—.

Most of my friends were deeply hurt
and haven't forgiven me yet;
I'd loaded the camel's back before
with dirt they couldn't forget.

And now, no really, the final straw
was words like sh— and f—!
I heard the camel's back go crack
beneath the weight of muck.

Then out of nowhere rushed John Bull,
that mildewed pup, good doggie!
squeakily bellowing for all he was worth,
and slavering wet and soggy.

He couldn't bite 'em, he was much too old,
but he made a pool of dribblings;
so while the other one heaved her sides,
with moans and hollow bibblings,

he did his best, the good old dog,
to support her, the hysterical camel,
and everyone listened and loved it, the
ridiculous bimmel-bammel.[55]

But still, one has no right to take
the old dog's greenest bones
that he's buried now for centuries
beneath England's garden stones.

And, of course, one has no right to lay
such words to the camel's charge,
when she prefers to have them left
in the WC writ large.

Poor homely words. I must give you back
to the camel and the dog,
for her to mumble and him to crack
in secret, great golliwog!

And hereby I apologise
to all my foes and friends
for using words they privately keep
for their own immortal ends.

And henceforth I will never use
more than the chaste, short dash;
so do forgive me! I sprinkle my hair
with grey, repentant ash.

The Little Wowser [56]

There is a little wowser
     John Thomas by name,
and for every bloomin', mortal thing
     that little blighter's to blame.

It was 'im as made the first mistake
     of putting us in the world,
forcin' us out of the unawake,
     an' makin' us come uncurled.

And then when you're gettin' nicely on
   an' life seems to begin,
that little bleeder comes bustin' in
   with: Hello boy! what about sin?

An' then he leads you by the nose
   after a lot o' women
as strips you stark as a monkey nut
   an' leaves you never a trimmin'.

An' then somebody has ter marry you
   to put him through 'is paces;
then when John Thomas don't worry you,
   it's your wife, wi' her airs an' graces.

I think of all the little brutes
   as ever was invented
that little cod's the holy worst.
   I've chucked him, I've repented.

The Young and Their Moral Guardians

O the stale old dogs who pretend to guard
the morals of the masses,
how smelly they make the great back-yard,
wetting after everyone that passes.

If a man goes by who doesn't give
a damn for their dirty kennels,
how they rush out and want to rive
him to pieces, the good-hearted spaniels!

And the young, the modern and jaunty young,
how scared they all are, even now
of the yellow dogs, how they slink away
in silence from the great bow-wow!

When a low bull-mongrel starts declaiming,
there's not a young man in the whole
of England with the guts to turn round on him, aiming
a good kick at his dirty old hole.

When I Read Shakespeare

When I read Shakespeare I am struck with wonder
that such trivial people should muse and thunder
in such lovely language.

Lear, the old buffer, you wonder his daughters
didn't treat him rougher,
the old chough, the old chuffer!

And Hamlet, how boring, how boring to live with,
so mean and self-conscious, blowing and snoring
his wonderful speeches, full of other folk's whoring!

And Macbeth and his Lady, who should have been choring,
such suburban ambition, so messily goring
old Duncan with daggers!

How boring, how small Shakespeare's people are!
Yet the language so lovely! like the dyes from gas-tar.

Salt of the Earth

Slowly the salt of the earth becomes salt of the sea.
Slowly the raindrops of appreciation
carry the salt of the earth, the wisdom of wise men, the gifts of
    the great
down to the ocean of the afterwards, where it remains as brine
in which to pickle the younger generations
who would be so much better without pickling.

Slowly the salt of the earth becomes salt of the sea.

Fresh Water

They say it is very difficult
to distil sea-water into sweet.

Perhaps that's why it is so difficult
to get a refreshing drink out of old wisdom,
old truth, old teaching of any sort.

Peace and War

People always make war when they say they love peace.
The loud love of peace makes one quiver more than any battle cry.
Why should one love peace? it is so obviously vile to make war.

Loud peace propaganda makes war seem imminent.
It is a form of war, even, self-assertion and being wise for other
    people.

Let people be wise for themselves. And anyhow
nobody can be wise except on rare occasions, like getting married
    or dying.

It's bad taste to be wise all the time, like being at a perpetual funeral.
For everyday use, give me somebody whimsical, with not too much
    purpose in life,
then we shan't have war, and we needn't talk about peace.

Many Mansions

When a bird flips his tail in getting his balance on a tree
he feels much gayer than if somebody had left him a fortune
or than if he'd just built himself a nest with a bathroom –
Why can't people be gay like that?

Glory

Glory is of the sun, too, and the sun of suns,
and down the shafts of his splendid pinions
run tiny rivers of peace.

Most of his time, the tiger pads and slouches in a burning peace.

And the small hawk high up turns round on the slow pivot of peace.

Peace comes from behind the sun, with the peregrine falcon, and
    the owl.

Yet all these drink blood.

Woe

Woe, woe to the world!
For we're all self-consciously aware of ourselves
yet not sufficiently conscious to be able to forget ourselves
and be whimsically at home in ourselves.

So everybody makes an assertion of himself,
and every self-assertion clashes on every other.

Attila

I would call Attila, on his little horse
a man of peace.

For after all, he helped to smash a lot of old Roman lies,
the lies, the treachery, the slippery cultured squalor of that
    sneaking court of Ravenna.

And after all, lying and base hypocrisy and treachery
are much more hellishly peaceless than a little straightforward
    bloodshed
which may occasionally be a preliminary to the peace that
    passes understanding.

So that I would call Attila, on his little horse
a man of peace.

What Would You Fight For?

I am not sure I would always fight for my life.
Life might not be worth fighting for.

I am not sure I would always fight for my wife.
A wife isn't always worth fighting for.

Nor my children, nor my country, nor my fellow men.
It all depends whether I found them worth fighting for.

The only thing men invariably fight for
is their money. But I doubt if I'd fight for mine, anyhow, not to
   shed a lot of blood over it.

Yet one thing I do fight for, tooth and nail, all the time.
And that is my bit of inward peace, where I am at one with myself.

And I must say, I am often worsted.

Choice

I would rather sit still in a state of peace on a stone
than ride in the motor-car of a multi-millionaire
and feel the peacelessness of the multi-millionaire
poisoning me.

Riches

When I wish I was rich, then I know I am ill.
Because, to tell the truth, I have enough as I am.
So when I catch myself thinking: Ah, if I was rich!
I say to myself: Hello! I'm not well. My vitality is low.

Poverty

The only people I ever heard talk about My Lady Poverty
were rich people, or people who imagined themselves rich.
St Francis himself was a rich and spoiled young man.

Being born among the working people
I know that poverty is a hard old hag,
and a monster, when you're pinched for actual necessities.
And whoever says she isn't, is a liar.

I don't want to be poor, it means I am pinched.
But neither do I want to be rich.
When I look at this pine tree near the sea,
that grows out of rock, and plumes forth, plumes forth,
I see it has a natural abundance.

With its roots it has a grand grip on its daily bread,
and its plumes look like green cups held up to sun and air
and full of wine.

I want to be like that, to have a natural abundance
and plume forth, and be splendid.

Noble

I know I am noble with the nobility of the sun.
A certain peace, a certain grace.
I would say the same if I were a chaffinch or a tree.

Wealth

Peace I have from the core of the atom, from the core of space,
and grace, if I don't lose it, from the same place.
And I look shabby, yet my roots go beyond my knowing,
deep beyond the world of man.
And where my little leaves flutter highest
there are no people, nor ever will be.

Yet my roots are in a woman too.
And my leaves are green with the breath of human experience.

Tolerance

One can be tolerant with a bore
and suffer fools, though not gladly
– why should a man pretend to be glad about his sufferings?

But it is hard to be tolerant with the smarties,
or to put up with the clever mess-makers,
or to endure the jazzy person;
one can't stand peaceless people any more.

Compari[57]

I would like a few men to be at peace with.
Not friends, necessarily, they talk so much.
Nor yet comrades, for I don't belong to any cause.
Nor yet 'brothers', it's so conceited.
Nor pals, they're such a nuisance.
But men to be at peace with.

Sick

I am sick, because I have given myself away.
I have given myself to the people when they came
so cultured, even bringing little gifts,
so they pecked a shred of my life, and flew off with a croak
of sneaking exultance.
So now I have lost too much, and am sick.

I am trying now to learn never
to give of my life to the dead,
never, not the tiniest shred.

Dead People

When people are dead and peaceless
they hate life, they only like carrion.

When people are dead and peaceless
they hate happiness in others
with thin, screaming hatred,
as the vulture that screams high up, almost inaudible,
hovering to peck out the eyes of the still-living creature.

Cerebral Emotions

I am sick of people's cerebral emotions
that are born in their minds and forced down by the will
on to their poor, deranged bodies.

People feeling things they intend to feel, they mean to feel,
they will feel,
just because they don't feel them.

For, of course, if you really feel something
you don't have to assert that you feel it.

Wellsian Futures

When men are made in bottles
and emerge as squeaky globules with no bodies to speak of,
and therefore nothing to have feelings with,

they will still squeak intensely about their feelings
and be prepared to kill you if you say they've got none.

To Women, as Far as I'm Concerned

The feelings I don't have I don't have.
The feelings I don't have I won't say I have.
The feelings you say you have, you don't have.
The feelings you would like us both to have, we neither of
     us have.

The feelings people ought to have, they never have.
If people say they've got feelings, you may be pretty sure they
     haven't got them.

So if you want either of us to feel anything at all
you'd better abandon all idea of feelings altogether.

Blank

At present I am a blank, and I admit it.
In feeling I am just a blank.
My mind is fairly nimble, and is not blank.
My body likes its dinner and the warm sun, but otherwise is blank.

My soul is almost blank, my spirits quite.
I have a certain amount of money, so my anxieties are blank.

And I can't do anything about it, even there I am blank.
So I am just going to go on being a blank, till something nudges
    me from within,
and makes me know I am not blank any longer.

Elderly Discontented Women

Elderly discontented women ask for intimate companionship,
by which they mean more talk, talk, talk
especially about themselves and their own feelings.

Elderly discontented women are so full of themselves
they have high blood pressure and almost burst.

It is as if modern women had all got themselves on the brain
and that sent the blood rushing to the surface of the body
and driving them around in frenzied energy

stampeding over everybody,
while their hearts become absolutely empty,
and their voices are like screwdrivers
as they try to screw everybody else down with their will.

Old People

Nowadays everybody wants to be young,
so much so, that even the young are old with the effort of being
    young.

As for those over fifty, either they rush forward in self-assertion
    fearful to behold,
or they bear everybody a grim and grisly grudge
because of their own fifty or sixty or seventy or eighty summers.

As if it's my fault that the old girl is seventy-seven!

The Grudge of the Old

The old ones want to be young, and they aren't young,
and it rankles, they ache when they see the young,
and they can't help wanting to spite it on them venomously.

The old ones say to themselves: We are not going to be old,
we are not going to make way, we are not going to die,
we are going to stay on and on and on and on
and make the young look after us
till they are old. We are stronger than the young.

We have more energy, and our grip on life is harder.
Let us triumph, and let the young be listless
with their puny youth.
We are younger even now than the young, we can put their youth
    in the shade.

And it is true.
And they do it.
And so it goes on.

Beautiful Old Age

It ought to be lovely to be old
to be full of the peace that comes of experience
and wrinkled ripe fulfilment.

The wrinkled smile of completeness that follows a life
lived undaunted and unsoured with accepted lies.
If people lived without accepting lies
they would ripen like apples, and be scented like pippins
in their old age.

Soothing, old people should be, like apples
when one is tired of love.
Fragrant like yellowing leaves, and dim with the soft
stillness and satisfaction of autumn.

And a girl should say:
It must be wonderful to live and grow old.
Look at my mother, how rich and still she is!

And a young man should think: By Jove,
my father has faced all weathers, but it's been a life!

Courage

What makes people unsatisfied
is that they accept lies.

If people had courage, and refused lies
and found out what they really felt and really meant
and acted on it.,

they would distil the essential oil out of every experience
and like hazel nuts in autumn, at last
be sweet and sound.

And the young among the old
would be as in the hazel woods of September
nutting, gathering nuts of ripe experience.

As it is, all that the old can offer
is sour, bitter fruit, cankered by lies.

Desire is Dead

Desire may be dead
and still a man can be
a meeting place for sun and rain,
wonder outwaiting pain
as in a wintry tree.

When the Ripe Fruit Falls

When the ripe fruit falls
its sweetness distils and trickles away into the veins of the earth.

When fulfilled people die
the essential oil of their experience enters
the veins of living space, and adds a glisten
to the atom, to the body of immortal chaos.

For space is alive
and it stirs like a swan
whose feathers glisten
silky with oil of distilled experience.

Elemental

Why don't people leave off being lovable
or thinking they are lovable, or wanting to be lovable,
and be a bit elemental instead?

Since man is made up of the elements
fire, and rain, and air, and live loam
and none of these is lovable
but elemental,
man is lop-sided on the side of the angels.

I wish men would get back their balance among the elements
and be a bit more fiery, as incapable of telling lies
as fire is.

I wish they'd be true to their own variation, as water is,
which goes through all the stages of steam and stream and ice
  without losing its head.

I am sick of lovable people,
somehow they are a lie.

Fire

Fire is dearer to us than love or food,
hot, hurrying, yet it burns if you touch it.

What we ought to do
is not to add our love together, or our goodwill, or any of that,
for we're sure to bring in a lot of lies,
but our fire, our elemental fire
so that it rushes up in a huge blaze like a phallus into hollow
  space
and fecundates the zenith and the nadir
and sends off millions of sparks of new atoms
and singes us, and burns the house down.

I Wish I Knew a Woman

I wish I knew a woman
who was like a red fire on the hearth
glowing after the day's restless draughts.

So that one could draw near her
in the red stillness of the dusk
and really take delight in her

without having to make the polite effort of loving her
or the mental effort of making her acquaintance.
Without having to take a chill, talking to her.

Talk

I wish people, when you sit near them
wouldn't think it necessary to make conversation
and send thin draughts of words
blowing down your neck and your ears
and giving you a cold in your inside.

The Effort of Love

I am worn out
with the effort of trying to love people
and not succeeding.

Now I've made up my mind
I love nobody, I am going to love nobody,
I'm not going to tell any lies about it
and it's final.

If there's a man here and there, or a woman
whom I can really like,
that's quite enough for me.

And if by a miracle a woman happened to come along
who warmed the cockles of my heart
I'd rejoice over the woman and the warmed cockles of my
    heart
so long as it didn't all fizzle out in talk.

Can't be Borne

Any woman who says to me
 – Do you really love me? –
earns my undying detestation.

Man Reaches a Point

I cannot help but be alone
for desire has died in me, silence has grown,
and nothing now reaches out to draw
other flesh to my own.

Grasshopper is a Burden

Desire has failed, desire has failed
and the critical grasshopper
has come down on the hearth in a burden of locusts
and stripped it bare.

Basta!

When a man can love no more
and feel no more
and desire has failed
and the heart is numb,

then all he can do
is to say: It is so!
I've got to put up with it
and wait.

This is a pause, how long a pause I know not,
in my very being.

Tragedy

Tragedy seems to me a loud noise
louder than is seemly.

Tragedy looks to me like man
in love with his own defeat.
Which is only a sloppy way of being in love with yourself.

I can't very much care about the woes and tragedies
of Lear and Macbeth and Hamlet and Timon:
they cared so excessively themselves.

And when I think of the great tragedy of our material-mechanical
    civilisation
crushing out the natural human life
then sometimes I feel defeated; and then again I know
my shabby little defeat would do neither me any good
nor anybody else.

After All the Tragedies are Over

After all the tragedies are over and worn out
and a man can no longer feel heroic about being a Hamlet –
When love is gone, and desire is dead, and tragedy has left the
    heart
then grief and pain go too, withdrawing
from the heart and leaving strange cold stretches of sand.

So a man no longer knows his own heart;
he might say into the twilight: What is it?
I am here, yet my heart is bare and utterly empty.
I have passed from existence, I feel nothing any more.
I am a nonentity.

Yet, when the time has come to be nothing, how good it is to be
    nothing!
a waste expanse of nothing, like wide foreshores where not a
    ripple is left
and the sea is lost
in the lapse of the lowest of tides.

Ah, when I have seen myself left by life, left nothing!
Yet even waste, grey foreshores, sand, and sorry, far-out clay
are sea-bed still, through their hour of bare denuding.
It is the moon that turns the tides.
The beaches can do nothing about it.

Nullus

I know I am nothing.
Life has gone away, below my low-water mark.

I am aware I feel nothing, even at dawn.
The dawn comes up with a glitter and a blueness, and I say: How
    lovely!
But I am a liar, I feel no loveliness, it is a mental remark, a cliché.

My whole consciousness is cliché
and I am null;
I exist as an organism
and a nullus.

But I can do nothing about it
except admit it and leave it to the moon.

There are said to be creative pauses,
pauses that are almost death, empty and dead as death, almost.

And in these awful pauses the evolutionary change takes place.
Perhaps it is so.
The tragedy is over, it has ceased to be tragic, the last pause is
    upon us.

Pause, brethren, pause!

Dies Irae

Even the old emotions are finished,
we have worn them out.
And desire is dead.
And the end of all things is inside us.

Our epoch is over,
a cycle of evolution is finished,
our activity has lost its meaning,
we are ghosts, we are seed;
for our Word is dead
and we know not how to live wordless.

We live in a vast house
full of inordinate activities,
and the noise, and the stench, and the dreariness and lack of
    meaning
madden us, but we don't know what to do.

All we can know, at this moment
is the fulfilment of nothingness.

Lo, I am nothing!
It is a consummation devoutly to be wished
in this world of mechanical self-assertion.

Dies Illa[58]

Dies irae, dies illa
solvet saeclum in favilla –
Day of wrath, O day of warning!
Flame devours the world.

It does, even if we don't see it.

For there are all sorts of flames:
slow, creeping cold ones
that burn inwardly
like flickering cancers.

And the slow cold flames
may burn for long years
before they've eaten through the joists and the girders
and the house comes down, with a subsiding crash.

Stop It

The one thing the old will never understand
is that you can't prevent change.
All flows, and even the old are rapidly flowing away.
And the young are flowing in the throes of a great alteration.

The Death of Our Era

Our era is dying
yet who has killed it?
Have we, who are it?

In the middle of voluted space
its knell has struck.
And in the middle of every atom, which is the same thing,
a tiny bell of conclusion has sounded.

The curfew of our great day
the passing-bell of our way of knowing
the knell of our bald-headed consciousness
the tocsin of this our civilisation.

Who struck the bell?
Who rang the knell?
Not I, not you,
yet all of us.

At the core of space the final knell
Of our era has struck, and it chimes
in terrible rippling circles between the stars
till it reaches us, and its vibrations shatter us
each time they touch us.

And they keep on coming, with greater force
striking us, the vibrations of our finish.

And all that we can do
is to die the amazing death
with every stroke, and go on
till we are blank.

And yet, as we die, why should not our vast mechanised day die
    with us
so that when we are reborn, we can be born into a fresh world?

For the new word is Resurrection.

The New Word

Shall I tell you again the new word
the new word of the unborn day?
It is Resurrection.
The resurrection of the flesh.

For our flesh is dead
only egoistically we assert ourselves.

And the new word means nothing to us,
it is such an old word,
till we admit how dead we are,
till we actually feel as blank as we really are.

Sun in Me

A sun will rise in me
I shall slowly resurrect
already the whiteness of false dawn is on my inner ocean.

A sun in me.

And a sun in heaven.

And beyond that, the immense sun behind the sun,
the sun of immense distances, that fold themselves together
within the genitals of living space.

And further, the sun within the atom
which is god in the atom.

Be Still!

The only thing to be done now,
now that the waves of our undoing have begun to strike on us,
is to contain ourselves.

To keep still, and let the wreckage of ourselves go,
let everything go, as the wave smashes us,
yet keep still, and hold
the tiny grain of something that no wave can wash away,
not even the most massive wave of destiny.

Among all the smashed debris of myself
keep quiet, and wait.
For the word is Resurrection.
And even the sea of seas will have to give up its dead.

At Last

When things get very bad, they pass beyond tragedy.
And then the only thing we can do is to keep quite still
and guard the last treasure of the soul, our sanity.

Since, poor individuals that we are,
if we lose our sanity
we lose that which keeps us individual
distinct from chaos.

In death, the atom takes us up
and the suns.

But if we lose our sanity
nothing and nobody in the whole vast realm of space
wants us, or can have anything to do with us.

We can but howl the lugubrious howl of idiots,
the howl of the utterly lost
howling their nowhereness.

Nemesis

The nemesis that awaits our civilisation
is social insanity
which in the end is always homicidal.
Sanity means the wholeness of the consciousness.
And our society is only part conscious, like an idiot.

If we do not rapidly open all the doors of consciousness
and freshen the putrid little space in which we are cribbed
the sky-blue walls of our unventilated heaven
will be bright red with blood.

The Optimist

The optimist builds himself safe inside a cell
and paints the inside walls sky-blue
and blocks up the door
and says he's in heaven.

The Third Thing

Water is H_2O, hydrogen two parts, oxygen one,
but there is also a third thing, that makes it water
and nobody knows what that is.
The atom locks up two energies
but it is a third thing present which makes it an atom.

The Sane Universe

One might talk of the sanity of the atom
the sanity of space
the sanity of the electron
the sanity of water –

For it is all alive
and has something comparable to that which we call sanity in
     ourselves.
The only oneness is the oneness of sanity.

Fear of Society is the Root of All Evil

Today, the social consciousness is mutilated
so everything is insane;
success is insane, and failure is insane,
chastity is insane, and debauchery is insane,
money is insane, and poverty is insane.

A fearful thing is the mutilated social consciousness.

God

Where sanity is
there God is.

And the sane can still recognise sanity
so they can still recognise God.

Sane and Insane

The puritan is insane
and the profligate is insane
and they divide the world.

The wealthy are insane
and the poverty-stricken are insane
and the world is going to pieces between them.

The puritan is afraid
and the profligate is afraid.

The wealthy are afraid
and the poverty-stricken are afraid.

They are afraid with horrible and opposing fears
which threaten to tear the world in two, between them.

A Sane Revolution

If you make a revolution, make it for fun,
don't make it in ghastly seriousness,
don't do it in deadly earnest,
do it for fun.

Don't do it because you hate people
do it just to spit in their eye.

Don't do it for the money,
do it and be damned to the money.

Don't do it for equality,
do it because we've got too much equality
and it would be fun to upset the apple-cart
and see which way the apples would go a-rolling.

Don't do it, anyhow, for international Labour.
Do it so that we can all of us be little aristocracies on our own
and kick our heels like jolly escaped asses.

Don't do it, anyhow, for international Labour.
Labour is the one thing a man has too much of.
Let's abolish Labour, let's have done with labouring!
Work can be fun, and men can enjoy it; then it's not labour.

Let's have it so! Let's make a revolution for fun!

Always This Paying

Nothing is really any fun today,
because you've always got to pay for everything.
And whatever costs you money, money, money, is really no fun.

That's why women aren't much fun. You're always having to pay
    for them.

Or else, poor things, they're having to pay for themselves,
which is perhaps worse.

Why isn't anything free, why is it always pay, pay, pay?

A man can't get any fun out of wife, sweetheart or tart
because of the beastly expense.

Why don't we do something about the money system?

Poor Young Things

The young today are born prisoners,
poor things, and they know it.

Born in a universal workhouse,
and they feel it.

Inheriting a sort of confinement
work, and prisoners' routine
and prisoners' flat, ineffectual pastime.

A Played-Out Game

Success is a played-out game, success, success!
because what have you got when you've got it?

The young aren't vitally interested in it any more.
Only third-rate swabs are pushing to get on, nowadays.

Getting the better of other people! Who cares? –
Getting the better of them! – Which better, what better, anyhow?

Our poor old daddies *got on*,
and then could never get off again.

If only we could make life a bit more just
so that we could all get along gaily
instead of getting on and not being able to get off again.

Triumph

It seems to me that for five thousand years at least
men have been wanting to triumph, triumph, triumph
triumph over their fellow men, triumph over obstacles, triumph
    over evil,
till now the very word is nauseating, we can't hear it any more

If we looked in our hearts, we should see
we loathe the thought of any sort of triumph,
we are sick of it.

The Combative Spirit

As a matter of fact, we are better than we know.
We trail behind us an endless tradition of combat, triumph, conquest
and we feel we've got to keep it up, keep on combating, triumphing,
    conquering.
When as a matter of fact, the thought of this endless imbecile struggle
    of combat
kills us, we are sick of it, to die.
We are fed up with combat,
we feel that if the whole combative, competitive system doesn't soon
    go bust,
we shall.

We want a new world of wild peace, where living is free.
Not this hyena tame peace where no man dare tell another he's a thief
and yet every man is driven into robbing every other man;
this pretty peace where every man has to fight, and fight foul
to get a living, in the dastardly mean combat
we call free competition and individual enterprise and equal
    opportunity.
Why should we have to fight for a living?
Living should be as free to a man as to a bird,
though most birds have to pay, with their lives, where men are.

Why should we brace ourselves up with mean emulation?
If we brace ourselves up, it should be for something we want to do
and we feel is worth doing.
The efforts of men, like the efforts of birds in spring,
would be lovely if they rose from the man himself, spontaneous
pure impulse to make something, to put something forth.
Even if it was only a tin pan.

I see the tin-man, the tinker, sitting day after day on the beach
mending and tinning the pans of all the village
and happy as a wagtail by a pool,
the same with the fishermen sitting darning their nets,
happy as perhaps kings used to be, but certainly aren't.
Work is the clue to a man's life.
But it must be free work, not done just for money, but for fun.

Why should we compete with one another?
As a matter of fact, when the tinker looks so happy tinkering
I immediately want to go and do something jolly too.
One free, cheerful activity stimulates another.
Men are not really mean.
Men are made mean, by fear, and a system of grab.

The young know these things quite well.
Why don't they prepare to act on them?
Then they'd be happy. For we are all so much better than the
    system allows us to be.

Wages

The wages of work is cash.
The wages of cash is want more cash.
The wages of want more cash is vicious competition.
The wages of vicious competition is – the world we live in.

The work-cash-want circle is the viciousest circle
that ever turned men into fiends.

Earning a wage is a prison occupation
and a wage-earner is a sort of gaol-bird.

Earning a salary is a prison overseer's job
a gaoler instead of a gaol-bird.

Living on our income is strolling grandly outside the prison
in terror lest you have to go in. And since the work-prison covers
almost every scrap of the living earth, you stroll up and down
on a narrow beat, about the same as a prisoner taking exercise.

This is called universal freedom.

Young Fathers

Young men, having no real joy in life and no hope in the future,
how can they commit the indecency of begetting children
without first begetting a new hope for the children to grow up to?

But then, you need only look at the modern perambulator
to see that a child, as soon as it is born,
is put by its parents into its coffin.

A Tale Told by an Idiot

Modern life is a tale told by an idiot;
flat-chested, crop-headed, chemicalised women, of indeterminate sex,
and wimbly-wambly[59] young men, of sex still more indeterminate,
and hygienic babies in huge hulks of coffin-like perambulators –

The great social idiot, it must be confessed,
tells dull, meaningless, disgusting tales
and repeats himself like the flushing of a WC.

Being Alive

The only reason for living is being fully alive;
and you can't be fully alive if you are crushed by secret fear,
and bullied with the threat: Get money or eat dirt! –
and forced to do a thousand mean things meaner than your nature,
and forced to clutch on to possessions in the hope they'll make you
    feel safe,
and forced to watch everyone that comes near you, lest they've come
    to do you down.

Without a bit of common trust in one another, we can't live.
In the end we go insane.
It is the penalty of fear and meanness, being meaner than our
    natures are.
To be alive, you've got to feel a generous flow,
and under a competitive system, that is impossible, really.

The world is waiting for a new great movement of generosity,
or for a great wave of death.

We must change the system, and make living free to all men,
or we must see men die, and then die ourselves.

Self-Protection

When science starts to be interpretive
it is more unscientific even than mysticism.

To make self-preservation and self-protection the first law of
    existence
is about as scientific as making suicide the first law of existence,
and amounts to very much the same thing.

A nightingale singing at the top of his voice
is neither hiding himself nor preserving himself nor propagating
    his species;
he is giving himself away in every sense of the word
and obviously, it is the culminating point of his existence.

A tiger is striped and golden for his own glory.
He would certainly be much more invisible if he were grey-green.

And I don't suppose the ichthyosaurus sparkled like the
    humming-bird,
no doubt he was khaki-coloured with muddy protective coloration,
so why didn't he survive?

As a matter of fact, the only creatures that seem to survive
are those that give themselves away in flash and sparkle
and gay flicker of joyful life;
those that go glittering abroad
with a bit of splendour.

Even mice play quite beautifully at shadows,
and some of them are brilliantly piebald.

I expect the dodo looked like a clod,
a drab and dingy bird.

A Man

All I care about in a man
is that unbroken spark in him
where he is himself
undauntedly.

And all I want is to see the spark flicker
vivid and clean.

But our civilisation, alas,
with lust crushes out the spark
and leaves men living clay.

Because when the spark is crushed in a man
he can't help being a slave, a wage-slave,
a money-slave.

Lizard

A lizard ran out on a rock and looked up, listening
no doubt to the sounding of the spheres.
And what a dandy fellow! the right toss of a chin for you
and swirl of a tail!

If men were as much men as lizards are lizards
they'd be worth looking at.

Relativity

I like relativity and quantum theories
because I don't understand them
and they make me feel as if space shifted about like a swan that
    can't settle,
refusing to sit still and be measured;
and as if the atom were an impulsive thing
always changing its mind.

Space

Space, of course, is alive
that's why it moves about;
and that's what makes it eternally spacious and unstuffy.

And somewhere it has a wild heart
that sends pulses even through me;
and I call it the sun;
and I feel aristocratic, noble, when I feel a pulse go through me
from the wild heart of space, that I call the sun of suns.

Sun-Men

Men should group themselves into a new order
of sun-men.
Each one turning his breast straight to the sun of suns
in the centre of all things,
and from his own little inward sun
nodding to the great one.

And receiving from the great one
his strength and his promptings,
and refusing the pettifogging promptings of human
weakness.

And walking each in his own sun-glory
with bright legs and uncringing buttocks.

Sun-Women

How strange it would be if some women came forward and said:
We are sun-women!
We belong neither to men nor our children nor even ourselves
but to the sun.

And how delicious it is to feel sunshine upon one!
And how delicious to open like a marigold
when a man comes looking down upon one
with sun in his face, so that a woman cannot but open
like a marigold to the sun,
and thrill with glittering rays.

Democracy

I am a democrat in so far as I love the free sun in men
and an aristocrat in so far as I detest narrow-gutted, possessive
    persons.

I love the sun in any man
when I see it between his brows
clear, and fearless, even if tiny.

But when I see these great successful men
so hideous and corpse-like, utterly sunless
like gross successful slaves grossly waddling,
then I am more than radical, I want to work a guillotine.

And when I see working men
pale and mean and insect-like, scuttling along
and living like lice on poor money
and never looking up,
then I wish, like Tiberius, the multitude had only one head
so that I could lop it off.

I feel that when people have gone utterly sunless
they shouldn't exist.

Aristocracy of the Sun

To be an aristocrat of the sun
you don't need one single social inferior to exalt you;
You draw your nobility direct from the sun
let other people be what they like.

I am that I am
from the sun,
and people are not my measure.

Perhaps, if we started right, all the children could grow up sunny
    and sun-aristocrats.
We need have no dead people, money-slaves, and social worms.

Conscience

Conscience
is sun-awareness
and our deep instinct
not to go against the sun.

The Middle Classes

The middle classes
are sunless.

They have only two measures:
mankind and money,
they have utterly no reference to the sun.

As soon as you let people be your measure
you are middle-class and essentially non-existent.

Because, if the middle classes had no poorer people to be superior to
they would themselves at once collapse into lower classness.

And if they had no upper classes either to be inferior to,
they'd become nothing.
For their middleness is only an unreality separating two realities.

No sun, no earth,
nothing that transcends the bourgeois middlingness,
the middle classes are more meaningless
than paper money when the bank is broke.

Immorality

It is only immoral
to be dead-alive
sun-extinct
and busy putting out the sun
in other people.

Censors

Censors are dead people
set up to judge between life and death.

For no live, sunny man would be a censor,
he'd just laugh.

But censors, being dead men,
have a stern eye on life.

– That thing's alive! It's dangerous. Make away with it! –
And when the execution is performed
you hear the stertorous, self-righteous heavy breathing of the
    dead men,
the censors, breathing with relief.

Man's Image

What a pity, when a man looks at himself in a glass
he doesn't bark at himself like a dog does,
or fluff up in indignant fury, like a cat!

What a pity he sees himself so wonderful,
a little lower than the angels!
and so interesting!

Immoral Man

Man is immoral because he has got a mind
and can't get used to the fact.

The deep instincts, when left alone, are quite moral,
and clear intuition is more than moral,
it really makes us men.

Why don't we learn to tame the mind
instead of the passions and the instincts and feelings?
It is the mind which is uncouth and overweening
and ruins our complex harmony.

Cowards

In all creation, only man cowers and is afraid of life.
Only man is terrified of his own possible splendour and delight.
Only is man agonised in front of the necessity to be something
        better than he is,
poor mental worm.

Though maybe the mammoth got too big in tusk and teeth,
and the extinct giant elk too big in antlers,
out of fear of the unknown enemy;
so perhaps they too died out from fear,
as man is likely to do.

Think – !

Imagine what it must have been to have existence
in the wild days when life was sliding whirlwinds, blue-hot weights,
in the days called chaos, which left us rocks, and gems!

Think that the sapphire is only alumina,[60] like kitchen pans
crushed utterly, and breathed through and through
with fiery weight and wild life, and coming out
clear and eternally blue!

Peacock

Think how a peacock in a forest of high trees
shimmers in a stream of blueness and long-tressed magnificence!
And women even cut their shimmery hair!

Paltry-Looking People

And think how the nightingale, who is so shy,
makes of himself a belfry of throbbing sound!
While people mince mean words through their teeth.

And think how wild animals trot with splendour
till man destroys them!
how vividly they make their assertion of life!

But how paltry, mingy and dingy and squalid people look
in their rag garments scuttling through the streets,
or sitting stuck like automata in automobiles!

Tarts

I suppose tarts are called tarts because they're tart,
meaning sour, make you pull a face after.

And I suppose most girls are a bit tarty today,
so that's why so many young men have long faces.

The father eats the pear, and the son's teeth are set on edge.

Latter-Day Sinners

The worst of the younger generation, those Latter-Day sinners,
is that they calmly assert: We only thrill to perversity, murder,
      suicide, rape –
bragging a little, really,
and at the same time expect to go on calmly eating good dinners
      for the next fifty years.

They say: *Après moi le déluge!* and calmly expect
that the deluge will never be turned on them, only *after* them.

Post me, nihil![61] – But perhaps, my dears,
nihil will come along and hit you on the head.

Why should the deluge wait while these young gentry go on eating
good dinners for fifty more long years?

Why should our Latter-Day sinners expect such a long smooth run
for their very paltry little bit of money?

If you are expecting a Second Advent in the shape of a deluge
you mustn't expect it also to wait for your convenience.

What Matters

As one of our brightest young intellectuals said to me:
It's not so much what we think,
or even what we like or dislike, or approve or disapprove that
      matters so very much.

What matters is what we thrill to.
We are ultimately determined by what we thrill to.
And, of course, thrilling is like loving, you have no choice about it.

Pondering this new truth of the sensational young, I said
But what do you thrill to? Do you know?
I suppose, as a matter of fact, it's getting a little difficult,
he replied, to thrill to anything.

A thrill rather easily exhausts itself – take even the war,
and look at the sodomitical and lesbian stuff – wearing rather thin.
Beauty, of course! Beauty is still a delicious escape.

And the pure intellect gives one a last, masturbating sense of
      excited freedom!
But, of course, one knows that both beauty and pure intellect are
      only escapes,
mild forms of cocaine; they're not life, exactly.

No, when it comes to thrills, there are really very few.
Judging from the fiction it is possible to read, I should say rape
    was rather thrilling
or being raped, either way, so long as it was consciously done,
    and slightly subtle.

Yes, if it's a keen match, rape is rather thrilling.
And then perhaps murder. That is to say
quite cold-blooded, intellectual murder, with a sufficient cool
    motive
and a complete absence of consequence to the murderer.

I should say that was rather thrilling,
rather thrilling to contemplate.

After that, of course, there's suicide – certain aspects perhaps,

Yes, I should say the contemplation of clever suicide *is* rather
    thrilling,
so long as the thing is done neatly, and the world is left looking
    very fooled.

Quite thrilling, I should say, at least to contemplate.
For the rest – no! I should say life held very few further thrilling
    possibilities.
So one of the brightest young intellectuals put it to me.
And I had to give him credit for his rather exhibitionist honesty.

And in the intervals of their thrills, I suppose
they must go on
they must go on scratching the eczema of their mental itch
with fingernails of septic criticising.

Fate and the Younger Generation

It is strange to think of the Annas, the Vronskys, the Pierres,
    all the Tolstoyan lot
wiped out.

And the Alyoshas and Dmitris and Myshkins and
    Stavrogins, the Dostoevsky lot
all wiped out.

And the Tchekov wimbly-wambly wet-legs all wiped out.

Gone! Dead, or wandering in exile with their feathers
    plucked,
anyhow, gone from what they were, entirely.

Will the Proustian lot go next?
And then our English imitation intelligentsia?
Is it the *Quos vult perdere Deus*[62] business?

Anyhow the Tolstoyan lot simply asked for extinction:
Eat me up, dear peasant! – So the peasant ate him.
And the Dostoevsky lot wallowed in the thought:
Let me sin my way to Jesus! So they sinned themselves off
    the face of the earth.
And the Tchekov lot: I'm too weak and lovable to live! So
    they went.
Now the Proustian lot: Dear darling death, let me wriggle
    my way towards you
like the worm I am! So he wriggled and got there.

Finally our little lot: I don't want to die, but by Jingo if I do!
 – Well, it won't matter so very much, either!

As for Me, I'm a Patriot

Whatever else they say of me
they'll never be able to say
I was one of the little blighters
who so brilliantly betray
the tough old England that made us
and in them is rotting away.

I'd betray the middle classes
and money and industry
and the intellectual asses
and cash christianity.

but not the England that made me
the stuff of a man,
the old England that doesn't upbraid me,
nor put me under a ban.

The Rose of England

Oh the rose of England is a single rose
and damasked red and white!

But roses, if they're fed too much,
change from being single and become gradually double,
and that's what's happened to the English rose.

The wild rose in a sheltered garden
when it need struggle no more
softly blows out its thin little male stamens
into broad sweet petals,
and through the centuries goes on and on
puffing its little male stamens out into sterile petal flames
till at last it's a full, full rose, and has no male dust any more,
it propagates no more.

So it is with Englishmen.
They are all double roses

and their true maleness is gone.
Oh the rose of England is a single rose
and needs to be raised from seed.

England in 1929

England was always a country of men
and had a brave destiny, even when she went wrong.

Now it's a country of frightened old mongrels
snapping out of fear,
and young wash-outs pretending to be in love with death
yet living on the fat of the land;

so, of course, the nation is swollen with insoluble problems
and like to become incurably diseased inside.

Liberty's Old Story

Men fight for liberty, and win it with hard knocks.
Their children, brought up easy, let it slip away again, poor fools.
And their grandchildren are once more slaves.

New Brooms

New brooms sweep clean
but they often raise such a dust in the sweeping
that they choke the sweeper.

Police Spies

Start a system of official spying
and you've introduced anarchy into your country.

Now It's Happened

One cannot now help thinking
how much better it would have been
If Vronsky and Anna Karenin
had stood up for themselves, and seen
Russia across her crisis,
instead of leaving it to Lenin.

The big, flamboyant Russia
might have been saved, if a pair
of rebels like Anna and Vronsky
had blasted the sickly air
of Dostoevsky and Tchekov,
and spy-government everywhere.

But Tolstoi was a traitor
to the Russia that needed him most,
the clumsy, bewildered Russia
so worried by the Holy Ghost.
He shifted his job on to the peasants
and landed them all on toast.

Dostoevsky, the Judas,
with his sham christianity
epileptically ruined
the last bit of sanity
left in the hefty bodies
of the Russian nobility.

So our goody-good men betray us
and our sainty-saints let us down,
and a sickly people will slay us
if we touch the sob-stuff crown
of such martyrs; while Marxian tenets
naturally take hold of the town.

Too much of the humble Willy wet-leg
and the holy can't-help-it touch,
till you've ruined a nation's fibre
and they loathe all feeling as such,
and want to be cold and devilish hard
like machines – and you can't wonder much –

Energetic Women

Why are women so energetic?
prancing their knees under their tiny skirts
like war-horses; or war-ponies at least?

Why are they so centrifugal?
Why are they so bursting, flinging themselves about?
Why, as they grow older, do they suffer from blood pressure?

Why are they never happy to be still?
Why did they cut off their long hair
which they could comb by the hour in luxurious quiet?

I suppose when the men all started being Willy wet-legs
they felt it was no longer any use being a linger-longer Lucy.

Film Passion

If all those females who so passionately loved
the film face of Rudolf Valentino
had had to take him for one night only, in the flesh,
how they'd have hated him!

Hated him just because he was a man
and flesh of a man.
For the luscious filmy imagination loathes the male substance
    with deadly loathing.

All the women who adored the shadow of the man on the
    screen
helped to kill him in the flesh.
Such adoration pierces the loins and perishes the man
worse than the evil eye.

Female Coercion

If men only fought outwards into the world
women might be devoted and gentle.
The fight's got to go in some direction.

But when men turn Willy wet-legs
women start in to make changes;
only instead of changing things that might be changed
they want to change the man himself
and turn the poor silk glove into a lusty sow's ear.

And the poor Willy wet-legs, the soft silk gloves,
how they hate the women's efforts to turn them
into sow's ears!

The modern Circe-dom!

Volcanic Venus

What has happened in the world?
the women are like little volcanoes
all more or less in eruption.

It is very unnerving, moving in a world of smouldering volcanoes.
It is rather agitating, sleeping with a little Vesuvius.
And exhausting, penetrating the lava-crater of a tiny Ixtaccihuatl[63]
and never knowing when you'll provoke an earthquake.

What Does She Want?

What does she want, volcanic Venus, as she goes fuming round?
What does she want?
She says she wants a lover, but don't you believe her.
She's seething like a volcano, and volcanoes don't want lovers.

Besides, she's had twenty lovers, only to find she didn't really
        want them.

So why should I, or you, be the twenty-first?
How are we going to appease her, maiden and mother
now a volcano of rage?
I tell you, the penis won't do it.
She bites him in the neck and passes on.

Wonderful Spiritual Women

The wonderful thoughtful women who make such good
        companions to a man
are only sitting tight on the craters of their volcano
and spreading their skirts.

Or like the woman who sat down on a sleeping mastodon
thinking he was a little hill, and she murmured such beautiful
        things
the men stood around like crocuses agape in the sun.

Then suddenly the mastodon rose with the wonderful lady
and trampled all the listeners to a smush.

Poor Bit of a Wench!

Will no one say hush! to thee
poor lass, poor bit of a wench?
Will never a man say: Come, my pigeon,
come an' be still wi' me, my own bit of a wench!

And would you peck out his eyes if he did?

What Ails Thee?

What ails thee then, woman, what ails thee?
doesn't ter know?
If tha canna say't, come then an' scraight[64] it out on my bosom!
Eh – Men doesna ha'e bosoms? 'appen not, on'y tha knows what
      I mean.
Come then, tha can scraight it out on my shirt-front
an' tha'lt feel better.

    – in the first place, I don't scraight.
    And if I did, I certainly couldn't *scraight it out*.
    And if I could, the last place I should choose
    would be your shirt-front
    or your manly bosom either.
    So leave off trying putting the Robbie Burns touch over me
    and kindly hand me the cigarettes
    if you haven't smoked them all,
    which you're much more likely to do
    than to shelter anybody from the cau-auld blast.

It's No Good!

It's no good, the women are in eruption
and those that have been good so far
now begin to steam ominously,
and if they're over forty-five, hurl great stones into the air
which are very likely to hit you on the head as you sit
on the very slopes of the matrimonial mountain
where you've sat peacefully all these years.

Vengeance is mine, saith the Lord,
but the women are my favourite vessels of wrath.

Don't Look at Me!

My dears, don't look at me, I am merely terrified of you.
I don't know what you want, but I certainly haven't got it to
    give you.

No, my poor little penis would be of no use to you
dear ladies, none whatsoever.
It's something else you are after, if you could but formulate it.

As for bearing my children – why there
I wouldn't insult you with the suggestion.

The son of man goes forth to war
no more, he sends his daughter
collecting foreskins.

But I consider I was sufficiently circumcised long ago.

My dears, if you want the skies to fall
they are established on the many pillars of the phallus,
so perhaps you'll do it.

Ships in Bottles

O ship in a bottle
with masts erect and spars all set and sails spread
how you remind me of my London friends,
O ships in bottles!

Little fleets
that put to sea on certain evenings,
frigates, barks and pinnaces, yawls
all beautifully rigged and bottled up
that put to sea and sink Armadas
in a pub parlour, in literary London, on certain evenings.

O small flotilla of sorry souls
sail on, over perilous seas of thought,
cast your little anchors in ports of eternity,
then weigh, and out to the infinities,
skirting the poles of being and of not-being.

Ah, in that parlour of the London pub
what dangers, ah, what dangers!
Caught between great icebergs of doubt
they are all but crushed
little ships.

Nipped upon the frozen floods of philosophic despair
high and dry.
Reeling in the black end of all beliefs
they sink.

Yet there they are, there they are,
little ships
safe inside their bottles!

Whelmed in profundities of profound conversation,
lost between great waves of ultimate ideas
they are – why there they are,
safe inside their bottles!

Safer than in the arms of Jesus!
Oh, safer than anything else is a well-corked, glassy ego,
and sounder than all insurance is a shiny mental conceit!

Sail, little ships in your glass bottles,
safe from every contact,
safe from all experience,
safe, above all, from life!

And let the nodding tempests of verbosity
weekly or twice-weekly whistle round your bottles.
Spread your small sails immune, little ships!
The storm is words, the bottles never break.

Know Thyself, and That Thou Art Mortal

If you want to know yourself
you've got to keep up with yourself.
Your self moves on, and is not today what it was yesterday;
and you've got to run, to keep up with it.

But sometimes we run ahead too fast
running after a figment of ourselves.
And that's what we've done today.

We think we're such clever little johnnies
with our sharp little eyes and our high-power machines
which get us ahead so much faster than our feet could ever carry us.

When, alas, it's only part of our clever little self that gets ahead!
Something is left behind, lost and howling, and we know it.

Ah, clever Odysseus, who outwitted the cyclop
and blinded him in his one big eye,
put out a light of consciousness and left a blinded brute.

Clever little ants in spectacles, we are,
performing our antics.

But what we also are, and we need to know it,
is blinded brutes of cyclops, with our cyclopean eye put out.

And we still bleed, and we grope and roar;
for spectacles and bulging clever ant-eyes are no good to the cyclop,
he wants his one great wondering eye, the eye of instinct and intuition.

As little social ants perhaps we function all right.
But, oh, our human lives, the lunging blind cyclops we are!
hitting ourselves against unseen rock, crashing our head against the
    roof
of the ancient cave, smashing into one another,
tearing each other's feelings, trampling each other's tenderest
    emotions to mud
and never knowing what we are doing, roaring blind with pain and
    dismay.

Ah, cyclops, the little ant-men can never enlighten you
with their bulging policeman's-lamp eyes.
You need your own great wondering eye that flashes with instinct
and gleams on the world with the warm dark vision of intuition!

Even our brilliantest young intellectuals
are also poor blind cyclops, moaning
with all the hurt to their instinctive and emotional selves,
over their mutilated intuitive eye.

What is Man Without an Income?

What is man without an income?
– Well, let him get on the dole!

Dole, dole, dole,
hole, hole, hole,
soul, soul, soul –

What is man without an income?
Answer without a rigmarole.

On the dole, dole, dole,
he's a hole, hole, hole,
in the nation's pocket.

– Now then, you leave a man's misfortunes alone!

He's got a soul, soul, soul
but the coal, coal, coal
on the whole, whole, whole
doesn't pay,
so the dole, dole, dole's
the only way.

And on the dole, dole, dole,
a man's a hole, hole, hole
in the nation's pocket,
and his soul, soul, soul
won't stop a hole, hole, hole
though his ashes might.

Immortal Caesar dead and turned to clay
would stop a hole to keep the wind away.

But a man without a job
isn't even as good as a gob
of clay.

Body and soul
he's just a hole
down which the nation's resources roll
away.

Canvassing for the Election

– Excuse me, but are you a superior person?
– I beg your pardon?
– Oh, I'm sure you'll understand. We're making a census of all the really
patriotic people – the right sort of people, you know – of course, you
understand what I mean – so *would* you mind giving me your word? –
and signing here, please – that you *are* a superior person – that's all we
need to know –
– Really, I don't know what you take me for!
– Yes, I know! It's too bad! Of course, it's perfectly superfluous to ask,
but the League insists. Thank you so much! No, sign here, please, and
there I countersign. That's right! Yes, that's all! – *I declare I am a*
superior person. – Yes, exactly! and here I countersign your declaration.
It's so simple, and really, it's *all* we need to know about anybody. And
do you know, I've never been denied a signature! We English *are* a solid
people, after all. This proves it. Quite! Thank you so much! We're
getting on simply splendidly – and it *is* a comfort, isn't it? –

Altercation

Now, look here,
if you were really superior,
really superior,
you'd have money, and you know it!

Well, what abaht it?

What about it?
what about it?
why isn't it obvious?
Here you are, with no money,
and here am I, paying income tax and god-knows-what
    taxes
just to support you and find you money,
and you stand there and expect me to treat you like an
    equal! –
Whereas, let me tell you, if you *were* my equal
you'd *have* money, you'd *have* it, enough to support your
    self, anyhow –
And there you stand with *nothing*, and expect me to hand
    it you out
as if it were your dues, and I didn't count at all –

All right, guv'nor! What abaht it?

Do you mean to say what about it?
My God, it takes some beating!
If you were a *man*, and up to my mark, you'd *have* money
    – can't you see it?
You're my inferior, that's what you are, you're my inferior.
And do you think it's my business to be handing out
    money to a lot of inferior swipe?
Eh? Answer me that!

Right ch' are, boss! An' what abaht it?

Finding Your Level

Down, down, down!
There must be a nadir somewhere
of superiority.

Down, and still
the superior persons, though somewhat inferior,
are still superior.

They are still superior, so there must be something they are
    superior to.
There must be a bed-rock somewhere, of people who are not
    superior,
one must come down to *terra firma* somewhere!

Or must one simply say:
All my inferiors are very superior.

There has been great progress
in superiority.

Fortunately though, some superior persons are still superior
to the quite superior persons who are not so superior as they are.

May I ask if you are *really* superior
or if you only look it so wonderfully?
Because we English *do* appreciate a *real* gentleman, or a *real* lady;
but appearances *are* deceptive nowadays, aren't they?

And if you only *look* so distinguished and superior
when really you are slightly inferior,
like a shop-lady or a lady-secretary,
you mustn't expect, my dear, to get away with it.
There's a list kept of the truly superior
and if you're not on the list, why there you are, my dear,
you're off it.

There are great numbers of quite superior persons who are not on
    the list,
poor things – but we can't help that, can we!
We must draw a line somewhere
or we should never know when we were crossing the equator.

What is man, that thou art mindful of him,
or the son of man, that thou pitiest him?
for thou hast made him a little lower than the angels
who are *very* superior people,
Oh *very*!

Climbing Up

When you climb up to the middle classes
you leave a lot behind you,
you leave a lot, you've lost a lot
and you've nobody to remind you
of all the things they squeezed out of you
when they took you and refined you.

When they took you and refined you
they squeezed out most of your guts;
they took away your good old stones
and gave you a couple of nuts;
and they taught you to speak King's English
and butter your slippery buts.

Oh, you've got to be like a monkey
if you climb up the tree!
You've no more use for the solid earth
and the lad you used to be.
You sit in the boughs and gibber
with superiority.

They all gibber and gibber and chatter,
and never a word they say
comes really out of their guts, lad,
they make it up halfway;
they make it up, and it's always the same,
if it's serious or if it's play.

You think they're the same as you are
and then you'll find they're not,
and they never were nor would be,
not one of the whole job lot.

And you have to act up like they do
or they think you're off your dot.

There isn't a man among 'em,
not one; they all seemed to me
like monkeys or angels or something, in a limited
liability company;
like a limited liability company
they are, all limited liability.

What they're limited to or liable
to, I could never make out.
But they're all alike, an' it makes you
want to get up an' shout
an' blast 'em forever; but they'd only
think you a lower-class lout.

I tell you, something's been done to 'em,
to the pullets up above;
there's not a cock bird among 'em
though they're always on about love,
an' you could no more get 'em a move on,
no! no matter how you may shove!

To Clarinda

Thank you, dear Clarinda,
for helping with Lady C,
It was you who gave her her first kiss
and told her not to be
afraid of the world, but to sally forth
and trip it for all she was worth.

So out she came, and she said she was Jane,
and you clapped your hands, and said: Say it again!
And you cried: 'Ooray! Play up, John Thomas!
Let's have no full stops, let's just manage with commas! –

And the white snow glistened, the white world was gay
up there at that height in the Diablerets.

And we slid, and you ski'd, and we came in to tea
and we talked and we roared and you typed Lady C.

And how jolly it was with us up in the snow
with the crest of the dirty drab world down below!

And how bitter it is to come down
to the dirty drab world,
and slowly feel yourself drown
in its mud, and its talk, slowly swirled
to the depths, to the depths
of London town!

Conundrums

Tell me a word
that you've often heard,
yet it makes you squint
if you see it in print!

Tell me a thing
that you've often seen,
yet if put in a book
it makes you turn green!

Tell me a thing
that you often do,
which described in a story
shocks you through and through!

Tell me what's wrong
with words or with you
that you don't mind the thing
yet the name is taboo.

A Rise in the World

I rose up in the world, 'Ooray!
rose very high, for me.
An earl once asked me down to stay
and a duchess once came to tea.

I didn't stay very long with the earl
and the duchess has done with me.
But still, I rose quite high in the world,
don't you think? – or don't you agree?

But now I am slithering down again
down the trunk of the slippery tree;
I find I'd rather get back to earth,
where I belong, you see.

Up there I didn't like it,
chattering, though not with glee,
the whole of the time, and nothing
mattering – at least, not to me.

God, let me get down to earth again
away from the upper ten
million – for there's millions of 'em
up there – but not any men.

Up He Goes!

Up I rose, my lads, an' I heard yer
sayin': Up he goes!

Up like a bloomin' little Excelsior[65]
In his Sunday clothes!

Up he goes, up the bloomin' ladder
about to the giddy top!
Who'd ever have thought it of that lad, a
pasty little snot! –

Never you mind, my lads, I left you
a long, long way behind.
You'll none of you rise in the world like I did;
an' if you did, you'd find

it damn well wasn't worth it,
goin' up an' bein' refined;
it was nowt but a dirty sell, that's all,
a *damn fraud*, underlined.

They're not any better than we are
the upper classes – they're worse.
Such bloomin' fat-arsed dool-owls,
they aren't even fit to curse!

There isn't a damn thing in 'em,
they're as empty as empty tins;
they haven't the spunk of a battle-twig,[66]
an' all they can think of is sins.

No, there's nowt in the upper classes
as far as I can find;
a worse lot of jujubey asses
than the lot I left behind.

They'll never do a thing, boys,
they can't, they're simply fused.
So if any of you's live wires, with wits
to use, they'd better be used.

It there's anything got to be done, why
get up an' do it yourselves!
Though God knows if you're any better,
sittin' there in rows on your shelves!

An' if you're not any better,
if you've none of you got more spunk
than they've got in the upper classes,
why, let's all do a bunk.

We're not fit for the earth we live on,
we're not fit for the air we breathe.
We'd better get out, an' make way for
the babes just beginning to teethe.

The Saddest Day

'We climbed the steep ascent to heaven
    Through peril, toil and pain.
O God, to us may strength be given
    to scramble back again.'

O I was born low and inferior
but shining up beyond
I saw the whole superior
world shine as the promised land.

So up I started climbing
to join the host on high,
but when at last I got there
I had to sit down and cry.

For it wasn't a bit superior,
it was only affected and mean;
though the house had a fine interior
the people were never in.

I mean, they were never entirely
there when you talked to them;
away in some private cupboard
some small voice went: *Ahem!*

Ahem! they went. *This fellow
is a little too open for me;
with such people one has to be careful,
though, of course, we won't let him see! —*

And they thought you couldn't hear them
privately coughing: *Ahem!*
And they thought you couldn't see them
cautiously swallowing their phlegm!

But of course I always heard them,
and every time the same.
They all of them always kept up their sleeve
their class-superior claim.

Some narrow-gutted superiority,
and trying to make you agree,
which, for myself, I couldn't,
it was all cat-piss to me.

And so there came the saddest day
when I had to tell myself plain;
the upper classes are just a fraud,
you'd better get down again.

Prestige

I never met a single
middle-class person whose
nerves didn't tighten against me
as if they'd got something to lose.

Though what it was, you can ask me;
some mysterious sort of prestige
that was nothing to me; though they always
seemed to think I was laying it siege.

It was something I never could fathom,
that mysterious prestige which they all
seemed to think they'd got, like a halo
around them, an invisible wall.

If *you* were willing to see it
they were only too eager to grant
you a similar glory, since you'd risen
to their levels, my holy aunt!

But never, no never, could I see it,
and so I could never feel
the proper unction about it,
and it worried me a good deal.

For years and years it bothered me
that I couldn't feel one of them,
till at last I saw the reason:
they were just a bloody sham.

As far as any superiority
or halo or prestige went
they were just a bloody collective fraud,
that was what their *ahem!* meant.

Their superiority was meanness,
they were cunning about the goods
and sly with a lot of after-thought,
and they put it over us, the duds!

And I'd let myself be swindled,
half believing 'em, till one day
I suddenly said: I've finished!
My God, let me get away!

Have Done with It

Once and for all, have done with it,
all the silly bunk
of upper-class superiority; that superior
stuff is just holy skunk.

Just you walk around them
and look at the fat-arsed lot
and tell me how they can put it across,
this superior rot!

All these gracious ladies,
graciously bowing down
from their pedestals! Holy Moses,
they've done you brown![67]

And all the sacred gentry,
so responsible and good,
feeling so *kind* towards you
and suckin' your blood!

My! the bloomin' pompoms!
Even as trimmings they're stale.
Still, if you don't want to bother,
I don't care myself a whale.

Henriette

O Henriette
I remember yet
how cross you were
over Lady C,
how you hated her
and detested me.

Yet now you see
you don't mind a bit.
You've got used to it,
and you feel more free.

And now you know
how good we were
up there in the snow
with Lady C,
though you hated her
at the first go.

Yet now you can see
how she set us free
to laugh, and to be
more spontaneous, and we
were happy, weren't we,
up there in the snow
with the world below!

So now, when you say
your prayers at night
you must sometimes pray:

Dear Lord of delight,
may I be Jane
tonight, profane

but sweet in your sight,
though last night I was Mary –

You said I might,
dear Lord of right,
be so contrary.
So may I be Jane
tonight and refrain
from being Mary? –

Vitality

Alas, my poor young men,
do you lack vitality?

Has the shell grown too heavy for the tortoise?
Does he just squirm?

Is the frame of things too heavy
for poor young wretched men?

Do they jazz and jump and wriggle
and rush about in machines
and listen to bodiless noises
and cling to their thin young women
as to the last straw

just in desperation,
because their spirit can't move?
Because their hope is pinned down by the system
and can't even flutter?

Well, well, if it is so it is so;
but remember, the undaunted gods
give vitality still to the dauntless.

And sometimes they give it as love,
ah love, sweet love, not so easy!
But sometimes they give it as lightning.

And it's no good wailing for love
if they only offer you lightning.

And it's no good mooning for sloppy ease
when they're holding out the thunderbolt
for you to take.

You might as well take the lightning
for once, and feel it go through you.
You might as well accept the thunderbolt
and prepare for storms.

You'll not get vitality any other way.

Willy Wet-Legs

I can't stand Willy wet-leg,
can't stand him at any price.
He's resigned, and when you hit him
he lets you hit him twice.

Maybe

Ah well, ah well, maybe
the young have learned some sense.
They ought at last to see through the game,
they've sat long enough on the fence.

Maybe their little bottoms
will get tired and sore at last
of sitting there on the fence, and letting
their good youth go to waste.

Maybe a sense of destiny
will rise in them one day,
maybe they'll realise it's time
they slipped into the fray.

Maybe they're getting tired
of sitting on the fence;
it dawns on them that the whole damn swindle
is played at their expense.

Stand Up!

Stand up, but not for Jesus!
It's a little late for that.
Stand up for justice and a jolly life,
I'll hold your hat.

Stand up, stand up for justice,
ye swindled little blokes!
Stand up and do some punching,
give 'em a few hard pokes.

Stand up for jolly justice,
you haven't got much to lose:
a job you don't like, and a scanty chance
for a dreary little booze.

Stand up for something different,
and have a little fun
fighting for something worth fighting for
before you've done.

Stand up for a new arrangement,
for a chance of life all round,
for freedom, and the fun of living
bust in, and hold the ground!

Demon Justice

If you want justice
let it be demon justice
that puts salt on the tails
of the goody good.

For the sins of omission,
for leaving things out,
not even a suspicion
of John Thomas about —

not even an inkling
that Lady Jane
is quietly twinkling
up the lane –

not even a hint
that a pretty bottom
has a gay little glint
quite apart from Sodom –

that you and I
were both begotten
when our parents felt spry
beneath the cotton –

that the face is not only
the mind's index,
but also the comely
shy flower of sex –

that a woman is always
a gate to the flood,
that a man is forever
a column of blood –

for these most vital
things omitted,
now make requital
and get acquitted.

Now bend you down
to demon justice,
and take sixty slashes
across your rusties.

Then with a sore
arse perhaps you'll remember
not quite to ignore
the jolly little member.

Be a Demon!

Oh be a demon
outside all class!
If you're a woman
or even an ass
still be a demon
beyond the mass.

Somewhere inside you
lives your own little fiend,
and woe betide you
if he feels demeaned,
better do him justice,
keep his path well cleaned.

When you've been being
too human, too long,
and your demon starts lashing out
going it strong,
don't get too frightened,
it's you who've been wrong.

You're not altogether
such a human bird,
you're as mixed as the weather,
not just a good turd,
so shut up pie-jaw blether,[68]
let your demon be heard.

Don't look for a saviour,
you've had some, you know!
Drop your sloppy behaviour
and start in to show
your demon rump twinkling
with a hie! hop below!

If, poor little bleeder,
you still feel you must follow
some wonderful leader
now the old ones ring hollow,
then follow your demon
and hark to his *holloa*!

The Jeune Fille

Oh the innocent girl
in her maiden teens
knows perfectly well
what everything means.

If she didn't, she oughter;
it's a silly shame
to pretend that your daughter
is a blank at the game.

Anyhow she despises
your fool pretence
that she's just a sheep
and can't see through the fence.

Oh every lass
should hear all the rough words
and laugh, let them pass;
and be used to the turds

as well as the grass;
and know that she's got
in herself a small treasure
that may yet give a lot

of genuine pleasure
to a decent man;
and beware and take care
of it while she can.

If she never knows
what is her treasure,
she grows and throws
it away, and you measure

the folly of that
from her subsequent woes.
Oh the innocent maid,
when she knows what's what

from the top of her head
to the tips of her toes
is more innocent far
than the blank-it-out girl

who gets into the car
and just fills you with hell.

Trust

Oh we've got to trust
one another again
in some essentials.

Not the narrow little
bargaining trust
that says: I'm for you
if you'll be for me.

But a bigger trust,
a trust of the sun
that does not bother
about moth and rust,
and we see it shining
in one another.

Oh don't you trust me,
don't burden me
with your life and affairs; don't thrust me
into your cares.

But I think you may trust
the sun in me
that glows with just
as much glow as you see
in me, and no more.

But if it warms
your heart's quick core
why then trust it, it forms
one faithfulness more.

And be, oh be
a sun to me,
not a weary, insistent
personality

but a sun that shines
and goes dark, but shines
again and entwines
with the sunshine in me

till we both of us
are more glorious
and more sunny.

NETTLES

A Rose is not a Cabbage

And still, in spite of all they do, I love the rose of England,
but the cabbages of England leave me cold.

Oh the cabbages of England leave me cold
even though they grow on genuine English mould,
with their caterpillars, and the care with which they fold
nothingness, pale nothingness in their hearts.

Now that the winter of our discontent
is settled on the land, roses are scarce in England, very scarce,
    there are none any more.
But look at the cabbages, Oh count them by the score!
Oh aren't they green. Oh haven't we, haven't we spent
a lot of money rearing them – !

Yet the cabbages of England leave me cold
no matter of what sort the cabbage be.

The Man in the Street

I met him in the street
I said: How do you do? –
He said: And who are you
when we meet? –

I sadly went my way
feeling anything but gay,
yet once more I met a man and had to stay –
May I greet – ?

He cut me very dead,
but then he turned and said:
I see you're off your head
thus to greet

in the street
a member of the British Public: don't you see
the policeman on his beat?
Well, he's there protecting *me*! –

But! said I,
but why – ?

And they ran me in, to teach me why.

Britannia's Baby

Oh Britannia's got a baby, a baby, a baby,
Britannia's got a baby, and she got it by and by.

It's called the British Public, the Public, the Public,
It's called the British Public, including you and I.

It's such a bonny baby, a baby, a baby,
It's such a bonny baby, we daren't let it cry.

So we've got a lot of nurses, of nurses, of nurses,
to feed the bonny baby, and keep its tara dry.

Eat your pap, little man, like a man!
Drink its minky-winky, then, like a man!

Does it want to go to bye-bye! there then, take its little dummy,
take its dummy, go to bye-bye like a man, little man!

Drop of whiskey in its minky? well it shall, yes it shall
if it's good, if it's going to be a *good* little man.

Want to go a little tattah? so it shall, of course it shall
go a banging little tattah with its Auntie
if it's good!
If it's good today, and tomorrow-day as well,
then when Sunday comes, it shall go a tattah with its Auntie
in a motor, in a pap-pap pap-pap motor, little man!

Oh isn't it a lucky little man!
to have whiskey in its minky
and to go a banging tattah with its Auntie
who loves her little man,
such a dear, kind Auntie, isn't she, to a lucky little man – !

For Oh, the British Public, the Public, the Public,
For Oh, the British Public is a lucky little man!

Change of Government [69]

We've got a change of government
if you know what I mean.
Auntie Maud has come to keep house
instead of Aunt Gwendoline.

They say that Auntie Maud, you know,
is rather common; she's not
so well brought up as Aunt Gwendoline is,
so perhaps she'll be more on the spot.

That's what we hope: we hope she'll be
a better manager; for Oh dear me
Aunt Gwen was a poor one! but Aunt Maud, you see,
was brought up poor, so she'll *have* to be

more careful. Though if she's not
won't it be awful! what shall we do?
Aunt Libby's really a feeble lot,
and I simply daren't think of Aunt Lou!

I've never seen her, but they say
she's a holy terror: she takes your best frock
and *all* your best things, and just gives them away
to the char, who's as good as you are, any day.

And she makes you go to work, even if
you've got money of your own.
And she shuts you in the cellar for the least little tiff,
and just loves to hear you sob and groan.

Oh I do hope Aunt Maud will manage all right!
Because they say, if she doesn't
Aunt Louie is almost bound to come
with all our horrible cousins

that we've never seen, coming stamping and swearing
and painting the woodwork red
just to show how dangerous they are!
Oh, Aunt Louie's the one I dread.

The British Workman and the Government

Hold my hand, Auntie, Auntie,
Auntie, hold my hand!
I feel I'm going to be naughty, Auntie
and you don't seem to understand.

Hold my hand and love me, Auntie,
love your little boy!
We want to be loved, especially, Auntie,
us whom you can't employ.

Idle we stand at the kerb-edge, Auntie,
dangling our useless hands.
But we don't mind so much if you love us, and we feel
that Auntie understands.

But wages go down, and really, Auntie,
we get a pretty thin time.
But so long as we know that Auntie loves us
we'll try to act up sublime.

Hold my hand, Auntie, Auntie,
Auntie, hold my hand!
Perhaps I'm going to be naughty, Auntie,
and you don't seem to understand.

Clydesider

If Maudie doesn't love us
then why should we be good?
Why shouldn't we steal the jam in the cupboard
and all the dainty food

as we never get a taste of! – really
it ought all to be Jock's and mine.
Maudie is nought but the housekeeper
and she kens it fine.

So if Maudie doesn't suit us
she's got to pack and go.
We're getting to be big lads now, an' soon
we can run our own show.

Flapper Vote

We voted 'em in, and we'll vote 'em out!
We'll show 'em a thing or two, never you doubt.

Lizzie and Lucy and me and Flossie
we'll show these old uncles who's going to be bossy!

Now then, Prime Minister, hold on a bit!
Remember who voted you into your seat!

But for Lizzie and Lucy and Flossie and me
you all of you know where you'd jolly well be.

But me and Lucy and Flossie and Lizzie
we thought we'd elect you to keep you all busy.

So be a nice uncle, be good to us girls;
just vote us some pin-money, to encourage our curls!

And Lizzie and me and Flossie and Lucy,
we'll back you up, uncle! We're young, and we're juicy! –

Songs I Learnt at School

I – NEPTUNE'S LITTLE AFFAIR WITH FREEDOM

Father Neptune one day to Freedom did say:
If ever I lived upon dry–y land,
The spot I should hit on would be little Britain –
Said Freedom: Why that's my own I–sland! –

   'Oh what a bright little I–sland!
   A right little, tight little I–sland!
   Seek all the world round there's none can be found
   So happy as our little I–sland!'

So Father Neptune walked up the shore
bright and naked aft and fore
as he's always been, since the Flood and before.

And instantly rose a great uproar
of Freedom shrieking till her throat was sore:
Arrest him, he's indecent, he's obscene what's more! –

Policemen and the British nation
threw themselves on him in indignation
with handcuffs, and took him to the police-station.

The sea-god said, in consternation:
But I came at Freedom's invitation! –
So then they charged him with defamation.

And all the sea-nymphs out at sea
rocked on the waves and sang lustily
thinking old Neptune was off on a spree
with giddy Freedom in the land of the Free:

   'Oh what a bright little I–sland!
   A right little, tight little I–sland! – '

II – MY NATIVE LAND

First verse:

> Of every land or east or west
> I love my native land the best, etc. etc.

Second verse:

> Of every tongue or east or west
> I love my native tongue the best
> Though not so smoothly spoken
> Nor woven with Italian art
> Yet when it speaks from heart to heart
> The spell is never broken
> The–e spell is–s never bro–o–ken!

Oh a man may travel both east and west
and still speak his native language the best.

But don't try it on, Oh never start
this business of speaking from heart to heart
in mother English, or you're in the cart.

For our honest and healthy English tongue
is apt to prove a great deal too strong

for our dainty, our delicate English ears.
Oh touch the harp, touch the harp gently, my dears!
We English are so sensitive, much more than appears. –

Oh don't for an instant ever dream
of speaking plain English to an Englishman; you'll seem

to him worse than a bolshevist Jew, or an utter
outsider sprung up from some horrible gutter.

Oh mince your words, and mince them well
if you don't want to break the sweet English spell.

For we English are really a race apart,
superior to everyone else: so don't start

being crude and straightforward, you'll only prove
you're a rank outsider of the fifth remove.

III – THE BRITISH BOY

First verse:

Oh I'm a British bo–oy, Sir,
A joy to–o tell it you.
God make me of it worthy
Life's toilsome journey through!
And when to man's estate I grow
My British blood the world shall know,
For I'm a British bo–oy, Sir,
A joy to–o tell it you! –

And so to man's estate he grew
and his British blood the world it knew.

And the world it didn't give a hoot
if his blood was British or Timbuctoot.

But with that British blood of his
he painted some pictures, real beauties

he thought them, so he sent them home
to Britain, where his blood came from.

But Britannia turned pale, and began to faint.
– Destroy, she moaned, these horrors in paint! –

He answered: Dear Britannia, why?
I'm your British boy, and I did but try – !

If my pictures are nude, so once were you,
and you will be again, therefore why look blue! –

Britannia hid behind her shield
lest her heel of Achilles should be revealed,

and she said: Don't dare, you wretch, to be lewd!
I never was nor will be nude! –

And she jabbed her British trident clean
through the poor boy's pictures: You see what I mean! –

But the British boy he turned and fled
for the trident was levelled at his head.

Henceforth he'll keep clear of her toasting-fork.
Pleasing Britannia is no light work.

13,000 People

Thirteen thousand people came to see
my pictures, eager as the honey bee

for the flowers; and I'll tell you what –
all eyes sought the same old spot

in every picture, every time,
and gazed and gloated without rhyme

or reason, where the leaf should be,
the fig-leaf that was not, woe is me!

And they blushed, they giggled, they sniggered, they leered,
or they boiled and they fumed, in fury they sneered

and said: Oh boy! I tell you what,
look at that one there, that's pretty hot! –

And they stared and they stared, the half-witted lot,
at the spot where the fig-leaf just was not!

But why, I ask you? Oh tell me why?
Aren't they made quite the same, then, as you and I?

Can it be they've been trimmed, so they've never seen
the innocent member that a fig-leaf will screen?

What's the matter with them? aren't they women and men?
or is something missing? or what's wrong with them then?

that they stared and leered at the single spot
where a fig-leaf might have been, and was not.

I thought it was a commonplace
that a man or a woman in a state of grace,

in puris naturalibus,[70] don't you see,
had normal pudenda, like you and me.

But it can't be so, for they behaved
like lunatics looking, they bubbled and raved

or gloated or peeped at the simple spot
where a fig-leaf might have been, but was not.

I tell you, there must be something wrong
with my fellow-countrymen; or else I don't belong.

Innocent England

Oh what a pity, Oh! don't you agree,
that figs aren't found in the land of the free!

Fig trees don't grow in my native land;
there's never a fig-leaf near at hand

when you want one; so I did without;
and that is what the row's about.

Virginal, pure policemen came
and hid their faces for very shame

while they carried the shameless things away
to gaol, to be hid from the light of day.

And Mr Mead, that old, old lily,
said: 'Gross! coarse! hideous!' – and I, like a silly,

thought he meant the faces of the police-court officials,
and how right he was, and I signed my initials

to confirm what he said; but alas, he meant
my pictures, and on the proceedings went.

The upshot was, my pictures must burn
that English artists might finally learn

when they painted a nude, to put a *cache sexe* on,
a cache sexe, a cache sexe, or else begone!

A fig-leaf; or, if you cannot find it,
a wreath of mist, with nothing behind it.

A wreath of mist is the usual thing
in the north, to hide where the turtles sing.

Though they never sing, they never sing,
don't you dare to suggest such a thing

or Mr Mead will be after you.
– But what a pity I never knew

A wreath of English mist would do
as a cache sexe! I'd have put a whole fog.

But once and forever barks the old dog,
so my pictures are in prison, instead of in the Zoo.

Give Me a Sponge

Give me a sponge and some clear, clean water
and leave me alone awhile
with my thirteen sorry pictures that have just been rescued
from durance vile.

Leave me alone now, for my soul is burning
as it feels the slimy taint
of all those nasty police-eyes like snail-tracks smearing
the gentle souls that figure in the paint.

Ah, my nice pictures, they are fouled, they are dirtied
not by time, but by unclean breath and eyes
of all the sordid people that have stared at them uncleanly
looking dirt on them, and breathing on them lies.

Ah my nice pictures, let me sponge you very gently
to sponge away the slime
that ancient eyes have left on you, where obscene eyes have
      crawled
leaving nasty films upon you every time.

Ah the clean waters of the sky, ah! can you wash
away the evil starings and the breath
of the foul ones from my pictures? Oh purify
them now from all this touch of tainted death!

Puss-Puss!

– Oh, Auntie, isn't he a beauty! And is he a gentleman or a lady?
– Neither, my dear! I had him fixed. It saves him from so many
    undesirable associations.

London Mercury

Oh when Mercury came to London
they 'had him fixed'.
It saves him from so many undesirable associations.

And now all the Aunties like him so much
because, you see, he is 'neither, my dear!'

My Little Critics

My little critics must all have been brought up by their Aunties
who petted them, and had them fixed
to save them from undesirable associations.

It must be so. Otherwise
the sight of an ordinary Tom wouldn't send them into such silly
    hysterics,
my little critics, dear, safe little pets.

Editorial Office

Applicant for post as literary critic: Here are my credentials, Sir! –
Editor: Er – quite. But – er – biologically! Have you been fixed? –
    arrangé – you understand what I mean?
Applicant: I'm afraid I don't.
Editor: (sternly) Have you been made safe for the great British
    Public? Has everything objectionable been removed from you?
Applicant: In what way, quite?
Editor: By surgical operation. Did your parents have you sterilised?
Applicant: I don't think so, Sir. I'm afraid not.
Editor: Good morning! Don't trouble to call again. We have the
    welfare of the British Public at heart.

The Great Newspaper Editor to his Subordinate

Mr Smith, Mr Smith,
haven't I told you to take the pith
and marrow and substance out of all
the articles passing beneath your scrawl?

And now look here what you've gone and done!
You've told them that life isn't really much fun,
when you know that they've got to think that they're happy,
as happy as happy, Oh, so happy, you sappy.

Think of the effect on Miss Harrison
when she reads that her life isn't really much fun.
She'll take off her specs, and she'll put down the paper
as if it was giving off poison vapour.

And she'll avoid it; she'll go and order
The Morning Smile, sure that it will afford her
comfort and cheer, sure that it will tell her
she's a marv'lous, delicious, high-spirited feller.

You must chop up each article, make it pappy
and easy to swallow; always tell them they're happy,
suggest that they're spicy, yet how *pure* they are,
and what a sense of true humour they've got, ha-ha!

Mr Smith, Mr Smith,
have you still to learn that pith
and marrow and substance are sure to be
indigestible to Miss Ponsonby!

Mr Smith, Mr Smith,
if you stay in my office, you've got to be kith
and kin with Miss Jupson, whose guts are narrow
and can't pass such things as substance and marrow.

Mr Smith, Mr Smith,
consider Miss Wilks, or depart forthwith.
For the British Public, once more be it said,
is summed up in a nice, narrow-gutted old maid.

Modern Prayer

Almighty Mammon, make me rich!
Make me rich quickly, with never a hitch
in my fine prosperity! Kick those in the ditch
who hinder me, Mammon, great son of a bitch!

Cry of the Masses

Give us back, Oh give us back
Our bodies before we die!

Trot, trot, trot, corpse-body, to work.
Chew, chew, chew, corpse-body, at the meal.
Sit, sit, sit, corpse-body, in the car.
Stare, stare, stare, corpse-body, at the film.
Listen, listen, listen, corpse-body, to the wireless.
Talk, talk, talk, corpse-body, newspaper talk.
Sleep, sleep, sleep, corpse-body, factory-hand sleep.
Die, die, die, corpse-body, doesn't matter!

Must we die, must we die
bodiless, as we lived?
Corpse-anatomies with ready-made sensations!
Corpse-anatomies, that can work.
Work, work, work,
rattle, rattle, rattle,
sit, sit, sit,
finished, finished, finished –

Ah no, Ah no! before we finally die
or see ourselves as we are, and go mad,
give us back our bodies, for a day, for a single day,
to stamp the earth and feel the wind, like wakeful men again.

Oh, even to know the last wild wincing of despair,
aware at last that our manhood is utterly lost,
give us back our bodies for one day.

What Have They Done to You?

What have they done to you, men of the masses
creeping back and forth to work?

What have they done to you, the saviours of the people?
Oh what have they saved you from?

Alas, they have saved you from yourself,
from your own body, saved you from living your own life.

And given you this jig-jig-jig
tick-tick-ticking of machines,
this life which is no-man's-life.

Oh a no-man's-life in a no-man's-land
this is what they've given you
in place of your own life.

The People

Ah the people, the people!
surely they are flesh of my flesh!

When, in the streets of the working quarters,
they stream past, stream past, going to work;

then, when I see the iron hooked in their faces,
their poor, their fearful faces,

then I scream in my soul, for I know I cannot
cut the iron hook out of their faces, that makes them so drawn,
nor cut the invisible wires of steel that pull them

back and forth to work,
back and forth, to work

like fearful and corpse-like fishes hooked and being played
by some malignant fisherman on an unseen, safe shore
where he does not choose to land them yet, hooked fishes of
    the factory world.

The Factory Cities

Oh, over the factory cities there seems to hover a doom
so dark, so dark, the mind is lost in it.

Ah, the industrial masses, with the iron hook through their gills,
when the evil angler has played them long enough,
another little run for their money, a few more turns of the reel
fixing the hook more tightly, getting it more firmly in –

Ah, when he begins to draw the line in tight, to land his fish,
the industrial masses – Ah, what will happen, what will happen?

Hark! the strange noise of millions of fish in panic,
in panic, in rebellion, slithering millions of fish
whistling and seething and pulling the angler down into boiling
    black death!

Leaves of Grass, Flowers of Grass

Leaves of grass, what about leaves of grass?
Grass blossoms, grass has flowers, flowers of grass,
dusty pollen of grass, tall grass in its midsummer maleness,
hay-seed and tiny grain of grass, graminiferae[71]
not far from the lily, the considerable lily;

even the blue-grass blossoms;
even the bison knew it;
even the stupidest farmer gathers his hay in bloom, in blossom
just before it seeds.

Only the best matters; even the cow knows it;
grass in blossom, blossoming grass, risen to its height and its
    natural pride
in its own splendour and its own feathery maleness
the grass, the grass.

Leaves of grass, what are leaves of grass, when at its best grass
    blossoms?

Magnificent Democracy

Oh, when the grass flowers, the grass
how aristocratic it is!
Cock's-foot, fox-tail, fescue and tottering-grass,
see them wave, see them wave, plumes
prouder than the Black Prince,
flowers of grass, fine men.

Oh, I am a democrat
of the grass in blossom,
a blooming aristocrat all round.

MORE PANSIES

Image-Making Love

And now
the best of all
is to be alone, to possess one's soul in silence.

Nakedly to be alone, unseen
is better than anything else in the world,
a relief like death.

Always
at the core of me
burns the small flame of anger, gnawing
from trespassed contacts, from red-hot finger bruises,
    on my inward flesh.

Always
in the eyes of those who loved me
I have seen at last the image of him they loved
and took for me,
mistook for me.

And always
it was a simulacrum, something
like me, and like a gibe at me.

So now I want, above all things,
to preserve my nakedness
from the gibe of image-making love.

People

I like people quite well
at a little distance.
I like to see them passing and passing
and going their own way,
especially if I see their aloneness alive in them.

Yet I don't want them to come near.
If they will only leave me alone
I can still have the illusion that there is room enough in the
world.

Desire

Ah, in the past, towards rare individuals
I have felt the pull of desire:
Oh come, come nearer, come into touch!
Come physically nearer, be flesh to my flesh –

But say little, oh say little,
and afterwards, leave me alone.
Keep your aloneness, leave me my aloneness.
I used to say this, in the past, but now no more.
It has always been a failure.
They have always insisted on love
and on talking about it
and on the me-and-thee and what we meant to each other.

So now I have no desire any more
Except to be left, in the last resort, alone, quite alone.

To a Certain Friend

You are so interested in yourself
that you bore me
thoroughly, I am unable to feel any interest in your interesting
self.

The Emotional Friend

He said to me: You don't trust me!
I said: Oh yes I do!
I know you won't pick my pocket,
I know you'll be very kind to me.
But it was not enough, he looked at me almost with hate.
And I failed entirely to see what he meant –
Since there was no circumstance requiring trust between us.

Correspondence in After Years

A man wrote to me: We missed it, you and I.
We were meant to mean a great deal to one another;
but we missed it.
And I could only reply:
A miss is as good as a mile,
mister!

The Egoists

The only question to ask today, about man or woman,
is: Has she chipped the shell of her own ego?
Has he chipped the shell of his own ego?
They are all perambulating eggs
going: 'Squeak! Squeak! I am all things unto myself,
yet I can't be alone, I want somebody to keep me warm.'

Chimaera

Most people, today, are chimaera
chimerical:
just fantasies of self-importance
their own self-importance
and sphinxes of self-consciousness.

Ultimate Reality

A young man said to me:
I am interested in the problem of reality.

I said: Really!
Then I saw him turn to glance, surreptitiously,
in the big mirror, at his own fascinating shadow.

Sphinx

But why do I feel so strangely about you?
said the lovely young lady, half wistful, half menacing.
I took to my heels and ran
before she could set the claws of her self-conscious questioning in me
or tear me with the fangs of disappointment
because I could not answer the riddle of her own self-importance.

Intimates

Don't you care for my love? she said bitterly.

I handed her the mirror, and said:
Please address these questions to the proper person!
Please make all requests to headquarters!
In all matters of emotional importance
please approach the supreme authority direct!
So I handed her the mirror.

And she would have broken it over my head,
but she caught sight of her own reflection
and that held her spellbound for two seconds
while I fled.

True Love at Last

The handsome and self-absorbed young man
looked at the lovely and self-absorbed girl.

The lovely and self-absorbed girl
looked back at the handsome and self-absorbed young man
and thrilled.

And in that thrill he felt:
Her self-absorption is even as strong as mine.
I must see if I can't break through it
and absorb her in me.

And in that thrill she felt:
His self-absorption is even stronger than mine!
What fun, stronger than mine!
I must see if I can't absorb this Samson of self-absorption.

So they simply adored one another
and in the end they were both nervous wrecks, because
in self-absorption and self-interest they were equally matched.

Andraitx [72] – Pomegranate Flowers

It is June, it is June,
the pomegranates are in flower,
the peasants are bending cutting the bearded wheat.

The pomegranates are in flower
beside the high road, past the deathly dust,
and even the sea is silent in the sun.

Short gasps of flame in the green of night, way off
the pomegranates are in flower,
small sharp red fires in the night of leaves.

And noon is suddenly dark, is lustrous, is silent and dark
men are unseen, beneath the shading hats;
only, from out the foliage of the secret loins
red flamelets here and there reveal
a man, a woman there.

I Dare Do All

'I dare do all that may become a man.'
But tell me, oh tell me, what is becoming to a man!
Tell me first what I am,
that I may know what is unbecoming to me.

Battle of Life

Is life strife, is it the long combat?
yes, it is true. I fight all the time.
I am forced to.
Yet I am not interested in fight, in strife, in combat,
I am only involved.

There are Too Many People

There are too many people on earth,
insipid, unsalted, rabbity, endlessly hopping.
They nibble the face of the earth to a desert.

The Heart of Man

There is the other universe, of the heart of man
that we know nothing of, that we dare not explore.
A strange grey distance separates
our pale mind still from the pulsing continent
of the heart of man.

Forerunners have barely landed on the shore
and no man knows, no woman knows
the mystery of the interior
when darker still than Congo or Amazon
flow the heart's rivers of fullness, desire and distress.

Moral Clothing

When I am clothed I am a moral man,
and unclothed, the word has no meaning for me.

When I put on my coat, my coat has pockets
and in the pockets are things I require,
so I wish no man to pick my pocket
and I will pick the pocket of no man.

A man's business is one of his pockets, his bank account too,
his credit, his name, his wife even may be just another of his
     pockets.
And I loathe the thought of being a pilferer,
a pick-pocket,
That is why business seems to me despicable,
and most love-affairs, just sneak-thief pocket-picking
of dressed-up people.

When I stand in my shirt I have no pockets
therefore no morality of pockets;
but still my nakedness is clothed with responsibility
towards those near and dear to me, my very next of kin.
I am not yet alone.

Only when I am stripped stark naked I am alone
and without morals, and without immorality.
The invisible gods have no moral truck with us.

And if stark naked I approach a fellow-man or fellow-woman
they must be naked too,
and none of us must expect morality of each other:
I am that I am, take it or leave it.
Offer me nothing but that which you are, stark and strange.
Let there be no accommodation at this issue.

Behaviour

It is well to be disciplined in all the social usages
and to have manners for all occasions
as we have clothes.
It is absurd for me to display my naked soul at the tea-table.

If we are properly clothed and disciplined in the dining-room or
    the street
then the private intimacy of friendship will be real and precious
and our naked contact will be rare and vivid and tremendous.

But when everybody goes round with soul half-bared, or quite
in promiscuous intimate appeal
then friendship is impossible
and naked embrace an anti-climax, humiliating and ridiculous.

The Hostile Sun

Sometimes the sun turns hostile to men
when the daytime consciousness has got overweening
when thoughts are stiff, like old leaves,
and ideas are hard, like acorns ready to fall.

Then the sun turns hostile to us
and bites at our throats and chests
as he bites at the stems of leaves in autumn, to make them fall.

Then we suffer, and though the sun bronzes us
we feel him strangling even more the issues of our soul
for he is hostile to all the old leafy foliage of our thoughts
and the old upward flowing of our sap, the pressure of our
    upward flow of feeling
is against him.

Then only under the moon, cool and unconcerned,
calm with the calm of scimitars and brilliant reaping hooks
sweeping the curve of space and moving the silence,
we have peace.

The Church

If I was a member of the Church of Rome
I should advocate reform:
the marriage of priests
the priests to wear rose-colour or magenta in the streets
to teach the Resurrection in the flesh
to start the year on Easter Sunday
to add the mystery of Joy-in-Resurrection to the Mass
to inculcate the new conception of the Risen Man.

The Protestant Churches

The Protestant Churches have had their day
and served their great purpose.
They knew the useful Godhead of Providence.
But now we have to go back to the Creative Godhead
which overshadows the other
and which we have lost.

Loneliness

I never know what people mean when they complain of loneliness.
To be alone is one of life's greatest delights, thinking one's own
    thoughts,
doing one's own little jobs, seeing the world beyond
and feeling oneself uninterrupted in the rooted connection
with the centre of all things.

The Uprooted

People who complain of loneliness must have lost something,
lost some living connection with the cosmos, out of themselves,
lost their life-flow
like a plant whose roots are cut.
And they are crying like plants whose roots are cut.

But the presence of other people will not give them new rooted
    connection
it will only make them forget.
The thing to do is in solitude slowly and painfully put forth new
    roots
into the unknown, and take root by oneself.

Delight of Being Alone

I know no greater delight than the sheer delight of being alone.
It makes me realise the delicious pleasure of the moon
that she has in travelling by herself: throughout time,
or the splendid growing of an ash tree
alone, on a hillside in the north, humming in the wind.

Refused Friendship

He said to me: Your life will be so much the poorer
since you refuse my friendship.

But I, honestly, don't know what he means.
I can't see that I refuse anything.
I like him. What else is there?

Future Relationships

The world is moving, moving still, towards further democracy.
But not a democracy of idea or ideal, nor of property, nor even of
    the emotion of brotherhood.
But a democracy of men, a democracy of touch.

Future Religion

The future of religion is in the mystery of touch.
The mind is touchless, so is the will, so is the spirit.
First come the death, then the pure aloneness, which is permanent,
then the resurrection into touch.

Future States

Once men touch one another, then the modern industrial form of
    machine civilisation will melt away
and universalism and cosmopolitanism will cease;
the great movement of centralising into oneness will stop
and there will be a vivid recoil into separateness;
many vivid small states, like a kaleidoscope, all colours
and all the differences given expression.

Future War

After our industrial civilisation has broken and the civilisation of
    touch has begun
war will cease, there will be no more wars.
The heart of man, in so far as it is budding, is budding warless
and budding towards infinite variety, variegation,
and where there is infinite variety, there is no interest in war.
Oneness makes war, and the obsession of oneness.

Signs of the Times

If you want to get a glimpse of future possibilities
look at the young men under thirty.
Those that are fresh and alive are the same in every country,
a certain carelessness, a certain tenderness, a certain instinctive
    contempt
for old values and old people:
a certain warlessness even moneylessness,
a waiting for the proper touch, not for any word or deed.

Initiation Degrees

No man, unless he has died, and learned to be alone
will ever come into touch.

Unhappy Souls

The unhappy souls are those that can't die and become silent
but must ever struggle on to assert themselves.

Full Life

A man can't fully live unless he dies and ceases to care
ceases to care.

People Who Care

People who care, who care, who care
and who dare not die for fear they should be nothing at all
probably are nothing at all.

Non-Existence

We don't exist unless we are deeply and sensually in touch
with that which can be touched but not known.

All-Knowing

All that we know is nothing, we are merely crammed waste-paper
    baskets
unless we are in touch with that which laughs at all our knowing.

Salvation

The only salvation is to realise that we know nothing about it
and there is nothing to save
and nothing to do
and effort is the ruin of all things.
Then, if we realise that we never were lost, we realise we couldn't
    be saved.

For you can't save that which was never lost,
at the worst, you can only save it up,
and once you realise that you never were lost
you realise the fatuity of saving up against possible loss.
The one thing easiest to lose is savings.

Old Archangels

And so the official archangels,
Orthodox Michael and that whispering Gabriel,
have had their term of office, they must go.
It is Lucifer's turn, the turn of the Son of the Morning,
to sway the earth of men,
the Morning Star.

Lucifer

Angels are bright still, though the brightest fell.
But tell me, tell me, how do you know
that he lost any of his brightness in falling?
He only fell out of your ken, you orthodox angels,
you dull angels, tarnished with centuries of conventionality.

The Mill of God

Why seek to alter people, why not leave them alone?
The mills of God will grind them small, anyhow, there is no escape.
The heavens are the nether millstone and our heavy earth
rolls round and round, grinding exceeding small.

Multitudes

The multitudes are like droppings of birds, like dung of sea-fowl
    that have flown away,
Oh they are grist for the mills of God, their bones ground down
to fertilise the roots of unknown men who are still to come in fresh
    fields.

Fallen Leaves

There is the organic connection, like leaves that belong to a tree,
and there is the mechanical connection, like leaves that are cast to
    the earth.

Winds of heaven fan the leaves of the tree like flames and tunes,
but winds of heaven are mills of God to the fallen leaves
grinding them small to humus, on earth's nether millstone.

The Difference

People are like leaves, fluttering and gay on the bush of the globe,
or they are like leaves, rustling thick, in crowds on the floor of
    the earth.
And the thick, fallen crowds crackle and crumble under the
    milling of the winds,
the winds of change that will not be still,
the breath of life.
But the living leaves in the breath of the wind are more lively,
they glisten and shake.

The Breath of Life

The breath of life and the sharp winds of change are the same
    thing.
But people who are fallen from the organic connection with the
    cosmos
feel the winds of change grind them down.

Vengeance is Mine

Vengeance is mine, saith the Lord, I will repay.
And the stiff-necked people, and the self-willed people, and self-
    important ones, the self-righteous, self-absorbed
all of them who wind their energy round the idea of themselves
and so strangle off their connection with the ceaseless tree of life,
and fall into sharp, self-centred self-assertion, sharp or soft,
they fall victim at once to the Vengeance of the unforgiving god
as their nerves are stretched till they twangle and snap
and irritation seethes secretly through their guts, as their tissue
    disintegrates
and flames of katabolistic energy alternate
with ashes of utter boredom, ennui, and disgust.

It is the Vengeance of the Lord, long and unremitting
till the soul of the stiff-necked is ground to dust, to fertilising meal
with which to manure afresh the roots of the tree of life.
And so the Lord of Vengeance pays back, repays life
for the defection of the self-centred ones.

Astronomical Changes

Dawn is no longer in the house of the Fish
Pisces, oh Fish, Jesus of the watery way,
your two thousand years are up.

And the foot of the Cross no longer is planted in the place of the
    birth of the Sun.
The whole great heavens have shifted over, and slowly pushed aside
the Cross, the Virgin, Pisces, the Sacred Fish
that casts its sperm upon the waters, and knows no intercourse;
pushed them all aside, discarded them, make way now for
    something else.

Even the Pole itself has departed now from the Pole Star
and pivots on the invisible,
while the Pole Star lies aside, like an old axle taken from the wheel.

Fatality

No one, not even God, can put back a leaf on to a tree
once it has fallen off.

And no one, not God nor Christ nor any other,
can put back a human life into connection with the living cosmos
once the connection has been broken
and the person has become finally self-centred.

Death alone, through the long process of disintegration,
can melt the detached life back
through the dark Hades at the roots of the tree
into the circulating sap, once more, of the tree of life.

Free Will

The human will is free, ultimately, to choose one of two things:
either to stay connected with the tree of life, and submit
the human will to the flush of the vaster impulsion of the tree;
or else to sever the connection, to become self-centred, self-willed,
self-motived –
and subject, really, to the draught of every motor-car or the kicking
     tread of every passer-by.

In a Spanish Tram-Car

She fanned herself with a violet fan
and looked sulky, under the thick straight brows.

The wisp of modern black mantilla
made her half Madonna, half Astarte.

Suddenly her yellow-brown eyes looked with a flare into mine;
– we could sin together! –

The spark fell and kindled instantly on my blood,
then died out almost as swiftly.

She can keep her sin
She can sin with some thick-set Spaniard.
Sin doesn't interest me.

Spanish Privilege

The inward cocky assertiveness of the Spaniard seems to say:
God is supreme,
but He can't stop me from sinning against Him if I want to,
and when I want to, I'm going to;
though you bloody outsiders had better not try it on.

So they go on sinning, though sin is obsolete,
and nobody but themselves is interested.

At the Bank in Spain

Even the old priest in his long black robe and silvery hair
came to the counter with his hat off, humble at the shrine,
and was immensely flattered when one of the fat little clerks of the
    bank
shook hands with him.

The Spanish Wife

When I saw her straying a little dazed through her untidy house
I realised the secret joy her young Spanish husband had
in frustrating her, just inwardly frustrating her,
this foreign woman of the wealthy north.

The Painter's Wife

She was tangled up in her own self-conceit, a woman,
and her passion could only flare through the meshes
towards other women, in communion;
the presence of a man made her recoil
and burn blue and cold, like the flame in a miner's lamp
when the after-damp is around it.

Yet she seemed to know nothing about it
and devoted herself to her husband
and made him paint her nude, time after time,
and each time it came out the same, a horrible, sexless, lifeless
    abstraction
of the female form, technically 'beautiful', actually a white
    machine drawing, more null than death.

And she was so pleased with it, she thought one day it would
    be recognised as 'great'.
And he thought so too.
Nobody else did.

Modern Problems

The worst of it is
When a woman can only love, flamily, those of her own sex
she has a secret, almost ecstatised hatred of maleness in any
    man
that she exudes like pearly white poison gas,
and men often succumb like white mice in a laboratory,
    around her,
specimens to be anatomised.

Dominant Women

Dominant women are as a rule so subtly and fiendishly
    domineering
that the young of their own sex revolt against them at last,
and turn once more to men to save them, Perseus, St George,
from the dragon of the modern female.

Men and Women

All this talk of equality between the sexes is merely an
    expression of sex-hate.
Men and women should learn tenderness to each other
and to leave one another alone.

The Scientific Doctor

When I went to the scientific doctor
I realised what a lust there was in him to wreak his so-called
    science on me
and reduce me to the level of a thing.
So I said: Good-morning! and left him.

Healing

I am not a mechanism, an assembly of various sections.
And it is not because the mechanism is working wrongly, that
    I am ill.
I am ill because of wounds to the soul, to the deep emotional self,
and the wounds to the soul take a long, long time, only time can
    help
and patience, and a certain difficult repentance,
long, difficult repentance, realisation of life's mistake, and the
    freeing oneself
from the endless repetition of the mistake
which mankind at large has chosen to sanctify.

En Masse

Today, society has sanctified
the sin against the Holy Ghost,
and all are encouraged into the sin
so that all may be lost together, *en masse*, the great word of our
    civilisation.

God and the Holy Ghost

There is no sinning against God, what does God care about sin!
But there is sinning against the Holy Ghost, since the Holy
    Ghost is with us
in the flesh, is part of our consciousness.

The Holy Ghost is the deepest part of our own consciousness
wherein we know ourself for what we are
and know our dependence on the creative beyond.

So if we go counter to our own deepest consciousness
naturally we destroy the most essential self in us,
and once done, there is no remedy, no salvation for this,
nonentity is our portion.

Humility

Nowadays, to talk of humility is a sin against the Holy Ghost.
It is a sneaking evasion of the responsibility
of our own consciousness.

Proper Pride

Everything that lives has its own proper pride
as a columbine flower has, or even a starling walking and
    looking around.

And the base things like hyenas or bed-bugs have least pride of
    being,
they are humble with a creeping humility, being parasites
    or carrion creatures.

Humility Mongers

When I hear a man spouting about humility today
I know he is either a bed-bug, battening on sleeping people,
or a hyena, eating corpses.

Tender Reverence

To be humble before other men is degrading, I am humble
    before no man
and I want no man to be humble before me.

But when I see the life-spirit fluttering and struggling in a man
I want to show always the human tender reverence.

Absolute Reverence

I feel absolute reverence to nobody and to nothing human,
neither to persons nor things nor ideas, ideals nor religions nor
    institutions,
to these things I feel only respect, and a tinge of reverence
when I see the fluttering of pure life in them.

But to something unseen, unknown, creative
from which I feel I am a derivative
I feel absolute reverence. Say no more!

Belief

Forever nameless
Forever unknown
Forever unconceived
Forever unrepresented
yet forever felt in the soul.

Bells

The Mohammedans say that the sound of bells,
especially big ones, is obscene.

That hard clapper striking in a hard mouth
and resounding after with a long hiss of insistence is obscene.

Yet bells call the Christians to God,
especially clapper bells, hard tongues wagging in hard mouths,
metal hitting on metal, to enforce our attention,
and bring us to God.

The soft thudding of drums,
of finger or fist or soft-skinned sticks upon the stretched
     membrane of sound,
sends summons in the old hollows of the sun.

And the accumulated splashing of a gong,
where tissue plunges into bronze with wide wild circles of sound
and leaves off,
belongs to the bamboo thicket, and the drake in the air flying past.

And the sound of a blast through the sea-curved core of a shell
when a black priest blows on a conch,
and the dawn cry from a minaret, God is great,
and the calling of the old Red Indian high on the pueblo roof
whose voice flies on, calling like a swan
singing between the sun and the marsh,
on and on, like a dark-faced bird singing alone,
singing to the men below, the fellow-tribesmen
who go by without pausing, soft-foot, without listening, yet
     they hear:
there are other ways of summons, crying: Listen! Listen!
     Come near!

The Triumph of the Machine

They talk of the triumph of the machine,
but the machine will never triumph.

Out of the thousands and thousands of centuries of man,
the unrolling of ferns, white tongues of the acanthus lapping
 at the sun,
for one sad century
machines have triumphed, rolled us hither and thither,
shaking the lark's nest till the eggs have broken.

Shaken the marshes till the geese have gone
and the wild swans flown away singing the swan-song of us.

Hard, hard on the earth the machines are rolling,
but through some hearts they will never roll.

The lark nests in his heart
and the white swan swims in the marshes of his loins,
and through the wide prairies of his breast a young bull herds
 the cows,
lambs frisk among the daisies of his brain.

And at last
all these creatures that cannot die, driven back
into the uttermost corners of the soul,
will send up the wild cry of despair.

The trilling lark in a wild despair will trill down from the sky,
the swan will beat the waters in rage, white rage of an enraged
 swan,
even the lambs will stretch forth their necks like serpents,
like snakes of hate, against the man in the machine:
even the shaking white poplar will dazzle like splinters of glass
 against him.

And against this inward revolt of the native creatures of the soul
mechanical man, in triumph seated upon the seat of his machine,
will be powerless, for no engine can reach into the marshes and
 depths of a man.

So mechanical man in triumph seated upon the seat of his machine
will be driven mad from himself, and sightless, and on that day
the machines will turn to run into one another,
traffic will tangle up in a long-drawn-out crash of collision
and engines will rush at the solid houses, the edifice of our life
will rock in the shock of the mad machine, and the house will
    come down.

Then, far beyond the ruin, in the far, in the ultimate, remote places
the swan will lift up again his flattened, smitten head
and look round, and rise, and on the great vaults of his wings
will sweep round and up to greet the sun with a silky glitter of a
    new day
and the lark will follow trilling, angerless again,
and the lambs will bite off the heads of the daisies for friskiness.
But over the middle of the earth will be the smoky ruin of iron,
the triumph of the machine.

Forte Dei Marmi[73]

The evening sulks along the shore, the reddening sun
reddens still more on the blatant bodies of these all-but-naked,
    sea-bathing city people.

Let me tell you that the sun is alive, and can be angry,
and the sea is alive, and can sulk,
and the air is alive, and can deny us as a woman can.

But the blatant bathers don't know, they know nothing;
the vibration of the motor-car has bruised their insensitive bottoms
into rubber-like deadness, Dunlop-inflated unconcern.

Sea-Bathers

Oh the handsome bluey-brown bodies, they might just as well be
    gutta percha,[74]
and the reddened limbs red india-rubber tubing, inflated,
and the half-hidden private parts just a little brass tap, rubinetto,[75]
turned on for different purposes.

They call it health, it looks like nullity.

Only here and there a pair of eyes, haunted, looks out as if asking:
where then is life?

Talk of Loyalty

I have noticed that people who talk a lot about loyalty
are always themselves by nature disloyal
and they fear the come-back.

Talk of Faith

And people who talk about faith
usually want to force somebody to agree with them,
as if there was safety in numbers, even for faith.

Amo Sacrum Vulgus[76]

Oh I am of the people!
the people, the people!
Oh I am of the people
and proud of my descent.

And the people always love me,
they love me, they love me,
the people always love me,
in spite of my ascent.

You must admit I've risen,
I've risen, I've risen,
you must admit I've risen
above the common run.

The middle classes hate it,
they hate it, they hate it,
the middle classes hate it
and want to put me down.

But the people always love me,
they love me, they love me,
the people always love me
because I've risen clean.

Therefore I know the people,
the people, the people
are still in bud, and eager
to flower free of fear.

And so I sing a democracy,
a democracy, a democracy
that puts forth its own aristocracy
like bearded wheat in ear.

Oh golden fields of people,
of people, of people,
oh golden field of people
all moving into flowers.

No longer at the mercy,
the mercy, the mercy
of middle-class mowing-machines, and
the middle-class money power.

Boredom, Ennui, Depression

And boredom, ennui, depression
are long slow vibrations of pain
that possess the whole body
and cannot be localised.

The Deadly Victorians

We hate the Victorians so much
because we are the third and fourth generation
expiating their sins
in the excruciating torment of hopelessness, helplessness,
    listlessness,
because they were such base and sordid optimists
successfully castrating the body politic,
and we are the gelded third and fourth generation.

What Are the Wild Waves Saying?

What are the wild waves saying
sister the whole day long?

It seems to me they are saying:
How disgusting, how infinitely sordid this humanity is
that dabbles its body in me
and daubs the sand with its flesh
in myriads, under the hot and hostile sun!
and so drearily 'enjoys itself!'
What are the wild waves saying?

Welcome Death

How welcome death would be
if first a man could have his full revenge
on our castrated society.

Dark Satanic Mills

The dark, satanic mills of Blake
how much darker and more satanic they are now!
But oh, the streams that stream white-faced, in and out,
in and out when the hooter hoots, white-faced, with a dreadful gush
of multitudinous ignominy,
what shall we think of these?
They are millions to my one!

They are millions to my one! But oh
what have they done to you, white-faced millions
mewed and mangled in the mills of man?
What have they done to you, what have they done to you,
what is this awful aspect of man?

Oh Jesus, didn't you see, when you talked of service
this would be the result!
When you said: Retro me, Satanas![77]
this is what you gave him leave to do
behind your back!

And now, the iron has entered into the soul
and the machine has entangled the brain, and got it fast,
and steel has twisted the loins of man, electricity has exploded
    the heart
and out of the lips of people jerk strange mechanical noises in
    place of speech.

What is man, that thou art no longer mindful of him?
and the son of man, that thou pitiest him not?
Are these no longer men, these millions, millions?
What are they then?

We Die Together

Oh, when I think of the industrial millions, when I see some of
    them,
a weight comes over me heavier than leaden linings of coffins
and I almost cease to exist, weighed down to extinction
and sunk into depression that almost blots me out.

Then I say to myself: Am I also dead? is that the truth?
Then I know
that with so many dead men in mills
I too am almost dead.
I know the unliving factory-hand, living-dead millions
is unliving me, living-dead me,
I, with them, am living dead, mechanical enslaved at the machine.

And enshrouded in the vast corpse of the industrial millions,
embedded in them, I look out on the sunshine of the South.

And though the pomegranate has red flowers outside the window
and oleander is hot with perfume under the afternoon sun
and I am 'Il Signore' and they love me here,
yet I am a mill-hand in Leeds
and the death of the Black Country is upon me
and I am wrapped in the lead of a coffin-lining, the living death of
    my fellow-men.

What Have They Done to You?

What have they done to you, men of the masses creeping back and
    forth to work?
What have they done to you, the saviours of the people, oh what
    have they saved you from, while they pocketed the money?

Alas, they have saved you from yourself, from your own frail dangers,
and devoured you with the machine, the vast maw of iron.

They saved you from squalid cottages and poverty of hand to mouth
and embedded you in the workmen's dwellings, where your wage is
    the dole of work, and the dole is your wage of nullity.

They took away, oh they took away your man's native instincts and
    intuitions
and gave a board-school education, newspapers, and cinema.

They stole your body from you, and left you an animated carcass
to work with, and nothing else:
unless goggling eyes, to goggle at the film,
and a board-school brain, stuffed up with the ha'penny press.
Your instincts gone, your intuition gone, your passion dead,
Oh carcass with a board-school mind and a ha'penny-newspaper
    intelligence,
what have they done to you, what have they done to you, oh what
    have they done to you?

Oh look at my fellow-men, oh look at them
the masses! Oh, what has been done to them?

What is a Man to Do?

Oh, when the world is hopeless
what is a man to do?

When the vast masses of men have been caught by the machine
into the industrial dance of the living death, the jigging of wage-
    paid work,
and fed on condition they dance this dance of corpses driven by
    steam.

When year by year, year in, year out, in millions, in increasing
    millions
they dance, dance, dance this dry industrial jig of the corpses
    entangled in iron
and there's no escape, for the iron goes through their genitals,
    brains, and souls,

then what is a single man to do?

For mankind is a single corpus, we are all one flesh
even with the industrial masses, and the greedy middle mass.

Is it hopeless, hopeless, hopeless?
has the iron got them fast?
are their hearts the hub of the wheel?
the millions, millions of my fellow-men!

Then must a single man die with them, in the clutch of iron?
Or must he try to amputate himself from the iron-entangled body
    of mankind
and risk bleeding to death, but perhaps escape into some
    unpopular place
and leave the fearful Laocöon of his fellow-man entangled in iron
to its fearful fate?

City-Life

When I am in a great city, I know that I despair.
I know there is no hope for us, death waits, it is useless to care.

For oh the poor people, that are flesh of my flesh,
I, that am flesh of their flesh,
when I see the iron hooked into their faces,
their poor, their fearful faces,
I scream in my soul, for I know I cannot
take the iron hook out of their faces, that makes them so drawn,
nor cut the invisible wires of steel that pull them
back and forth, to work,
back and forth, to work,
like fearful and corpse-like fishes hooked and being played
by some malignant fisherman on an unseen shore
where he does not choose to land them yet, hooked fishes of the
    factory world.

Thirteen Pictures

O my Thirteen pictures are in prison!
O somebody bail them out!
I don't know what they've done, poor things, but justice has arisen
in the shape of half a dozen stout
policemen and arrested them, and hauled them off to gaol.

O my Boccaccio, O how goes your pretty tale
locked up in a dungeon cell
with Eve and the Amazon, the Lizard and the frail
Renascence,[78] all sent to hell
at the whim of six policemen and a magistrate whose stale
sensibilities hate everything that's well?

Auto-Da-Fé [79]

Help! Help! they want to burn my pictures,
they want to make an *auto-da-fé*!
They want to make an *act of faith*, and burn my pretty pictures.
They've seized and carried them away!

Help! Help! I am calling in English –
is the language dead and empty of reply?
The Unholy Inquisition has arrested all my pictures,
a magistrate, and six fat smaller fry.

Six fat smaller bobbies are the inquisitors minor
who've decided that Boccaccio must burn.
But the Grand Inquisitor is a stale magistrate
in Marlborough Road, and it is now his turn.

Oh he has put his pince-nez on, and stoutly has stepped down
to the police-station cell
where my darling pictures, prisoners, await his deadly frown
and his grand-inquisitorial knell.

Oh he knows all about it, he casts a yellow eye
on the gardener whose shirt's blown back:
Burn that! – he sees Eve running from the likes of him: I
order you, destroy the whole vile pack. –

All my pretty pictures huddled in the dark awaiting
their doom at the hands of Mr Meade.
But the day they burn my pictures they burn the rose of England
and fertilise the weeds on every mead.

Help! Oh help! they want to burn my pictures:
we've got the Inquisition back
with a set of cankered magistrates and busy-busy bobbies.
Look out, my lad, you've got 'em on your track.

Shows

Today, if a man does something pretentious and deliberate
let him show it to the crowd, probably they will applaud
and anyhow they can't do any hurt.

But if he produces something beautiful, with the frail beauty of life,
let him hide it away, so it can go on blossoming.
If he show it, the eyes and the breath of the crowd
will defile it, and spoil its beauty.

Even the very flowers in the shops or parks
are deflowered by being looked at by so many unclean eyes.

Rose and Cabbage

And still I look for the men who will dare to be
roses of England
wild roses of England
men who are wild roses of England
with metal thorns, beware!
but still more brave and still more rare
the courage of rosiness in a cabbage world
fragrance of roses in a stale stink of lies
rose-leaves to bewilder the clever fools
and rose-briars to strangle the machine.

The Gulf

Now again and now for ever breaks the great illusion
of human oneness.

Sons of earth, sons of fire, sons of air and water,
sons of the living elements, sons of the unthinking gods,
women, women the same.

And then the hordes of the spawn of the machine,
the hordes of the egocentric, the robots.

For listen! the egocentric self is the same as the machine,
the ego running in its own complex and disconnected motion
using all life only as power, as an engine uses steam or gas
powers to repeat its own egocentric motions,
this is the machine incarnate:
and the robot is the machine incarnate,
and the slave is the machine incarnate,
and the hopeless inferior, he is the machine incarnate,
an engine of flesh, useless unless he is a tool
of other men.

The great industrialists know it.
Mr Ford knows it.
The brain of the machine knows the limbs and trunk of the
　　　machine.

But oh, men, men still unmechanised,
sons of the elements and the unspeaking gods,
sons of the wind and rain, sons of the fire and rock,
what are you going to do, entangled among all the engines?

Behold the gulf, impassable
between machine-spawn, myriads
mechanical and intellectual,
and the sons of men, with the wind and the fire of life
in their faces, and motion never mechanical in their limbs.

The Cross

Behold your Cross, Christians!
With the upright division into sex,
men on this side, women on that side,
without any division into inferiority and superiority
only differences,
divided in the mystic, tangible and intangible difference.

And then, truth much more bitter to accept,
the horizontal division of mankind
into that which is below the level, and that which is above . . .

That which is truly man, and that which is robot,
the ego-bound.

On this cross of division, division into sex,
division into slave and freeman,
Christ, the human consciousness,
was crucified
to set all men free
to make all men noble
to wipe away the mystic barriers of sex.

In vain, in vain, in vain, oh vastly in vain
this horrific crucifixion.
Now risen Man and risen lord,
risen from the dead, after this crucifixion
must learn the supreme lesson –

That sex is an eternal upright division, before which we must bow
and live in the acceptance of it,
it can never be wiped out;
the gods that made us are greater than our consciousness
and we, we are mostly unexplored hinterland
and our consciousness is a spot of light in a great but living
     darkness.

And then, risen, we must learn the most cruel lesson
of the horizontal division of mankind,
the eternal division between the base and the beautiful.
The base, those that are below the bar of the cross,
the small ones, ego-bound, little machines running in an enclosed
     circle of self
the inferiors.

The inferiors, the inferiors, there they are, in hordes.
And they will destroy all, unless they are made to submit
and to serve that which is flamey or pure and watery or swift wind
     or sound ringing rock,
that which is elemental and of the substantial gods in man.
Mankind is lost and lost forever
unless men swiftly divide again, and the base are thrust down
into service, like the roots of trees.

For today, the base, the robots sit on the thrones of the world
in all the high places, and they are masters of industry
and rulers of millions of robots, being robots themselves, the same
only the brainy sort:
But brainy robot, or aesthetic robot, or merely muscular or
  mechanical robot
it is all the same,
less than real men, inferiors, inferiors.

How then are the few men, men of the wind and rain,
men of the fire and rock, how are they going to come forth
from the robot mass of rich and poor, mechanical ego-bound
  myriads?

Life will find a way.
Life always finds a way.
Only. Oh man, stare, stare into the gulf
between you and the robot-hordes, misnamed your fellow-men.

Fellow-Men

A few are my fellow-men,
a few, only a few:
the mass are not.

The mass are not my fellow-men,
I repudiate them as such.
Let them serve.

The Sight of God

Men are not alike in the sight of God.
Oh no, oh no!
Men are anything but alike in the sight of God.

In the sight of God and the unknown gods
most men don't matter at all, any more than ants matter to men:
only the few, the very few, matter in the sight of God, and the living
  substantial gods.

Souls to Save

You tell me every man has a soul to save?
I tell you, not one man in a thousand has even a soul to lose.
The automat has no soul to lose
so it can't have one to save.

When Most Men Die

When most men die, today,
when most women die,
it is merely a machine breaks down
and can't be mended.

Hold Back!

Oh men, living men, vivid men, ocean and fire,
don't give any more life to the machines!
Draw it away, draw it away, for these horrible machine-people
can't live any more, except for a spell, when the living cease to
    accept them as brothers
and give them life.

Machines of iron must be tended by hands of flesh
and robots must have encouragement from men of the vivid life
or they break down.

Oh men of life and of living,
withdraw, withdraw your flow
from the grinning and insatiable robots.

Impulse

You can count on anything, but you can't count on impulse.
You can't even count on the mechanical impulse for money and
    motor-cars
which rules the robot-classes and the robot-masses, now.

Once disillusion falls on living men, and they feel the illusion ebb
    away,
the illusion of mankind, the illusion of a hopeful future for these
    masses and classes of men,
once disillusion falls on living men, and illusion of brotherhood
    and hope bleeds right away,

Then, then comes the great moment of choice.
Oh, life is nothing if not choice.
And that which is choice alone matters.

In the moment of choice, the soul rolls back
away from the robot-classes and the robot-masses
and withdraws itself, and recognises a flower or the morning-star
but utterly fails to recognise any more the grey rat-hordes of classes
    and masses.

And then, when the soul of living men repudiates them,
then at once the impulse of the greedy classes and masses breaks
    down
and a chaos of impulse supervenes
in which is heard the crashing splinter of machines
and the dull breaking of bones.

For the robot classes and masses are only kept sane
by the kindness of living women and men.

Now living women and men are threatened with extinction
and the time has come to cease to be kind any more
to the robot classes and masses.

Oh, if the huge tree dies
save some shoots, some lovely flowering shoots,
to graft on another tree.

Trees raised from seed have wild and bitter fruits,
they need grafting:
and even the loveliest flowers, you must graft them on a new stock.

Men Like Gods

Men wanted to be like gods
so they became like machines
and now even they're not satisfied.

Men and Machines

Man invented the machine
and now the machine has invented man.
God the Father is a dynamo
and God the Son a talking radio
and God the Holy Ghost is gas that keeps it all going.

And men have perforce to be little dynamos
and little talking radios
and the human spirit is so much gas, to keep it all going.

Man invented the machine
so now the machine has invented man.

Masses and Classes

There are masses and there are classes
but the machine it is that has invented them both.

The classes are so superior
because they are the brains of the machine.
And the masses are also superior
because they are the arms and legs of the machine.

An old Frenchman uttered the truism:
God cannot do without me!
Certainly the god in the machine cannot!
It has all the time to be soothed and consoled by the hands of life.

Give Us the Thebaïd

Modern society is a mill
that grinds life very small.
The upper millstone of the robot-classes,
the lower millstone of the robot-masses,
and between them, the last living human beings
being ground exceeding small.

Turn away, O turn away, man of flesh!
Slip out, O slip out from between the millstones,
extract and extricate yourself
and hide in your own wild Thebaïd.
Then let the millstones grind, for they cannot stop grinding, so
    let them grind
without grist.
Let them grind on one another, upper-class robot weight upon
    lower-class robot weight,
till they grow hot, and burst, as even stone can explode.

Side-Step, O Sons of Men!

Sons of men, from the wombs of wistful women,
not piston-mechanical-begotten,
sons of men, with the wondering eyes of life,
hark! hark! step aside silently and swiftly.

The machine has got you, is turning you round and round
and confusing you, and feeding itself on your life.
Softly, subtly, secretly, in soul first, then in spirit, then in body,

slip aside, slip out
from the entanglement of the giggling machine
that sprawls across the earth in iron imbecility.

Softly, subtly, secretly, saying nothing,
step aside, step out of it, it is eating you up,
O step aside, with decision, sons of men, with decision.

On and On and On

The machine will run on and on and on –
then let it!

Oh, never fight the machine,
nor its mechanised robots, robot classes and masses!
Lift never a finger against them, that they can see,
Let them run on and on and on –
It is their heaven and their doom.

Oh Wonderful Machine!

Oh wonderful machine, so self-sufficient, so sufficient unto
    yourself!
You who have no feeling of the moon as she changes her quarters!
You who don't hear the sea's uneasiness!
You to whom the sun is merely something that makes the
    thermometer rise!

Oh wonderful machine, you are man's idea of godliness,
you who feel nothing, who know nothing, who run on absolved
from any other connection!
Oh you godly and smooth machine, spinning on in your own
    Nirvana,
turning the blue wheels of your own heaven;
almighty machine,
how is it you have to be looked after by some knock-kneed wretch
at two pounds a week?

Oh great god of the machine,
what lousy archangels and angels you have to surround yourself
    with!
And you can't possibly do without them!

But I Say Unto You: Love One Another

Oh I have loved my fellow-men –
and lived to learn they are neither fellow nor men
but machine-robots.

Oh I have loved the working class
where I was born,
and lived to see them spawn into machine-robots
in the hot-beds of the board-schools and the film.

Oh how I loved the thought of thoughtful people,
gentle and refined,
and lived to find out
that their last thought was money
and their last refinement bluff, a hate disguised,
and one trapped one's fingers in their brassy, polished works!

Love Thy Neighbour

I love my neighbour
but
are these things my neighbours?
these two-legged things that walk and talk
and eat and cachinnate, and even seem to smile,
seem to smile, ye gods!

Am I told that these things are my neighbours?
All I can say is Nay! nay! nay! nay!

As Thyself!

Supposing I say: dogs are my neighbours
I will love dogs as myself!

Then gradually I approximate to the dogs,
wriggle and wag and slaver, and get the mentality of a dog!
This I call a shocking humiliation.

The same with my robot neighbours.
If I try loving them, I fall into their robot jig-jig-jig,
their robot cachinnation comes rattling out of my throat —
and I had better even have approximated to the dog.

Who then, O Jesus, is my neighbour?
If you point me to that fat money-smelling man in a motor-car
or that hard-boiled young woman beside him
I shall have to refuse entirely to accept either of them.

My neighbour is not the man in the street, and never was:
he jigs along in the imbecile cruelty of the machine
and is implacable.

My neighbour, O my neighbour!
Occasionally I see him, silent, a little wondering,
with his ears pricked and his body wincing,
threading his way among the robot machine-people.

O my neighbour,
sometimes I see her, like a flower, nodding her way and shrinking
from the robot contact on every hand!

How can that be my neighbour
which I shrink from!

Lonely, Lonesome, Loney – O!

When I hear somebody complain of being lonely
or, in American, lonesome
I really wonder and wonder what they mean.

Do they mean they are a great deal alone?

But what is lovelier than to be alone?
escaping the petrol fumes of human conversation
and the exhaust-smell of people
and be alone!

Be alone, and feel the trees silently growing.
Be alone, and see the moonlight outside, white and busy and
    silent.
Be quite alone, and feel the living cosmos softly rocking,
soothing and restoring and healing.

Soothed, restored and healed
when I am alone with the silent great cosmos
and there is no grating of people with their presences gnawing
at the stillness of the air.

Trees in the Garden

Ah in the thunder air
how still the trees are!

And the lime tree, lovely and tall, every leaf silent,
hardly looses even a last breath of perfume.

And the ghostly, creamy coloured little tree of leaves,
white, ivory white among the rambling greens,
how evanescent, variegated elder, she hesitates on the green
    grass
as if, in another moment, she would disappear
with all her grace of foam!

And the larch that is only a column, it goes up too tall to see:
and the balsam-pines that are blue with the grey-blue blueness
    of things from the sea,
and the young copper beech, its leaves red-rosey at the ends,
how still they are together, they stand so still
in the thunder air, all strangers to one another
as the green grass glows upwards, strangers in the garden.

Lichtental

Storm in the Black Forest

Now it is almost night, from the bronzey soft sky
jugful after jugful of pure white liquid fire, bright white,
tipples over and spills down
and is gone
and gold-bronze flutters bent through the thick upper air.

And as the electric liquid pours out, sometimes
a still brighter white snake wriggles among it, spilled
and tumbling wriggling down the sky:
and then the heavens cackle with uncouth sounds.

And the rain won't come, the rain refuses to come!

This is the electricity that man is supposed to have mastered,
chained, subjugated to his use!
supposed to!

Revolution as Such!

Curiously enough, actual revolutions are made by robots,
living people never make revolutions,
they can't, life means too much to them.

Robot Feelings

It is curious, too, that though the modern man in the street
is a robot and incapable of love
he is capable of an endless, grinding, nihilistic hate:
that is the only strong feeling he is capable of;
and therein lies the danger of robot-democracy and all the men in
    the street,
they move in a great grind of hate, slowly but inevitably.

Real Democracy

If the robot can recognise the clean flame of life
in men who have never fallen in life
then he repents, and his will breaks, and a great love of life
brings him to his knees, in homage and pure passion of service.

Then he receives the kiss of reconciliation
and ceases to be a robot, and becomes a servant of life,
serving with delight and with reverence those men whose flame
of life undimmed delights him, so even he is lit up.

Robot-Democracy

In a robot-democracy, nobody is willing to serve,
even work is unwilling, the worker is unwilling, unwilling.
The great grind of unwillingness, the slow undergrind of hate
and democracy is ground into dust
then the millstones burst with the internal heat of their own
    friction.

Worship

All men are worshippers
unless they have fallen, and become robots.

All men worship the wonder of life
until they collapse into egoism, the mechanical, self-centred system
    of the robot.

But even in pristine men, there is the difference:
some men can see life clean and flickering all around,
and some can only see what they are shown.

Some men look straight into the eyes of the gods
and some men can see no gods, they only know
the gods are there because of the gleam on the faces of the men
    who see.

Most men, even unfallen, can only live
by the transmitted gleam from the faces of vivider men
who look into the eyes of the gods.
And worship is the joy of the gleam from the eyes of the gods,
and the robot is denial of the same,
even the denial that there *is* any gleam.

Classes

There are two classes of men;
those that look into the eyes of the gods, and these are few,
and those that look into the eyes of the few other men
to see the gleam of the gods there, reflected in the human eyes.

All other class is artificial.
There is, however, the vast third homogeneous amorphous class of
    anarchy,
the robots, those who deny the gleam.

Democracy is Service

Democracy is service, but not the service of demos.
Democracy is demos serving life
and demos serves life as it gleams on the face of the few,
and the few look into the eyes of the gods, and serve the sheer gods.

False Democracy and Real

If man only looks to man, and no one sees beyond,
then all is lost, the robot supervenes.

The few must look into the eyes of the gods, and obey the look
in the eyes of the gods:
and the many must obey the few that look into the eyes of the gods;
and the stream is towards the gods, not backwards, towards man.

Service

Ah yes, men must learn to serve
not for money, but for life.

Ah yes, men must learn to obey
not a boss, but the gleam of life on the face of a man
who has looked into the eyes of the gods.

Man is only perfectly human
when he looks beyond humanity.

What are the Gods?

What are the gods, then, what are the gods?

The gods are nameless and imageless
yet looking in a great full lime tree of summer
I suddenly saw deep into the eyes of gods:
it is enough.

The Gods! The Gods!

People were bathing and posturing themselves on the beach
and all was dreary, great robot limbs, robot breasts,
robot voices, robot even the gay umbrellas.

But a woman, shy and alone, was washing herself under a tap
and the glimmer of the presence of the gods was like lilies,
and like water-lilies.

Name the Gods!

I refuse to name the gods, because they have no name.
I refuse to describe the gods, because they have no form nor shape
     nor substance.

Ah, but the simple ask for images!
Then for a time at least, they must do without.

But all the time I see the gods:
the man who is moving the tall white corn,
suddenly, it curves, as it yields, the white wheat,
and sinks down with a swift rustle, and a strange, falling flatness,
ah! the gods, the swaying body of god!
ah the fallen stillness of god, autumnus, and it is only July
the pale-gold flesh of Priapus dropping asleep.

There Are No Gods

There are no gods, and you can please yourself –
have a game of tennis, go out in the car, do some shopping, sit and
     talk, talk, talk
with a cigarette browning your fingers.
There are no gods, and you can please yourself –
go and please yourself –

But leave me alone, leave me alone, to myself!
and then in the room, whose is the presence
that makes the air so still and lovely to me?

Who is it that softly touches the sides of my breast
and touches me over the heart
so that my heart beats soothed, soothed, soothed and at peace?

Who is it smooths the bed-sheets like the cool
smooth ocean when the fishes rest on edge
in their own dream?

Who is it that clasps and kneads my naked feet, till they unfold,
till all is well, till all is utterly well? the lotus-lilies of the feet!

I tell you, it is no woman, it is no man, for I am alone.
And I fall asleep with the gods, the gods
that are not, or that are
according to the soul's desire,
like a pool into which we plunge, or do not plunge.

Food of the North

The food of the north tastes too much of the fat of the pig,
fat of the pig!
Take me south again, to the olive trees
and oil me with the lymph of the silvery trees
oil me with the lymph of trees
not with the fat of the pig.

Retort to Whitman[80]

And whoever walks a mile full of false sympathy
walks to the funeral of the whole human race.

Retort to Jesus

And whoever forces himself to love anybody
begets a murderer in his own body.

The Deepest Sensuality

The profoundest of all sensualities
is the sense of truth
and the next deepest sensual experience
is the sense of justice.

Sense of Truth

You must fuse mind and wit with all the senses
before you can feel truth.
And if you can't feel truth you can't have any other
satisfactory sensual experience.

Satisfaction

The profound sensual experience of truth: Yea, this is!
alone satisfies us, in the end.

Vibration of Justice

The profound and thrilling vibration of justice, sense of ultimate
    justice
makes the heart suddenly quiver with love.

Lies

Lies are not a question of false fact
but of false feeling and perverted justice.

Poison

What has killed mankind – for the bulk of mankind is dead –
is lies:
the nasty lying pretence of seeming to feel what we don't feel.

Commandments

When Jesus commanded us to love our neighbour
he forced us to live a great lie, or to disobey:
for we can't love anybody, neighbour or no neighbour, to order,
and faked love has rotted our marrow.

Emotional Lies

You hear a woman say: I love my husband dearly –
and you look in her eyes and see it is a lie.
Even it is a trick: but she is not ashamed.

Laughter

Listen to people laughing
and you will hear what liars they are
or cowards.

Drawing-Room

You sit talking in all earnestness to a woman,
hearing her talk, that is:
and you know all the while
that every syllable, every accent, every intonation and every cadence
is a lie:
yet you go on talking, in all earnestness.

Cabbage-Roses

You may smell the breath of the gods in the common roses,
and feel the splendour of the gods go through you, even as you see
the greenfly on the stems,
in the summer morning:
or you may not.

If you don't then don't pretend you do –
but if you don't you are suffering from an amnesia
of the senses:
you are like to die of malnutrition of the senses:
and your sensual atrophy
will at last send you insane.

Cold Blood

In cold blood, I cannot feel goddesses in the summer evening
trafficking mysteriously through the air.
But what right has my blood to be cold
before I am dead?
If I cut my finger, my blood is hot, not cold.

And even in cold blood I know this:
I am more alive, more aware and more wise
when my blood is kindled:
and when in the summer evening
I feel goddesses trafficking mysteriously through the air.

Sunset

There is a band of dull gold in the west, and say what you like
again and again some god of evening leans out of it
and shares being with me, silkily
all of twilight.

Listen to the Band!

There is a band playing in the early night,
but it is only unhappy men making a noise
to drown their inner cacophony: and ours.

A little moon, quite still, leans and sings to herself
through the night
and the music of men is like a mouse gnawing,
gnawing in a wooden trap, trapped in.

The Human Face

Hardly ever, now, has a human face
the baffling light or the strange still gleam of the gods
within it, upon it.

Even from the face of the children, now,
that spangled glisten is gone, that at-oneness without afterthought,
and they are bridled with cunning, and bitted
with knowledge of things that shall never be admitted,
even the fact of birth: even little children.

Holbein and Titian and Tintoret could never paint faces, now:
because those faces were windows to the strange horizons, even
     Henry VIII;
whereas faces now are only human grimaces,
with eyes like the interiors of stuffy rooms, furnished.

Portraits

Portraits are now supremely uninteresting
because all the faces contain sets of emotional and mental furniture
all more or less alike,
as all drawing-rooms are, arranged!

Furniture

Some women live for the idiotic furniture of their houses,
some men live for the conceited furniture of their minds,
some only live for their emotional furnishing –

and it all amounts to the same thing, furniture,
usually in 'suites'.

Children Singing in School

Class-children are singing in school
and what an awful concatenation of sounds it is!
They have no song in their souls, none in their spirits,
none in their little throats or classroom bodies
only they are made to utter these cog-wheel sounds
which are meant to be the old folk-song: Strawberry Fair!

Keep It Up

People go on singing when they have no song in them.
People go on talking when they have nothing to say.
People go on walking when they have nowhere to go.
People keep it up, because they daren't stop.

So here we go round the mulberry bush,
mulberry bush, mulberry bush!
Here we go round the mulberry bush
never having seen a mulberry bush in our lives.

Race and Battle

The race is not to the swift
but to those that can sit still
and let the waves go over them.

The battle is not to the strong
but to the frail, who know best
how to efface themselves
to save the streaked pansy of the heart from being trampled
    to mud.

Nothing to Save

There is nothing to save, now all is lost,
but a tiny core of stillness in the heart
like the eye of a violet.

British Sincerity

They tell me that these British moral birds
all the great jixery[81] up in the fixery
are 'perfectly sincere'
and 'perfectly honest'.

If it is perfectly sincere to deny your own make-up
and perfectly honest to pretend to be unbegotten
may I ask you then, where insincerity and dishonesty begin.

The jixery perhaps never picked a man's pocket
but my god, they sneak-thiefed his very genitals away from him:
going a bit further than his pocket, what?

And the poor man never knew he was jixed,
fixed, fixed, fixed!
He feels for his purse, and finds it there, and says,
Oh my jixer, my fixer,
oh he's an honest man! anyhow!

Is British hypocrisy a form of softening of the brain?
Or what is it that my nation is suffering from?

The English are So Nice!

The English are so nice
so awfully nice
they are the nicest people in the world.

And what's more, they're very nice about being nice,
about your being nice as well!
If you're not nice they soon make you feel it.

Americans and French and Germans and so on
they're all very well
but they're not *really* nice, you know.
They're not nice in *our* sense of the word, are they now?

That's why one doesn't have to take them seriously.
We must be nice to them, of course,
of course, naturally.
But it doesn't really matter what you say to them,
they don't really understand,
you can just say anything to them:
be nice, you know, just nice,
but you must never take them seriously, they wouldn't understand,
just be nice, you know! oh, fairly nice,
not too nice of course, they take advantage,
but nice enough, just nice enough
to let them feel they're not quite as nice as they might be.

The Hills

I lift up mine eyes unto the hills
and there they are, but no strength comes from them to me.
Only from darkness
and ceasing to see
strength comes.

Tourists

There is nothing to look at any more,
everything has been seen to death.

Seekers

Oh seekers, when you leave off seeking
you will realise there was never anything to seek for.

You were only seeking to lose something,
not to find something,
when you went forth so vigorously in search.

Search for Love

Those that go searching for love
only make manifest their own lovelessness,
and the loveless never find love,
only the loving find love,
and they never have to seek for it.

Search for Truth

Search for nothing any more, nothing
except truth.
Be very still, and try and get at the truth.

And the first question to ask yourself is:
How great a liar am I?

Lies about Love

We are all liars, because
the truth of yesterday becomes a lie tomorrow,
whereas letters are fixed,
and we live by the letter of truth.

The love I feel for my friend, this year,
is different from the love I felt last year.
If it were not so, it would be a lie.
Yet we reiterate love! love!
as if it were coin with a fixed value
instead of a flower that dies, and opens a different bud.

Travel is Over

I have travelled, and looked at the world, and loved it.
Now I don't want to look at the world any more,
there seems nothing there.
In not-looking, and in not-seeing
comes a new strength
and undeniable new gods share their life with us, when we
    cease to see.

Old Men

Whom the gods love, die young.
How the gods must hate most of the old, old men today,
the rancid old men that don't die
because the gods don't want them
won't have them
leave them to stale on earth.

Old people fixed in a rancid resistance
to life, fixed to the letter of the law.

The gods, who are life, and the fluidity of living change
leave the old ones fixed to their ugly, cogged self-will
which turns on and on, the same, and is hell on earth.

Death

Death is no escape, ah no! only a doorway to the inevitable.
That's why the dogged, resistant old ones dare not die,
dare not die! – they daren't go through the door.

They dare not die, because they know
in death they cannot any more escape
the retribution for their obstinacy.
Old men, old obstinate men and women
dare not die, because in death
their hardened souls are washed with fire, and washed and seared
till they are softened back to life-stuff again, against which they
hardened themselves.

Bourgeois and Bolshevist

The bourgeois produces the bolshevist, inevitably
as every half-truth at length produces the contradiction of itself
in the opposite half-truth.

Property and No-Property

The bourgeois asserts that he owns his property by divine right
and the bolshevist asserts that by human right no man shall own
    property
and between the two blades of this pair of shears, property and
    no-property,
we shall all be cut to bits.

Cowardice and Impudence

Bourgeois cowardice produces bolshevist impudence
in direct ratio.
As the bourgeois gets secretly more cowardly, knowing he is in the
    wrong,
the bolshevist gets openly more impudent, also knowing he is in
    the wrong.
And between the cowardice and impudence of this pair who are in
    the wrong,
this pair of property mongrels,
the world will be torn in two.

Lord Tennyson and Lord Melchett [82]

'Dost tha hear my horse's feet, as he canters away?
Property! Property! Property! tha's what they seems to say!'

Do you hear my Rolls Royce purr, as it glides away?
 – I lick the cream off property! that's what it seems to say!

Choice of Evils

If I have to choose between the bourgeois and the bolshevist
I choose the bourgeois,
he will interfere with me less.

But in choosing the bourgeois one brings to pass
only more inevitably the bolshevist,
since the bourgeois is the direct cause of the bolshevist,
as a half-lie causes the immediate contradiction of the half-lie.

Hard-Boiled Conservatives

O you hard-boiled conservatives and you soft-boiled liberals
don't you *see* how you make bolshevism inevitable?

Solomon's Baby

Property is now Solomon's baby
and whoever gets it, it'll be a dead baby,
a corpse, even of property.

The Property Question

In settling the property question between them,
bourgeois and bolshevist,
they'll merely destroy all property and a great many people,
like the two lions who devoured one another, and left the tail-tufts
    wagging.
Let's hope there'll be more sense in the tail-tufts
than there was in the lions.

The Way Out

The only way to settle the property question
is to cease to be interested in it; to be so interested in something
    else
that the property problem solves itself by the way.

St George and the Dragon

The more you tackle the property dragon
the more deadly and dangerous it becomes.
Whereas if you ride away and become deeply concerned in
    something else
the old dragon will dwindle down to the size of a stray cat,
    neglected,
whom some recalcitrant old maid will adopt, as a hobby.

It is all a question of being profoundly interested in property, or
    not.
And quite a lot of people are not.
But they let themselves be overwhelmed by those that are.

The Half-Blind

The bourgeois and the bolshevist are both blind
hence the ridiculous way they rush in where angels fear to tread.
They can't see it.

But among the bourgeois and the bolshevist bounders
one notices men here and there, going hesitatingly, faltering
with the pathos of those who can see, but whose sight is dim.
And these, the minority of men who can still see the light of life,
give way all the time before the mechanical rushing of the ugly
    stone-blind ones.

Minorities in Danger

Now above all is the time for the minorities of men,
those who are neither bourgeois nor bolshevist, but true life,
to gather and fortify themselves, in every class, in every country, in
    every race.

Instead of which, the minorities that still see the gleams of life
submit abjectly to the blind mechanical traffic-streams of those
    horrors
the stone-blind bourgeois and the stone-blind bolshevist
and pander to them.

If You are a Man

If you are a man and believe in the destiny of mankind
then say to yourself: we will cease to care
about property and money and mechanical devices,
and open our consciousness to the deep, mysterious life
that we are now cut off from.

The machine shall be abolished from the earth again;
it is a mistake that mankind has made;
money shall cease to be, and property shall cease to perplex,
and we will find the way to immediate contact with life
and with one another.

To know the moon as we have never known
yet she is knowable.
To know a man as we have never known
a man, as never yet a man was knowable, yet still shall be.

Terra Incognita

There are vast realms of consciousness still undreamed of,
vast ranges of experience, like the humming of unseen harps,
we know nothing of, within us.

Oh when man has escaped from the barbed-wire entanglement
of his own ideas and his own mechanical devices
there is a marvellous rich world of contact and sheer fluid beauty
and fearless face-to-face awareness of now-naked life
and me, and you, and other men and women
and grapes, and ghouls, and ghosts and green moonlight
and ruddy-orange limbs stirring the limbo
of the unknown air, and eyes so soft,
softer than the space between the stars,
and all things, and nothing, and being and not-being
alternately palpitant,
when at last we escape the barbed-wire enclosure
of *Know Thyself*, knowing we can never know,
we can but touch, and wonder, and ponder, and make our effort

and dangle in a last fastidious fine delight
as the fuchsia does, dangling her reckless drop
of purple after so much putting forth
and slow mounting marvel of a little tree.

Climbing Down

They are afraid of climbing down from this idiotic tin-pot heaven
    of ours
because they don't know what they'll find when they do get down.

They needn't bother, most of them will never get down at all,
they've got to stay up.
And those that do descend have got to suffer a sense-change
into something new and strange.

Become aware as leaves are aware
and fine as flowers are fine
and fierce as fire is fierce
and subtle, silvery, tinkling and rippling
as rainwater
and still a man,
but a man reborn from the rigidity of fixed ideas
resurrected from the death of mechanical motion and emotion.

Only the Best Matters

Only the best matters, in man especially.
True, you can't produce the best without attending to the whole,

but that which is secondary is only important
in so far as it goes to the bringing forth of the best.

To Pino

O Pino
What a bean-o!
when we printed Lady C!

Little Giuntina
couldn't have been a
better little bee!

When you told him
perhaps they'd scold him
for printing those naughty words
All he could say:
'But we do it every day!
like the pigeons and the other little birds!'

And dear old Lady Jean:
'I don't know what you mean
by publishing such a book.

We're all in it, all my family –
me and Ekkerhart and Somers and Pamelie –
you're no better than a crook – !'

'Wait, dear Lady Jean, wait a minute!
What makes you think that you're all in it?
Did you ever open the book?
Is Ekke Sir Clifford? it's really funny!
And you, dear Lady Jean, are you Connie?
Do open the book and look! – '

But off she went, being really rattled,
and there's a battle that's still to be battled
along with the others! what luck!

Broadcasting to the GBP

'Hushaby baby, on a tree top,
when the wind blows, the cradle shall rock,
when the bough breaks – '
                    Stop that at once!
You'll give the Great British Public a nervous shock!

'Goosey goosey gander,
whither do you wander,
upstairs, downstairs,
in my lady's – '
                    Stop! where's your education?
Don't you know that's obscene?
Remember the British Public!

'Baa-baa black sheep,
have you any wool?
yes sir! yes sir!
three bags full!
One for the master, and one for the dame,
and one for the little boy that lives down the —'
                                        No!
You'd better omit that, too communistic!
Remember the state of mind of the British Public.

'Pussy-cat pussy-cat where have you been?
I've been up to London to see the fine queen!
Pussy-cat pussy-cat what did you there?
I frightened a little mouse – '
                    Thank you! thank you!
There are no mice in our Royal Palaces. Omit it!

We Can't Be Too Careful

We can't be too careful
about the British Public.
It gets bigger and bigger
and its perambulator has to get bigger and bigger
and its dummy-teat has to be made bigger and bigger and bigger
and the job of changing its diapers gets bigger and bigger and
    bigger and bigger
and the sound of its howling gets bigger and bigger and bigger
    and bigger and bigger
and the feed of pap that we nurses and guardian angels of the
    press have to deal out to it
gets bigger and bigger and bigger and bigger and bigger and
    bigger
yet its belly-ache seems to get bigger too
and soon even God won't be big enough to handle that infant.

Glimpses

What's the good of a man
unless there's the glimpse of a god in him?
And what's the good of a woman
unless she's a glimpse of a goddess of some sort?

All Sorts of Gods

There's all sorts of gods, all sorts and every sort,
and every god that humanity has ever known is still a god today –
the African queer ones and Scandinavians' queer ones,
the Greek beautiful ones, the Phoenician ugly ones, the Aztec
    hideous ones,
goddesses of love, goddesses of dirt, excrement-eaters or lily virgins,
Jesus, Buddha, Jehovah and Ra, Egypt and Babylon,
all the gods, and you see them all if you look, alive and moving
    today,
and alive and moving tomorrow, many tomorrows, as yesterdays.

Where do you see them, you say?
You see them in glimpses, in the faces and forms of people, in
    glimpses.
When men and women, when lads and girls are not thinking,
when they are pure, which means when they are quite clean from
    self-consciousness,
either in anger or tenderness, or desire or sadness or wonder or
    mere stillness,
you may see glimpses of the gods in them.

For a Moment

For a moment, at evening, tired, as he stepped off the tram-car,
– the young tram-conductor in a blue uniform, to himself
    forgotten, –
and lifted his face up, with blue eyes looking at the electric rod
    which he was going to turn round,
for a moment, pure in the yellow evening light, he was Hyacinthus.

In the green garden darkened the shadow of coming rain
and a girl ran swiftly, laughing breathless, taking in her white
    washing
in rapid armfuls from the line, tossing it in the basket,
and so rapidly, and so flashing, fleeing before the rain,
for a moment she was Io, Io, who fled from Zeus, or the Danaë.

When I was waiting and not thinking, sitting at a table on the hotel
    terrace,
I saw suddenly coming towards me, lit up and uplifted with
    pleasure,
advancing with the slow-swiftness of a ship backing her white sails
    into port,
the woman who looks for me in the world
and for the moment she was Isis, gleaming, having found her Osiris.

For a moment, as he looked at me through his spectacles,
pondering, yet eager, the broad and thick-set Italian who works in
    with me,
for a moment he was the Centaur, the wise yet horse-hoofed Centaur
in whom I can trust.

Goethe and Pose

When Goethe becomes an Apollo, he becomes a plaster cast.
When people pose as gods, they are Crystal Palace statues,
Made of cement poured into a mould, around iron sticks.

Men Like Gods

When men think they are like gods
they are usually much less than men
being conceited fools.

Thought

Thought, I love thought.
But not the jaggling and twisting of already existent ideas,
I despise that self-important game.
Thought is the welling up of unknown life into consciousness
Thought is the testing of statements on the touchstone of the
      conscience
Thought is gazing on to the face of life, and reading what can be
      read,
Thought is pondering over experience, and coming to a conclusion.
Thought is not a trick, or an exercise, or a set of dodges,
Thought is a man in his wholeness wholly attending.

Be It So

O, if a flame is in you, be it so!
When your flame flickers up, and flickers forth in sheer purity,
for a moment free from all conceit of yourself, and all after-thought,
you are for that moment one of the gods, Jesus or Fafnir or Priapus
      or Siva.

Conceit

It is conceit that kills us
and makes us cowards instead of gods.

Under the great Command: Know thyself, and that thou art mortal!
we have become fatally self-conscious, fatally self-important, fatally
    entangled in the Laocoön coils of our conceit.

Now we have to admit we *can't* know ourselves, we can only know
    about ourselves.
And I am not interested to know about myself any more,
I only entangle myself in the knowing.

Now let me be myself,
now let me be myself, and flicker forth,
now let me be myself, in the being, one of the gods.

Man is More Than Homo Sapiens

Man is not quite a man
unless he has his pure moments, when he is surpassing.
I saw an angry Italian seize an irritating little official by the throat
and all but squeeze the life out of him:
and Jesus himself could not have denied that at that moment the
    angry man
was a god, in godliness pure as Christ, beautiful
but perhaps Ashtaroth, perhaps Siva, perhaps Huitzilopochtli
with the dark and gleaming beauty of the messageless gods.

Self-Conscious People

O are you tangled up in yourself,
poor little man, poor little man!

Is she tangled up in herself then,
poor woman, poor woman!

But beware!
They are like cats with unclean claws, tangled up in nets,
and if you try to get them out
they will tear you terribly, and give you blood-poisoning.

Two Ways of Living and Dying

While people live the life
they are open to the restless skies, and streams flow in and out
darkly from the fecund cosmos, from the angry red sun, from the moon,
up from the bounding earth, strange pregnant streams, in and out of
    the flesh,
and man is an iridescent fountain, rising up to flower
for a moment godly, like Baal or Krishna, or Adonis or Balder, or
    Lucifer.

But when people are only self-conscious and self-willed
they cannot die, their corpse still runs on,
while nothing comes from the open heaven, from earth, from the sun
    and moon
to them, nothing, nothing;
only the mechanical power of self-directed energy
drives them on and on, like machines,
on and on, and their triumph in mere motion
full of friction, full of grinding, full of danger to the gentle passengers
of growing life,
but on and on, on and on, till the friction wears them out
and the machine begins to wobble
and with hideous shrieks of steely rage and frustration
the worn-out machine at last breaks down:
it is finished, its race is over.

So self-willed, self-centred, self-conscious people die
the death of nothingness, worn-out machines, kaput!

But when living people die in the ripeness of their time,
terrible and strange the god lies on the bed, wistful, coldly wonderful,
beyond us, now beyond, departing with that purity
that flickered forth in the best hours of life,
when the man was himself, so a god in his singleness,
and the woman was herself, never to be duplicated, a goddess there
gleaming her hour in life as she now gleams in death
and departing inviolate, nothing can lay hand on her,
she who at her best hours was herself, warm, flickering, herself,
    therefore a goddess,
and who now draws slowly away, cold, the wistful goddess receding.

So Let Me Live

So let me live that I may die
eagerly passing over from the entanglement of life
to the adventure of death, in eagerness
turning to death as I turn to beauty,
to the breath, that is, of new beauty unfolding in death.

Gladness of Death

Oh death,
about you I know nothing, nothing –
about the afterwards
as a matter of fact, we know nothing.

Yet oh death, oh death,
also I know so much about you,
the knowledge is within me, without being a matter of fact.

And so I know
after the painful, painful experience of dying
there comes an after-gladness, a strange joy
in a great adventure,
oh the great adventure of death, where Thomas Cook cannot
    guide us.

I have always wanted to be as the flowers are,
so unhampered in their living and dying,
and in death I believe I shall be as the flowers are.
I shall blossom like a dark pansy, and be delighted
there among the dark sun-rays of death.
I can feel myself unfolding in the dark sunshine of death
to something flowery and fulfilled, and with a strange sweet
    perfume.
Men prevent one another from being men
but in the great spaces of death
the winds of the afterwards kiss us into blossom of manhood.

Humanity Needs Pruning

Humanity needs pruning,
It is like a vast great tree with a great lot of sterile, dead, rotting
    wood
and an amount of fungoid and parasitic growth.
The tree of humanity needs pruning, badly,
it needs thoroughly pruning, not as in the late war, blasting
with unintelligent and evil destruction,
but pruning, severely, intelligently and ruthlessly pruning.

The tree of human existence badly needs pruning
or the whole tree may fall rotten.

Self-Sacrifice

Self-sacrifice, after all, is a wrong and mistaken idea.
It cannot be anything but wrong to sacrifice
good, healthy, natural feelings, instincts, passions or desires,
just as it cannot be anything but wrong to cut the throats
of doves for Venus, or steers for Hermes,
if it is merely Venus or Hermes you are thinking of.

Venus would rather have live doves than dead, if you want to
    make an offering.
If you want to make her an offering, let the doves fly from her altar.

But what we may sacrifice, if we call it sacrifice, from the self,
are all the obstructions to life, self-importance, self-conceit,
    egoistic self-will,
or all the ugly old possessions that make up the impediments of
    life,
ugly old furniture, ugly old books, ugly old buildings, ugly old 'art',
anything that belongs to us, and is ugly and an impediment to the
    free motion of life –
sacrifice that to the bright gods, and satisfy the destructive instinct.

Shedding of Blood

'Without shedding of blood there is no remission of sin.'
What does it mean?
Does it mean that life which has gone ugly and unliving is sin
and the blood of it must be spilt?

O spill the blood, not of your firstling lamb, without spot or
    blemish,
but kill the scabbed and ugly lamb, that spreads contagion.

O slay, not the bright proud life that is in you, that can be happy,
but the craven, the cowardly, the creeping you, that can only
    be unhappy, kill it, the unliving thing.

O sacrifice, not that which is noble and generous and spontaneous
    in humanity
but that which is mean and base and squalid and degenerate,
destroy it, shed its unclean blood, kill it, put it out of existence.
O shed the unclean, mean, cowardly, greedy, egoistic, degenerate
    blood
and let mankind make new blood, fresh and bright.

The Old Idea of Sacrifice

The old idea of sacrifice was this:
that blood of the lower life must be shed
for the feeding and strengthening of the handsomer, fuller life.

O when the old world sacrificed a ram
it was to the gods who make us splendid
and it was for a feast, a feast of meat, for men and maids
on a day of splendour, for the further splendour of being men.

It was the eating up of little lives,
even doves, even small birds,
into the dance and splendour of a bigger life.

There is no such thing as sin.
There is only life and anti-life.

And sacrifice is the law of life which enacts
that little lives must be eaten up into the dance and splendour
of bigger lives, with due reverence and acknowledgement.

Self-Sacrifice

Self-sacrifice is perhaps the vilest deed a man can do.
The self that we are, at its best, is all that we are,
is the very individual flame of life itself
which is the man's pure self.

And to sacrifice that, to anything or anybody whatsoever,
is the vilest cowardice and treachery.
Yet a woman can add her flame to a man's
or a man can add his flame to the flame of another man
as a gift of gladness, seeing the glamour of life go up
swifter and higher and brighter, for the yielding and the adding
    together.

[Thomas Earp]

I heard a little chicken chirp:
My name is Thomas, Thomas Earp!
And I can neither paint nor write,
I only can set other people right.

All people that can write or paint
do tremble under my complaint.
For I am a chicken, and I can chirp,
and my name is Thomas, Thomas Earp.

'Gross, Coarse, Hideous'

(*Police description of my pictures*)

Lately I saw a sight most quaint:
London's lily-like policemen faint
in virgin outrage as they viewed
the nudity of a Lawrence nude!

[Mr Squire] [83]

Dearly-beloved Mr Squire,
so long as you lead the gawky choir
of critical cherubs that chirrup and pipe
in the weekly press their self-satisfied swipe –

Oh London's Mercury, Sunday-School Squire,
so long as you tune your turn-turn lyre
with its tinkle-winkle and tweedle-dee
to the lesser fry in the hierarchy –

So long will they lift their impertinent voices
and chirrup their almost indecent noises
almost as empty as belching or hiccup
in grand chorale to your monthly kick-up.

So now we beg you, Mr Squire,
do now, once and forever, retire
and leave the critical piggy-wiggies.

Let There be Light!

If ever there was a beginning
there was no god in it
there was no Verb
no Voice
no Word.

There was nothing to say:
Let there be light!
All that story of Mr God switching on day
is just conceit.

Just man's conceit!
– Who made the Sun?
– My child, I cannot tell a lie,
I made it!

George Washington's Grandpapa!

All we can honestly imagine in the beginning
is the incomprehensible plasm of life, of creation
struggling
and *becoming* light.

God is Born

The history of the cosmos
is the history of the struggle of becoming.
When the dim flux of unformed life
struggled, convulsed back and forth upon itself,
and broke at last into light and dark,
came into existence as light,
came into existence as cold shadow,
then every atom of the cosmos trembled with delight.
Behold, God is born!
He is bright light!
He is pitch dark and cold!

And in the great struggle of intangible chaos
when, at a certain point, a drop of water began to drip
    downwards
and a breath of vapour began to wreathe up,
lo! again the shudder of bliss through all the atoms!
Oh, God is born!
Behold, He is born wet!
Look, He hath movement upward! He spirals!

And so, in the great aeons of accomplishment and débâcle
from time to time the wild crying of every electron:
Lo! God is born.

When sapphires cooled out of molten chaos:
See, God is born! He is blue, He is deep blue, He is for ever blue!

When gold lay shining, threading the cooled-off rock:
God is born! God is born! bright yellow and ductile He is born.

When the little eggy amoeba emerged out of foam and nowhere
then all the electrons held their breath:
Ach! Ach! Now indeed God is born! He twinkles within.

When from a world of mosses and of ferns
at last the narcissus lifted a tuft of five-point stars
and dangled them in the atmosphere,
then every molecule of creation jumped and clapped its hands:
God is born! God is born perfumed and dangling and with a
      little cup!

Throughout the aeons, as the lizard swirls his tail finer than water,
as the peacock turns to the sun, and could not be more splendid,
as the leopard smites the small calf with a spangled paw, perfect,
the universe trembles: God is born! God is here!

And when at last man stood on two legs and wondered,
then there was a hush of suspense at the core of every electron:
Behold, now very God is born!
God Himself is born!
And so we see, God is not
until He is born.

And also we see
there is no end to the birth of God.

The White Horse

The youth walks up to the white horse to put its halter on
and the horse looks at him in silence.
They are so silent they are in another world.

Flowers and Men

Flowers achieve their own floweriness and it is a miracle.
Men don't achieve their own manhood, alas, oh alas! alas!

All I want of you, men and women,
all I want of you
is that you shall achieve your beauty
as the flowers do.

Oh leave off saying I want you to be savages.
Tell me, is the gentian savage, at the top of its coarse stem?
Oh what in you can answer to this blueness?
. . . as the gentian and the daffodil . . .
Tell me! tell me! is there in you a beauty to compare
to the honeysuckle at evening now
pouring out his breath?

Prayer

Give me the moon at my feet
Put my feet upon the crescent, like a Lord!
O let my ankles be bathed in moonlight, that I may go
sure and moon-shod, cool and bright-footed
towards my goal.

For the sun is hostile, now
his face is like the red lion,

LAST POEMS

The Greeks Are Coming

Little islands out at sea, on the horizon,
keep suddenly showing a whiteness, a flash and a furl, a hail
of something coming, ships a-sail from over the rim of the sea.

And every time, it is ships, it is ships,
it is ships of Cnossos coming, out of the morning and the sea,
it is Aegean ships, and men with archaic pointed beards
coming out of the Eastern end.

But it is far-off foam.
And an ocean liner going east, like a small beetle walking the edge,
is leaving a long thread of dark smoke
like a bad smell.

The Argonauts

They are not dead, they are not dead!
Now that the sun, like a lion, licks his paws
and goes slowly down the hill:
now that the moon, who remembers, and only cares
that we should be lovely in the flesh, with bright, crescent feet,
pauses near the crest of the hill, climbing slowly, like a queen
looking down on the lion as he retreats.

Now the sea is the Argonauts' sea, and in the dawn
Odysseus calls the commands, as he steers past those foamy
     islands;
wait, wait, don't bring the coffee yet, nor the *pain grillé*.[84]
The dawn is not off the sea, and Odysseus' ships
have not yet passed the islands, I must watch them still.

Middle of the World

This sea will never die, neither will it ever grow old,
nor cease to be blue, nor in the dawn
cease to lift up its hills
and let the slim black ship of Dionysos come sailing in
with grape-vines up the mast, and dolphins leaping.

What do I care if the smoking ships
of the P&O and the Orient Line and all the other stinkers
cross like clockwork the Minoan distance!
They only cross, the distance never changes.

And now that the moon who gives men glistening bodies
is in her exaltation, and can look down on the sun,
I see descending from the ships at dawn
slim naked men from Cnossos, smiling the archaic smile
of those that will without fail come back again,
and kindling little fires upon the shores
and crouching, and speaking the music of lost languages.

And the Minoan Gods and the Gods of Tiryns
are heard softly laughing and chatting, as ever;
and Dionysos, young, and a stranger,
leans listening on the gate, in all respect.

For the Heroes Are Dipped in Scarlet

Before Plato told the great lie of ideals,
men slimly went like fishes, and didn't care.

They had long hair, like Samson,
and clean as arrows they sped at the mark
when the bow-cord twanged.

They knew it was no use knowing
their own nothingness:
for they were not nothing.

So now they come back! Hark!
Hark! the low and shattering laughter of bearded men
with the slim waists of warriors, and the long feet
of moon-lit dancers.

Oh, and their faces scarlet, like the dolphin's blood!
Lo! the loveliest is red all over, rippling vermilion
as he ripples upwards!
laughing in his black beard!

They are dancing! they return, as they went, dancing!
For the thing that is done without the glowing as of god,
    vermilion,
were best not done at all.
How glistening red they are!

Demiurge

They say that reality exists only in the spirit
that corporal existence is a kind of death
that pure being is bodiless
that the idea of the form precedes the form substantial.

But what nonsense it is!
as if any Mind could have imagined a lobster
dozing the under-deeps, then reaching out a savage and
    iron claw!

Even the mind of God can only imagine
those things that have become themselves:
bodies and presences, here and now, creatures with a
    foothold in creation
even if it is only a lobster on tiptoe.

Religion knows better than philosophy.
Religion knows that Jesus never was Jesus
till he was born from a womb, and ate soup and bread
and grew up, and became, in the wonder of creation, Jesus,
with a body and with needs, and a lovely spirit.

The Work of Creation

The mystery of creation is the divine urge of creation,
but it is a great strange urge, it is not a Mind.
Even an artist knows that his work was never in his mind,
he could never have *thought* it before it happened.
A strange ache possessed him, and he entered the struggle,
and out of the struggle with his material, in the spell of the urge,
his work took place, it came to pass, it stood up and saluted
    his mind.

God is a great urge, wonderful, mysterious, magnificent,
but he knows nothing beforehand.
His urge takes shape in flesh, and lo!
it is creation! God looks himself on it in wonder, for the first time.
Lo! there is a creature, formed! How strange!
Let me think about it! Let me form an idea!

Red Geranium and Godly Mignonette

Imagine that any mind ever *thought* a red geranium!
As if the redness of a red geranium could be anything but a sensual
    experience
and as if sensual experience could take place before there were any
    senses.
We know that even God could not imagine the redness of a red
    geranium
nor the smell of mignonette
when geraniums were not, and mignonette neither.
And even when they were, even God would have to have a nose
to smell at the mignonette.
You can't imagine the Holy Ghost sniffing at cherry-pie heliotrope.
Or the Most High, during the coal age, cudgelling his mighty brains
even if he had any brains: straining his mighty mind
to think, among the moss and mud of lizards and mastodons,
to think out, in the abstract, when all was twilit green and muddy:
'Now there shall be tum-tiddly-um, and tum-tiddly um,
hey-presto! scarlet geranium! '

We know it couldn't be done.
But imagine, among the mud and the mastodons,
God sighing and yearning with tremendous creative yearning, in
    that dark green mess,
oh, for some other beauty, some other beauty
that blossomed at last, red geranium, and mignonette.

Bodiless God

Everything that has beauty has a body, and is a body;
everything that has being has being in the flesh:
and dreams are only drawn from the bodies that are.

And God?
Unless God has a body, how can he have a voice
and emotions, and desires, and strength, glory or honour?
For God, even the rarest God, is supposed to love us
and wish us to be this that and the other.
And he is supposed to be mighty and glorious.

The Body of God

God is the great urge that has not yet found a body
but urges towards incarnation with the great creative urge.

And becomes at last a clove carnation: lo! that is god!
and becomes at last Helen, or Ninon: any lovely and
    generous woman
at her best and her most beautiful, being god, made manifest,
any clear and fearless man being god, very god.

There is no god
apart from poppies and the flying fish,
men singing songs, and women brushing their hair in the sun.
The lovely things are god that has come to pass, like Jesus came.
The rest, the undiscoverable, is the demiurge.

The Rainbow

Even the rainbow has a body
made of the drizzling rain
and is an architecture of glistening atoms
built up, built up
yet you can't lay your hand on it,
nay, nor even your mind.

Maximus

God is older than the sun and moon
and the eye cannot behold him
nor voice describe him.

But a naked man, a stranger, leaned on the gate
with his cloak over his arm, waiting to be asked in.
So I called him: Come in, if you will! –
He came in slowly, and sat down by the hearth.
I said to him: And what is your name? –
He looked at me without answer, but such a loveliness
entered me, I smiled to myself, saying: He is God!
So he said: *Hermes!*
God is older than the sun and moon
and the eye cannot behold him
nor the voice describe him:
and still, this is the God Hermes, sitting by my hearth.

The Man of Tyre

The man of Tyre went down to the sea
pondering, for he was a Greek, that God is one and all alone and
     ever more shall be so.

And a woman who had been washing clothes in the pool of rock
where a stream came down to the gravel of the sea and sank in,
who had spread white washing on the gravel banked above the bay,
who had lain her shift on the shore, on the shingle slope,

who had waded to the pale green sea of evening, out to a shoal,
pouring sea-water over herself,
now turned, and came slowly back, with her back to the evening
    sky.

Oh lovely, lovely with the dark hair piled up, as she went deeper,
    deeper down the channel, then rose shallower, shallower,
with the full thighs slowly lifting of the wader wading shorewards
and the shoulders pallid with light from the silent sky behind,
both breasts dim and mysterious, with the glamorous kindness of
    twilight between them,
and the dim notch of black maidenhair like an indicator,
giving a message to the man –

So in the cane-brake he clasped his hands in delight
that could only be god-given, and murmured:
Lo! God is one god! But here in the twilight
godly and lovely comes Aphrodite out of the sea
towards me!

They Say the Sea is Loveless

They say the sea is loveless, that in the sea
love cannot live, but only bare, salt splinters
of loveless life.
But from the sea
the dolphins leap round Dionysos' ship
whose masts have purple vines,
and up they come with the purple dark of rainbows
and flip! they go! with the nose-dive of sheer delight;
and the sea is making love to Dionysos
in the bouncing of these small and happy whales.

Whales Weep Not!

They say the sea is cold, but the sea contains
the hottest blood of all, and the wildest, the most urgent.

All the whales in the wider deeps, hot are they, as they urge
on and on, and dive beneath the icebergs.
The right whales, the sperm-whales, the hammer-heads, the killers
there they blow, there they blow, hot wild white breath out of the sea!

And they rock, and they rock, through the sensual ageless ages
on the depths of the seven seas,
and through the salt they reel with drunk delight
and in the tropics tremble they with love
and roll with massive, strong desire, like gods.
Then the great bull lies up against his bride
in the blue deep of the sea
as mountain pressing on mountain, in the zest of life:
and out of the inward roaring of the inner red ocean of whale blood
the long tip reaches strong, intense, like the maelstrom-tip, and comes
    to rest
in the clasp and the soft, wild clutch of a she-whale's fathomless body.

And over the bridge of the whale's strong phallus, linking the wonder
    of whales
the burning archangels under the sea keep passing, back and forth,
keep passing archangels of bliss
from him to her, from her to him, great Cherubim
that wait on whales in mid-ocean, suspended in the waves of the sea,
great heaven of whales in the waters, old hierarchies.
And enormous mother whales lie dreaming, suckling their whale-
    tender young
and dreaming with strange whale eyes wide open in the waters of the
    beginning and the end.

And bull-whales gather their women and whale-calves in a ring
when danger threatens, on the surface of the ceaseless flood,
and range themselves like great fierce Seraphim facing the threat,
encircling their huddled monsters of love.
And all this happens in the sea, in the salt

where God is also love, but without words:
and Aphrodite is the wife of whales
most happy, happy she!
and Venus among the fishes skips and is a she-dolphin,
she is the gay, delighted porpoise sporting with love and the sea,
she is the female tunny-fish, round and happy among the males
and dense with happy blood, dark rainbow bliss in the sea.

Invocation to the Moon

You beauty, O you beauty
you glistening garmentless beauty!
great lady, great glorious lady
greatest of ladies
crownless and jewelless and garmentless
because naked you are more wonderful than anything we can
    stroke.

Be good to me, lady, great lady of the nearest
heavenly mansion, and last!
Now I am at your gate, you beauty, you lady of all nakedness!
Now I must enter your mansion, and beg your gift,
Moon, O Moon, great lady of the heavenly few.

Far and forgotten is the Villa of Venus the glowing
and behind me now in the gulfs of space lies the golden house of
    the sun,
and six have given me gifts, and kissed me god-speed
kisses of four great lords, beautiful, as they held me to their bosom
    in farewell,
and kiss of the far-off lingering lady who looks over the distant
    fence of the twilight,
and one warm kind kiss of the lion with golden paws.

Now, lady of the Moon, now open the gate of your silvery house
and let me come past the silver bells of your flowers and the
    cockle-shells
into your house, garmentless lady of the last great gift:

who will give me back my lost limbs
and my lost white fearless breast
and set me again on moon-remembering feet
a healed, whole man, O Moon!

Lady, lady of the last house down the long, long street of the stars,
be good to me now, as I beg you, as you've always been good to
     men
who begged of you and gave you homage
and watched for your glistening feet down the garden path!

Butterfly

Butterfly, the wind blows seaward, strong beyond the garden wall!
Butterfly, why do you settle on my shoe, and sip the dirt on my shoe,
Lifting your veined wings, lifting them? big white butterfly!

Already it is October, and the wind blows strong to the sea
from the hills where the snow must have fallen, the wind is polished
     with snow.
Here in the garden, with red geraniums, it is warm, it is warm
but the wind blows strong to seaward, white butterfly, content on
     my shoe!

Will you go, will you go from my warm house?
Will you climb on your big soft wings, black-dotted,
as up an invisible rainbow, an arch,
till the wind slides you sheer from the arch-crest
and in a strange level fluttering you go out to seaward, white speck!

Farewell, farewell, lost soul!
you have melted in the crystalline distance,
it is enough! I saw you vanish into air.

Bavarian Gentians

Not every man has gentians in his house
in Soft September, at slow, Sad Michaelmas.

Bavarian gentians, big and dark, only dark
darkening the daytime, torch-like with the smoking blueness of
    Pluto's gloom,
ribbed and torch-like, with their blaze of darkness spread blue
down flattening into points, flattened under the sweep of white day
torch-flower of the blue-smoking darkness, Pluto's dark-blue daze,
black lamps from the halls of Dis, burning dark blue,
giving off darkness, blue darkness, as Demeter's pale lamps give
    off light,
lead me then, lead me the way.

Reach me a gentian, give me a torch!
let me guide myself with the blue, forked torch of this flower
down the darker and darker stairs, where blue is darkened on blueness
even where Persephone goes, just now, from the frosted September
to the sightless realm where darkness is awake upon the dark
and Persephone herself is but a voice
or a darkness invisible enfolded in the deeper dark
of the arms Plutonic, and pierced with the passion of dense gloom,
among the splendour of torches of darkness, shedding darkness on
    the lost bride and her groom.

Lucifer

Angels are bright still, though the brightest fell.
But tell me, tell me, how do you know
he lost any of his brightness in the falling?
In the dark-blue depths, under layers and layers of darkness,
I see him more like the ruby, a gleam from within
of his own magnificence,
coming like the ruby in the invisible dark, glowing
with his own annunciation, towards us.

The Breath of Life

The breath of life is in the sharp winds of change
mingled with the breath of destruction.
But if you want to breathe deep, sumptuous life
breathe all alone, in silence, in the dark,
and see nothing.

Silence

Come, holy Silence, come
great bride of all creation.

Come, holy Silence! reach, reach
from the presence of God, and envelop us.

Let the sea heave no more in sound,
hold the stars still, lest we hear the heavens dimly ring with
    their commotion!
fold up all sounds.

Lo! the laugh of God!
Lo! the laugh of the creator!
Lo! the last of the seven great laughs of God!
Lo! the last of the seven great laughs of creation!

Huge, huge roll the peals of the thundrous laugh,
huge, huger, huger and huger pealing
till they mount and fill and all is fulfilled of God's last and
    greatest laugh
till all is soundless and senseless, a tremendous body of silence
enveloping even the edges of the thought-waves,
enveloping even me, who hear no more,
who am embedded in a shell of silence,
of silence, lovely silence
of endless and living silence
of holy silence
the silence of the last of the seven great laughs of God.

Ah! the holy silence – it is meet!
It is very fitting! there is nought beside!
For now we are passing through the gate, stilly,
in the sacred silence of gates,
in the silence of passing through doors,
in the great hush of going from this into that,
in the suspension of wholeness, in the moment of division
    within the whole!

Lift up your heads, O ye Gates!
for the silence of the last great thundrous laugh
screens us purely, and we can slip through.

The Hands of God

It is a fearful thing to fall into the hands of the living God.
But it is a much more fearful thing to fall out of them.

Did Lucifer fall through knowledge?
oh then, pity him, pity him that plunge!

Save me, O God, from falling into the ungodly knowledge
of myself as I am without God.
Let me never know, O God,
let me never know what I am or should be
when I have fallen out of your hands, the hands of the living God.

That awful and sickening endless sinking, sinking
through the slow, corruptive levels of disintegrative knowledge
when the self has fallen from the hands of God
and sinks, seething and sinking, corrupt
and sinking still, in depth after depth of disintegrative
    consciousness,
sinking in the endless undoing, the awful katabolism into the
    abyss!
even of the soul, fallen from the hands of God!

Save me from that, O God!
Let me never know myself apart from the living God!

Pax

All that matters is to be at one with the living God,
to be a creature in the house of the God of Life.

Like a cat asleep on a chair,
at peace, in peace
and at one with the master of the house, with the mistress,
at home, at home in the house of the living,
sleeping on the hearth, and yawning before the fire.

Sleeping on the hearth of the living world,
yawning at home before the fire of life,
feeling the presence of the living God
like a great reassurance,
a deep calm in the heart,
a presence
as of the master sitting at the board
in his own and greater being,
in the house of life.

Abysmal Immortality

It is not easy to fall out of the hands of the living God.
They are so large, and they cradle so much of a man.
It is a long time before a man can get himself away.
Even through the greatest blasphemies, the hands of the
    living God still continue to cradle him.

And still through knowledge and will, he can break away,
man can break away, and fall from the hands of God
into himself alone, down the godless plunge of the abyss,
a god-lost creature turning upon himself
in the long, long fall, revolving upon himself
in the endless writhe of the last, the last self-knowledge
which he can never reach till he touch the bottom of the abyss
which he can never touch, for the abyss is bottomless.

And there is nothing else, throughout time and eternity,
but the abyss, which is bottomless,
and the fall to extinction, which can never come,
for the abyss is bottomless,
and the turning down plunge of writhing of self-knowledge,
    self-analysis
which goes further and further, and yet never finds an end
for there is no end,
it is the abyss of the immortality
of those that have fallen from God.

Only Man

Only man can fall from God.
Only man.

No animal, no beast nor creeping thing,
no cobra nor hyena nor scorpion nor hideous white ant
can slip entirely through the fingers of the hands of god
into the abyss of self-knowledge,
knowledge of the self-apart-from-god.

For the knowledge of the self-apart-from-God
is an abyss down which the soul can slip
writhing and twisting in all the revolutions
of the unfinished plunge
of self-awareness, now apart from God, falling
fathomless, fathomless, self-consciousness wriggling
writhing deeper and deeper in all the minutiae of self-knowledge,
downwards, exhaustive,
yet never, never coming to the bottom, for there is no bottom;
zigzagging down like the fizzle from a finished rocket,
the frizzling falling fire that cannot go out, dropping wearily,
neither can it reach the depth
for the depth is bottomless,
so it wriggles its way even further down, further down
at last in sheer horror of not being able to leave off
knowing itself, knowing itself apart from God, falling.

Return of Returns

Come in a week.
Yes, yes, in the seven-day week!
for how can I count in your three times three
of the sea-blown week of nine.

Come then, as I say, in a week,
when the planets have given seven nods,
'It shall be! It shall be!' assented seven times
by the great seven, by Helios the brightest
and by Artemis the whitest,
by Hermes and Aphrodite, flashing white glittering words,
by Ares and Kronos and Zeus,
the seven great ones, who must all say yes.

When the moon from out of the darkness
has come like a thread, like a door just opening
opening, till the round white doorway of delight
is half open.

Come then!
Then, when the door is half open.
In a week!
The ancient river week, the old one.
Come then!

Stoic

Groan then, groan.
For the sun is dead, and all that is in heaven
is the pyre of blazing gas.

And the moon that went
so queenly, shaking her glistening beams,
is dead too, a dead orb wheeled once a month round
    the park.

And the five others, the travellers,
they are all dead!
In the hearse of night you see their tarnished coffins
travelling, travelling still, still travelling
to the end, for they are not yet buried.

Groan then, groan!
Groan then, for even the maiden earth
is dead, we run wheels across her corpse.

Oh groan,
groan with mighty groans!

But for all that, and all that,
'in the centre of your being, groan not'.
In the centre of your being, groan not, do not groan.
For perhaps the greatest of all illusions
is this illusion of the death of the undying.

In the Cities

In the cities
there is even no more any weather,
the weather in town is always benzine, or else petrol fumes,
lubricating oil, exhaust gas.

As over some dense marsh, the fumes
thicken, miasma, the fumes of the automobile
densely thicken in the cities.

In ancient Rome, down the thronged streets
no wheels might run, no insolent chariots.
Only the footsteps, footsteps
of people
and the gentle trotting of the litter-bearers.

In Minos, in Mycenae,
in all the cities with lion gates
the dead threaded the air, lingering
lingering in the earth's shadow
and leaning towards the old hearth.

In London, New York, Paris,
in the bursten cities
the dead tread heavily through the muddy air,
through the mire of fumes
heavily, stepping weary on our hearts.

Lord's Prayer

For thine is the kingdom,
the power, and the glory.

Hallowed be thy name then,
Thou who art nameless.

Give me, Oh give me
besides my daily bread
my kingdom, my power, and my glory.

All things that turn to thee
have their kingdom, their power, and their glory.
Like the kingdom of the nightingale at twilight
whose power and glory I have often heard and felt.

Like the kingdom of the fox in the dark,
yapping in his power and his glory
which is death to the goose.

Like the power and the glory of the goose in the mist
hawking over the lake.

And I, a naked man, calling
calling to thee for my mana,
my kingdom, my power, and my glory.

Mana of the Sea

Do you see the sea, breaking itself to bits against
          the islands
yet remaining unbroken, the level great sea?

Have I caught from it
the tide in my arms
that runs down to the shallows of my wrists, and breaks
abroad in my hands, like waves among the rocks of
          substance?

Do the rollers of the sea
roll down my thighs
and over the submerged islets of my knees
with power, sea-power,
sea-power
to break against the ground
in the flat, recurrent breakers of my two feet?

And is my body ocean, ocean
whose power runs to the shores along my arms
and breaks in the foamy hands, whose power rolls out
to the white-treading waves of two salt feet?

I am the sea, I am the sea!

Salt

Salt is scorched water that the sun has scorched
into substance and flaky whiteness
in the eternal opposition
between the two great ones, Fire, and the Wet.

The Four

To our senses, the elements are four
and have ever been, and will ever be
for they are the elements of life, of poetry, and of perception,
the four Great Ones, the Four Roots, the First Four
of Fire and the Wet, Earth and the wide Air of the world.

To find the other many elements, you must go to the laboratory
and hunt them down.
But the four we have always with us, they are our world.
Or rather, they have us with them.

The Boundary Stone

So, salt is the boundary mark between Fire that burns, and
    the Wet.
It is the white stone of limits, the term, the landmark between
the two great and moving Ones, Fire and the yielding Wet.
It is set up as a boundary, and blood and sweat
are marked out with the boundary of salt, between Fire and
    the Wet.

Spilling the Salt

Don't spill the salt, for it is the landmark,
and cursed be he that removeth his neighbour's landmark.

And the watchers, the dividers, those swift ones with dark
    sharp wings
and keen eyes, they will hover, they will come between you,
between you and your purpose like a knife's edge shadow
cutting you off from your joy.

For the unseen witnesses are the angels of creation
but also the sunderers, the angels with black, sharp wing-tips.

Walk Warily

Walk warily, walk warily, be careful what you say:
because now the Sunderers are hovering round,
the Dividers are close upon us, dogging our every breath
and watching our every step.
and beating their great wings in our panting faces.

The angels are standing back, the angels of the Kiss.
They wait, they give way now
to the Sunderers, to the swift ones,
the ones with the sharp black wings
and the shudder of electric anger
and the drumming of pinions of thunder
and hands like salt
and the sudden dripping down of the knife-edge cleavage
    of the lightning
cleaving, cleaving.

Lo, we are in the midst of the Sunderers,
the cleavers, that cleave us forever apart from one another,
and separate heart from heart, and cut away all caresses
with the white triumphance of lightning and electric delight,
the Dividers, the Thunderers, the Swift Ones, blind with speed,
who put salt in our mouths
and currents of excitement in our limbs
and hotness, and then more crusted brine in our hearts.

It is the day of the Sunderers
and the angels are standing back.

Mystic

They call all experience of the senses *mystic*, when the
    experience is considered.
So an apple becomes *mystic* when I taste in it
the summer and the snows, the wild welter of earth
and the insistence of the sun.
All of which things I can surely taste in a good apple.

Though some apples taste preponderantly of water,
      wet and sour
and some of too much sun, brackish sweet
like lagoon-water, that has been too much sunned.
If I say I taste these things in an apple, I am called *mystic*,
      which means a liar.
The only way to eat an apple is to hog it down like a pig
and taste nothing
that is *real*.

But if I eat an apple, I like to eat it with all my senses awake.
Hogging it down like a pig I call the feeding of corpses.

Anaxagoras[85]

When Anaxagoras says: Even the snow is black!
he is taken by the scientists very seriously
because he is enunciating a 'principle', a 'law'
that all things are mixed, and therefore the purest white snow
has in it an element of blackness.

That they call science, and reality.
I call it mental conceit and mystification
and nonsense, for pure snow is white to us,
white and white and only white
with a lovely bloom of whiteness upon white
in which the soul delights and the senses
have an experience of bliss.

And life is for delight, and for bliss
and dread, and the dark, rolling ominousness of doom,
then the bright dawning of delight again
from off the sheer white snow, or the poised moon.

And in the shadow of the sun the snow is blue, so blue-aloof
with a hint of the frozen bells of the scylla flower
but never the ghost of a glimpse of Anaxagoras' funeral black.

Kissing and Horrid Strife

I have been defeated and dragged down by pain
and worsted by the evil world-soul of today.

But still I know that life is for delight
and for bliss
as now when the tiny wavelets of the sea
tip the morning light on edge, and spill it with delight
to show how inexhaustible it is.

And life is for delight, and bliss
like now where the white sun kisses the sea
and plays with the wavelets like a panther playing with its cubs,
cuffing them with soft paws,
and blows that are caresses,
kisses of the soft-balled paws, where the talons are.

And life is for dread,
for doom that darkens, and the Sunderers
that sunder us from each other,
that strip us and destroy us and break us down
as the tall foxgloves and the mulleins and mallows
are torn down by dismembering autumn
till not a vestige is left, and bleak winter has no trace
of any such flowers;
and yet the roots below the blackness are intact:
the Thunderers and the Sunderers have their term,
their limit, their thus far and no further.

Life is for kissing and for horrid strife.
Life is for the angels and the Sunderers.
Life is for the daimons and the demons,
those that put honey on our lips, and those that put salt.
But life is not
for the dead vanity of knowing better, nor the blank
cold comfort of superiority, nor silly
conceit of being immune,
nor puerility of contradictions
like saying snow is black, or desire is evil.

Life is for kissing and for horrid strife,
the angels and the Sunderers.
And perhaps in unknown Death we perhaps shall know
Oneness and poised immunity.
But why then should we die while we can live?
And while we live
the kissing and communing cannot cease
nor yet the striving and the horrid strife.

When Satan Fell

When Satan fell, he only fell
because the Lord Almighty rose a bit too high,
a bit beyond himself.

So Satan only fell to keep a balance.
'Are you so lofty, O my God?
Are you so pure and lofty, up aloft?
Then I will fall, and plant the paths to hell
with vines and poppies and fig trees
so that lost souls may eat grapes
and the moist fig
and put scarlet buds in their hair on the way to hell,
on the way to dark perdition.'

And hell and heaven are the scales of the balance of life
which swing against each other.

Doors

But evil is a third thing.
No, not the ithyphallic demons
not even the double Phallus of the devil himself
with his key to the two dark doors
is evil.

Life has its palace of blue day aloft
and its halls of the great dark below,

and there are the bright doors where souls go gaily in:
and there are the dark doors where souls pass silently
holding their breath, naked and darkly alone,
entering into the other communion.

There is a double sacredness of doors.
Some you may sing through, and all men hear,
but others, the dark doors, oh hush! hush!
let nobody be about! slip in! go all unseen.
But evil, evil is another thing! in another place!

Evil is Homeless

Evil has no home,
only evil has no home,
not even the home of demoniacal hell.
Hell is the home of souls lost in darkness,
even as heaven is the home of souls lost in light.
And like Persephone or Attis
there are souls that are at home in both homes.
Not like grey Dante, colour-blind
to the scarlet and purple flowers at the doors of hell.

But evil,
evil has no dwelling-place,
the grey vulture, the grey hyena, corpse-eaters
they dwell in the outskirt fringes of nowhere
where the grey twilight of evil sets in.

And men that sit in machines
among spinning wheels, in an apotheosis of wheels
sit in the grey mist of movement which moves not
and going which goes not
and doing which does not
and being which is not:
that is, they sit and are evil, in evil,
grey evil, which has no path, and shows neither light nor dark
and has no home, no home anywhere.

What Then is Evil?

Oh, in the world of the flesh of man
iron gives the deadly wound
and the wheel starts the principle of all evil.

Oh, in the world of things
the wheel is the first principle of evil.

But in the world of the soul of man
there, and there alone lies the pivot of pure evil
only in the soul of man, when it pivots upon the ego.

When the mind makes a wheel which turns on the hub of the ego
and the will, the living dynamo, gives the motion and the speed
and the wheel of the conscious self spins on in absolution, absolute
absolute, absolved from the sun and the earth and the moon,
absolute consciousness, absolved from strife and kisses
absolute self-awareness, absolved from the meddling of creation
absolute freedom, absolved from the great necessities of being
then we see evil, pure evil
and we see it only in man
and in his machines.

The Evil World-Soul

Oh, there is evil, there is an evil world-soul.
But it is the soul of man only and his machines
which has brought to pass the fearful thing called evil,
hyenas only hint at it.

Do not think that a machine is without a soul.
Every wheel on its hub has a soul, evil,
it is part of the evil world-soul, spinning.

And every man who has become a detached and self-activated ego
is evil, evil, part of the evil world-soul
which wishes to blaspheme the world into greyness,
into evil neutrality, into mechanism.
The Robot is the unit of evil.
And the symbol of the Robot is the wheel revolving.

The Wandering Cosmos

Oh, do not tell me the heavens as well are a wheel.
For every revolution of the earth around the sun
is a footstep onwards, onwards, we know not whither
and we do not care,
but a step onwards in untravelled space,
for the earth, like the sun, is a wanderer.
Their going round each time is a step
onwards, we know not whither,
but onwards, onwards, for the heavens are wandering,
the moon and the earth, the sun, Saturn and Betelgeuse,
    Vega and Sirius and Altair,
they wander their strange and different ways in heaven
past Venus and Uranus and the signs.

For life is a wandering, we know not whither, but going.

Only the wheel goes round, but it never wanders.
It stays on its hub.

Death is not Evil, Evil is Mechanical

Only the human being, absolved from kissing and strife,
goes on and on and on, without wandering,
fixed upon the hub of the ego,
going, yet never wandering, fixed, yet in motion,
the kind of hell that is real, grey and awful,
sinless and stainless going round and round,
the kind of hell grey Dante never saw
but of which he had a bit inside him.

Know thyself, and that thou art mortal.
But know thyself, denying that thou art mortal:
a thing of kisses and strife
a lit-up shaft of rain
a calling column of blood
a rose tree bronzey with thorns
a mixture of yea and nay
a rainbow of love and hate
a wind that blows back and forth

a creature of conflict, like a cataract:
know thyself, in denial of all these things.

And thou shalt begin to spin round on the hub of
    the obscene ego
a grey void thing that goes without wandering
a machine that in itself is nothing
a centre of the evil world.

Strife

When strife is a thing of two
each knows the other in struggle
and the conflict is a communion
a twoness.

But when strife is a thing of one
a single ego striving for its own ends
and beating down resistances
then strife is evil, because it is not strife.

The Late War

The War was not strife
it was murder
each side trying to murder the other side
evilly.

Murder

Killing is not evil.
A man may be my enemy to the death,
and that is passion and communion.

But murder is always evil
being an act of one
perpetrated upon the other
without cognisance or communion.

Murderous Weapons

So guns and strong explosives
are evil, evil
they let death upon unseen men
in sheer murder.

And most murderous of all devices
are poison gases and air-bombs
refinements of evil.

Departure

Now some men must get up and depart
from evil, or all is lost.

The evil will in many evil men
makes an evil world-soul, which purposes
to reduce the world to grey ash.
Wheels are evil
and machines are evil
and the will to make money is evil.

All forms of abstraction are evil:
finance is a great evil abstraction
science has now become an evil abstraction
education is an evil abstraction.

Jazz and film and wireless
are all evil abstractions from life.

And politics, now, are an evil abstraction from life.

Evil is upon us and has got hold of us.
Men must depart from it, or all is lost.
We must make an isle impregnable
against evil.

The Ship of Death

I

Now it is autumn and the falling fruit
and the long journey towards oblivion.

The apples falling like great drops of dew
to bruise themselves an exit from themselves.

And it is time to go, to bid farewell
to one's own self, and find an exit
from the fallen self.

II

Have you built your ship of death, O have you?
O build your ship of death, for you will need it.

The grim frost is at hand, when the apples will fall
thick, almost thundrous, on the hardened earth.

And death is on the air like a smell of ashes!
Ah! can't you smell it?
And in the bruised body, the frightened soul
finds itself shrinking, wincing from the cold
that blows upon it through the orifices.

III

And can a man his own quietus make
with a bare bodkin?

With daggers, bodkins, bullets, man can make
a bruise or break of exit for his life;
but is that a quietus, O tell me, is it quietus?

Surely not so! for how could murder, even self-murder
ever a quietus make?

IV

O let us talk of quiet that we know,
that we can know, the deep and lovely quiet
of a strong heart at peace!

How can we this, our own quietus, make?

V

Build then the ship of death, for you must take
the longest journey, to oblivion.

And die the death, the long and painful death
that lies between the old self and the new.

Already our bodies are fallen, bruised, badly bruised,
already our souls are oozing through the exit
of the cruel bruise.

Already the dark and endless ocean of the end
is washing in through the breaches of our wounds,
already the flood is upon us.

Oh build your ship of death, your little ark,
and furnish it with food, with little cakes, and wine
for the dark flight down oblivion.

VI

Piecemeal the body dies, and the timid soul
has her footing washed away, as the dark flood rises.

We are dying, we are dying, we are all of us dying
and nothing will stay the death-flood rising within us
and soon it will rise on the world, on the outside world.

We are dying, we are dying, piecemeal our bodies are dying
and our strength leaves us,
and our soul cowers naked in the dark rain over the flood,
cowering in the last branches of the tree of our life.

VII

We are dying, we are dying, so all we can do
is now to be willing to die, and to build the ship
of death to carry the soul on the longest journey.

A little ship, with oars and food
and little dishes, and all accoutrements
fitting and ready for the departing soul.

Now launch the small ship, now as the body dies
and life departs, launch out, the fragile soul
in the fragile ship of courage, the ark of faith
with its store of food and little cooking pans
and change of clothes,
upon the flood's black waste
upon the waters of the end
upon the sea of death, where still we sail
darkly, for we cannot steer, and have no port.

There is no port, there is nowhere to go,
only the deepening blackness darkening still
blacker upon the soundless, ungurgling flood,
darkness at one with darkness, up and down
and sideways utterly dark, so there is no direction any more
and the little ship is there; yet she is gone.
She is not seen, for there is nothing to see her by.
She is gone! gone! and yet
somewhere she is there.
Nowhere!

VIII

And everything is gone, the body is gone
completely under, gone, entirely gone.
The upper darkness is heavy as the lower,
between them the little ship
is gone.

It is the end, it is oblivion.

IX

And yet out of eternity a thread
separates itself on the blackness,
a horizontal thread
that fumes a little with pallor upon the dark.

Is it illusion? or does the pallor fume
A little higher?
Ah wait, wait, for there's the dawn,
the cruel dawn of coming back to life
out of oblivion.

Wait, wait, the little ship
drifting, beneath the deathly ashy grey
of a flood-dawn.

Wait, wait! even so, a flush of yellow
and strangely, O chilled wan soul, a flush of rose.

A flush of rose, and the whole thing starts again.

X

The flood subsides, and the body, like a worn sea-shell,
emerges strange and lovely..
And the little ship wings home, faltering and lapsing
on the pink flood,
and the frail soul steps out into the house again
filling the heart with peace.

Swings the heart renewed with peace
even of oblivion.

Oh build your ship of death. Oh build it!
for you will need it.
For the voyage of oblivion awaits you.

Difficult Death

It is not easy to die, O it is not easy
to die the death.

For death comes when he will
not when we will him.

And we can be dying, dying, dying
and longing utterly to die
yet death will not come.

So build your ship of death, and let the soul drift
to dark oblivion.
Maybe life is still our portion
after the bitter passage of oblivion.

All Souls' Day

Be careful, then, and be gentle about death.
For it is hard to die, it is difficult to go through
the door, even when it opens.

And the poor dead, when they have left the walled
and silvery city of the now hopeless body
where are they to go, Oh where are they to go?

They linger in the shadow of the earth.
The earth's long conical shadow is full of souls
that cannot find the way across the sea of change.

Be kind, Oh be kind to your dead
and give them a little encouragement
and help them to build their little ship of death

For the soul has a long, long journey after death
to the sweet home of pure oblivion.
Each needs a little ship, a little ship
and the proper store of meal for the longest journey.

Oh, from out of your heart
provide for your dead once more, equip them
like departing mariners, lovingly.

The Houseless Dead

Oh pity the dead that are dead, but cannot take
the journey, still they moan and beat
against the silvery adamant walls of life's exclusive city.

Oh pity the dead that were ousted out of life
all unequipped to take the long, long voyage.
Gaunt, gaunt they crowd the grey mud-beaches of shadow
that intervene between the final sea
and the white shores of life.

The poor gaunt dead that cannot die
into the distance with receding oars,
but must roam like outcast dogs on the margins of life!
Oh think of them, and encourage them to build
the bark of their deliverance from the dilemma
of non-existence to far oblivion.

Beware the Unhappy Dead!

Beware the unhappy dead, thrust out of life
unready, unprepared, unwilling, unable
to continue on the longest journey.

Oh, now as November draws near
the grey, grey reaches of earth's shadow,
the long mean marginal stretches of our existence
are crowded with lost souls, the uneasy dead
that cannot embark on the slinking sea beyond.

Oh, now they moan and throng in anger, and press back
through breaches in the walls of this our by-no-means
        impregnable existence

seeking their old haunts with cold ghostly rage,
old haunts, old habitats, old hearths,
old places of sweet life from which they are thrust out
and can but haunt in disembodied rage.

Oh, but beware, beware the angry dead.
Who knows, who knows how much our modern woe
is due to the angry unappeased dead
that were thrust out of life, and now come back at us
malignant, malignant, for we will not succour them.
Oh, on this day for the dead, now November is here
set a place for the dead, with a cushion and soft seat,
and put a plate, and put a wine-glass out
and serve the best of food, the fondest wine
for your dead, your unseen dead, and with your hearts
speak with them and give them peace and do them honour.

Or else beware their angry presence, now
within your walls, within your very heart.
Oh, they can lay you waste, the angry dead.
Perhaps even now you are suffering from the havoc they make
unknown within your breast and your deadened loins.

After All Saints' Day

Wrapped in the dark-red mantle of warm memories,
the little, slender soul sits swiftly down, and takes the oars
and draws away, away, towards dark depths,
wafting with warm love from still-living hearts
breathing on his small frail sail, and helping him on
to the fathomless deeps ahead, far, far from the grey shores
of marginal existence.

Song of Death

Sing the song of death, O sing it!
for without the song of death, the song of life
becomes pointless and silly.

Sing then the song of death, and the longest journey,
and what the soul takes with him, and what he leaves behind,
and how he enters fold after fold of deepening darkness
for the cosmos even in death is like a dark whorled shell
whose whorls fold round to the core of soundless silence and
    pivotal oblivion
where the soul comes at last, and has utter peace.

Sing then the core of dark and absolute
oblivion where the soul at last is lost
in utter peace.
Sing the song of death, O sing it!

The End, The Beginning

If there were not an utter and absolute dark
of silence and sheer oblivion

at the core of everything,
how terrible the sun would be,
how ghastly it would be to strike a match, and make a light.

But the very sun himself is pivoted
upon a core of pure oblivion,
so is a candle, even as a match.

And if there were not an absolute, utter forgetting
and a ceasing to know, a perfect ceasing to know
and a silent, sheer cessation of all awareness
how terrible life would be!
how terrible it would be to think and know, to have
    consciousness!

But dipped, once dipped in dark oblivion
the soul has peace, inward and lovely peace.

Sleep

Sleep is the shadow of death, but not only that.
Sleep is a hint of lovely oblivion.
When I am gone, completely lapsed and gone
and healed from all this ache of being.

Sleep and Waking

In sleep I am not, I am gone,
I am given up.
And nothing in the world is lovelier than sleep,
dark, dreamless sleep, in deep oblivion!
Nothing in life is quite so good as this.

Yet there is waking from the soundest sleep,
waking, and waking new.

Did you sleep well?
Ah yes, the sleep of God!
The world is created afresh.

Fatigue

My soul has had a long, hard day
she is tired,
she is seeking her oblivion.

O, and in the world
there is no place for the soul to find her oblivion,
the after darkness of her peace,
for man has killed the silence of the earth
and ravished all the peaceful oblivious places
where the angels used to alight.

Forget

To be able to forget is to be able to yield
to God who dwells in deep oblivion.
Only in sheer oblivion are we with God.
For when we know in full, we have left off knowing.

Know-All

Man knows nothing
till he knows how not-to-know.

And the greatest of teachers will tell you:
The end of all knowledge is oblivion,
sweet, dark oblivion, when I cease
even from myself, and am consummated.

Tabernacle

Come, let us build a temple to oblivion
with seven veils, and an innermost
Holy of Holies of sheer oblivion.

And there oblivion dwells, and the silent soul
may sink into god at last, having passed the veils.

But anyone who shall ascribe attributes to god or oblivion
let him be cast out, for blasphemy.
For god is a deeper forgetting far than sleep
and all description is a blasphemy.

Temples

Oh, what we want on earth
is centres here and there of silence and forgetting,
where we may cease from knowing, and, as far as we know,
may cease from being
in the sweet wholeness of oblivion.

Shadows

And if tonight my soul may find her peace
in sleep, and sink in good oblivion,
and in the morning wake like a new-opened flower
then I have been dipped again in God, and new-created.

And if, as weeks go round, in the dark of the moon
my spirit darkens and goes out, and soft strange gloom
pervades my movements and my thoughts and words,
then I shall know that I am walking still
with God, we are close together now the moon's in shadow.

And if, as autumn deepens and darkens
I feel the pain of falling leaves and stems that break in storms
and trouble and dissolution and distress
and then the softness of deep shadows folding, folding
around my soul and spirit, around my lips
so sweet, like a swoon, or more like the drowse of a low, sad song
singing darker than the nightingale, on, on to the solstice
and the silence of short days, the silence of the year, the shadow,
then I shall know that my life is moving still
with the dark earth, and drenched
with the deep oblivion of earth's lapse and renewal.

And if, in the changing phases of man's life,
I fall in sickness and in misery
my wrists seem broken and my heart seems dead
and strength is gone, and my life
is only the leavings of a life:

and still, among it all, snatches of lovely oblivion, and snatches of
     renewal,
odd, wintry flowers upon the withered stem, yet new, strange
     flowers
such as my life has not brought forth before, new blossoms of me –

then I must know that still
I am in the hands of the unknown God,
he is breaking me down to his own oblivion
to send me forth on a new morning, a new man.

Change

Do you think it is easy to change?
Ah, it is very hard to change and be different.
It means passing through the waters of oblivion.

Phoenix

Are you willing to be sponged out, erased, cancelled,
made nothing?
Are you willing to be made nothing?
dipped into oblivion?

If not, you will never really change.

The phoenix renews her youth
only when she is burnt, burnt alive, burnt down
to hot and flocculent ash.
Then the small stirring of a new small bub in the nest
with strands of down like floating ash
Shows that she is renewing her youth like the eagle,
Immortal bird.

APPENDIX

Preface to the American Edition of
New Poems *(1920)*

It seems when we hear a skylark singing as if sound were running forward into the future, running so fast and utterly without consideration, straight on into futurity. And when we hear a nightingale, we hear the pause and the rich, piercing rhythm of recollection, the perfected past. The lark may sound sad, but with the lovely lapsing sadness that is almost a swoon of hope. The nightingale's triumph is a paean, but a death-paean.

So it is with poetry. Poetry is, as a rule, either the voice of the far future, exquisite and ethereal, or it is the voice of the past, rich, magnificent. When the Greeks heard the *Iliad* and the *Odyssey*, they heard their own past calling in their hearts, as men far inland sometimes hear the sea and fall weak with powerful, wonderful regret, nostalgia; or else their own future rippled its time-beats through their blood, as they followed the painful, glamorous progress of the Ithacan. This was Homer to the Greeks: their Past, splendid with battles won and death achieved, and their Future, the magic wandering of Ulysses through the unknown.

With us it is the same. Our birds sing on the horizons. They sing out of the blue, beyond us, or out of the quenched night. They sing at dawn and sunset. Only the poor, shrill, tame canaries whistle while we talk. The wild birds begin before we are awake, or as we drop into dimness out of waking. Our poets sit by the gateways, some by the east, some by the west. As we arrive and as we go out our hearts surge with response. But whilst we are in the midst of life, we do not hear them.

The poetry of the beginning and the poetry of the end must have that exquisite finality, perfection which belongs to all that is far off. It is in the realm of all that is perfect. It is of the nature of all that is complete and consummate. This completeness, this consummateness, the finality and the perfection are conveyed in exquisite form: the perfect symmetry, the rhythm which returns upon itself like a dance where the hands link and loosen and link for the supreme moment of the end. Perfected bygone moments, perfected moments in the glimmering futurity, these are the treasured gemlike lyrics of Shelley and Keats.

But there is another kind of poetry: the poetry of that which is at hand: the immediate present. In the immediate present there is no perfection, no consummation, nothing finished. The strands are all flying, quivering, intermingling into the web, the waters are shaking the moon. There is no round, consummate moon on the face of running water, nor on the face of the unfinished tide. There are no gems of the living plasm. The living plasm vibrates unspeakably, it inhales the future, it exhales the past, it is the quick of both, and yet it is neither. There is no plasmic finality, nothing crystal, permanent. If we try to fix the living tissue, as the biologists fix it with formation, we have only a hardened bit of the past, the bygone life under our observation.

Life, the ever-present, knows no finality, no finished crystallisation. The perfect rose is only a running flame, emerging and flowing off, and never in any sense at rest, static, finished. Herein lies its transcendent loveliness. The whole tide of all life and all time suddenly heaves, and appears before us as an apparition, a revelation. We look at the very white quick of nascent creation. A water-lily heaves herself from the flood, looks round, gleams, and is gone. We have seen the incarnation, the quick of the ever-swirling flood. We have seen the invisible. We have seen, we have touched, we have partaken of the very substance of creative change, creative mutation. If you tell me about the lotus, tell me of nothing changeless or eternal. Tell me of the mystery of the inexhaustible, forever-unfolding creative spark. Tell me of the incarnate disclosure of the flux, mutation in blossom, laughter and decay perfectly open in their transit, nude in their movement before us.

Let me feel the mud and the heavens in my lotus. Let me feel the heavy, silting, sucking mud, the spinning of sky winds. Let me feel them both in purest contact, the nakedness of sucking weight, nakedly passing radiance. Give me nothing fixed, set, static. Don't give me the infinite or the eternal: nothing of infinity, nothing of eternity. Give me the still, white seething, the incandescence and the coldness of the incarnate moment: the moment, the quick of all change and haste and opposition: the moment, the immediate present, the Now. The immediate moment is not a drop of water running downstream. It is the source and issue, the bubbling up of the stream. Here, in this very instant moment, up bubbles the stream of time, out of the wells of futurity, flowing on to the oceans of the past. The source, the issue, the creative quick.

There is poetry of this immediate present, instant poetry, as well as poetry of the infinite past and the infinite future. The seething poetry of the incarnate Now is supreme, beyond even the everlasting gems of the before and after. In its quivering momentaneity it surpasses the crystalline, pearl-hard jewels, the poems of the eternities. Do not ask for the qualities of the unfading timeless gems. Ask for the whiteness which is the seethe of mud, ask for that incipient putrescence which is the skies falling, ask for the never-pausing, never-ceasing life itself. There must be mutation, swifter than iridescence, haste, not rest, come-and-go, not fixity, inconclusiveness, immediacy, the quality of life itself, without dénouement or close. There must be the rapid momentaneous association of things which meet and pass on the forever incalculable journey of creation: everything left in its own rapid, fluid relationship with the rest of things.

This is the unrestful, ungraspable poetry of the sheer present, poetry whose very permanency lies in its wind-like transit. Whitman's is the best poetry of this kind. Without beginning and without end, without any base and pediment, it sweeps past forever, like a wind that is forever in passage, and unchainable. Whitman truly looked before and after. But he did not sigh for what is not. The clue to all his utterance lies in the sheer appreciation of the instant moment, life surging itself into utterance at its very well-head. Eternity is only an abstraction from the actual present. Infinity is only a great reservoir of recollection, or a reservoir of aspiration: man-made. The quivering nimble hour of the present, this is the quick of Time. This is the immanence. The quick of the universe is the *pulsating, carnal self*, mysterious and palpable. So it is always.

Because Whitman put this into his poetry, we fear him and respect him so profoundly. We should not fear him if he sang only of the 'old unhappy far-off things', or of the 'wings of the morning'. It is because his heart beats with the urgent, insurgent Now, which is even upon us all, that we dread him. He is so near the quick.

From the foregoing it is obvious that the poetry of the instant present cannot have the same body or the same motion as the poetry of the before and after. It can never submit to the same conditions. It is never finished. There is no rhythm which returns upon itself, no serpent of eternity with its tail in its own mouth. There is no static perfection, none of that finality which we find so satisfying because we are so frightened.

Much has been written about free verse. But all that can be said, first and last, is that free verse is, or should be, direct utterance from the instant, whole man. It is the soul and the mind and body surging at once; nothing left out. They speak all together. There is some confusion, some discord. But the confusion and the discord only belong to the reality as noise belongs to the plunge of water. It is no use inventing fancy laws for free verse, no use drawing a melodic line which all the feet must toe. Free verse toes no melodic line, no matter what drill-sergeant. Whitman pruned away his clichés – perhaps his clichés of rhythm as well as of phrase. And this is about all we can do, deliberately, with free verse. We can get rid of the stereotyped movements and the old hackneyed associations of sound or sense. We can break down those artificial conduits and canals through which we do so love to force our utterance. We can break the stiff neck of habit. We can be in

ourselves spontaneous and flexible as flame, we can see that utterance rushes
out without artificial foam or artificial smoothness. But we cannot positively
prescribe any motion, any rhythm. All the laws we invent or discover – it
amounts to pretty much the same – will fail to apply to free verse. They will
only apply to some form of restricted, limited unfree verse.

All we can say is that free verse does *not* have the same nature as restricted
verse. It is not of the nature of reminiscence. It is not the past which we
treasure in its perfection between our hands. Neither is it the crystal of the
perfect future, into which we gaze. Its tide is neither the full, yearning flow of
aspiration, nor the sweet, poignant ebb of remembrance and regret. The past
and the future are the two great bournes of human emotion, the two great
homes of the human days, the two eternities. They are both conclusive, final.
Their beauty is the beauty of the goal, finished, perfected. Finished beauty
and measured symmetry belong to the stable, unchanging eternities.

But in free verse we look for the insurgent naked throb of the instant
moment. To break the lovely form of metrical verse, and to dish up the
fragments as a new substance, called *vers libre*, this is what most of the free-
versifiers accomplish. They do not know that free verse has its own *nature*,
that it is neither star nor pearl, but instantaneous like plasm. It has no goal in
either eternity. It has no finish. It has no satisfying stability, satisfying to
those who like the immutable. None of this. It is the instant; the quick; the
very jetting source of all will-be and has-been. The utterance is like a spasm,
naked contact with all influences at once. It does not want to get anywhere.
It just takes place.

For such utterance any externally-applied law would be mere shackles and
death. The law must come new each time from within. The bird is on the
wing in the winds, flexible to every breath, a living spark in the storm, its very
flickering depending upon its supreme mutability and power of change.
Whence such a bird came: whither it goes: from what solid earth it rose up,
and upon what solid earth it will close its wings and settle, this is not the
question. This is a question of before and after. Now, *now*, the bird is on the
wing in the winds.

Such is the rare new poetry. One realm we have never conquered: the pure
present. One great mystery of time is *terra incognita* to us: the instant. The
most superb mystery we have hardly recognised: the immediate, instant self.
The quick of all time is the instant. The quick of all the universe, of all
creation, is the incarnate, carnal self. Poetry gave us the clue: free verse:
Whitman. Now we know.

The ideal – what is the ideal? A figment. An abstraction. A static
abstraction, abstracted from life. It is a fragment of the before or the after. It
is a crystallised aspiration, or a crystallised remembrance: crystallised, set,

finished. It is a thing set apart, in the great storehouse of eternity, the storehouse of finished things.

We do not speak of things crystallised and set apart. We speak of the instant, the immediate self, the very plasm of the self. We speak also of free verse.

All this should have come as a preface to *Look! We Have Come Through!* But is it not better to publish a preface long after the book it belongs to has appeared? For then the reader will have had his fair chance with the book, alone.

Introductory Note to Collected Poems (1928)

The volume of *Rhyming Poems* is collected from four little books, *Love Poems and Others*, *Amores*, *New Poems* and *Bay*. Of these *Love Poems and Others* was the first, and was published in 1913.

I have now tried to arrange the poems, as far as possible, in chronological order, the order in which they were written. The first poems I ever wrote, if poems they were, was when I was nineteen: now twenty-three years ago. I remember perfectly the Sunday afternoon when I perpetrated those first two pieces: 'To Guelder-Roses' and 'To Campions'; in springtime, of course, and, as I say, in my twentieth year. Any young lady might have written them and been pleased with them; as I was pleased with them. But it was after that, when I was twenty, that my real demon would now and then get hold of me and shake more real poems out of me, making me uneasy. I never 'liked' my real poems as I liked 'To Guelder-Roses'.

I have tried to establish a chronological order, because many of the poems are so personal that, in their fragmentary fashion, they make up a biography of an emotional and inner life. Many of the poems, again, are what one might call fictional, poems like 'Love on the Farm', 'Wedding Morn', 'Two Wives', and the dialect poems. They have no necessary chronological sequence. But the poems to Miriam, and to my mother, and to Helen, and to the other woman, the woman of 'Kisses in the Train' and 'Hands of the Betrothed', they need the order of time, as that is the order of experience. So, perhaps, do the subjective poems like 'Virgin Youth'.

The first change in scene comes when for the first time I left Nottinghamshire, at the age of twenty-three, to go to teach in a new school on the fringes of South London. From the playground we could look north at the blue bubble of the Crystal Palace, fairy-like to me. Then the poems to Helen begin, and the school poems, and London.

Some of the earliest poems, like 'The Wild Common' and 'Virgin Youth', are a good deal rewritten. They were struggling to say something which it takes a man twenty years to be able to say. Some of the fictional poems are changed, to make the 'fiction' more complete. A young man is afraid of his demon and puts his hand over the demon's mouth sometimes and speaks for him. And the things the young man says are very rarely poetry. So I have tried to let the demon say his say, and to remove the passages where the young man intruded. So that, in the first volume, many poems are changed, some entirely rewritten, recast. But usually this is only because the poem started out to be something which it didn't quite achieve, because the young man interfered with his demon.

The crisis of Volume I is the death of the mother, with the long haunting of death in life, which continues to the end, through all the last poems, which come from *Bay*, and which belong to the war. *Bay* appeared in 1919, but the poems were written mostly in 1917 and 1918, after I left Cornwall perforce.

A big break in scene, however, had happened before then, in 1912, when I left England for the first time. In 1912 begins the new cycle of *Look! We Have Come Through!* Of this volume the first few poems belong to England and the end of the death-experience, but 'Bei Hennef', written in May 1912, by a river in the Rhineland, starts the new cycle, which ends with 'Frost Flowers', written in Cornwall at the end of the bitter winter of 1916–17. It seems to me that no poetry, not even the best, should be judged as if it existed in the absolute, in the vacuum of the absolute. Even the best poetry, when it is at all personal, needs the penumbra of its own time and place and circumstance to make it full and whole. If we knew a little more of Shakespeare's self and circumstance how much more complete the Sonnets would be to us, how their strange, torn edges would be softened and merged into a whole body! So one would like to ask the reader of *Look! We Have Come Through!* to fill in the background of the poems, as far as possible, with the place, the time, the circumstance. What was uttered in the cruel spring of 1917 should not be dislocated and heard as if sounding out of the void.

The poems of *Birds, Beasts and Flowers* were begun in Tuscany, in the autumn of 1920, and finished in New Mexico in 1923, in my thirty-eighth year. So that from first to last these poems cover all but twenty years.

Introduction to Collected Poems

Instead of bewailing a lost youth, a man nowadays begins to wonder, when he reaches my ripe age of forty-two, if ever his past will subside and be comfortably bygone. Doing over these poems makes me realise that my teens and my twenties are just as much me, here and now and present, as ever they were, and that pastness is only an abstraction. The actuality, the body of feeling, is essentially alive and here.

And I remember the slightly self-conscious Sunday afternoon, when I was nineteen, and I 'composed' my first two 'poems'. One was to 'Guelder-Roses', and one to 'Campions', and most young ladies would have done better: at least I hope so. But I thought the effusions very nice, and so did Miriam.

Then much more vaguely I remember subsequent half-furtive moments when I would absorbedly scribble at verse for an hour or so, and then run away from the act and the production as if it were secret sin. It seems to me that 'knowing oneself' was a sin and a vice for innumerable centuries before it became a virtue. It seems to me it is still a sin and vice when it comes to new knowledge. In those early days – for I was very green and unsophisticated at twenty – I used to feel myself at times haunted by something, and a little guilty about it, as if it were an abnormality. Then the haunting would get the better of me, and the ghost would suddenly appear, in the shape of a usually rather incoherent poem. Nearly always I shunned the apparition once it had appeared. From the first, I was a little afraid of my real poems – not my 'compositions', but the poems that had the ghost in them. They seemed to me to come from somewhere, I didn't quite know where, out of a me whom I didn't know and didn't want to know, and to say things I would much rather not have said: for choice. But there they were. I never read them again. Only I gave them to Miriam, and she loved them, or she seemed to. So when I was twenty-one, and went to Nottingham University as a day-student, I began putting them down in a little college notebook, which was the foundation of the poetic me. *Sapientiae Urbs Conditur* it said on the cover. Never was anything less true. The city is founded on a passionate unreason.

To this day, I still have the uneasy haunted feeling, and would rather not write most of the things I do write – including this Note. Only now I know my demon better, and, after bitter years, respect him more than my other, milder and nicer self. Now I no longer like my 'compositions'. I once thought the poem 'Flapper' a little masterpiece: when I was twenty: because the demon isn't in it. And I must have burnt many poems that had the demon fuming in them. The fragment 'Discord in Childhood' was a long poem, probably was good, but I destroyed it. Save for Miriam, I perhaps should have destroyed them all. She encouraged my demon. But alas, it was me, not he, whom she loved. So for her too it was a catastrophe. My demon is not easily loved: whereas the ordinary me is. So poor Miriam was let down. Yet in a sense, she let down my demon, till he howled. And there it is. And no more *past* in me than my blood in my toes or my nose.

I have tried to arrange the poems in chronological order: that is, in the order in which they were written. The first are either subjective, or Miriam poems. 'The Wild Common' was very early and very confused. I have rewritten some of it, and added some, till it seems complete. It has taken me twenty years to say what I started to say, incoherently, when I was nineteen, in this poem. The same with 'Virgin Youth', and others of the subjective poems with the demon fuming in them smokily. To the demon, the past is not past. The wild common, the gorse, the virgin youth are here and now. The same: the same me, the same one experience. Only now perhaps I can give it more complete expression.

The poems to Miriam, at least the early ones like 'Dog-Tired' and 'Cherry-Robbers' and 'Renascence', are not much changed. But some of the later ones had to be altered, where sometimes the hand of commonplace youth had been laid on the mouth of the demon. It is not for technique these poems are altered: it is to say the real say.

Other verses, those I call the imaginative, or fictional, like 'Love on the Farm' and 'Wedding Morn,' I have sometimes changed to get them into better form, and take out the dead bits. It took me many years to learn to play with the form of a poem: even if I can do it now. But it is only in the less immediate, the more fictional poems that the form has to be played with. The demon, when he's really there, makes his own form willy-nilly, and is unchangeable.

The poems to Miriam run into the first poems to my mother. Then when I was twenty-three, I went away from home for the first time, to the south of London. From the big new red school where I taught, we could look north and see the Crystal Palace: to me, who saw it for the first time, in lovely autumn weather, beautiful and softly blue on its hill to the north. And past the school, on an embankment, the trains rushed south to Brighton or to Kent. And round the school the country was still only just being built over, and the elms of Surrey stood tall and noble. It was different from the Midlands.

Then began the poems to Helen, and all that trouble of 'Lilies in the Fire': and London, and school, a whole new world. Then starts the rupture with home, with Miriam, away there in Nottinghamshire. And gradually the long illness, and then the death of my mother; and in the sick year after, the collapse of Miriam, of Helen, and of the other woman, the woman of 'Kisses in the Train' and 'The Hands of the Betrothed'.

Then, in that year, for me everything collapsed, save the mystery of death, and the haunting of death in life. I was twenty-five, and from the death of my mother, the world began to dissolve around me, beautiful, iridescent, but passing away substanceless. Till I almost dissolved away myself, and was very ill: when I was twenty-six.

Then slowly the world came back: or I myself returned: but to another world. And in 1912, when I was still twenty-six, the other phase commenced, the phase of *Look! We Have Come Through!* – when I left teaching, and left England, and left many other things, and the demon had a new run for his money.

But back in England during the war, there are the War poems from the little volume: *Bay*. These, beginning with 'Tommies in the Train', make up the end of the volume of *Rhyming Poems*. They are the end of the cycle of purely English experience and death experience.

The first poems I had published were 'Dreams Old' and 'Dreams Nascent', which Miriam herself sent to Ford Madox Hueffer, in 1910, I believe, just when the *English Review* had started so brilliantly. Myself, I had offered the little poem 'Study' to the *Nottingham University Magazine*, but they returned it. But Hueffer accepted the 'Dreams' poems for the *English Review*, and was very kind to me, and was the first man I ever met who had a real and a true feeling for literature. He introduced me to Edward Garnett, who, somehow, introduced me to the world. How well I remember the evenings at Garnett's house in Kent, by the log fire. And there I wrote the best of the dialect poems. I remember Garnett disliked the old ending to 'Whether or Not'. Now I see he was right, it was the voice of the commonplace me, not the demon. So I have altered it. And there again, those days of Hueffer and Garnett are not past at all, once I recall them. They were good to the demon, and the demon is timeless. But the ordinary mealtime me has yesterdays.

And that is why I have altered 'Dreams Nascent', that exceedingly funny and optimistic piece of rhymeless poetry which Ford Hueffer printed in the *English Review*, and which introduced me to the public. The public seemed to like it. The MP for schoolteachers said I was an ornament to the educational system, whereupon I knew it must be the ordinary me which had made itself heard, and not the demon. Anyhow, I was always uneasy about it.

There is a poem added to the second volume, which had to be left out of *Look! We Have Come Through!* when that book was first printed, because the publishers objected to mixing love and religion, so they said, in the lines:

> But I hope I shall find eternity
> With my face down buried between her breasts . . .

But surely there are many eternities, and one of them Adam spends with his face buried and at peace between the breasts of Eve: just as Eve spends one of her eternities with her face hidden in the breast of Adam. But the publishers coughed out that gnat, and I was left wondering, as usual.

Some of the poems in *Look!* are rewritten, but not many, not as in the first volume. And *Birds, Beasts and Flowers* are practically untouched. They are what they are. They are the same me as wrote 'The Wild Common', or 'Renascence'.

Perhaps it may seem bad taste to write this so personal foreword. But since the poems are so often personal themselves, and hang together in a life, it is perhaps only fair to give the demon his body of mere man, as far as possible.

Introduction to the Unexpurgated Edition of Pansies (1929)

This little bunch of fragments is offered as a bunch of *pensées*, anglicé pansies; a handful of thoughts. Or, if you will have the other derivation of pansy, from *panser*, to dress or soothe a wound; these are my tender administrations to the mental and emotional wounds we suffer from. Or you can have heartsease if you like, since the modern heart could certainly do with it.

Each little piece is a thought; not a bare idea or an opinion or a didactic statement, but a true thought, which comes as much from the heart and the genitals as from the head. A thought, with its own blood of emotion and instinct running in it like the fire in a fire opal, if I may be so bold. Perhaps if you hold up my pansies properly to the light, they may show a running vein of fire. At least, they do not pretend to be half-baked lyrics or melodies in American measure. They are thoughts which run through the modern mind and body, each having its own separate existence, yet each of them combining with all the others to make up a complete state of mind.

It suits the modern temper better to have its state of mind made up of apparently irrelevant thoughts that scurry in different directions, yet belong to the same nest; each thought trotting down the page like an independent creature, each with its own small head and tail, trotting its own little way, then curling up to sleep. We prefer it, at least the young seem to prefer it, to those solid blocks of mental pabulum packed like bales in the pages of a proper heavy book. Even we prefer it to those slightly didactic opinions and slices of wisdom which are laid horizontally across the pages of Pascal's *Pensées* or La Bruyère's *Caractères*, separated only by *pattes de mouches*, like faint sprigs of parsley. Let every *pensée* trot on its own little paws, not be laid like a cutlet trimmed with a *patte de mouche*.

Live and let live, and each pansy will tip you its separate wink. The fairest thing in nature, a flower, still has its roots in earth and manure; and in the perfume there hovers still the faint strange scent of earth, the under-earth in all its heavy humidity and darkness. Certainly it is so in pansy-scent, and in violet-scent; mingled with the blue of the morning the black of the corrosive humus. Else the scent would be just sickly sweet.

So it is: we all have our roots in earth. And it is our roots that now need a little attention, need the hard soil eased away from them, and softened so that a little fresh air can come to them, and they can breathe. For by pretending to have no roots, we have trodden the earth so hard over them that they are starving and stifling below the soil. We have roots, and our roots are in the sensual, instinctive and intuitive body, and it is here we need fresh air of open consciousness.

I am abused most of all for using the so-called 'obscene' words. Nobody quite knows what the word 'obscene' itself means, or what it is intended to mean: but gradually all the *old* words that belong to the body below the navel have come to be judged obscene. Obscene means today that the policeman thinks he has a right to arrest you, nothing else.

Myself, I am mystified at this horror over a mere word, a plain simple word that stands for a plain simple thing. 'In the beginning was the Word, and the Word was God and the Word was with God.' If that is true then we are very far from the beginning. When did the Word 'fall'? When did the Word become unclean 'below the navel'? Because today, if you suggest that the word arse was in the beginning and was God and was with God, you will just be put in prison at once. Though a doctor might say the same of the word *ischial tuberosity*, and all the old ladies would piously murmur, 'Quite'! Now that sort of thing is idiotic and humiliating. Whoever the God was that made us, He made us complete. He didn't stop at the navel and leave the rest to the devil. It is too childish. And the same with the Word which is God. If the Word is God – which in the sense of the human mind it is – then you can't suddenly say that all the words which belong below the navel are obscene. The word arse is as much God as the word face. It must be so, otherwise you cut off your God at the waist.

What is obvious is that the words in these cases have been dirtied by the mind, by unclean mental associations. The words themselves are clean, so are the things to which they apply. But the mind drags in a filthy association, calls up some repulsive emotion. Well, then, cleanse the mind, that is the real job. It is the mind which is the Augean stables, not language. The word arse is clean enough. Even the part of the body it refers to is just as much me as my hand and my brain are me. It is not for *me* to quarrel with my own natural make-up. If I am, I am all that I am. But the impudent and dirty mind won't have it. It hates certain parts of the body, and makes the words representing these parts scapegoats. It pelts them out of the consciousness with filth, and there they hover, never dying, never dead, slipping into the consciousness again unawares, and pelted out again with filth, haunting the margins of the consciousness like jackals or hyenas. And they refer to parts of our own living bodies, and to our most essential acts. So that man turns himself into a thing of shame and horror. And his consciousness shudders with horrors that he has made for himself.

That sort of thing has got to stop. We can't have the consciousness haunted any longer by repulsive spectres which are no more than poor simple scapegoat words representing parts of man himself; words that the cowardly and unclean mind has driven out into the limbo of the unconscious, whence they return upon us looming and magnified out of all proportion, frightening us beyond all reason. We must put an end to that. It is the self divided against itself most dangerously. The simple and natural 'obscene' words must be cleaned up of all their depraved fear-associations, and readmitted into the consciousness to take their natural place. Now they are magnified out of all proportion, so is the mental fear they represent. We must accept the word arse as we accept the word face, since arses we have and always shall have. We can't start cutting off the buttocks of unfortunate mankind, like the ladies in the Voltaire story, just to fit the mental expulsion of the word.

This scapegoat business does the mind itself so much damage. There is a poem of Swift's which should make us pause. It is written to Celia, his Celia – and every verse ends with the mad, maddened refrain: 'But – Celia, Celia, Celia shits!' Now that, stated baldly, is so ridiculous it is almost funny. But when one remembers the gnashing insanity to which the great mind of Swift was reduced by that and similar thoughts, the joke dies away. Such thoughts poisoned him, like some terrible constipation. They poisoned his mind. And why, in heaven's name? The *fact* cannot have troubled him, since it applied to himself and to all of us. It was not the fact that Celia shits which so deranged him, it was the *thought*. His mind couldn't bear the thought. Great wit as he was, he could not see how ridiculous his revulsions were. His arrogant mind overbore him. He couldn't even see how much worse it would be if Celia didn't shit. His physical sympathies were too weak, his guts were too cold to sympathise with poor Celia in her natural functions. His insolent and sicklily squeamish mind just turned her into a thing of horror, because she was merely natural and went to the WC. It is monstrous! One feels like going back across all the years to poor Celia, to say to her: It's all right, don't you take any notice of that mental lunatic.

And Swift's form of madness is very common today. Men with cold guts and over-squeamish minds are always thinking those things and squirming. Wretched man is the victim of his own little revulsions, which he magnifies into great horrors and terrifying taboos. We are all savages, we all have taboos. The Australian black may have the kangaroo for his taboo. And then he will probably die of shock and terror if a kangaroo happens to touch him. Which is what I would call a purely unnecessary death. But modern men have even more dangerous taboos. To us, certain words, certain ideas are taboo, and if they come upon us and we can't drive them away, we die or go mad with a degraded sort of terror. Which is what happened to Swift. He was such a great wit. And the modern mind altogether is falling into this form of degraded taboo-insanity. I call it a waste of sane human consciousness. But it is very dangerous, dangerous to the individual and utterly dangerous to society as a whole. Nothing is so fearful in a mass-civilisation like ours as a mass-insanity.

The remedy is, of course, the same in both cases: lift off the taboo. The kangaroo is a harmless animal, the word shit is a harmless word. Make either into a taboo, and it becomes most dangerous. The result of taboo is insanity. And insanity, especially mob-insanity, mass-insanity, is the fearful danger that threatens our civilisation. There are certain persons with a sort of rabies, who live only to infect the mass. If the young do not watch out, they will find themselves, before so very many years are past, engulfed in a howling manifestation of mob-insanity, truly terrifying to think of. It will be better to be dead than to live to see it. Sanity, wholeness, is everything. In the name of piety and purity, what a mass of disgusting insanity is spoken and written. We shall have to fight the mob, in order to keep sane, and to keep society sane.

Foreword to the Expurgated Edition of Pansies (1929)

These poems are called Pansies because they are rather Pensées than anything else. Pascal and La Bruyère wrote their Pensées in prose, but it has always seemed to me that a real thought, a single thought, not an argument, can only exist easily in verse, or in some poetic form. There is a didactic element about prose thoughts which makes them repellent, slightly bullying. 'He who hath wife and children hath given hostages to fortune.' There is a thought well put; but it immediately irritates by its assertiveness. It applies too direct to actual practical life. If it were put into poetry it wouldn't nag at us so practically. We don't want to be nagged at.

So I should wish these Pansies to be taken as thoughts rather than anything else; casual thoughts that are true while they are true and irrelevant when the mood or circumstance changes. I should like them to be as fleeting as pansies, which wilt so soon, and are so fascinating with their varied faces, while they last. And flowers, to my thinking, are not merely pretty-pretty. They have in their fragrance an earthiness of the humus and the corruptive earth from which they spring. And pansies, in their streaked faces, have a look of many things besides heartsease.

Some of the poems are perforce omitted – about a dozen from the bunch. When Scotland Yard seized the manuscript in the post, at the order of the Home Secretary, no doubt there was a rush of detectives, postmen and Home Office clerks and heads to pick out the most lurid blossoms. They must have been very disappointed. When I now read down the list of the omitted poems, and recall the dozen amusing, not terribly important, bits of pansies which have had to stay out of print for fear a policeman might put his foot on them, I can only grin once more to think of the nanny-goat, nanny-goat-in-a-white-petticoat silliness of it all. It is like listening to a Mrs Caudle's curtain lecture in the next house, and wondering whether Mrs Caudle is funnier, or Mr Caudle; or whether they aren't both merely stale and tedious.

Anyhow I offer a bunch of pansies, not a wreath of *immortelles*. I don't want everlasting flowers, and I don't want to offer them to anybody else. A flower passes, and that perhaps is the best of it. If we can take it in its transience, its breath, its maybe mephistophelian, maybe palely ophelian face, the look it gives, the gesture of its full bloom, and the way it turns upon us to depart – that was the flower, we have had it, and no *immortelle* can give us anything in comparison. The same with the pansy poems; merely the breath of the moment, and one eternal moment easily contradicting the next eternal moment. Only don't nail the pansy down. You won't keep it any better if you do.

NOTES

Lawrence is perhaps the most accessible of modern poets. I have limited myself here to glossing only those words or phrases which cannot be easily found by a reader armed with the *Shorter OED* and a decent dictionary of mythology.

For help with one or two of these notes I would like to thank John Worthen and Christopher Pollnitz

1 (p. 8) *Biuret*   a name for a chemical compound (whose characteristics the narrator is apparently trying to master)
2 (p. 11) *mard-arsed kid, / E'll gie thee socks!*   soft, namby-pamby, / I'll give you a good hiding
3 (p. 12) *scraightin'*   crying
4 (p. 14) *weird*   probably used in the sense of a magical chant like those of *Macbeth*'s 'weird sisters'
5 (p. 19) *David and Dora*   two characters from Dickens's *David Copperfield*
6 (p. 20) *aqua regia*   a solution of nitric and hydrochloride acids capable of dissolving most metals
7 (p. 27) *slive*   sneak about
8 (p. 27) *a clout*   a rag
9 (p. 36) *the Shalimar*   Lawrence is perhaps remembering the beginning of one of the *Indian Love Lyrics* by the late nineteenth-century Anglo-Indian poet Laurence Hope (Adela Nicolson): 'Pale hands I loved beside the Shalimar, / Where are you now?' There are Shalimar gardens in Lahore.
10 (p. 43) *otchel*   a humpbacked person
11 (p. 44) *smock-ravelled*   perplexed
12 (p. 44) *Larropin'*   Rushing
13 (p. 46) *swelted*   fainted away
14 (p. 46) *clawkin'*   tear or scratch
15 (p. 47) *colleyfoglin'*   deceptive, untrustworthy
16 (p. 48) *'affle an' caffle*   to shilly-shally and to cavil
17 (p. 50) *gen*   gave
18 (p. 95) *neckar*   Lawrence almost certainly meant to write 'neckan', the name for a water spirit in Northern mythology. See Matthew Arnold's poem 'The Neckan' (1852).
19 (p. 102) *flig*   quick or eager to fly off
20 (p. 105) *Iacchos*   one of the forms of Dionysus, the Greek god of wine and revelry

21 (p. 136) *the mowie*   presumably an area of mown grass

22 (p. 152) *Bei Hennef*   *bei*, German for near

23 (p. 158) *Frohnleichnam*   the German word for the festival of Corpus Christi

24 (p. 162) *Tuatha De Danaan*   gods worshipped by the Celts

25 (p. 167) *orts and slarts*   leavings, leftovers

26 (p. 177) *Wehmut, ist dir weh*   sadness, are you sad? (German)

27 (p. 218) *rock left bare by the viciousness of Greek women*   an uncharacteristically obscure reference to the death of some young Athenian prisoners of war who were kept in a stone quarry near Syracuse after their defeat in battle. It is not clear where Lawrence found the reference to the local women exulting in their sufferings.

28 (p. 220) *so morbid, as the Italians say*   *morbido*, the Italian word for soft

29 (p. 221) *Jamque vale! . . . ego sum . . . sono io*   and now farewell (Latin) . . . I am (Latin) . . . I am (Italian)

30 (p. 248) *Erechtheion*   The Erechtheum is the name of a temple in Athens.

31 (p. 249) *forestière*   French version of the Italian word for a foreigner or tourist (*forestiero*)

32 (p. 255) *The Evangelistic Beasts*   The four gospel writers became associated with the four beasts of the Apocalypse described in Revelation 6–8.

33 (p. 255) *Filius Meus*   my son (Latin)

34 (p. 256) ΙΧΘΥΣ   The association of Christ with a fish may come from the fact that the Greek letters which make up the word here can be made to stand for Jesus Christ, Son of God, Saviour.

35 (p. 270) *Quelle joie de vivre / Dans l'eau!*   What joy of living in the water! (French)

36 (p. 275) *Pipistrello*   bat (Italian)

37 (p. 280) *a sghembo!*   erratically (Italian)

38 (p. 286) *Buon viaggio*   Have a good trip. (Italian)

39 (p. 290) *Basta!*   Enough! (Italian)

40 (p. 302) *Dross-jabot*   the frill formerly worn by men around the edge of their shirts

41 (p. 309) *noli me tangere*   touch me not (Latin). See John, 20:17.

42 (p. 309–10) *Asinello, Ciuco, Somaro . . . burro*   various words in Italian for the ass or donkey

43 (p. 311) *sierra roqueña*   rocky mountain range

44 (p. 314) *Tace, tu, crapa, bestia!*   Keep quiet, you beastly she-goat! (Italian)

45 (p. 315) *Le bestie non parlano, poverine!*   Animals can't speak, poor things! (Italian)

46   (p. 318) *Ich dien*   I serve. (German)

47   (p. 321) *Dient Ihr! Dient! / Omnes, vos omnes, servite*   The sense is obey and serve me, all of you, first in German and then in Latin.

48   (p. 325) *miserere*   for *miserere mei*, i.e. pity me (Latin)

49   (p. 330) *Qué tiene, amigo? / León*   What have you got there, friend, a lion? (Spanish)

50   (p. 331) *Hermoso es*   It's beautiful. (Spanish)

51   (p. 356) *Sum, ergo non cogito*   I am therefore I don't [have to] think (Latin), a comic reversal of Descartes's famous *cogito ergo sum*, I think therefore I am.

52   (p. 376) *nesh*   tender, sensitive

53   (p. 378) *maquillage*   the French word for comestics, make-up

54   (p. 392) *foraminiferae*   belonging to the lowest class of protozoa, i.e. the lowest, unicellular form of animal

55   (p. 406) *bibblings . . . bimmel-bammel*   Bibble-babble is idle, childish talk and bimmel-bammel is probably something similar.

56   (p. 406) *wowser*   Australian slang for a puritanical enthusiast or fanatic

57   (p. 413) *Compari*   Italian for confederates, old friends

58   (p. 424) *Dies Illa*   The Latin words which begin this poem, and which have already been called upon for the title of the preceding one, are from a famous medieval hymn on the Last Judgement. The two lines which follow them are Lawrence's rough translation. Scott had already incorporated them into his *Lay of the Last Minstrel*, a poem Lawrence knew well.

59   (p. 435) *wimbly-wambly*   To wimble-wamble is to roll about when walking.

60   (p. 442) *alumina*   the chief constituent of all clays found crystallised in sapphires

61   (p. 444) *Après moi le déluge . . . Post me, nihil!*   The French words are attributed to one of Louis XV's mistresses, reproached for her extravagance, and mean that she didn't care what happened after she was gone. The Latin words which follow – 'After me, nothing' – can carry the same implication.

62   (p. 446) *Quos vult perdere Deue* [*prius dementat*]   Those whom God wishes to destroy He first deprives of their senses. (Latin)

63   (p. 451) *Ixtaccihuatl*   one of the volcanoes near Mexico City

64   (p. 453) *scraight*   See Note 3 above.

65   (p. 464) *Excelsior*   Latin for higher but also the title of an uplifting poem by Longfellow

66   (p. 465) *dool-owls . . . battle-twig*   hobgoblins . . . earwig

67   (p. 468) *done you brown*   perhaps a misprint for 'done you down'

68 (p. 474) *pie jaw blether*   magpie chatter
69 (p. 480) *Change of Government*   The Labour government elected in May 1929 is here portrayed as 'Auntie Maud'. 'Aunt Gwendoline' represents the Conservatives, 'Aunt Libby' the Liberals and 'Aunt Lou' the Communists.
70 (p. 486) *in puris naturalibus*   in the natural state, i.e. naked (Latin)
71 (p. 493) *graminiferae*   grass-producing plants
72 (p. 499) *Andraitx*   a town in Majorca
73 (p. 518) *Forte Dei Marmi*   a holiday resort in Italy
74 (p. 519) *gutta percha*   the gum of trees found in Malaysia and used for the insulation of electric wires
75 (p. 519) *rubinetto*   *rubinetto* is Italian for tap.
76 (p. 519) *Amo sacrum vulgus*   I love the sacred crowd (Latin), a direct reversal of Horace's well-known declaration, *Odi profanum vulgus*.
77 (p. 522) *Retro me, Satanas!*   Get thee behind me, Satan! (Latin)
78 (p. 525) *Boccaccio . . . Eve and the Amazon . . . the Lizard . . . Renascence* These are all references to particular paintings by Lawrence.
79 (p. 526) *Auto-Da-Fé*   Portuguese for an act of faith or justice (the condemnation of a heretic)
80 (p. 544) *Retort to Whitman*   The lines from Whitman's poetry to which Lawrence is replying are: 'And whoever walks a furlong without sympathy / walks to his own funeral.'
81 (p. 550) *jixery*   Joynson-Hicks, the Home Secretary instrumental in promoting the censorship of Lawrence's writing and painting in 1929, was known by his opponents as Jix.
82 (p. 554) *Lord Melchett*   title taken by Alfred Mond, leading industrialist of Lawrence's time and founder of ICI
83 (p. 569–70) *Thomas Earp . . . Mr Squire*   Neither of these poems has a title in the notebook. They refer to two journalists Lawrence disliked.
84 (p. 574) *pain grillé*   toast
85 (p. 595) *Anaxagoras*   a pre-Socratic Greek philosopher

INDEX OF POEM TITLES

INDEX OF FIRST LINES